Programming Java 2
Micro Edition
on Symbian OS

Programming Java 2 Micro Edition on Symbian OS

A developer's guide to MIDP 2.0

Martin de Jode

With
**Jonathan Allin, Darren Holland, Alan Newman
and Colin Turfus**

Reviewed by
**Ivan Litovski, Roy Hayun, George Sewell, Simon Lewis,
Michael Aubert and Hana Bisada**

Managing Editor
Phil Northam

Assistant Editor
Freddie Gjertsen

John Wiley & Sons, Ltd

Published by John Wiley & Sons Ltd, The Atrium, Southern Gate, Chichester,
West Sussex PO19 8SQ, England
Telephone (+44) 1243 779777

Email (for orders and customer service enquiries): cs-books@wiley.co.uk
Visit our Home Page on www.wileyeurope.com or www.wiley.com

Other Wiley Editorial Offices

John Wiley & Sons Inc., 111 River Street, Hoboken, NJ 07030, USA

Jossey-Bass, 989 Market Street, San Francisco, CA 94103-1741, USA

Wiley-VCH Verlag GmbH, Boschstr. 12, D-69469 Weinheim, Germany

John Wiley & Sons Australia Ltd, 33 Park Road, Milton, Queensland 4064, Australia

John Wiley & Sons (Asia) Pte Ltd, 2 Clementi Loop #02-01, Jin Xing Distripark, Singapore 129809

John Wiley & Sons Canada Ltd, 22 Worcester Road, Etobicoke, Ontario,
Canada M9W 1L1

Wiley also publishes its books in a variety of electronic formats. Some content that
appears in print may not be available in electronic books.

Library of Congress Cataloging-in-Publication Data

Jode, Martin de.
 Programming the Java 2 micro edition for symbian OS: a developer's guide to MIDP 2.0/
 Martin de Jode ... [et al.].
 p. cm.
 ISBN 0-470-09223-8
 1. Java (Computer program language). 2. Operating systems (Computers) 3. Wireless
 communication systems–Programming.
 I. Title.
 QA76.73.J38J615 2004
 005.13'3 – dc22

2004007312

British Library Cataloguing in Publication Data

A catalogue record for this book is available from the British Library

ISBN 0-470-09223-8

Typeset in 10/12pt Optima by Laserwords Private Limited, Chennai, India
Printed and bound in Great Britain by Biddles Ltd, King's Lynn
This book is printed on acid-free paper responsibly manufactured from sustainable
forestry in which at least two trees are planted for each one used for paper production.

Contents

About This Book   ix

Author Biographies   xiii

Author's Acknowledgements   xvii

Symbian Press Acknowledgements   xix

Foreword   xxi

Innovation Through Openness   xxiii

Section 1: J2ME and MIDP   1

1 Introduction to J2ME   3
   1.1   Configurations and Profiles   3
   1.2   CLDC and MIDP   7
   1.3   CDC and Personal Profile   16
   1.4   J2ME on Symbian OS   21
   1.5   Summary   22

2 Getting Started   23
   2.1   Introduction to MIDP   23
   2.2   Helloworld, Turbo Edition   46
   2.3   Introduction to Tools for MIDP   54
   2.4   Installing and Running a MIDlet   82
   2.5   MIDP on Symbian OS Phones   89
   2.6   Summary   89

3 MIDP 2.0 and the JTWI   91
3.1   Introduction to the JTWI   91
3.2   The CLDC on Symbian OS   94
3.3   MIDP 2.0   95
3.4   Optional J2ME APIs in the JTWI   155
3.5   MIDP 2.0 and Symbian OS Phones   201
3.6   Summary   202

4 Java APIs for Bluetooth Wireless Technology   205
4.1   Introduction to Bluetooth   205
4.2   Introduction to the Bluetooth APIs   206
4.3   Programming the Bluetooth APIs   208
4.4   L2CAP Protocol   224
4.5   Security   227
4.6   Java Bluetooth API and the MIDP 2.0 Security Model   229
4.7   Sample Code   230
4.8   Development Tools   241
4.9   Java Bluetooth APIs and Symbian OS   244
4.10 Summary   244

5 MIDP 2.0 Case Studies   247
5.1   Introduction   247
5.2   The Expense Application   248
5.3   The Demo Racer Game   282
5.4   The Picture Puzzle   294

Section 2: Writing Quality Code for Smartphones   317

6 Making Java Code Portable   319
6.1   Introduction   319
6.2   Design Patterns   320
6.3   Portability Issues   326
6.4   Summary   333

7 Writing Optimized Code   335
7.1   Introduction   335
7.2   What Are We Starting With?   336
7.3   Benchmarking   336
7.4   General Guidelines for Optimization   337
7.5   Feedback and Responsiveness   338
7.6   Object Creation   338
7.7   Method Modifiers and Inlining   340
7.8   Strings   343

7.9   Using Containers   348
7.10 How Not To Do It   349
7.11 Copying an `Array`   351
7.12 Thoughts on Looping   352
7.13 Graphics   358
7.14 LifeTime Case Study   366
7.15 Arithmetic Operations   385
7.16 Design Patterns   386
7.17 Memory Management   388
7.18 JIT and DAC Compilers   390
7.19 Obfuscators   391
7.20 Summary   392

Section 3: The Evolution of the Wireless Java Market 393

8 The Market, the Opportunities and Symbian's Plans 395

8.1   Introduction   395
8.2   The Wireless Java Market   395
8.3   Meeting Market Needs   400
8.4   Providing Advanced Services   402
8.5   Why Java?   406
8.6   Symbian and Java   409
8.7   Java and Digital Rights Management   418
8.8   The Java Verified Program   420
8.9   Beyond Advanced Consumer Services   421
8.10 Trends in Technology   421

Appendix 1: CLDC Core Libraries 423

Appendix 2: MIDP Libraries 429

Appendix 3: Using the Wireless Toolkit Tools at the Command Line 437

Appendix 4: Developer Resources and Bibliography 439

Appendix 5: Specifications of Symbian OS Phones 445

Index 461

About This Book

In 2001, Symbian's first book devoted to Java on Symbian OS was published. Jonathan Allin's *Wireless Java for Symbian Devices* (WJSD) provided an in-depth exposition targeted at programming PersonalJava on Symbian OS. The embedded Java story has moved on a lot in two years and so has Symbian's implementation, so once again we decided to put pen to paper to produce a new book aimed at helping developers program Java on the latest generation of Symbian OS phones.

This book is not intended to supersede Jonathan Allin's WJSD, which dealt very thoroughly with Symbian's PersonalJava implementation and still remains the definitive guide for developers programming PersonalJava on Symbian devices such as the Nokia 9200 or Sony Ericsson P800 and P900. Instead, this new book covers very different territory, focusing on programming MIDP, particularly MIDP 2.0, on Symbian OS.

Symbian's Java implementation has evolved over the years from a JDK 1.1.4-based implementation in Symbian OS Version 5.0, through PersonalJava on Symbian OS Version 6.0 and is now moving, with Symbian OS Version 7.0 and subsequent releases, to a single Java 2 Micro Edition (J2ME) CLDC/MIDP-based implementation. The latest generation of Symbian OS phones support MIDP 2.0 plus a range of additional, optional APIs, all conforming to Java Specification Requests (JSRs) arrived at through the Java Community Process.

Phones based on the latest releases of Symbian OS, such as the Nokia 6600 and Sony Ericsson P900, support MIDP 2.0 as well as implementations of the Wireless Messaging API (JSR 120), Java Bluetooth API (JSR 82) and also, in the case of the Nokia 6600, the Mobile Media API (JSR 135).

This book is not just about MIDP 2.0. Instead we will show developers how to get the best out of the latest generation of Symbian OS phones, by providing a practical, in-depth, guide to programming J2ME on these devices. In addition to a thorough discussion of MIDP we have also included an in-depth exposition of all the optional J2ME APIs that can be found on phones such as the Sony Ericsson P900 and Nokia 6600.

Our approach has been to illustrate the new MIDP 2.0 features and optional APIs by way of concrete examples tested on real devices. In addition to extensive sample code we include a chapter of case studies that develop more or less complete applications. By adopting this approach developers will be equipped with code that they know will run on real devices. Where specifications allow optional functionality we indicate whether this is supported on Symbian phones. We also point out known bugs and possible work-arounds. In addition we aim to use the considerable experience available within Symbian to show the reader how to write efficient and effective code for constrained devices. To complete the picture we also discuss what Java has to offer in the wireless space and how it may enrich the wireless value chain. We also provide an insight into how Java is likely to evolve on Symbian OS in the future.

In writing this book, our desire has been to give enough information in one volume for developers to make the most of the Java 2 Micro Edition on Symbian OS, enabling them to provide the compelling content that will enrich the wireless ecosystem.

The book is divided three sections:

- Section 1: J2ME and MIDP

- Section 2: Writing Quality Code for Smartphones

- Section 3: The Evolution of the Wireless Java Market

In Section 1 we introduce the Java 2 Micro Edition and the ideas behind configurations and profiles. We then concentrate on programming MIDP and the additional APIs that make up the Java platform on the latest generation of Symbian OS phones.

Section 2 investigates design and implementation considerations involved in writing high-quality code, focusing on the issues of portability and efficiency.

The final section looks at the strategic importance of Java to the wireless ecosystem and provides a glimpse as to how Wireless Java may evolve on Symbian OS.

Who Is This Book For?

The book is aimed at Java developers already programming in the wireless space or interested in moving into the wireless space and who wish to know what can be achieved with J2ME on the latest Symbian OS phones. Enough introductory information and examples are provided for newcomers to J2ME to get going with MIDP programming, while the thorough treatment of the new MIDP 2.0 and optional APIs provides more weighty fare for the experienced MIDP programmer.

Conventions

To help you get the most from the text and keep track of what's happening, we've used a number of simple conventions throughout this book.

When we refer to words you use in your code, such as classes, attributes and methods, or to the name of a file, we use this style:

Person class: we obtain the name attribute by invoking the getName method on our Person instance

When we list code, or the contents of files, we use the following convention:

```
SocketConnection conn = (SocketConnection)Connector.open(url);
DataOutputStream out = conn.openDataOutputStream();
byte[] buf= request.getBytes();
out.write(buf);
out.flush();
out.close();
```

We show commands typed at the command line like this:

```
C:\WTK20\apps\Example\src>javac -d tmpclasses -bootclasspath %MIDPAPI%
        -classpath %J2MECLASSPATH% *.java
```

URLs are written: ***www.symbian.com/developer***

Author Biographies

Martin de Jode

Martin graduated from the University of York with a BSc in Physics and, after a brief spell in industry, returned to academia to undertake research in the field of non-linear optics at Essex University. Graduating with a PhD, Martin spent eight years working in research at the London Hospital Medical College, studying the use of lasers to treat cancer. During this time he developed a particular interest in using Monte Carlo simulation to model the interaction of light with biological tissue using Fortran.

Martin joined Symbian in 2000, after completing an MSc in Object Oriented Software Systems from City University. As a Java Developer Consultant in Symbian's Developer Network he spends his time providing support to Symbian's Java developer community. In addition to writing technical papers on PersonalJava and J2ME for Symbian's website, Martin has developed numerous utility and sample applications showing how to make the most of Symbian's Java platform. Other activities include delivering training, evangelizing Java on Symbian OS and trying to keep up with the proliferation of J2ME JSRs.

Outside of work, Martin is passionate about cricket, having spent what seems like a lifetime playing competitive club cricket in and around the home counties.

Jonathan Allin

Jonathan is Symbian's Product Manager for Java Technology. His role is to ensure that Symbian OS provides a first class Java platform for mobile phones, and covers Symbian's Java strategy and implementation roadmap, partnerships, and, of course, how Java relates to other development environments. Jonathan was the lead author of *Wireless Java for Symbian Devices*, authored the "Developing with Java" chapter in

Professional Symbian Programming, and presents regularly on wireless Java opportunities and optimizing Java code for mobile devices.

Jonathan has a BSc in Electronics and a DSc in Biomedical Engineering. He picked up an MBA when working for Acorn Computers, where he helped develop computers and software for schools. Prior to joining Symbian in 1999, he worked for Origin BV for three years, where he first became interested in Java and particularly the role it can play within the enterprise.

Jonathan is married to Lauren, who is a social worker and essential for keeping in order their three children: Benjamin, Daniel, and Victoria, who are into rugby, music, and hockey respectively. Java reminds Jonathan that computing can be fun, interesting and useful.

Darren Holland

Darren joined Symbian in 2002. He graduated in 1995 with a BSc in Computing Systems Technology and started his career developing telephone billing and enterprise fax software in C++ before starting to work with Java in 1999.

Darren would like to thank the IS department of Symbian who provided support throughout the development of the Expense application prototype, ensuring that the resources and infrastructure required were in place. More importantly, they supported the project remit and supplied the encouragement that ultimately ensured success. In particular Olivia Hawkins, Belen Ares Paredes and Tarek Meliti contributed greatly.

Darren would also like to thank his wife Solène for her continual support and for helping to keep him sane during life's more stressful moments. No matter how much Darren enjoys work he would always rather be sailing!

Alan Newman

Alan Newman is a technology consultant and freelance technical writer, living in Brighton with his partner Abi and his son, Freddie, who was born in the summer of 2003. He has been programming since he was 8 years old when he acquired his first computer, a Sinclair ZX81, before moving on to the Commodore Pet, and BBC B Micro.

After graduating with a business degree, he began working in the NHS as an analyst, automating many previously manual data entry tasks for his department. He then moved into banking and programmed trade entry and loan collateral management systems on the trade floor of the Republic National Bank of New York where, in 1998, he took a keen interest in learning Java and its interaction with the Internet. He then spent a year with Internet sports magazine Sportal.com, before setting up his own company, Sensible Development, which created and now runs a multiplayer football manager game, which can be found at ***www.effeffelle.com***.

He is an advocate of plain speaking as a means of preventing that glazed-over look consumers often show when confronted with technology. He also believes that technology should not dictate but instead enhance consumer and business tasks.

Colin Turfus

Colin graduated from the University of Dundee, Scotland with a BSc (Hons) in maths and physics, and from the University of Cambridge with a PhD in applied mathematics. He has researched and lectured at universities in the UK and in South Korea, publishing papers in fluid dynamics and computational astrophysics. He became interested in Java programming while developing intranet-based maths teaching resources and lecturing about Internet technology in South Korea.

He joined Symbian shortly after its inception in the summer of 1998, and has been involved since in establishing and building the Symbian Developer Network, which he now heads. He was a contributing author to *Wireless Java for Symbian Devices*.

Colin's interests include jogging, hill-walking and classical guitar. He is married to Keum-ye from South Korea. They have three girls: Selina, Sonya and Emily.

Author's Acknowledgements

First and foremost I would like to thank my co-authors Alan Newman, Jonathan Allin, Colin Turfus and Darren Holland without whose help we would not have been able to create this book.

I must also thank Phil Northam of Symbian Press, whose initial idea this book was and who lobbied hard for its realization. Also thanks to his assistant Freddie Gjertsen for his painstaking work in ensuring consistency in the style and grammar of our work and who kept us all on the straight and narrow.

I'm also very indebted to the reviewers from Symbian's Java Engineering team: Hana Bisada, Roy Hayun, Simon Lewis, Michael Aubert, Ivan Litovski and George Sewell, the real experts, who develop Symbian's Java implementation. They have all spent considerable time ensuring the correctness and quality of the author's contributions.

I'm grateful to the guys at Rococo Software for providing us with their Impronto Simulator for JSR 82, and in particular to Steven Crane for suggesting numerous improvements to Chapter 5. I'd also like to thank Jarmo Lahtinen and Janne Levula from Nokia for their advice on aspects of the MIDP implementation running on the Nokia 6600.

I would also like to extend my thanks to Gaynor Redvers-Mutton who has ably managed the publication of the book at John Wiley.

Last, but far from least, I must mention the Symbian work placement students Xi Chen and Sunny Khaila, who provided much of the groundwork for this book. As well as exploring the MIDP 2.0 specification, they also produced early prototypes of several of the example applications featured in the text.

Symbian Press Acknowledgements

Symbian licenses, develops and supports Symbian OS, the platform for next-generation data-enabled mobile phones. Symbian is headquartered in London, with offices worldwide. For more information see the Symbian website, **www.symbian.com**. 'Symbian', 'Symbian OS' and other associated Symbian marks are all trademarks of Symbian Ltd. Symbian acknowledges the trademark rights of all third parties referred to in this material.

Thanks to all who have had input into this book, including the many whose behind-the-scenes work ensured the book was delivered on time! Let's not forget the Laughing Gravy and the Stage Door either...

About the cover

The cover concept, designed by Jonathan Tastard, was inspired by David Levin, CEO of Symbian, in a 2003 keynote presentation at Exposium, where he pronounced:

> The mobile phone has traditionally connected the mouth to the ear. Symbian develops Symbian OS to enable a new generation of connected communications devices to connect the mouth to the ear to the eye. To realize this vision, the mobile phone industry is working together to develop the latest technologies, support open industry standards, and ensure interoperability between advanced mobile phones as networks evolve from 2.5G to 3G.

Foreword

Tim Lindholm, Architect of the J2ME platform at Sun Microsystems, Inc.

The rate of adoption of the Java platform in wireless devices is unprecedented, but more important is the change in perspective that the adoption reflects.

The desktop and server have relatively long histories as open platforms and, as such, have evolved developer communities and vibrant markets for third-party software. In contrast, until recently, wireless devices were as closed as the legendary mainframes of decades past; the only developers of software for the early mobile phones were hidden away in the laboratories of the large companies who made those phones.

Coupled with advances in the raw computational capabilities of the devices themselves, the development and adoption of the Java 2 Micro Edition (J2ME) platform has changed all that. Within the last few years, wireless devices have emerged as a new, open, networked computing platform deployed on a massive scale. Its effectiveness has been in large part facilitated by the availability of a standard software architecture, one that reduces the difficulty and cost of developing applications while supporting a broad and competitive market for implementations.

Symbian has been a key player in the creation of this new ecosystem. The most recent version of Symbian OS incorporates the most current J2ME platform targeting mobile devices: MIDP 2.0. Symbian OS and MIDP 2.0 together form an integrated, compelling package spanning the software stack of a wireless device.

This book focuses on MIDP programming of Symbian OS phones. Far from just reciting a litany of API descriptions, it uses example applications to make practical points. It digs into the details that are relevant to good application design and getting good performance. As well as covering MIDP 2.0 programming, the book also covers programming for MIDP 1.0, the platform in many already-deployed devices. Finally, the book explores many of the standard J2ME optional packages that Symbian OS currently supports, or will support in the near future. The examples are developed completely, through to their installation and execution on real devices.

Although presented in the context of Symbian OS, the worldwide availability of MIDP on wireless devices means that the lessons of this book are not tied to any particular operating system. This book should appeal to all developers who want to take better advantage of the wireless J2ME platform.

Innovation Through Openness

The success of an open operating system for smartphones is closely linked to the degree to which the functionality of lower levels of software and hardware can be accessed, modified, and augmented by add-on software and hardware. Java MIDP 1.0 allowed only modest access to underlying Symbian OS functionality. Java MIDP 2.0 exploits it much more fully and this book brings you the most up-to-date information available for programming Java MIDP 2.0 for Symbian OS. As Java MIDP 2.0 smartphones begin to ship in volume in 2004, we are witnessing the coming of a third wave of mobile phones.

The first wave was voice-centric mobile phones. Mobile phone manufacturers have performed wonders of optimization on the core feature of these phones – their ability to provide great mobile voice communications. Successive generations of products improved their portability, battery life, reliability, signal handling, voice quality, ergonomics, price, and usability. In the process, mobile phones became the most successful consumer electronics product in history.

The second wave was rich-experience mobile phones. Instead of just conveying voice conversations between mouth and ear, these phones provided a much richer sensory experience than their predecessors. High-resolution color screens conveyed data vividly and graphically. High-fidelity audio systems played quality music through such things as ringtones and audio files. These phones combined multimedia with information and communications, to dramatic effect.

But the best was still to come. The primary characteristic of the third wave of mobile phones is their openness. Openness is an abstract concept, but one with huge and tangible consequences for developers. The key driver is that the growing on-board intelligence in modern phones – the smartness of the hardware and software – can now be readily accessed by add-on hardware and software. The range of applications and services that can be used on a phone is not fixed at the time of manufacture, meaning new applications and services can be added afterwards. The phone can be tailored by an operator to suit its customers and these customers can then add further customizations, reflecting specific needs or interests.

The Symbian Ecosystem

Open phones allow a much wider array of companies and individuals to contribute to the value and attractiveness of smartphones. The attractiveness of a phone to an end-user is no longer determined only by the various parties involved in the creation of that phone. Over-the-air downloads and other late-binding mechanisms allow additional companies and individuals to try out new ideas, delivering their applications and services directly to end-users. Many of these ideas may not seem viable at the time of manufacture. However, the advantage of open phones is that there is more time and more opportunity for all these new and innovative ideas to mature into advantageous, usable applications that can make a user's life easier – whether it be over-the-air synchronization with a PC, checking traffic or having fun with 3D games or photo editing.

The real power of open phones arises when add-on services on one phone are re-used as add-on services on other phones. This allows an enormous third-party development ecosystem to flourish. These third parties are no longer tied to the fortunes of any one phone, or any one phone manufacturer. Moreover, applications that start their lives as add-ons for one phone can find themselves incorporated at time of manufacture in subsequent phones, including phones from other manufacturers. This depends on the commonality of the underlying operating system. Open standards drive a virtuous cycle of research and development: numerous companies can leverage the prowess, skills, experience and success of the Symbian ecosystem.

Symbian OS Phones

Symbian OS phones are currently based on the following user interfaces open to C++ and Java programmers: the Series 80 Platform (Nokia 9200 Communicator series), the Series 90 Platform (Nokia 7700), the Series 60 Platform (Nokia 6600, 6620, 7650, 3650, 3660, 3620, N-Gage, Siemens SX1 and Sendo X), and UIQ (Sony Ericsson P800, P900, BenQ P30, Motorola A920 and A925). The Nokia 6600 was the first smartphone to include Java MIDP 2.0. Read on for a brief summary of the user interface families now available.

Mobile Phones with a Numeric Keypad
These phones are designed for one-handed use and require a flexible UI that is simple to navigate with a joystick, softkeys, jogdial, or any

combination of these. Examples of this come from the Series 60 Platform which, in addition to the manufacturers listed above, is also licensed to Panasonic and Samsung. Fujitsu produces a user interface for a range of phones including the F2102v, F2051 and F900i for NTT DoCoMo's FOMA network. Pictured is the Siemens SX1.

Mobile Phones with Portrait Touch Screens

These mobile phones tend to have larger screens than those in the previous category and can dispense with a numeric keypad altogether. A larger screen is ideal for viewing content or working on the move, and pen-based interaction gives new opportunities to users and developers. The best current example of this form factor is UIQ, which is the platform for the Sony Ericsson P800 and P900, as well as BenQ P30 and Motorola's A920 and A925. The P800, P900 and P30 actually combine elements of full screen access and more traditional mobile phone use by including a numeric keypad, while the Motorola smartphones dispense with a keypad altogether. Pictured is the Sony Ericsson P900.

Mobile Phones with Landscape Screens

These mobile phones have the largest screens of all Symbian OS phones and can have a full keyboard and may also include a touch screen. With this type of mobile phone, developers may find enterprise applications particularly attractive. A current example of the keyboard form factor is the Series 80 Platform. This is the basis of the Nokia 9200 Communicator series, and has been used in the Nokia 9210i and Nokia 9290. Based on the Series 90 Platform, the Nokia 7700 is an example of a touch screen mobile phone without keyboard, aimed more at high multimedia usage.

When you're ready to use the Java programming skills you've learned in this book, you'll want an up-to-the-minute overview of available phones, user interfaces and tools. For the latest information, start at **www.symbian.com/developer** for pointers to partner websites, other books, white papers and sample code. If you're developing technology that could be used on any Symbian OS phone, you can find more information about partnering with Symbian at **www.symbian.com/partners**.

We wish you an enjoyable experience programming with Symbian OS and lots of commercial success.

Section 1

J2ME and MIDP

1

Introduction to J2ME

In order to understand how Java 2 Micro Edition (J2ME) lies within the wider Java landscape it is best to explore the overall Java architecture. J2ME has been developed primarily as a technology for the execution of applications on constrained devices. In this case, constrained devices are mobile phones, PDAs, TV set-top boxes, in-vehicle telemetry, residential gateways and other embedded devices.

J2ME as a whole can be described as the technology that caters for all these devices. Given that many of them have limited resources, it would be imprudent to expect all of these devices to be able to deliver all of the functionality of the few. The Java community therefore decided that these devices should be grouped to best reflect their purpose and capabilities. This would provide a lowest common denominator for each device group and arrange them into **configurations**. To further differentiate these devices and to accommodate vertical markets within each configuration, **profiles** were created, refining the Java APIs for each device type.

The following analyzes how J2ME is positioned within the Java architecture and how the J2ME configurations and profiles complement each other. It also describes the packages and classes within the commonly used environments, with special emphasis on MIDP 2.0.

1.1   Configurations and Profiles

1.1.1   Architecture

J2ME is the newest and smallest addition to the Java family. It is the smaller brother of J2SE (Standard Edition) and the server-based J2EE (Enterprise Edition). As mentioned, J2ME provides a development environment for a range of small, constrained devices. Even though J2ME is targeted at devices with limited capabilities, it has been derived from J2SE and shows all the characteristics of the Java language. We have already

Programming Java 2 Micro Edition on Symbian OS: A developer's guide to MIDP 2.0.   Martin de Jode
© 2004 Symbian Ltd   ISBN: 0-470-09223-8

introduced the concepts of configurations and profiles; the rest of this chapter will explain how and why these concepts have been derived and implemented.

Each combination of configuration and profile matches a group of products specifically optimized to match the memory, processing power and I/O capabilities of each device.

The full Java architecture can be seen in Figure 1.1. It shows how the technology has developed to offer a platform for a range of circumstances. Enterprise applications can be developed using the J2EE packages, taking full advantage of the power of large servers capable of transmitting large chunks of data across networks. The J2SE edition complements J2EE and provides the basis for desktop-type applications. Already we can see that these two versions of Java are defined with consideration of processor power, memory and communication ability: it would be inefficient for the virtual machine running on a desktop machine (J2SE) to also include large packages targeted towards an enterprise application (J2EE).

Further inspection of the Java architecture reveals that there are two groups of special interest to us, under the banner of J2ME. J2ME provides an environment for developers wishing to develop applications for smaller devices. This environment has been specialized to cater for machines with even less capacity.

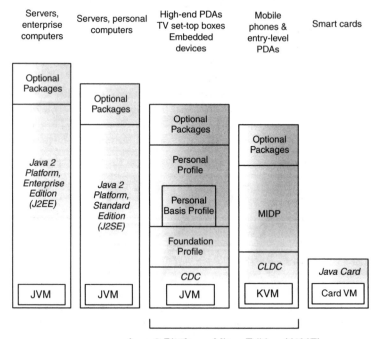

Figure 1.1 The Java landscape.

1.1.2   Configurations

So far we have examined the bigger Java picture and looked at how J2ME fits within that. We have also established that J2ME provides an environment for the development and execution of applications for constrained devices. These devices cover a broad range of functionality and use: we may want to program devices that provide telemetry data from a vehicle, or create data applications for a TV set-top box; but we might instead want to develop applications for mobile phones.

These three examples show immediately why we might want to split J2ME into configurations. While an application sitting in a motor vehicle transmitting data back to a server has much in common with a gaming application transmitting high scores to a server, one thing that becomes apparent is the differential in power source available to both. One device is able to draw on the car battery, whereas a mobile phone has to rely on a rechargeable battery. The requirements in the cost and size of the hardware are also different. This provides particular constraints on the capabilities of the processor and therefore the virtual machine within the device. While all these devices have common attributes, not all of them are the same. It is therefore necessary to provide a set of base classes appropriate to each grouping of devices.

A configuration consists of a combination of a virtual machine and a minimal set of class libraries designed to provide the base functionality for a distinct set of devices with similar characteristics, such as network connectivity, processor power and memory. There are two such current configurations, defined as follows:

- Connected Device Configuration (CDC)
  This configuration is designed for devices with more memory, faster processors and greater network bandwidth. It is appropriate, at least in the near term, for home automation and automotive entertainment, navigation, and telemetry systems. A programming model closer to J2SE simplifies porting existing desktop clients for enterprise systems to mobile devices that support CDC.

- Connected Limited Device Configuration (CLDC)
  This configuration is intended for devices with intermittent network connections, small processors and limited memory. Expected targets included two-way pagers, mobile phones and entry-level PDAs. However, in practice, the functionality delivered by CLDC and the associated profiles and optional packages is very close to that of CDC. As a consequence it is used today on most high-end mobile phones, or smartphones, which are replacing PDAs in the marketplace.

1.1.3   Profiles

Whereas a configuration provides the lowest common denominator for a group of devices, the profile adds an additional layer on top of the configuration providing APIs for a specific class of device. This creates the ability for each configuration to be adapted and targeted towards vertical markets. That is to say, while some devices may appear to have similar functionality, they do in fact have different requirements in terms of the available APIs and interfaces to their own hardware. Some mobile phones, for example, offer more memory, CPU speed or I/O interfaces than others and therefore might want to offer more in terms of an interface between the programmer and the hardware.

Currently, four Java Community Process profiles exist across the two J2ME configurations, but only one of those is a CLDC profile. However, an additional profile called 'DoJa', defined by NTT DoCoMo, operates on the J2ME CLDC APIs and is used on i-mode devices. With only one JCP profile currently defined, a developer new to J2ME might ask themselves: why is a profile required at all?

Using the example of two-way pagers as a possible type of CLDC device, it becomes easier to understand the need for another profile. We can see there are similarities between two-way pagers and mobile phones. Both usually connect intermittently over a wireless network, both can communicate via text type messaging and, possibly, both may store a certain level of information, such as phone numbers. They will both also have a screen of some description. However, the user interface (UI) signals the beginning of the diversity between the two types of device. The method by which data input is captured and indeed displayed will be very different. Each device should have a UI in tune with its own capabilities. While both types of device are CLDC, each will require a separate profile so that the most appropriate APIs are available to the developer.

Mobile Information Device Profile (MIDP)

This profile offers the core functionality required by mobile applications, such as the user interface, network connectivity, local data storage and, importantly, application lifecycle management. As well as the reference implementation for mobile phones and pagers, there is a second implementation that caters for the Palm OS. It is known as MIDP for Palm OS and it provides for the different user interface on such devices.

Information Module Profile (IMP)

This profile is based upon the MIDP 1.0 profile. IMP combined with CLDC provides a Java application environment targeted at resource-constrained and embedded networked devices. These devices do not have rich graphical user interfaces, but their relationship to MIDP 1.0 means that developer skills can be easily transferred to IMP.

Foundation Profile

This profile is the first of three, tiered CDC profiles. It provides a network-capable implementation without a user interface. It can be combined with the Personal Profile and Personal Basis Profile when devices require a UI.

Personal Profile

This profile is aimed at devices that require full GUI or Internet applet support, such as high-end PDAs or communicator-type devices. It provides a full Abstract Window Toolkit (AWT) library and offers web fidelity. It is capable of running web-based applets designed for the desktop environment.

Personal Basis Profile

This profile is a subset of the Personal Profile and provides a network-based environment for network-connected devices that support a limited GUI or require specialized graphical interfaces. Devices include set-top boxes and in-vehicle systems.

The Personal Basis Profile and Personal Profile have replaced Personal Java technology and provide a clear migration path for PersonalJava applications to J2ME. Although Personal Information Management and Telephony APIs are not mandatory in this profile, replacements are being specified for J2ME use. Both the Personal Basis Profile and Personal Profile are layered on top of the CDC and Foundation Profile.

1.2 CLDC and MIDP

1.2.1 CLDC

A developer wishing to create applications for mobile devices may be tempted to ignore the full specification of CLDC. A developer may initially be interested in getting acquainted with MIDP as a standalone technology. It is, however, important to understand the underlying technology that forms MIDP.

The CLDC, as specified by Java Specification Request (JSR) 30 (**http://jcp.org/en/jsr/detail?id=30**), is the smaller of the two configurations and sets out to define a standard for devices with the following capabilities:

- 160 KB to 512 KB of total memory budget available for the Java platform

- 16-bit or 32-bit processor

- low power consumption, often operating on battery power

- intermittent network connection, possibly wireless and limited to a bandwidth of 9600 bps or less.

The 160 KB memory budget is derived from the minimum hardware requirements, as follows:

- at least 128 KB of non-volatile memory available for the Java Virtual Machine and CLDC libraries

- 32 KB of volatile memory for the Java runtime object memory.

CLDC itself defines the minimum required Java technology in terms of libraries and components for small-connected devices. Specifically, this addresses the Java language itself, the virtual machine definition, core libraries, I/O capabilities, networking and security.

Interestingly, from an early stage, one of the focuses for the CLDC definition was to recognize that much of the content for these devices would come from third-party developers. Another was that the idea of being able to create applications portable across a range of devices should be adhered to. This would provide an easier path to revenue generation and therefore proliferate content for more devices. The nature of Java means that a programmer can create applications that use the device's features without having to actually understand the working of the device. The developer only needs to comprehend the interface to the device. CLDC does not guarantee portability and it does not implement any optional features. Variants of devices within CLDC should be specified through profiles, rather than the configuration. It must be said that true application portability can only be obtained if a few principles are applied during the application design stage. We shall be looking at these issues later in this book.

1.2.1.1   K-Virtual Machine

Sun's original VM for CLDC was known as the KVM (which stood for Kauai Virtual Machine, sometimes also known as the Kilo Virtual Machine). The CLDC VM is, apart from a few differences which we shall outline shortly, compliant with the Java Virtual Machine Specification and the Java Language Specification.

The libraries available are typically split into two categories: those defined by CLDC and those defined by a profile and its optional packages such as MMAPI and WMA. Figure 1.2 demonstrates at a high level how these components fit together.

So that the CLDC virtual machine can run within a small footprint and also to take into account additional security requirements for CLDC devices, CLDC differs from CDC in the following respects:

- no floating point support (although it has been added for CLDC 1.1) – this means that `float` and `double` numbers cannot be used and alternative means of storing these values have to be found, for example, "string math"

- no finalization – the `Object.finalize()` method does not exist (`Object.finalize()` is used to carry out any tidying up that may

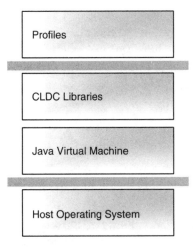

Figure 1.2 High-level architecture.

be needed when an object is collected by the garbage-collector. However, there is little, if any, practical need for this method.)

- limited error handling – only three error classes exist: `java.lang.Error`, `java.lang.OutOfMemory` and `java.lang.VirtualMachineError`

- no Java Native Interface (JNI) – this is due to security concerns and the overhead exerted by JNI on the device memory

- no user-defined class loaders – the built-in class loader cannot be overridden, for security reasons

- no reflection

- no thread groups and daemon threads – although threading is available, thread groups cannot be created (however, `Thread` arrays can be created if a similar effect is required)

- no weak references, although these will be added to CLDC 1.1.

1.2.1.2 Core Libraries

A number of classes have been inherited from J2SE. To maintain the relationship between J2ME configurations and J2SE, it was decided that each class has to have the same name and that each package name must be identical or a subset of the corresponding J2SE class. The semantics of the class must remain the same; methods included in the subset shall not be changed. This means that classes may not be added to a package if they do not exist in J2SE.

The following outlines the classes that are available in CLDC 1.0 (a full listing of these packages can be found in Appendix 1):

- system classes – J2SE includes several classes that are closely tied into the Java virtual machine; for example, the `javac` compiler requires certain functions from the `String` and `StringBuffer` classes

- data type classes – `Boolean`, `Byte`, `Short`, `Integer`, `Long` and `Character` are supported under CLDC; `Double` and `Float` are not supported

- collection classes – `Vector`, `Stack` and `Hashtable` are available, together with interfaces such as `Enumeration`

- input/output classes – `Reader`, `Writer`, `InputStreamReader` and `InputStreamWriter` are required in order to support internationalization

- calendar and time classes – a small subset of the `java.util` classes `Calendar`, `Date` and `TimeZone` are included; only one time zone is supported by default, although device manufacturers may implement additional ones

- additional utility classes – the `java.util` classes `Random` and `Math` have been included to provide a pseudo-random number generator and methods such as `min`, `max` and `abs`, respectively

- exception classes – as the CLDC classes are compatible with J2SE libraries, CLDC classes throw the same exceptions as J2SE classes; there is, therefore, a fairly comprehensive list of exception classes (see Appendix 1)

- error classes – in contrast to the exception classes, the error handling capabilities of CLDC are limited to the three error classes seen previously

- internationalization – CLDC provides support for the translation of Unicode characters to and from byte streams; just as J2SE uses readers and writers, J2ME uses the following constructors:

```
new InputStreamReader(InputStream is);
new InputStreamReader(InputStream is, String name);
new OutputStreamReader(OutputStream os);
new OutputStreamReader(OutputStream os, String name);
```

The constructors that define a string parameter can name the encoding scheme. If it is not named, the default encoding (stored in the system property `microedition.encoding`) is used. Additional converters may be used by certain implementations. An `UnsupportedEncodingException` will be thrown if the specified converter is not present. CLDC does not support localization such as time and currency formatting. If necessary, these can be added to an application's logic.

- property support – `java.util.Properties` provides support for the limited set of properties available in CLDC.

The properties are obtained by making a call to `System.getProperty(String, key)`. This method returns some limited property information about the device itself, such as the configuration version, platform name, character encoding and supported profiles. It also returns the values of the properties defined by each optional package supported by the device.

1.2.1.3   *Networking and I/O*

Networking on CLDC devices has been streamlined so that the programmer does not have to fully understand the underlying device capabilities. The Generic Connection Framework (GCF) has been created, streamlining the implementation of networking within applications. This also helps provide a smaller footprint.

Networking and I/O are implemented using the same interface. All connections are created using a single static method in a system class called `Connector`. There are six basic interface types addressed by this framework, although the actual implementation of any of these protocols is governed by the profile rather than by CLDC:

- basic serial input
- basic serial output
- datagram communication
- connection-orientated, i.e. TCP/IP
- notification mechanism for client–server communications
- basic web server connections.

Creating the connections is rather simple and, regardless of the type of connection, the format is the same. Here is a list of some common examples:

- HTTP:
  `Connector.open("www.foo.com");`
- Sockets:
  `Connector.open("socket://192.168.0.1:9000");`
- Datagrams:
  `Connector.open("datagram://192.168.0.1");`

This minimizes the differences between one protocol and another and uses a text string (the parameter to the `open()` method) to categorize the type of connection required. This approach means abstractions within application modules remain the same when communication changes from one form to another. Essentially, the binding of the protocols is

carried out at runtime. At implementation level, the open() parameter
(up to the first ":") instructs the system to obtain the desired protocol
from the location where the protocol implementations are stored. This
late binding allows an application to dynamically adapt to use different
protocols at runtime.

1.2.1.4 Security

Implementing a full J2SE-style security policy requires a large amount of
memory that is not available to typical CLDC devices. CLDC therefore
implements a simpler domain-based security model, which specifies:

- Java classes are properly verified and guaranteed to be valid Java
  applications; the classes are pre-verified at build time, which means
  that the CLDC implementation has much less to do to verify a JAR file

- only a limited, predefined set of Java APIs is available to the
  application programmer: those defined by CLDC, the profiles and
  optional packages

- the downloading and management of applications on the device
  takes place at the native code level inside the virtual machine; no
  user-definable class loaders are provided

- the set of native functions accessible to the virtual machine is closed,
  meaning that the programmer cannot download new libraries containing native functionality; native functions other than those associated
  with the Java libraries provided by the configuration or profile cannot
  be accessed

- the programmer cannot override the system classes provided in the
  packages java.*, javax.microedition.* and other profile or
  system-specific packages; this is governed by a class lookup which
  is performed during class verification and provides the reason for the
  pre-verification stage of MIDlet (the basic MIDP application structure) packaging.

Further security measures may, of course, be implemented by the profile,
as shall be seen in Section 1.2.2.

1.2.2 MIDP

The Mobile Information Device Profile (MIDP) combined with CLDC
provides a more focused platform for mobile information devices, such
mobile phones and entry-level PDAs. MIDP provides the vertical integration required to make the Java runtime environment applicable to
these devices by providing direction for the base environment provided
by CLDC.

The MIDP specification has been revised under JSR 118 (Symbian is
one of the contributors to the JSR 118 expert group). MIDP 2.0 extends

the original definition in a number of ways and provides a platform which enables developers to create highly graphical, audio-capable, networked applications for mobile devices. A maintenance release, MIDP 2.1, is being specified.

Supported by many integrated development environments, MIDP has become a widely-accepted platform and has been deployed on many mobile devices around the world. If developers take the approach that they can "write once and tweak everywhere", they can leverage the underlying technology to distribute enterprise, utility and entertainment applications to a wide and varied audience.

The introduction of over-the-air provisioning has standardized the method by which applications may be deployed to end-users. Users can browse web or WAP sites to locate applications and the Application Manager System (AMS) checks for versioning and compatibility with the host device and manages local installation. MIDP is also optimized to provide a graphical user interface for mobile devices, regardless of input method and screen size.

1.2.2.1 MIDP Packages

The MIDP 2.0 specification offers developers seven packages with which they may create applications. The packages are derived from CLDC as well as providing additional classes, which can be found under `javax.microedition.*`. This follows the rule that all packages and classes inherited from J2SE must follow the same naming conventions. All new classes not inherited from J2SE must be given a new naming convention, hence the creation of the `javax.microedition` package nomenclature.

Inherited classes

These classes are inherited from J2SE via CLDC:

- `java.lang`
- `java.io`
- `java.util`

MIDP 2.0 classes

These classes extend the CLDC environment and provide user interface, gaming, MIDlet application framework, persistent storage, multimedia, network and security classes. Details of these classes can be found in Appendix 2:

- `javax.microedition.io` provides networking support based upon the Generic Connection Framework defined in CLDC
- `javax.microedition.lcdui` provides a standard set of user interface classes

- `javax.microedition.lcdui.game` is new to MIDP 2.0 and provides a game development framework aimed at speeding up the game development process

- `javax.microedition.media` is new to MIDP 2.0 and provides basic audio functionality such as playback and simple tone generation

- `javax.microedition.media.control` is new to MIDP 2.0 and defines the specific `Control` types that can be used with a media `Player`

- `javax.microedition.midlet` provides the MIDlet framework

- `javax.microedition.rms` provides persistent storage for applications, even when the MIDlet is not running; a "best effort" is also made by the device implementation to retain data during power loss

- `javax.microedition.pki` is new to MIDP 2.0 and provides end-to-end security for MIDlets by the introduction of registered domains; trusted MIDlets can be installed and given extra access to the device.

1.2.2.2 Core Functionality

Mobile User Interface (LCDUI)

MIDP provides a set of standard components to aid the creation of portable, intuitive user interfaces. These classes reduce the development time and also reduce the size of the final application.

The standard classes include screen objects, which hold objects such as choice groups, lists, pop-up alerts and progress bars. Forms can be created to capture user input via text entry components, read-only fields and custom items. All screen and form objects are device-aware and provide support for native display, input and navigation techniques. MIDP 2.0 also sees the introduction of the `CustomItem` class, which allows developers to define their own form items.

Multimedia and Game Functionality

MIDP provides an ideal opportunity for developers to create game and other entertainment content for mobile devices. A set of low-level APIs allows the developer to take control of the screen at pixel level. Graphics can be animated and user input can be captured. The Game API adds game-specific control over animation with its framework implementation managing sprites, collision detection, layers and tiled layers. Built-in multimedia support is also provided with the Mobile Media API (MMAPI), an optional MIDP package that adds video and other multimedia functionality. MIDP also has a subset of the MMAPI which provides support for simple tone generation and playback of WAV files.

The Game API has been added as part of MIDP 2.0 and further consolidates the case for Java being a game development platform for mobile devices. Coupled with over-the-air provisioning, this offers a strong business case for generating revenue streams from users obtaining entertaining applications whilst on the move. The provision of this game development framework leaves the designer more time to work on game-play, rather than having to repurpose home-made animation classes to suit another application. This also reduces application size and optimizes animation routines by permitting extensive use of native code, hardware acceleration and device-specific image data formats, as required.

The Game API provides a manager for sprites and layers, as well as providing an implementation for creating complex tiled layers. The layer manager keeps an index of all screen objects registered with it and renders them on screen as required when calls are made to its paint() method.

The Media API has been created for MIDP 2.0 as a subset of the larger Mobile Media API (MMAPI), developed under the Java Community Process JSR 135. When the MMAPI was developed it was recognized that smaller constrained devices, such as mobile phones, would not be able to accommodate its full complement. Wisely, it was recognized that not all mobile devices would, for example, have cameras so making this compulsory would be ineffective. The MIDP 2.0 Media API therefore sets out to provide upwards audio compatibility with MMAPI. The Media API provides the ability to perform simple tone generation, audio play-back of WAV files, and general media controls such as start, stop and volume control.

Extensive Connectivity

Developers can enable their applications to communicate over a network as required (see Section 2.1.3.2). Interfaces are available for communication over http, https, datagrams, sockets and serial ports. MIDP also supports the SMS capabilities of GSM and CDMA networks through the optional Wireless Messaging API (WMA). WMA 2.0 even supports MMS capabilities. A specific device may not provide support for all of these protocols.

Communication with third parties can also be created using an event-based networking model. MIDP supports a server push model based upon a push registry which keeps track of registered third party inbound communications from the network. When information arrives, the device can start the registered MIDlet (this may depend on user approval). This enables developers to create turn-based games, for example, or to create enterprise applications which receive alert-based data such as financial or field sales information, and integrate that information directly with an application.

Over-the-Air Provisioning

Although MIDP 1.0 did not officially encapsulate an over-the-air provisioning (OTA) definition, it did recommend a practice that was adopted as an addendum to the original specification and has now been made a part of the MIDP 2.0 specification. This means that deployment and updating of applications over-the-air now falls within the MIDP specification. It has therefore been standardized and defines how applications are discovered, installed and removed on MIDP devices. The most useful consequence of this is that status reports can now be produced. This greatly enhances the revenue model for MIDP applications because applications can be tracked as they are installed, updated or removed.

Persistent Storage

MIDP also implements a simple record-based database management system. The data will remain present across multiple invocations of a MIDlet. The platform is responsible for making its best effort to maintain the integrity of the data throughout normal use of the device, including rebooting and battery changes. However, when the associated MIDlet suite is removed, so are the record stores. MIDP 2.0 now allows explicit sharing of data across MIDlet suites, assuming the serving data store has given permission for this sharing.

End-to-End Security

With greater network connectivity and the nature of common application installation methods, a robust security model has been specified. HTTPS leverages existing standards such SSL and WTLS and enables the transmission of encrypted data. Security domains are used to identify trusted and untrusted MIDlets. By default, all applications are untrusted and are prevented from accessing any privileged functionality. Access can be gained by signing the MIDlet to specific domains defined on the device using the X.509 PKI standard.

This allows mobile phone operators and manufacturers to improve the user experience by limiting the capabilities of unknown applications. Developers see application credibility and user confidence increased by having their applications reviewed, and deemed trusted, by operators or manufacturers in order to access advanced capabilities. Depending on the security policy of the device, a user may also choose to allow unknown applications full or temporary access to advanced capabilities.

1.3   CDC and Personal Profile

1.3.1   CDC

The Connected Device Configuration (CDC) has been developed under the Java Community Process, by JSR 36. Symbian was a member of the expert group that developed it. The configuration has been designed for devices with more memory, faster processors and greater network bandwidth than those using CLDC. Examples of such devices include TV set-top boxes, residential gateways, in-vehicle telemetry and high-end PDAs.

With this in mind, it is easier to understand that CDC was designed with the aim of being based upon the J2SE 1.3 APIs while providing support for resource-constrained devices. This leaves a route open for existing J2SE developers to leverage their skills and also provides a path for the creation of secure enterprise-type applications for constrained devices.

CDC offers more facilities than CLDC. It provides a full Java 2 virtual machine including floating point and core library features, such as custom class loading, thread support and security. Like CLDC, it is a subset of the full J2SE implementation; the classes have been optimized to create a smaller memory footprint and some J2SE libraries have modified interfaces. An example of this is that the `javax.microedition.io` package provides the generic connection interface for input/output and networking.

Target devices are expected to have the following minimum specification:

- 32-bit CPU

- 2 MB RAM

- 2 MB ROM.

The Java environment for these devices is completed with the addition of one of three profiles which sit on top of the CDC classes to form the complete implementation. The CDC profiles, which are layered, are as follows:

- the Foundation Profile (JSR 46) is the most basic CDC profile; it provides the basic application support classes such as network and I/O support but does not provide a graphical user interface

- the Personal Basis Profile (JSR 129) provides all of the Foundation Profile APIs and a structure for building lightweight component toolkits and support for the Xlet application model

- the Personal Profile (JSR 62) provides full AWT, applet and limited bean support as well as the Foundation and Personal Basis Profiles; it represents a migration path for PersonalJava technology.

We shall have a close look at the Personal Profile in Section 1.3.2.

1.3.1.1 Core Libraries

The following core packages are available within the CDC configuration:

- `java.io` provides the system input and output through data streams, serialization and the file system

- `java.lang` provides the classes that are fundamental to the design of the Java language, for example, `Object`, which is the root of the class hierarchy

- `java.lang.ref` provides the reference-object classes, which support a limited degree of interaction with the garbage collector

- `java.lang.reflect` provides the classes and interfaces for obtaining reflective information about classes and objects

- `java.math` provides classes for performing arbitrary-precision integer (`BigInteger`) and decimal (`BigDecimal`) arithmetic

- `java.net` provides the classes for implementing networking applications

- `java.security` provides the classes and interfaces for the security framework

- `java.security.cert` provides the classes and interfaces for parsing and managing certificates

- `java.text` provides classes and interfaces for handling text, dates, numbers and messages in a manner independent of natural languages

- `java.util` provides the classes which contain the collections framework, legacy collection classes, event model, date and time facilities, internationalization and miscellaneous utility classes such as the string tokenizer and random number generator

- `java.util.jar` provides classes for reading and writing the JAR file format, which is based upon the standard ZIP file format with an optional manifest file

- `java.util.zip` provides classes for reading and writing the standard ZIP and GZIP file formats

- `javax.microedition.io` provides the classes for generic connections.

1.3.1.2 Optional Packages

The optional packages give device manufacturers the ability to support additional technologies if they so wish:

- RMI provides a subset of the J2SE RMI for Java-based network devices; it exposes distributed application protocols (through Java interfaces, classes and method invocations) and shields the application developer from the details of network communications

- JDBC provides a subset of the JDBC 3.0 API, which can be used to access flat files and tabular data sources such as spreadsheets; it also provides cross-DBMS connectivity to a range of SQL databases.

1.3.2   Personal Profile

The Personal Profile provides a further way of specifying the subset of APIs for a CDC-based device. Its definition is based upon the Java Community Process JSR 62, for which Symbian was a member of the expert advisory group.

As we have seen earlier, profiles provide a more specialized environment for devices common to a particular configuration. The Personal Profile is aimed at devices that require full GUI or internet applet support, such as communicators or game consoles. It is the successor to Personal-Java, which was developed prior to the formalization of J2ME, and therefore provides a clear migration path for PersonalJava applications to the J2ME platform.

The Personal Profile builds upon the Foundation Profile and the Personal Basis Profile by adding graphical user interface classes to the environment. It inherits networking and Xlet capabilities from the other two profiles. It has been designed to provide full graphical support and the ability to run web-based applets designed for the desktop to mobile device applications with web fidelity. The following outlines the core packages included in the Personal Profile and from where they are derived.

Added by the Foundation Profile
The following packages provide full J2SE 1.3.1 support for basic class library packages:

- `java.io`

- `java.lang`

- `java.lang.ref`

- `java.net`

- `java.security`

- `java.security.acl`

- `java.security.cert`

- `java.security.interfaces`

- `java.security.spec`

- `java.text`

- `java.util`

- `java.util.jar`

- `java.util.zip`

The following package provides compatibility for the CLDC 1.0 generic connection framework:

- `javax.microedition.io`

Added by the Personal Basis Profile
The following packages provide support for lightweight components and some 2D Java graphics:

- `java.awt`

- `java.awt.color`

- `java.awt.event`

- `java.awt.image`

The following package provides bean support by an external bean editor (IDE) running on a J2SE-based JRE:

- `java.beans`

The following packages provide limited RMI support for Xlets and are not intended for general-purpose use:

- `java.rmi`

- `java.rmi.registry`

The following packages provide Xlet support:

- `javax.microedition.xlet`

- `javax.microedition.clet.ixc`

Added by the Personal Profile
The following package provides support for applets:

- `java.applet`

The following packages provide support for heavyweight components and 2D graphics:

- `java.awt`

- `java.awt.datatransfer`

1.4   J2ME on Symbian OS

Java on Symbian OS has a long history dating back to Symbian OS Version 5 (released in 1999). This initial Java offering was based on Sun's JDK 1.1.4 platform. For the next major release, Symbian decided to take advantage of the reduced memory footprint offered by PersonalJava (compared to the burgeoning JDK) and used the PersonalJava 1.1.1 specification as the basis for the Java implementation. This release, Symbian OS Version 6.0, became available in 2000.

PersonalJava was the forerunner of J2ME and the first attempt by Sun to provide a Java environment for the more resource-constrained embedded device. It is the direct antecedent of the CDC-based Personal Profile.

In 1999, acknowledging that "one size doesn't fit all", Sun announced the splitting of Java into three versions:

- Java 2 Enterprise Edition (J2EE)
- Java 2 Standard Edition (J2SE)
- Java 2 Micro Edition (J2ME).

Symbian immediately became involved in shaping the Micro Edition via the expert groups of the Java Community Process. Soon it was clear that J2ME MIDP was gaining momentum in the wireless space as phone manufacturers endorsed the idea of a lightweight Java environment suitable for mass-market phones. Symbian recognized the strength of the MIDP movement by including J2ME CLDC/MIDP 1.0 as its standard Java offering in Symbian OS Version 7.0, released in 2002, as well as back-porting the technology to earlier versions. Currently, all Symbian OS phones available in Western markets support at least MIDP 1.0.

Although MIDP 1.0 generated considerable enthusiasm amongst the wireless Java community, it was also realized that MIDP 1.0 on its own was limited in its capabilities to access the functionality offered by a typical smartphone from within a MIDlet. Consequently, soon after the release of MIDP 1.0, the wireless Java community started work on enhancing the capabilities of MIDP. This has manifested in MIDP 2.0 (JSR 118), released in its final form in November 2002, and a range of extension API JSRs, all forming part of the Java Community Process.

These developments provide a substantial increase in the functionality available to MIDlets. As a consequence, the latest release of Symbian OS (Version 7.0s) and UIQ 2.1 move to a single Java technology stream based on J2ME CLDC and MIDP 2.0 (plus additional optional J2ME APIs).

J2ME MIDP is now established as the ubiquitous Java platform in the mobile phone arena and, as such, Symbian will continue to evolve and enhance its CLDC/MIDP offering. For more insight into future developments of J2ME on Symbian OS, including Symbian's position with regard to CDC-based technologies, the reader is referred to Chapter 8.

1.5   Summary

This chapter has introduced the J2ME architecture in order to indicate
the position of MIDP 2.0 within that structure. We have examined the
various configurations and profiles and shown why they are necessary in
providing a structure for the various needs and requirements of a J2ME
device now and in the future. We have outlined the packages and classes
of CLDC 1.0 and MIDP 2.0 to show their core functionality and have also
shown how J2ME and Symbian sit together.

In Chapter 2 we are going to examine MIDP 2.0 in more depth, start
programming a simple MIDP 2.0 application and look at the some of the
various tools on offer.

2

Getting Started

2.1 Introduction to MIDP

In the previous chapter we examined the core MIDP functionality and outlined the CLDC and MIDP classes that form the development environment. Before we start writing our first piece of code, we need to look at the basic concepts of MIDP, the most commonly used packages and methods, and how it all fits together. We'll also look at the various development options, what they can do, and how they are installed.

MIDP allows the execution of multiple MIDP applications, known as MIDlets. The model defines how the MIDlet is packaged, what runtime environment is available, and how it should behave with respect to the, sometimes, constrained resources of the MIDP device. The model also defines how MIDlets can be packaged together in suites and share one another's resources, such as graphics and data stored in the small database facility known as the RMS. Each MIDlet suite also has a descriptor file called the JAD file, which allows the application management software on the device to identify what it is about to install prior to installation. The model also defines a lifecycle for a MIDlet, which allows for orderly starting, stopping and cleanup of a MIDlet.

2.1.1 The MIDP Model and Lifecycle

The MIDlet forms the application framework that executes on CLDC devices under the Mobile Information Device Profile (MIDP). Every application must extend the MIDlet class found in the `javax.microedition.midlet` package. The application management software (AMS) manages the MIDlet itself. The AMS is a part of the device's operating environment and guides the MIDlet through its various states during the execution process. Unlike desktop or server applications, MIDlets should not have a `public static void main()` method. If

Programming Java 2 Micro Edition on Symbian OS: A developer's guide to MIDP 2.0.   Martin de Jode
© 2004 Symbian Ltd   ISBN: 0-470-09223-8

one is found then the AMS ignores it. MIDlets are initialized when the AMS provides the initial class needed by CLDC to start the MIDlet. The AMS then guides the MIDlet through its various changes of state. We shall look at these states next.

2.1.1.1   MIDlet States

Once a MIDlet has been instantiated, it resides in one of three possible states. A state is designed to ensure that the behavior of an application is consistent with the expectations of the end-users and device manufacturer. Initialization of the application should be short; it should be possible to put an application in a non-active state; and it should also be possible to destroy an application at any time. Therefore, three valid MIDlet states exist:

PAUSED
The MIDlet has been initialized, but is in a dormant state. This state is entered in one of four ways:

- after the MIDlet has been instantiated by the AMS invoking its constructor; if an exception occurs, the DESTROYED state is entered

- from the ACTIVE state, if the `pauseApp()` method is called by the AMS

- from the ACTIVE state, if the `startApp()` method has been called but an exception has been thrown

- from the ACTIVE state, if the `notifyPaused()` method has been invoked and successfully returned.

When a well-written MIDlet is paused, it should generally release any shared resources.

ACTIVE
The MIDlet is functioning normally. This state is entered after the AMS has called the `startApp()` method. The `startApp()` method can be called on more than one occasion during the MIDlet lifecycle.

DESTROYED
The MIDlet has released all resources and terminated. This state, which can only be entered once, is entered for the following two reasons:

- the `destroyApp(boolean unconditional)` method has been called by the AMS and returned successfully; if the `unconditional` argument is `false` a `MIDletStateChangedException` may be thrown and the MIDlet will not move to the DESTROYED state; the implementation of the `destroyApp()` method should release all resources and terminate any running threads

- when the `notifyDestroyed()` method successfully returns; the application should release all resources and terminate any running threads prior to calling `notifyDestroyed()`.

2.1.1.2 MIDlet Lifecycle Methods

The `javax.microedition.midlet.MIDlet` abstract class defines three lifecycle methods:

- `pauseApp()` – this method is called by the AMS to indicate to the MIDlet that it should enter the PAUSED state, releasing all shared resources and becoming passive

- `startApp()` – this method is invoked by the AMS to signal to the MIDlet that it has moved from the PAUSED to the ACTIVE state. The application should acquire any resources it requires to run and then set the current display

- `destroyApp()` – this method is called by the AMS to indicate to the MIDlet that it should enter the DESTROYED state; all persistent and state data should be saved and all resources that have been acquired during its lifecycle should be released at this point; generally, a well-written MIDlet will start up in the state it was in prior to being shut down.

2.1.1.3 Notifying and Requesting the AMS

The AMS manages the MIDlet suite installation and lifecycle. There are a number of methods that the MIDlet may use to notify the AMS of the state it is in:

- `notifyDestroyed()` – the MIDlet notifies the AMS that it has released all resources held during execution, moved into the DESTROYED state and may be reclaimed by the system

- `notifyPaused()` – the MIDlet notifies the AMS that it has moved into the PAUSED state, releasing any shared resources it held

- `resumeRequest()` – a paused MIDlet asks the AMS to be started again

- `getAppProperty()` – provides a MIDlet with a mechanism to retrieve named properties from the AMS.

2.1.1.4   *The Lifecycle Model*

The various states of the MIDlet (see Figure 2.1) show how the AMS and the MIDlet interface combine to form the lifecycle of the MIDlet:

1. The AMS creates a new instance of a MIDlet. The MIDlet's constructor is called with no argument and the application is put into the PAUSED state. If any exception is thrown during this phase then the application is put into the DESTROYED state.

2. The AMS calls `startApp()` to move the MIDlet into the ACTIVE state. The MIDlet itself will at this point acquire any resources it needs and begin executing.

3. Once the application is running, the MIDlet can move to two other states:

    *   the `MIDlet` can be put into the PAUSED state by a call from the AMS to the `pauseApp()` method
        The MIDlet will cease to be in the ACTIVE state and choose to release some of the resources it currently holds. If the programmer requires the MIDlet to pause, then the MIDlet should first release shared resources (possibly stopping any running threads) and then call the `notifyPaused()` method.

    *   the MIDlet can move to the DESTROYED state
        The user or the AMS decides that the application no longer needs to be running. Game play may be finished, for example, or the AMS may have decided that a process of a higher priority needs to claim the resources being used by the MIDlet.

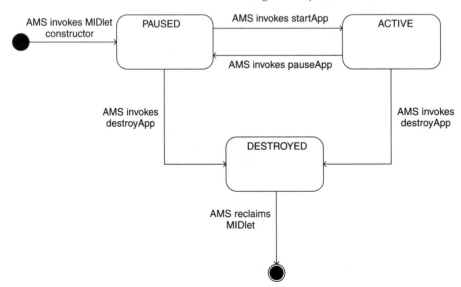

Figure 2.1   State transition diagram of the MIDlet lifecycle.

2.1.1.5 Example MIDlet

The basic structure of a MIDlet is very simple. As outlined earlier, there is no static `main` method. The MIDlet is instantiated by the AMS, which provides the initial class for the MIDlet to initialize.

The following skeleton code shows this basic MIDlet structure:

```
import javax.microedition.midlet.*;
public class MyMidlet extends MIDlet {
    public MyMidlet() {
    }
    public void startApp() throws MIDletStateChangeException {
    }
    public void pauseApp() {
    }
    public void destroyApp(boolean unconditional) {
    }
}
```

2.1.1.6 Creating MIDlets

Once the MIDlet has been created we are ready to compile, pre-verify and package the MIDlet into a suite for deployment to a target device or a device emulator.

CLDC provides a two-pass implementation of the bytecode verifier. Not only is the standard J2SE verifier bigger than the whole of a typical CLDC implementation, it also requires over 100 KB of dynamic memory for a typical application. CLDC therefore requires a pre-verifier, which is typically run on the machine used to build the application, to carry out the space- and performance-intensive parts of verification. The pre-verifier annotates the bytecode so that all the client device has to do is check the results for correctness: the annotations cannot be spoofed and code signing is not required. The on-device footprint is about 10 KB and requires fewer than one hundred bytes of runtime memory. The downside is a 5 % increase in class file size.

Typically, compilation, pre-verification and packaging are automated by tools, such as the KToolbar, available with Sun's J2ME Wireless Toolkit, as we will discuss later in this chapter. The toolkits provide an interface for the compiler, `javac`; pre-verification, `preverify.exe`; and the packaging tool, `jar`. These commands are also available on the command line (see Appendix 3).

Once this process has been completed we are nearly ready to run the MIDlet suite. There is, however, one final task to complete: the creation of the application descriptor (JAD) file. This file is required to notify the AMS of the contents of the JAR file. The following attributes must be included in a JAD file:

- `MIDlet-Name` – the name of the suite that identifies the MIDlets to the user

- `MIDlet-Version` – the version number of the MIDlet suite; this is used by the AMS to identify whether this version of the MIDlet suite is already installed or whether it is an upgrade, and communicate this information to the user
- `MIDlet-Vendor` – the organization that provides the MIDlet suite
- `MIDlet-Jar-URL` – the URL from which the JAR file can be loaded; both absolute and relative URLs must be supported; the context for relative URLs is from where the JAD file was loaded
- `MIDlet-Jar-Size` – the number of bytes in the JAR file.

It is also useful to include the following attributes in a JAD file:

- `MIDlet-n` – the name, icon and class of the *n*th MIDlet in the JAR file (separated by commas); the lowest value of *n* must be 1 and all following values must be consecutive; the name is used to identify the MIDlet to the user and must not be null; the icon refers to a PNG file in the resource directory and may be omitted; the class parameter is the name of the class extending the MIDlet class
- `MIDlet-Description` – a description of the MIDlet suite
- `MicroEdition-Configuration` – the J2ME configuration required, in the same format as the `microedition.configuration` system property, e.g. "CLDC-1.0"
- `MicroEdition-Profile` – the J2ME profiles required, in the same format as the `microedition.profiles` system property, e.g. "MIDP-1.0" or "MIDP-2.0" depending on the version of MIDP against which the MIDlet is built; if the value of the attribute is set to "MIDP-2.0", the device onto which the MIDlet is to be installed must implement the MIDP 2.0 profile otherwise the installation will fail; MIDlets compiled against the MIDP 1.0 profile will install successfully on a device implementing MIDP 2.0.

The following represents a sample JAD file for a hypothetical application called "MyMidlet":

```
MIDlet-1:MyMidlet, MyIcon.png, com.symbian.MyMidlet
MIDlet-Description: Example MIDP 2.0 MIDlet
MIDlet-Jar-Size: 3707
MIDlet-Jar-URL: MyMidlet.jar
MIDlet-Name: MyMidlet
MIDlet-Vendor: Symbian Ltd
MIDlet-Version: 2.0
MicroEdition-Configuration: CLDC-1.0
MicroEdition-Profile: MIDP-2.0
```

Once the JAD file has been created the MIDlet is ready to be executed. The following command line is used to initiate the MIDlet within the emulator supplied with the Wireless Toolkit, via its JAD file.

```
C:\WTK20\bin>emulator -
       Xescriptor:C:\WTK20\apps\Example\bin\MyMidlet.jad
```

Of course, much of this is simplified if the developer uses the Wireless Toolkit KToolbar application, which provides a convenient GUI to these functions. However, it may not always be possible to do this, especially in the case of Solaris and Linux machines.

2.1.2 User Interfaces

A user interface for mobile information devices would have proved something of a challenge for those sitting around the table during the early stages of creating the MIDP 1.0 specification. Confronted with a device of limited power, display and storage capabilities, those participants, including Symbian, who were a part of the Java Community Process for JSR 37 (MIDP 1.0) would have thought long and hard about how best to tackle this problem.

MIDP devices do, of course, pose quite a challenge for those tasked with developing applications. Much of the challenge in the application design is trying to create a sophisticated, productive application intuitive enough for the enterprise user to grasp easily or engaging enough for the gamer. It must also be capable of running in a restricted environment.

Java developers may at this point be asking themselves, "I can see how much of the J2ME technology has been adapted or truncated from J2SE, so why not do the same with the user interface?" There are numerous reasons, many of which are concerned with the device paradigm itself. AWT was designed for desktop applications. The desktop paradigm draws upon inherited usage from other applications: the purpose and use of certain components, and the navigation between them, is understood by the user and, therefore, doesn't have to be re-learnt. It is also intuitive: more space allows the GUI to have fuller, more explanatory labels and a pointer device provides a convenient way to initiate those commands.

One of the main considerations for mobile applications has to be portability. There are many different devices in the marketplace, all with different screen sizes and keypads. Some have pointer devices, some have joysticks and others have full keyboards. MIDP has had to cater for all these devices.

Mobile devices do not have a great need for window management or re-sizing. Clearly an AWT-type interface would be overkill on a device so small. Features such as overlapping windows, toggling between forms and then resizing them would be wasted. Buttons are also placed in specific places. The mobile UI needs to be more fluid and dynamic.

Since much time has been spent by manufacturers testing out their devices on users, with focus groups, usability studies and other market research, it would be a waste to then expect users to learn another method of entering and reading data from the device's screen. Remember the inherited knowledge a PC user gains from using the PC user interface? Well, the same applies to a mobile UI. The implementation of each of the high-level UI components is therefore left to the devices themselves and as a result the MIDP GUI (known as the LCDUI) was designed to take into account the following:

- a portable user interface

- a consideration of the form factor of small devices, the size of the screen, the data input methods and the processor size: processing AWT objects and dealing with their garbage collection would not be appropriate for a constrained device

- many people will use the devices while on the move or when not fully concentrating on the task in hand; many of the devices will be used with one hand, although some may use a pointing device

- the UI of the applications should be comparable to the native applications on the device.

2.1.2.1   Structure of the MIDP UI API and Class Overview

The LCDUI is split into high-level and low-level APIs, both of which have event-handling capabilities.

The high-level API is designed for applications that are required to be portable across many devices, regardless of screen size and input method. These applications can generally be aware of the device they are running on and make adjustments accordingly. A simple example of this would be whether a pointing device was present or not. This set of classes has a high level of abstraction and therefore the developer has little control over the look and feel. More specifically, the programmer has no control over the color, font and style of the components; scrolling and navigation of the on-screen image is left to the underlying implementation.

Conversely, the low-level API provides very little abstraction and gives the programmer precise control over where objects are placed on the screen. Typical examples of such applications would be games, where graphics require pixel-level placement on screen. As well as providing precise control over object positioning, event listeners will monitor for primitive events such as key presses and releases. The developer also has access to concrete keys and pointer actions. The `Canvas` and `Graphics` objects are the basis for the low-level API classes.

Typically, these applications are less portable than those developed using the high-level API. That does not mean, however, that these applications cannot be made to be portable. Some careful design to separate the UI from the main game logic can yield economies of scale and a number of these techniques and theories will be investigated in Chapter 6. The `Canvas` object provides methods for querying the size of the screen and also for identifying keys with the use of game-key mapping, which provides a generic method for accessing certain keys on the keypad. This mapping helps identify many of the actions required by games developers and maps the layout of certain keys on the pad to logical positions a game player might assume when playing.

2.1.2.2   The LCDUI Model

At the basic abstraction level of the MIDP user interface is the `Displayable` object. This encapsulates device-specific graphics rendering, along with the user input, and only one `Displayable` object can be visible at any one time. There are three types of `Displayable` object across the two APIs:

- complex, predefined, immutable user interface components, such as `List` or `TextBox`

- generic objects that may contain other objects or user interface components, such as a `Form`; input objects such as text fields can be appended to provide screens capable of capturing user input, entry of a password, for example

- user-defined screens, such as `Canvas`, a part of the low-level API.

The first two are inherited from `Screen`, which is itself derived from `Displayable` and handles all the user interaction between the high-level components and the application. The `Screen` object also manages all the rendering, interaction, traversal and on-screen scrolling, regardless of the device and the underlying implementation and it forms the basis for portability of the applications using these APIs. In the case of the third type of `Displayable` object, `Canvas` takes care of providing the basis of a UI with the low-level API classes.

The `Display` class acts as the display manager for the MIDlet. Each MIDlet is initialized with a `Display` object. There can only be one display in action at any one time and user interaction can only be made with the current display. The application sets the current display by calling the `Display.setCurrent(Displayable)` method; it can, of course, be any of the three `Displayable` object types.

The display manager interacts with the AMS to render the current display on the screen. To understand how to structure the application in the correct way, we need to look back at the MIDlet initialization process and lifecycle we examined in Section 2.1.1. The MIDlet is initialized in the paused state. Once the AMS has decided that the MIDlet is ready, it makes a call to the `startApp()` method. It should be remembered that the startApp() method can be called many times during the lifecycle of a MIDlet, so the developer should be aware of what display is made current and at what time. In MIDP 1.0, it was advised that the Displayable object was not truly visible until startApp() had returned. However, this requirement has been relaxed in MIDP 2.0. The Display.setCurrent(Displayable) method can, therefore, be carried out at MIDlet initialization and put in the MIDlet constructor. This also alleviates any problems the developer may experience with unwanted re-initialization of the application and its display after resuming from the paused state.

2.1.2.3   The Event Model

The javax.microedition.lcdui package implements an event model that runs across both the high- and low-level APIs. This handles such things as user interaction and calls to redraw the display. The implementation is notified of such an event and responds by making a corresponding call back to the MIDlet. There are four types of UI event:

- events that represent abstract commands that are part of the high-level API

- low-level events that represent single key presses or releases, or pointer events in the case of pointer-based devices

- calls to the paint() method of the Canvas class, generated for instance by a call to repaint()

- calls to a Runnable object's run() method requested by a call to callSerially() of class Display.

All callbacks are serialized and never occur in parallel. More specifically, a new callback will never start while another is running. The next one will only start once the previous one has finished, this will even be true when there is a series of events to be processed. In this case the callbacks are processed as soon as possible after the last UI callback has returned. The implementation also guarantees that a call to run(), requested by a call to callSerially(), is made after any pending repaint() requests have been satisfied.

There is, however, one exception to this rule: this occurs when the Canvas.serviceRepaints() method is called by the MIDlet. The call to this method causes the Canvas.paint() method to be invoked by the implementation and then waits for it to complete. This will occur whenever the serviceRepaints() method is called, regardless of where the method was called from, even if that source was an event callback itself.

Abstract commands are used to avoid having to implement concrete command buttons; semantic representations are used instead. The commands are attached to `Displayable` objects such high-level `List` or `Form` objects or low-level `Canvas` objects. The `addCommand()` method attaches a `Command` to the `Displayable` object. The `Command` specifies the label, type and priority. The `commandListener` then implements the actual semantics of the command. The native style of the device may prioritize where certain commands appear on the UI. For example, "Exit" is always placed above the right softkey on Nokia devices.

There are also some device-provided operations that help contribute towards the operation of the high-level API. For example, screen objects, such as `List` and `ChoiceGroup`, will have built-in events that return user input to the application for processing.

2.1.2.4 The High-Level API

Since MIDP 1.0, the LCDUI classes have vastly improved, helping the developer to create more intuitive, portable applications. Figure 2.2 shows the class diagram for both the high- and low-level APIs.

Command Class

The `Command` class is a construct that encapsulates the semantic meaning of an action. The behavior or response to the action is not itself specified by the class, but rather by a `CommandListener`. The command listener is attached to a `Displayable` object. The display of this command will depend upon the number and type of the other commands for that displayable object. The implementation is responsible for the representation

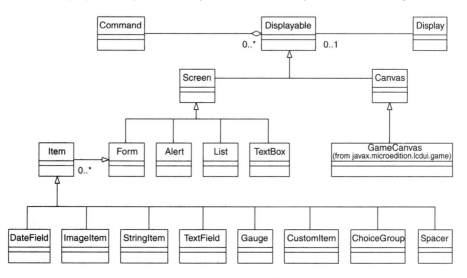

Figure 2.2 The architecture of the LCDUI.

of the command semantic information on screen; Command itself merely contains the following four pieces of information about the command:

- short label
  This string is mandatory. The application can request the user to be shown a label. Dependent upon the current layout and available screen space, the implementation will decide which is more appropriate. For command types other than SCREEN, a system-specific label considered more appropriate for this command on this device may override the labels provided.

- long label – this longer label is optional; it will be used if there is enough space to display it

- type – BACK, CANCEL, EXIT, HELP, ITEM, OK, SCREEN and STOP
  This is used to indicate the command's intent, so that the implementation can follow the style of the device. For example, the "back" operation on one device may always be placed over the right softkey.

- priority
  This integer value describes the importance of the command relative to other commands on the same screen. The implementation makes the choice as to the actual order and placement of commands on the screen. The implementation may, for example, first examine the command type to check for any particular style requirements and then use the priority values to distinguish between the remaining commands.

Screen Objects

Alert, List, Form and TextBox are all derived from Screen, itself derived from Displayable. Screen objects are high-level UI components that can be displayed. They provide a complete user interface in their own right, the specific look and feel of which is determined by the implementation.

Alert Object

An Alert object shows a message to the user, waits for a certain period and then disappears, at which point the next Displayable object is shown. This object is intended as a way of informing the user of any errors or exceptional conditions.

An Alert may be used by the developer to inform the user that an error or other condition has been reached. To emphasize these states to the user, the AlertType can be set to convey the context or importance of the message. For example, a warning sound may be played with the alert to draw the user's attention to an error. A different sound can then be played when the alert is advisory. This can be achieved using the AlertType.playSound() method. Other types may also be set, such as ALARM, CONFIRMATION, ERROR and INFO. These manifest as titles at the top of the alert screen.

As well as providing text, an image can also be used to indicate the nature of the alert. An exclamation mark may indicate an error, for example. To ensure the user reads the message, the alert may be made modal (the user must dismiss it before the next Displayable object is shown). This is effectively achieved by setting an infinite timeout on the alert: setTimeout(Alert.FOREVER).

An alert can also be used to show activity to the user. A gauge can be added to the alert to indicate progress, for example, for loading a new level in a game or connecting to a remote server over HTTP. An indicator is added by using the method setIndicator(Gauge). The gauge object is subject to certain limitations: it cannot be interactive, owned by another Form or have Commands attached to it; nor can it be an ItemCommandListener.

List Object

A List object is a screen that contains a list of choices for the user. It has much in common with ChoiceGroup (it shares the same interface, Choice). However, a List cannot be added to a Form and is, in fact, a Displayable object in its own right. This means it is very good for implementing a choice-based menu for the user. The Series 60 and UIQ platforms have a default "Select" mechanism, which means a separate CommandListener does not have to be added to the list. A List can be created by using one of the following two constructors:

```
List menu = new List(String title, int listType)
List menu = new List(String title, int listType, String[] stringElements,
        Image[] imageElements)
```

The second constructor allows the developer to specify the items within the list at creation rather than having to append, insert or set elements within the list.

The list type can be EXCLUSIVE, where only one choice can be made and one choice is selected at a time; MULTIPLE, which allows for more than one selection; or IMPLICIT, in which case the currently focused element is selected when a command is initiated.

Once the selection has been made, the index value or values of the selection can be captured by the application using one of two methods:

- getSelectedIndex() returns the results of a list returning one selection

- getSelectedFlags(boolean[]) returns the flags for all the elements in a MULTIPLE list; the application can then loop through the flags to determine the user's selections.

Form Object

This `Displayable` object is designed to contain a small number of closely-related user interface elements. Those elements are, in general, any subclass of the `Item` class and we shall be investigating these objects in more detail below. The `Form` manages the traversal, scrolling and layout of the form. It is defined by two constructors:

```
Form (String title)
Form (String title, Item[] items)
```

Items enclosed within a `Form` may be edited using the `append()`, `delete()`, `insert()` and `set()` methods and they are referred to by their indexes, starting at zero and ending with `size()`−1. A distinct `Item` may only be placed upon one `Form` at a time. If an attempt is made to put the same instance of `Item` on another `Form`, an `Illegal-StateException` will be thrown.

Items are organized via a layout policy that is based around rows. The rows typically relate to the width of the screen and are constant throughout. Forms grow vertically and a scroll bar will be introduced as required. If a form becomes too large, it may be better for the developer to create another screen. The layout algorithm used in MIDP 2.0 will be discussed in greater detail in Chapter 3.

Users can, of course, interact with a `Form`, and a `CommandListener` can be attached to capture this input using the `setCommandLis-tener()` method. An individual `Item` can be given an `ItemCom-mandListener` if a more contextual approach is required by the UI.

TextBox Object

A `TextBox` is a `Screen` object that allows the user to enter and edit text in a separate space away from the form. This is a `Displayable` object and can, therefore, be displayed on the screen in its own right. Its maximum size can be set at creation, but the number of characters displayed at any one time is unrelated to this size and is determined by the device itself.

Item Class

This is the superclass for all items that can be added to a `Form`. Every `Item` has a label, which is a string. This label is displayed by the implementation as near as possible to the `Item`, either on the same horizontal row or above.

When an `Item` is created, by default it is not owned by any container and does not have a `Command` or `ItemCommandListener`. However, default commands can be attached to an `Item`, using the `setDefault-Command()` method, which means the developer can make the user interface more intuitive for the user. A user can then use a standard gesture, such as pressing a dedicated selection key or tapping on the item with a pointer. Symbian devices support both interfaces through Series 60 and UIQ respectively. As a side issue, it should be noted that the use of default commands can disrupt the use of layout directives. Normal commands can also be attached to items using the `setDefaultCommand(Command)` method. Developers who use the low-level API will be quite familiar with this method.

A new set of properties that determine the minimum and preferred width and height of an `Item` has been added in MIDP 2.0. This can be used by the device implementation to determine how best to render the item on the screen and will be discussed further in Chapter 3.

The following types are derived from `Item`.

ChoiceGroup

A `ChoiceGroup` is a group of selectable objects. It may be used to capture single or multiple choices placed upon a `Form`. It is a subclass of `Item` and most of its methods are implemented via the `Choice` interface. It can be created using one of two constructors:

```
ChoiceGroup (String title, int type);
ChoiceGroup (String title, int type, String[] elements,
        Image[] image Elements);
```

The first, a simpler constructor, allows the developer to create an empty choice group, specifying its title and type, and append elements afterwards. The type can be either `EXCLUSIVE` (to capture one option from the group) or `MULTIPLE` (to capture many selections).

A developer who already knows the contents of the choice group may choose to use the second constructor. This has the advantage that all entries are created at the same time but, of course, the contents of the group may still be dynamic. Just as a `List` can be changed after creation, so the contents of the choice group can be changed. Insert, append and replace functionality is present. Each choice is indexed, incrementing by 1 from the first item being 0.

It is the responsibility of the device implementation to provide the graphical representation of the option group. For example, one device may use ticks to represent selected options in a multiple choice group and radio buttons to denote an exclusive selection. Another device, however, may choose to display these items another way. The point here is that the developer does not have control over the appearance of these items on the screen.

CustomItem

This is one of the most interesting MIDP 2.0 additions to the high-level API. It operates in a similar way to `Canvas`, in that the developer is able to specify what content appears where within the `CustomItem`. The developer has free rein to create an item that suits the purposes of the application.

Some of the standard items may not give quite the required functionality, so it may be better to define home-made ones instead. The only drawback to this approach is that, as well as having to draw all the contents using the item's `paint()` method, the programmer has to process and manage all events, such as user input, through `keyPressed()`.

Custom items may interact with either keypad or pointer-based devices. Both are optional within the specification and the underlying implementation will signal to the item which has been implemented. In the case of Symbian, these can be either UIQ or Series 60 devices.

Deriving from `Item`, `CustomItem` also inherits such methods as `getMinContentWidth()` and `getPrefContentHeight()` which help the implementation to determine the best fit of items within the screen layout. If the `CustomItem` is too large for the screen dimensions, it will resize itself to within those preferred, minimum dimensions. These changes will be notified to the `CustomItem` via the `sizeChanged()` and `paint()` methods.

As we have seen, the developer has total control over what appears on a `CustomItem` and the item is responsible for rendering itself to the display. Additionally, the developer can use the `Display.getColor(int)` and `Font.getFont(int)` methods to determine the underlying properties for items already displayed in the form of which the `CustomItem` will be a part. This will ensure that a consistent appearance is maintained.

DateField

This is an editable component that may be placed upon a `Form` to capture and display date and time (calendar) values. When the item is added to the form it can be set with or without an initial value. If the value is not set, a call to the `getDate()` method will return null. The field can handle `DATE` values, `TIME` values or both, `DATE_TIME` values. Where both are specified, the user interface will manage one after the other when looking for input. Calendar calculations made from this field are based upon the default locale and time zone definitions stored on the device.

ImageItem

The `ImageItem` is a reference to a mutable or immutable image that can be displayed on a `Form`. We shall look at the `Image` object in detail when we examine the low-level API classes. Suffice to say that the `Image` is retrieved from the MIDlet suite's JAR file in order to be displayed upon the form. This is performed by calling the following method, in this case from the root directory:

```
Image image = Image.createImage("/myImage.png");
```

This returns an `Image` object that can be used to create the `ImageItem`. An `ImageItem` is created by calling one of two constructors:

```
ImageItem imageItem = new ImageItem (String label, Image image,
        int layout, String altText);
ImageItem imageItem = new ImageItem (String label, Image image,
        int layout, String altText, in appearanceMode);
```

A title for the item can be defined along with a combination of layout constants that determine how the image should be laid out. The `altText` parameter will be displayed by the implementation if it establishes that the image is too large for the current display. The second constructor adds another parameter that determines the appearance of the `ImageItem`. The `appearanceMode` parameter values may be PLAIN, HYPERLINK or BUTTON. The preferred and minimum sizes may be affected if the second or third options are used.

Spacer

This is a blank non-interactive item with a definable minimum size, which was added as part of the MIDP 2.0 specification. It is used for allocating flexible amounts of space between items on a form and gives the developer much more control over the appearance of a form. The minimum width and height for each spacer can be defined to provide space between items within a row or between rows of items on the form.

StringItem

This is an item that can contain a string. It is a display-only item and the user cannot edit the contents. Both the label and content of the `StringItem` can, however, be changed by the application. As with `ImageItem`, its appearance can be specified at creation as one of PLAIN, HYPERLINK or BUTTON. The developer is able to set the text using the `setText()` method and its appearance using `setFont()`.

TextField

A `TextField` is an editable text component that may be placed upon a `Form`. It can be given an initial piece of text to display. It has a maximum size, set by `setSize(int size)`, and an input mask, which can be set when the item is constructed.

An input mask is used to ensure that end-users enter the correct data. This can reduce user frustration which, considering the input methods available to mobile devices, is very useful. The following masks can be used: ANY, EMAILADDR, NUMERIC, PHONENUMBER, URL, DECIMAL. These constraints can be set using the `setConstraints()` method and retrieved using `getConstraints()`. The constraint settings should be used in conjunction with the following set of

modifier flags using the bit-wise AND (&) operator: PASSWORD, SEN-
SITIVE, UNEDITABLE, NON_PREDICTIVE, INITIAL_CAPS_WORD,
INITIAL_CAPS_SENTENCE.

Ticker
This implements a ticker-tape object – a piece of text that runs continuously across the display. The direction and speed of the text is determined
by the device. The ticker scrolls continuously and there is no interface to
stop and start it. The implementation may pause it when there has been
a period of inactivity on the device, in which case the ticker will resume
when the user recommences interaction with the device.

The Ticker is created using the constructor Ticker(String
text); the currently displayed text is returned by getString(); and
the text is set or reset using setString(String text).

Interfaces
Four interfaces are provided by the user interface package, javax.mi-
croedition.lcdui. They are available to both the high- and low-
level APIs.

- Choice defines an API for user interface components such as List
  and ChoiceGroup
  The contents of these components are represented by strings and
  images which provide a defined number of choices for the user. The
  user's input can be one or more choices and they are returned to the
  application upon selection.

- CommandListener is used by applications that need to receive
  high-level events from the implementation; the listener is attached to
  a Displayable object within the application using the addCom-
  mand() method

- ItemCommandListener is a listener type for receiving notification
  of commands that have been invoked on Item objects
  This provides the mechanism for associating commands with specific
  Form items, thus contextualizing user input and actions according to
  the current active item on the Form, making it more intuitive.

- ItemStateListener is used by applications that need to receive
  events that indicate changes in the internal state of the interactive items
  within a Form; for example, a notification is sent to the application
  when the set of selected values within a ChoiceGroup changes.

2.1.2.5   The Low-Level API

Graphics and the Canvas
The low-level API provides the developer with a much more flexible
approach to user interface development. Whereas the high-level classes

leave the implementation to manage the display, the low-level API provides fine-grained control of the display to the developer. The programmer has pixel-level control over the positioning of objects on the screen and can also define objects through the extensive graphics facilities available.

Canvas, the main base class for low-level application programming, allows the developer total control over the display. The developer may specify down to pixel level the position of objects on the screen. To implement Canvas, the application should subclass it to create a new Displayable screen object. As it is Displayable, it is interchangeable with other screen objects such as List and Form. The developer may choose to use the high-level user interface classes when creating the UI by toggling between the two types.

Canvas is most commonly used by game developers when creating sprite animation, and it also forms the basis of GameCanvas, which is part of the new MIDP 2.0 Game API and will be examined later in this chapter and in more detail in the next. Canvas can be used in two modes. Normal mode allows for the display of other information such as softkey labels, title and other device information screen furniture. In full screen mode, set by calling the setFullScreenMode(boolean mode) method, the Canvas takes up as much of the display as the implementation will allow. In either mode, the dimensions of the Canvas can be accessed using the getWidth() and getHeight() methods.

Graphics are drawn to the screen by implementing code in the abstract paint() method. This method must be present in the subclass and will be called as part of the event model. The event model provides a series of methods that include user input methods such as keyPressed() and pointerPressed(), depending upon the device's data input implementation. All the methods are called serially except serviceRepaints() which blocks all other events until paint() has returned. In other words, if serviceRepaints() is called, then it will be serviced before calls to the others are resumed.

The paint(Graphics g) method provides a graphics object, which is used to draw to the display. The Graphics object provides a simple 2D geometric rendering capability. Rendering operations are based upon pixel replacement. Source pixels from the graphics context replace the destination pixels in the display object. Transparency is also supported and is implemented by leaving the pixel in an unchanged state. The color context can be set using the setColor (int red, int green, int blue) method.

An Image is drawn using the drawImage(Image image, int x, int y, int anchor) method of the Graphic class, which specifies the location of an Image object on the display. Other primitives may also be drawn: strings are drawn using drawstring(String string, int x, int y, int anchor) and rectangles using drawRectangle(int x, int y, int width, int height).

Such methods as keyPressed() and pointerPressed() represent the interface methods for the CommandListener. When a key is pressed, it returns a keyCode to the command listener. These key-Codes are mapped to keys on the keypad. The keyCode values are unique for each hardware key, unless keys are obvious synonyms for one another. These codes are equal to the Unicode encoding for the character representing the key. Examples of these are KEY_NUM0, KEY_NUM1, KEY_STAR, KEY_POUND, to mention a few. The problem with these key codes is that they are not necessarily portable across devices: other keys may be present on the keypad and will perhaps form a distinct list from those described previously. It is therefore better, and more portable, to use game actions instead.

Each keyCode can be mapped to a game action using the getGameAction(int keyCode) method. This translates the key code into constants such as LEFT, RIGHT, FIRE, GAME_A and GAME_B. Codes can translated back to keyCodes by using getKeyCode(int gameAction). Apart from making the application portable across devices, these game actions are mapped in such a way as to suit gamers. For example, the LEFT, RIGHT, UP and DOWN game actions might be mapped to the 4, 6, 2 and 8 keys on the keypad, making game-play instantly intuitive.

Typically, a simple Canvas class might look like this:

```
import javax.microedition.lcdui.*;
public class SimpleCanvas extends Canvas {
    public void paint(Graphics g) {
        // set color context to be black
        g.setColor(255, 255, 255);
        // draw a black filled rectangle
        g.fillRect(0, 0, getWidth(), getHeight());
        // set color context to be white
        g.setColor(0, 0, 0);
        // draw a string in the top left corner of the display
        g.drawString("This is some white text", 0, 0, g.TOP | g.LEFT);
    }
}
```

Threading

While we are looking at the low-level API, it is worth having a quick look at threading. Threading can be used to create animation within an application; there are many ways in which this can be done.

Timers can be used, but the most common way to create a thread is to implement a Runnable interface. Typically, it would be best to make the Canvas class Runnable and use this as the central core of any animated application. Implementing this interface specifies that the abstract run() method must be implemented and this is where the main work of the thread will be carried out. Normally, a Thread object is instantiated and the Runnable class itself is passed as the target. The following shows a framework that might be adopted:

```
import javax.microedition.lcdui.*;
public class ThreadedCanvas extends Canvas implements Runnable {
    private Thread thread;
    private boolean isRunning;
    private final int SLEEP = 50;
    ThreadedCanvas() {
        // initialize the class here.
    }
    synchronized void start() {
        isRunning = true;
        thread = new Thread(this);
        thread.start();
    }
    synchronized void stop() {
        isRunning = false;
    }
    public void run() {
        // put the main game logic in here
        while (isRunning) {
            // perform thread tasks
            // repaint
        }
        try {
            Thread.sleep(SLEEP);
        }
        catch (Exception e) {}
    }
    public void paint(Graphics g) {
        // paint Graphics object to the screen
    }
}
```

The Game API

Probably one of the most useful additions to the MIDP 2.0 programming environment is the creation of the Game API. It specifies a framework with which programmers can create rich gaming applications. The API has been designed to improve the performance of gaming applications on mobile devices that have, by definition, limited processor power. Application size is greatly reduced because much of the code required to produce sprite animation has been wrapped within the API's classes.

The API consists of five classes, which are as follows and will be given greater attention in Chapter 3:

- GameCanvas – a subclass of Canvas that provides the basic screen functionality for game development
  As well as inheriting methods from Canvas, it also provides some game-centric functionality, such as being able to query the current state of game keys, synchronous graphics flushing and an off-screen graphics buffer, which improve overall performance and simplify development.

- Layer – the visual element in a game such as a Sprite or a
  TiledLayer; it forms the basis for the Layer framework and affords
  necessary features such as location, size and visibility

- LayerManager – an index of all the layers present in the game
  It provides the ability to create a "view" or "viewport" to the game,
  which is useful when the developer is creating a large virtual world. As
  the user navigates through the world, the LayerManager manages
  what should be seen at each particular moment. It then renders that
  view to the display.

- Sprite – a basic animated Layer that can display one of several frames
  The really useful functionality of Sprite is that it creates a number
  of equal-sized frames based upon the input of a Sprite film-strip,
  provided at creation. It therefore becomes self-aware and is able to
  provide a custom or default sequential animation of all of its frames.
  Transformations may also be carried out and collision detection
  methods are available to simplify the development.

- TiledLayer – a class that enables the developer to create a large
  area of graphical content, without having to use the huge resources
  that a large image would require.
  The TiledLayer consists of a grid of cells that can be populated
  with one of several small tile images. In the Demo Racer application
  (see Chapter 5), we use a TiledLayer to create the background.
  These tiles are repeated across the screen to create a larger, screen
  sized image. If, for example, we want some of these tiles to change we
  could create dynamic cells to provide animation for a specific cell.
  For example, we may want to add a "glaring sun" to the sky area of
  the screen.

2.1.3 RMS Storage

One of the main problems for any application, especially in the enterprise
sector, is the question of storing data after the application has been closed.
MIDP applications may be used by sales people on the road, snapshots
of financial data may be downloaded via a secure server to the device or
it may be that high scores for a game need to be stored. Implementing
a full-scale JDBC database on a small, constrained device would be
adventurous, not to mention resource-draining on power and processor.
However, at the other end of the scale the data cannot be written directly
to the device's file system as this breaks the MIDP sandbox security
model. Therefore MIDP provides a simple record-based persistent storage
mechanism known as the Record Management System (RMS). The RMS
allows the MIDlet application to store persistent data within a controlled

environment, while maintaining system security. It provides a simple, non-volatile data store for MIDlets while they are not running.

The classes making up the RMS are contained in the `javax.micro-edition.rms` package. Essentially, the RMS is a very small, basic database. It stores binary data in a `Record` within a `RecordStore`. MIDlets can add, remove and update the records in a `RecordStore`. The persistent data storage location is implementation-dependent and is not exposed to the MIDlet.

A `RecordStore` is accessible across all MIDlets within a suite, and MIDP 2.0 extends access to MIDlets with the correct access permissions from other MIDlet suites. However, when the parent MIDlet suite is removed from the device, its recordstores are also removed regardless of whether a MIDlet in another suite is making use of them.

The RMS recordstore is discussed in more detail in Chapter 3 and will also feature in a couple of the case studies described in Chapter 5.

2.1.3.1   *Media API in MIDP 2.0*

MIDP 2.0 includes a small audio-only media capability, known as the Media API. The Media API is a subset of the much richer optional J2ME Mobile Media API (JSR 135). The Mobile Media API does ship on some Symbian OS phones, such as the Nokia 3650 and Nokia 6600, but it is an additional API and not part of MIDP 2.0.

The MIDP 2.0 Media API provides support for tone generation and audio playback of WAV files if the latter is supported by the underlying hardware. Since MIDP 2.0 is targeted at the widest possible range of devices, not just feature rich smartphones, the aim of the Media API is to provide a lowest common denominator functionality suitable for the capabilities of all MIDP 2.0 devices.

We will discuss programming the Media API and the Mobile Media API in detail in Chapter 3.

2.1.3.2   *Networking*

In Chapter 1 we looked at how the CLDC has defined a streamlined approach to networking, known as the Generic Connection Framework. The framework seeks to provide a consistent interface for every network connection between the MIDP classes and the underlying network protocols. Every time a network connection is made, no matter what protocol is being used, the interface remains the same. To open a connection, the static `open()` method in the `Connector` class is used.

In MIDP 1.0, the only protocol for which support was required was HTTP. MIDP 2.0 has made many more protocols available, although HTTP and HTTPS are the only two mandatory protocols. The optional protocols include sockets, server sockets and datagrams.

MIDP 2.0 adds an interesting new feature in the Push Registry. The Push Registry maintains a list of incoming network connections registered by MIDlets. When an incoming connection is received by the device a lookup of the port and MIDlet name is performed. If the MIDlet is not currently running then, if permitted by the security policy, the MIDlet will be launched.

Networking and the Push Registry will be discussed in more detail in Chapter 3.

2.2   Helloworld, Turbo Edition

By this stage in the book it is about time we started showing you some real code. So let's have a look at a sample application.

Helloworld has been the stalwart for authors time and time again because it serves to show the developer the basics and is also simple to program. We thought, however, we might stretch the reader a little more here. We want to give you something a little more useful, something that serves to demonstrate some points already made and also illustrates points we wish to make once we delve deeper into this book.

This application is still called Helloworld, but the tag "Turbo Edition" has been added to give it some glamour! Whereas previous Helloworld applications have only really served to display some text on the screen, this version sets out to unlock some of the more useful additions included in MIDP 2.0. The Game API seemed the most likely candidate.

2.2.1   Overview

As has been outlined above, rather than recreate the wheel, we decided that it would be interesting to show what can be achieved by using the Game API and some sprite graphics. It was thought that the techniques used here might serve as a splash screen, just to let the user know that everything is well in the world and the application is loading. When it is running, the Symbian logo is displayed, before splitting into four (see Figure 2.3). The four pieces rotate and the display becomes "Helloworld, Turbo Edition" (see Figure 2.4). The animation then runs in reverse.

In addition to being a rather sophisticated animation, this demonstrates the application lifecycle and what it really means for the developer. It also illustrates one of the basic principles of the Game API, sprite animation. So let's have an initial look at what is actually inside it.

This application is made up of four classes and one PNG format graphics file. It has been tested using the Nokia 6600 and we did, of course, use some of the tools outlined later in this chapter to achieve the end product.

Figure 2.3 Helloworld: Symbian.

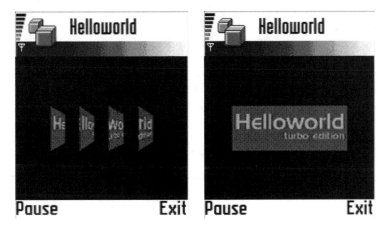

Figure 2.4 Helloworld: Turbo Edition.

2.2.2 MIDlet Class: `Helloworld.java`

This is the main class for the application. This class represents the MIDlet lifecycle of the application. Earlier in this chapter we described the process a MIDlet goes through from initialization to being destroyed. You may remember we talked about the relationship between the application software manager and the MIDlet itself. The AMS provides the class which initializes the MIDlet class. When it is ready to do so, a call is made to the `startApp()` method (every MIDlet has one).

It must be remembered that the `startApp()` method can be called more than once during the lifecycle of the MIDlet. The developer has, therefore, to be careful what code is put in this method. If, for example, the application were paused during execution, it would be unwise to display the wrong screen to the user. It would cause confusion and it is better to let the user know what is happening. It would also be unwise to put all initialization for a recordstore into the MIDlet constructor because the data does not have to be re-initialized when the MIDlet is re-executed after being released during the `pauseApp()` process. A balance has to be struck at this point to create a well-structured application.

Why not just set the current display, say a `Canvas` object, directly in the `setCurrent()` method in `startApp()`? More flexibility can be given to the application if we set a global `displayable` object at this point. It means that when the application is paused, whether by the AMS or the user, the global `displayable` object is set, for example to a pause screen which is more informative. After setting the `displayable` and therefore the current display to this temporary "paused" screen, the `displayable` object can then be set to the screen you wish the user to see once execution resumes. Therefore when `startApp()` is called and the MIDlet resumes execution, the user will return to the place where they were when they paused.

While we have been concerning ourselves with displaying the correct screen to the user, we also have to remember that the `MyGameCanvas` object is `Runnable`. During the `startApp()` process we have made a call to start the `MyGameCanvas` thread running. This enables the thread that provides the animation for that class. While the application is in the paused state, this resource should be released. Although the application can pause execution, it must be remembered that the device, through the AMS, may require the MIDlet to pause and release resources to deal with more important issues, such as receiving a phone call or text message.

```
import javax.microedition.lcdui.*;
import javax.microedition.midlet.*;
import java.io.IOException;
public class Helloworld extends MIDlet implements CommandListener {
    private MyGameCanvas gameCanvas;
    private MyPauseCanvas pauseCanvas;
    private Command exit;
    private Command pause;
    private Command resume;
    private Display display;
    private Displayable displayable;
    public Helloworld() {
        display = Display.getDisplay(this);
        pauseCanvas=new MyPauseCanvas();
        getCanvasDisplay();
        // create the commands for both the gameCanvas and pauseCanvas
        exit=new Command("Exit",Command.EXIT,1);
        pause=new Command("Pause",Command.ITEM,2);
        gameCanvas.addCommand(exit);
        gameCanvas.addCommand(pause);
        gameCanvas.setCommandListener(this);
        resume=new Command("Resume",Command.ITEM,2);
        pauseCanvas.addCommand(resume);
```

```
            pauseCanvas.setCommandListener(this);
    }
    protected void startApp() throws MIDletStateChangeException {
        getCanvasDisplay();
        display.setCurrent(displayable);
    }
    protected void pauseApp() {
        System.out.println("Pausing...");
        if(displayable!=null){
            display.setCurrent(displayable);
        }
    }
    public void destroyApp(boolean unconditional) {
        releaseResource();
    }
    private void releaseResource() {
        if(gameCanvas!=null){
            gameCanvas.stop();
        }
    }
    private void getCanvasDisplay(){
        try{
            if(gameCanvas==null){
                gameCanvas=new MyGameCanvas(this);
            }
            if(!gameCanvas.isRunning()){
                gameCanvas.start();
            }
            displayable=gameCanvas;
        }
        catch(IOException ioe){
        }
    }
    public void commandAction(Command command, Displayable d)    {
        if (command==exit){
            releaseResource();
            notifyDestroyed();
        }
        else if (command==pause){
            displayable=pauseCanvas;
            releaseResource();
            notifyPaused();
        }
        else if(command==resume){
            try{
                startApp();
            }
            catch (MIDletStateChangeException msce){}
        }
    }
}
```

2.2.3   GameCanvas Class: `MyGameCanvas.java`

Whereas the `Helloworld.java` class might be described as the heart-beat of this application, the `MyGameCanvas.java` class is probably the brains behind the operation! It is called at the very beginning of execution by the MIDlet and it only stops "thinking" when the MIDlet is paused or destroyed.

MyGameCanvas is responsible for instigating a thread that provides animation to the current display. However, prior to that it loads the graphics from the resource directory within the MIDlet suite; these are then used to form the sprite object, MySprite.java. A LayerManager, also created by the game canvas, manages this sprite object. As each sprite is created, it is added to the layer manager's index.

Once the thread is up and running, having been started by the startApp() method of the MIDlet, it is responsible through each cycle for painting sprites to the screen and making sure that the correct sprite frame is ready to be displayed at the correct time. The thread actually leaves the frame management to the sprite itself, but we shall look at this later. The layer manager makes a call to its own graphics context and draws the sprites to the screen. This cycle creates the illusion that is animation.

This process can be seen in the code below. The run() method provides the engine room for the thread cycle. First, it draws all the objects in its graphics context to the screen, using the draw() method. draw() receives the graphics context from the thread and uses it to create a black rectangular background the size of the screen dimensions. Having calculated the center of the screen, it then uses the layer manager to also paint the sprites within its index to the screen and makes the call to the flushGraphics() method, which notifies the screen that the graphics are ready for drawing and that they should be drawn now.

Before resting for a short while, a call is made to the tick() method, which asks the sprite to manage which frame should be displayed next. This interface needs to remain the same if any changes are made to the underlying logic that determines the frame display.

```java
import javax.microedition.lcdui.game.*;
import javax.microedition.lcdui.*;
import java.io.IOException;
public class MyGameCanvas extends GameCanvas implements Runnable {
    private Command exit;
    private Helloworld midlet;
    private MySprite sprite;
    private LayerManager layerManager;
    private Thread thread;
    private boolean running;
    private final int SLEEP = 100;
    public MyGameCanvas(Helloworld midlet) throws IOException {
        super(true);
        this.midlet = midlet;
        sprite = createSprite();
        // initialize the layer manager
        layerManager = new LayerManager();
        // append the sprite to the layer manager
        layerManager.append(sprite);
    }
```

```java
public boolean isRunning(){return running;}
synchronized void start(){
    running=true;
    thread=new Thread(this);
    thread.start();
}
public void run(){
    Graphics graphics=getGraphics();
    try{
        while (running){
            draw(graphics);
            tick();
            Thread.sleep(SLEEP);
        }
    }
    catch(InterruptedException ie){
        System.out.println(ie.toString());
    }
}
synchronized void stop(){
    running=false;
}
private void tick(){
        sprite.tick();
}
private void draw(Graphics g){
    // calculate the center of the screen based upon the
    // the images and canvas size
    int x = (getWidth()/2-sprite.getWidth()/2);
    int y = (getHeight()/2-sprite.getHeight()/2);
    // set and draw the background
    g.setColor(0,0,0);
    g.fillRect(0,0,getWidth(),getHeight());
    // paint the sprite on the screen
    layerManager.paint(g,x,y);
    flushGraphics();
}
private MySprite createSprite(){
    Image image=null;
    int height=0;
    int width=0;
    try{
        image = Image.createImage("/Splash.png");
        width = image.getWidth();
        height = image.getHeight() / MySprite.RAW_FRAMES;
    }
    catch(IOException io){
        io.printStackTrace();
    }
    return new MySprite(image, width, height);
}
}
```

2.2.4 Sprite Class: `MySprite.java`

While the metaphor of the body is being used to describe this application, this class most probably represents a limb! It is a relatively simple class, but it is clever enough to recognize what it is and act according to the information it has at its disposal. It subclasses the Game API class Sprite, which is itself an extension of Layer.

In order to make our GameCanvas as flexible as possible we need to make MySprite.java an intelligent class so that it can morph according to what it is holding – in other words, it reacts to the frames it has at its disposal. This is best achieved by making it responsible for making sure the correct frame is current when the game canvas cycles through its loop.

Upon initialization, the object is passed some basic information about itself. First, it is told what image to use. This image is full of the individual sprite images required to provide the animation for the application. This is where the Game API comes into its own. If you pass it an image of a certain height and tell it the height of the individual frames, the Sprite class is clever enough to create the frames for you. This really saves on development time and allows the developer to concentrate on the game logic of the application rather than getting bogged down in sprite definition. Therefore, the other items in the sprite's constructor are width and height.

The sprite in this case is left to determine its own frame order, based upon the order in which the frames are laid out in the graphic image passed to it at initialization. Essentially, the frames are sequenced in one direction and then reversed to provide the opposite effect, forming the animation of the Symbian image rotating to become the Helloworld image.

The beauty of this self-determination approach is that we now have a reusable object, as long as the functionality of the object is to remain the same. If we want to change the appearance of the animation, all we have to do is create a new set of frames and the sprite will do the rest. It is, of course, important to remember that we have to maintain the same interface with the game canvas which makes the calls to the class to set the next frame. It is, however, fair to say that this represents portable code that can be reused to create a different animation without any change to the game canvas.

```
import javax.microedition.lcdui.Image;
import javax.microedition.lcdui.game.Sprite;
public class MySprite extends Sprite {
    protected final int SLEEP=1000;
    protected static final int RAW_FRAMES=13;
    protected static final int HELLOWORLD_FRAME=12;
    protected static final int SYMBIAN_FRAME=0;
    protected boolean direction=false;
    public MySprite(Image image, int width, int height){
        super (image,width,height);
    }
    public void tick(){
        this.getDirection();
        if(direction){
```

```
            this.nextFrame();
        }
        else{
            this.prevFrame();
        }
    }
    private void getDirection(){
        if (this.getFrame() == SYMBIAN_FRAME |
                this.getFrame()== HELLOWORLD_FRAME){
            getDelay();
            if(direction){
                direction=false;
            }
            else{
                direction=true;
            }
        }
    }
    private void getDelay(){
        try{
            Thread.sleep(SLEEP);
        }
        catch(InterruptedException ie){
            System.out.println(ie.toString());
        }
    }
}
```

2.2.5   Paused Message Class: `MyPausedCanvas.java`

This is a very simple class, which requires little explanation. It is merely a
`Canvas` which is set as the current `Displayable` when the Helloworld
MIDlet is paused (see Figure 2.5).

Figure 2.5   Helloworld paused state.

```
import javax.microedition.lcdui.*;
public class MyPauseCanvas extends Canvas {
    private Font font = Font.getFont(Font.FACE_PROPORTIONAL,
          Font.STYLE_BOLD, Font.SIZE_LARGE);
    public void paint(Graphics g) {
        // show the user a screen with "PAUSED" in the center
        g.setColor(0,0,0);
        g.fillRect(0,0,getWidth(),getHeight());
        g.setColor(255,255,255);
        g.setFont(font);
        g.drawString("PAUSED",getWidth()/2,getHeight()/2,
              Graphics.TOP|Graphics.HCENTER);
    }
}
```

2.3 Introduction to Tools for MIDP

2.3.1 Toolkits

2.3.1.1 J2ME Wireless Toolkit 2.1

Overview

The J2ME Wireless Toolkit 2.1 provides basic tools for developers to create MIDP 2.0 applications. The Wireless Toolkit (WTK) was created by Sun to facilitate MIDP development. At the time of writing, the production release can be obtained free of charge from Sun's website (*http://java.sun.com/products/j2mewtoolkit/download-2_1.html*).

Amongst more advanced features, it provides the developer with the ability to compile, pre-verify and package MIDlet suites on the command line, as well as providing a simple GUI to manage MIDP application creation. The "Build" button on the KToolbar combines all the command line functionality described in Section 2.1.1.6, apart from packaging. The packaging command in the Projects menu provides this extra step. A handy interface for creating the JAD file is also supplied and accessed via the Settings button.

The J2ME WTK does not, however, provide a text editor or sophisticated debugging facilities, so users may find development a slightly cumbersome process. It does, however, remain a useful tool as it provides developers with device emulators and a development infrastructure and it captures system output and other debug information such as error messages (see Figure 2.6).

Versions of this tool are available for Windows and Unix-based systems. At the time of writing, the J2ME Wireless Toolkit 2.1 is available in production releases for the following operating systems:

- Microsoft Windows XP or Microsoft Windows 2000

- Microsoft Windows 98/NT (unsupported)

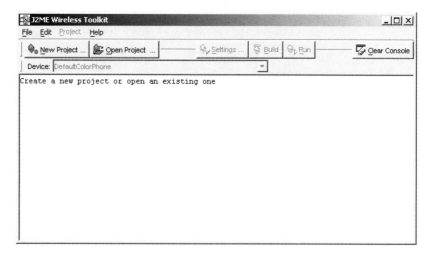

Figure 2.6 J2ME Wireless Toolkit.

- Solaris 8

- Red Hat Linux kernel 2.4.2-2. glibc version 2.2.2 (unsupported).

Also required for development is Java 2 SDK Standard Edition (J2SE SDK) of at least version 1.4 (this is available at the following location: *http://java.sun.com/j2se/downloads.html*).

Although support is only given for the more recent Windows platforms, this still represents a good opportunity for Java developers to test wireless applications on their favored development platforms.

The toolkit offers the developer support in the following development areas:

- OTA emulation
  The toolkit takes the developer through the steps a user experiences when discovering and downloading an application to the device. The emulator displays JAD file information, which allows the end-user to decide whether to install locally or not. The application is then downloaded and verified by the emulator device and installed. The application is then run "locally".

- MIDlet signing
  MIDlet signing is new to the MIDP environment. The toolkit allows a developer to browse for a J2SE keystore file (an SKS file) and use it to sign a MIDlet suite

- WMA emulation for SMS (and CBS broadcasts)

- new skins for QWERTY and media devices

- certificate management – an interface for the developer to manage security certificate files (CER files) and view the contents of J2ME keystore files (KS files)

- Push Registry emulation – this emulates a MIDlet's reaction to an inbound network connection or timer-based alarm; the registry is set up using the Push Registry tab within the Project > Settings dialog

- access to J2ME Web Services – the user can generate a stub connector to access J2ME Web Services from the toolbar; the user provides a Web Service Descriptor Language file (a WDSL file)

- monitoring for all protocols – HTTPS, socket, datagram, COMM, SSL, SMS/CBS

- compile-time and runtime selection of API extensions (WMA, MMAPI)

- switching between MMAPI and MIDP 2.0 Media API – this allows the developer to set the abilities of the underlying API implementation on the emulator device (some devices ship with the full MMAPI, so developers may wish to configure the emulator to reflect more powerful devices)

- new demos – demos such as the Mobile Media MIDlet (mmademo) and SMSDemo MIDlet allow the developer to gain an idea of how the toolkit handles SMS messaging between emulators within the same instance of the toolkit

- support for the ProGuard obfuscator
  Obfuscation provides a level of protection against reverse engineering. It also reduces the final file size of MIDlet suites. This is very useful when most end-users will be downloading their MIDlets remotely over the air. Smaller files mean more efficient execution and less space taken up in the device. ProGuard provides software that performs the obfuscation. It is available, under General Public License, at **http://proguard.sourceforge.net**.

- method profiling (from v1.0)

- memory and network monitoring (from v1.0) – this includes message filtering, sorting messages and viewing network traffic

- device speed emulation (from v1.0).

Installation
To enable installation of the J2ME Wireless Toolkit 2.1, the host PC will need to have the Java 2 SDK 1.4.1 installed. Installation on the PC can be carried out as follows.

1. Execute the file `j2me_wireless_toolkit-2_1-windows.exe` which is available from the download areas on the Java Sun website (see above).

2. The user will be prompted to confirm the location of the Java Runtime Environment (Figure 2.7). Version 1.4.1 or higher is required. If this is not present, it should be installed before continuing with the installation of the toolkit.

3. The destination of the toolkit can then be chosen and confirmed (Figure 2.8). In this case we deviated from the default location. Note that, at least for the current Toolkit, this name cannot contain spaces.

4. The installation program then prompts for the confirmation of a Program Folder name (Figure 2.9). On Windows machines, this is the name of the folder as it appears on the Start menu. It may be desirable to enter a shorter name.

5. A dialog reviewing the installation details is displayed. Press Next to begin installation.

6. The installer will then display a dialog to tell the user that installation has been completed (Figure 2.10).

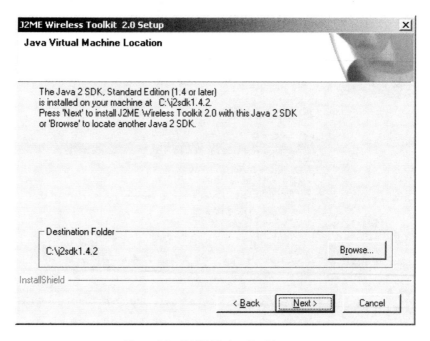

Figure 2.7 J2ME Wireless Toolkit setup.

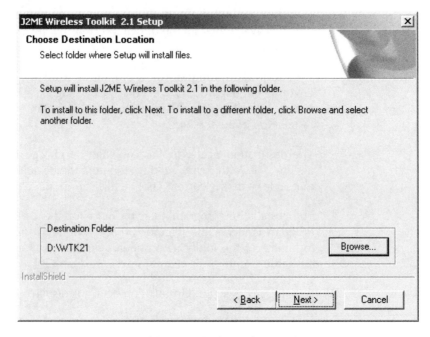

Figure 2.8 Confirming location.

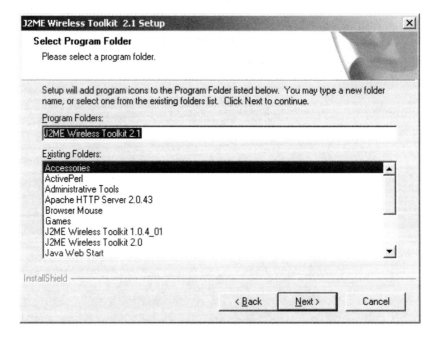

Figure 2.9 Selecting a program folder.

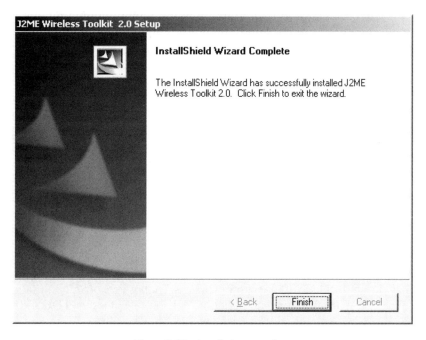

Figure 2.10   Installation complete.

2.3.1.2 Apache Ant

Overview

The Apache Ant project is a part of Apache's Jakarta project (**http://jakarta.apache.org**) and is a Java-based building tool distributed under the Apache license. It has been developed by the Java community and is described as "kind of like Make, but without the wrinkles". It can be obtained from the Apache Ant website (**http://ant.apache.org/index.html**). We are going to use it in conjunction with another tool, Antenna, which provides specific Ant tasks for building MIDP 1.0 and 2.0 applications. This is distributed under the GNU Lesser GPL and can be obtained from the SourceForge website (**http://antenna.sourceforge.net**).

It is a reasonably easy tool to use and, in a similar way to the Wireless Toolkit, it automates the compiling, pre-verifying and packaging of a MIDlet suite. The execution of an emulator can also be added on to the end of the XML configuration file for extra convenience. Whereas the KToolbar provides the developer with adequate tools for MIDlet creation, Ant gives the developer fine-grained control over how the MIDlet suite should be put together. The really great thing about Ant is that it comes fully integrated with Borland's JBuilder, Sun's ONE Studio and can also be integrated with other IDEs such as JCreator (**www.jcreator.com**), JEdit (**www.jedit.org**), and Eclipse (**www.eclipse.org**). However, this section will look at Ant as a standalone tool.

Ant reads an XML configuration file and uses this information to carry out whatever commands are inside it. In this case, it uses the Antenna's built-in tasks, such as compile, pre-verify and package. Commands can be set to `true`, or `false` when they are not required. This gives the developer the option of adding in an obfuscation step between compiling and pre-verification. An extra target could be inserted as well, to deal with packages from third-party developers. Ant really is flexible, and this is one of the reasons why it has been embraced by a growing number of Java developers. It facilitates the handling of builds for different applications or numerous builds for the same application, saving developer time during development as well as smoothing the communication between different members of a development team. Whichever way it is used it provides a defined and reproducible build for a MIDlet (with the use of Antenna) or for any other Java application for that matter.

Before we look at installation and execution let's have a look at an example `build.xml` file. We have built one for use with the Demo Racer application discussed in Chapter 5. Configuration of Ant and Antenna for MIDP 2.0 using the Wireless Toolkit version 2.1 is a little more difficult than for previous editions. Version 2.1 splits the CLDC and MIDP packages into JAR files for each version. Therefore the `<wtk home>/lib` directory contains `cldcapi10.jar`, `cldcapi11.jar`, `midpapi10.jar` and `midpapi20.jar` files. This split has to be reflected in the `build.xml` file, such as the one below. This build file was taken from the "hello" example included in the Antenna source ZIP file and then adapted for our needs.

```xml
<?xml version="1.0"?>
<project name="DemoRacer" default="build" basedir=".">
<!-- Define the WTK home directory, needed by the tasks. -->
    <property name="wtk.home" value="D:/WTK21"/>
    <!-- Define the MIDP API: either 1.0 or 2.0 can be used. -->
    <property name="wtk.midpapi" value="${wtk.home}/lib/midpapi20.jar"/>
    <!-- Define optional properties for this project. -->
    <property name="midlet.name" value="DemoRacer"/>
    <property name="midlet.home"
            value="${wtk.home}/apps/${midlet.name}"/>

    <!-- Define the tasks. -->
    <taskdef resource="antenna.properties"/>

    <target name="clean">
        <delete failonerror="false" dir="classes"/>
        <delete failonerror="false">
            <fileset dir=".">
                <exclude name="build.xml"/>
            </fileset>
        </delete>
    </target>

    <target name="build">
```

```
<!-- Copy a JAD file from the WTK demo applications.
     Caution: Ant only copies this the first time. Also
     make a directory to compile into. -->

<copy file="${midlet.home}/bin/${midlet.name}.jad" todir="."/>
<mkdir dir="classes"/>
<!-- Compile everything, but don't preverify (yet). -->
<wtkbuild srcdir="${midlet.home}/src"
          destdir="classes"
          preverify="false"/>

<!-- Package everything. Most of the necessary information is
     contained in the JAD file. Also preverify the result this
     time. To obfuscate everything, set the corresponding
     parameter to "true" (requires RetroGuard or ProGuard).
     The version parameter increments the MIDlet-Version by
     one. -->
<wtkpackage jarfile="${midlet.name}.jar"
            jadfile="${midlet.name}.jad"
            classpath="${wtk.home}/lib/cldcapi10.jar"
            obfuscate="false"
            preverify="true"
            autoversion="true">
    <!-- Package our newly compiled classes and the
         resources from the WTK demo application. -->
    <fileset dir="classes"/>
    <fileset dir="${midlet.home}/res"/>
</wtkpackage>

<!-- Start the MIDlet suite -->
<wtkrun jadfile="${midlet.name}.jad"
        device="DefaultColorPhone"
        trace="class,gc" wait="true"/>
    </target>
</project>
```

There are seven areas of interest in this build.xml file:

- Wireless Toolkit location – in the property wtk.home; Antenna relies upon functionality provided by the WTK, so this property is essential

- MIDP API location – the WTK 2.1 defines two sets of API, to allow for backwards compatibility when building MIDlets; we have chosen the midpapi20.jar file

- the Antenna properties file – defined in a task definition as a resource and set to antenna.properties, this file specifies the classpath of the antenna classes within the antenna-bin-0.9.11.jar file

- the build target – as the default build (we can define more than one within the same configuration file), this defines what the build will actually include
  In this case, we copy the existing JAD file to a new location, although we could use this build.xml file to create a new one. The MIDlet

source is defined along with the destination for the compiled classes. The emulator execution and packaging are wrapped in this build.

- the `wtkpackage` command – this creates the JAR and if the JAD file is present, it tries to update the `MIDlet-Jar-Size` and `MIDlet-Jar-URL` attributes; it performs obfuscation and pre-verification (if those attributes are set to `true`) and increments the version number of the MIDlet

- the build classpath – the WTK 2.1 splits the CLDC classes into CLDC 1.0 and CLDC 1.1, so we need to specify the classes against which the pre-verifier should verify; we have chosen CLDC 1.0; the pre-verifier won't execute successfully if this property is not set correctly

- running in an emulator – once all this has been completed successfully the specified emulator will be run according to the device set in the device property.

Installation

Builds are available from the Ant website for both Windows and Linux/Unix developers, though we are only concerned with Windows installation. Developers can choose either a binary (***http://ant.apache.org/index.html***) or source (***http://ant.apache.org/srcdownload.cgi***) download. For simplicity we shall examine the binary download. Once the Ant ZIP or TAR file has been downloaded (***http://antenna.sourceforge.net***), its contents should be extracted to a suitable location. Once this has been done, there are a number of environment variables that need to be set, before Ant can be used.

You will also need to download the `antenna-bin-0.9.11.jar` and `antenna-src-0.9.11.zip` files. Place the JAR file in Ant's `lib` directory. Extract the source files to a location under the existing Ant installation, for example `<ant installation>\antenna\` and then place the Antenna JAR file in Ant's `lib` directory. This will ensure that the Antenna package is in the classpath.

Assume, for this example, that Ant is installed in c:\ant\. The following sets up the environment:

```
set ANT_HOME=c:\ant
set JAVA_HOME=c:\jdk1.2.2
set PATH=%PATH%;%ANT_HOME%\bin
```

Alternatively these can be set permanently via the System command within the Control Panel on the PC.

Using Ant

Once these environment variables have been set up, Ant is ready to go. To run with the default arguments, simply navigate to the directory containing the build.xml file and type ant at the command prompt. As each target is met, its name will be echoed to the screen, so progress can be monitored. Any errors will also be written to the screen. While build.xml is the default build file, different configurations may have been created for each project. To specify which build file to use, set the –buildfile argument to identify an alternative file:

```
ant -buildfile <path to build file>
```

Alternatively the developer may only want to run up to a certain target or perhaps they have a build file containing many targets. This can be specified by adding the target name as an option. If a particular target has a dependency (our example hasn't, but they can be added), then it will run those first, before running itself. Executing the emulator may be taken out of the build target in our example, put into a separate target and executed on its own.

```
ant -buildfile <path to build file> <target name>
```

These are just two useful options. Ant help provides a list of the other options available and it can be called by typing:

```
ant -help
```

2.3.1.3 Nokia Developer's Suite 2.0 for J2ME

Overview
The Nokia Developer's Suite 2.0 for J2ME (NDS) has been created by Nokia and is available from the Forum Nokia website (download from the Tools & SDKs section at **www.forum.nokia.com**). It is a tool designed primarily to enhance existing development tools, although it can run as a standalone tool. Incidentally, there are versions available for both Windows and Linux platforms.

The suite provides developers with class libraries, APIs and Nokia device emulators used to create both MIDP 1.0 and MIDP 2.0 Java applications. Once it is integrated with an IDE, such as Borland's JBuilder or Sun's Studio ONE, it becomes a very useful tool in the development of mobile applications.

The NDS offers many features to the developer:

- support for Series 60 MIDP Concept SDK Beta 0.3 Nokia Edition
  Series 60 is a major Symbian OS platform, which has been developed by Nokia and licensed to manufacturers such as Sendo, Siemens, Samsung and Panasonic. This SDK provides a Nokia device reference implementation of that platform

- deployment on devices using infrared, USB and RS-232 (available on Windows platforms only)
  The suite provides a convenient interface with which to deploy JAR files to the device during development. During testing it is wise to make intermittent checks on the quality of the application code on the target device. This will greatly reduce the frustration and time spent.

- FTP uploading capability with WML deck creation

- application signing with a public/private key

- an integrated audio converter for MIDI and ringtone XML files.

For developers new to the Java environment, Figure 2.11 shows how the NDS can be used to speed up the creation of new classes. Imported packages and interface references can be set up using a dialog box. This also gives the developer the ability to browse the MIDP packages to find various APIs.

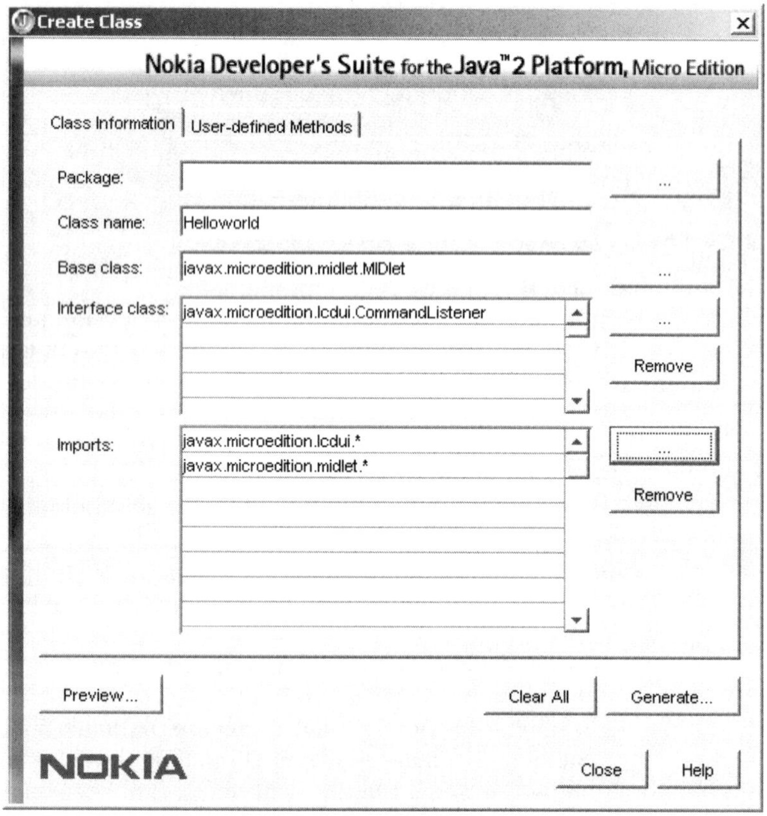

Figure 2.11 Create Class dialog.

Installation

Although the NDS can be installed in standalone mode, it is probably best used when integrated with an IDE. We shall, therefore, walk through the necessary steps required to integrate the product with Borland's JBuilder 9 Personal Edition. (Note that the NDS can also be integrated with Sun ONE Studio 4, Mobile Edition.)

The Nokia Developer's Suite requires JBuilder 9 and the Mobile Set 3.01 to be installed first. We will outline the installation of them in Section 2.3.2.1.

The steps to install the NDS on Windows are as follows:

1. Download the ZIP file from the Forum Nokia website and extract it to a suitable location.

2. To register the software and obtain a serial number for installation, you must have a valid registration with Forum Nokia. The serial number will be sent to the registered email address. Request the registration key and click either "sent" or "already supplied" on the dialog box.

3. Execute the file `setup.exe` in the extraction directory. After the splash screen, the terms and conditions of use have to be agreed to. A prompt then appears requesting the entry of the serial number for the software (Figure 2.12).

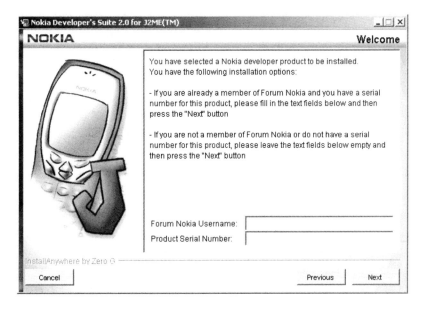

Figure 2.12 NDS installation.

Figure 2.13   Choosing configuration type.

4. Once the serial number has been entered, the next decision to be made is how you will actually install the suite, integrated either with JBuilder or Sun ONE Studio, or as a Standalone tool (Figure 2.13).

5. The locations of the JBuilder IDE need to be confirmed along with the destination of the NDS, in successive dialog boxes.

6. The installation is now ready to begin. Press "Install" to install the software. Once the installation has completed, the PC will require restarting.

The NDS has now been fully integrated with the JBuilder IDE. Go to the Tools menu within the Borland IDE and see that "Nokia Developers Suite for J2ME" has appeared near the bottom.

2.3.2   Integrated Development Environments

2.3.2.1   *JBuilder 9*

Overview
Borland has created a number of tools for the developer, with varying degrees of functionality, ranging from the basic personal edition through to enterprise level.

The IDE provides a thorough interface for creating Java applications. The text editor provides auto-completion of methods and class members. It also provides a graphical overview of all the methods and class members in the currently displayed class. Classes can be navigated and viewed easily using the Project and Structure windows.

Compilation highlights where errors have occurred and, by simply double-clicking the message, the user will be taken to the error. Libraries and other APIs can be easily imported and added to projects, negating the need to worry about classpaths on the PC itself. Version 9 also includes team collaboration utilities with version control software such as CVS.

As each new edition of the IDE is released, the previous one is available from the Borland website for non-commercial evaluation purposes (*www.borland.com/products/downloads/download_jbuilder.html*). The Personal version can be found here and, of course, can only be used for non-commercial evaluation purposes.

Borland also provides an additional module, the Mobile Set, which extends the IDE into mobile development, providing the functionality of the WTK. The Borland Mobile Set 3.01 has been created essentially to enable the JBuilder IDE to also be a wireless development tool. It integrates with the Wireless Toolkit and provides visual design tools for the creation of MIDlets. It can also provide support for the NDS and other manufacturer add-ins, and the Mobile Set includes support for OTA provisioning. JBuilder 9 also provides support for the unified emulator interface (UEI), which is described in greater detail later in this chapter. JBuilder 9 supports class obfuscation, using RetroGuard version 1.1. This process occurs as part of the archive process and reduces the final size of the JAR files. The process of obfuscation reduces class file sizes when it scrambles the source code. The Mobile Set also uses RetroGuard.

RetroGuard rolls the creation of JAD and JAR files into a more accessible interface as well as giving developers debugging capabilities and testing of applications on device emulators. It is available under the GNU Lesser General Public License from *www.retrologic.com*.

Installation

We will now give an overview of how to install JBuilder 9 Personal Edition IDE. A non-commercial Personal edition of each version of JBuilder is made available for evaluation purposes. The latest version is called JBuilderX and includes support for MIDP 2.0 application development.

First, download two installation files (jb9_windows.zip and mobileset_301.zip) from the Borland website: *www.borland.com/products/downloads/download_jbuilder.html*. A valid registration and email address will be required to successfully complete the installation.

1. Extract both ZIP files to a suitable location. The JBuilder ZIP will produce a file called per_install.exe. This file should be executed.

2. After the Borland splash appears, the destination for the tool will be requested (see Figure 2.14). When this has been entered press Next.

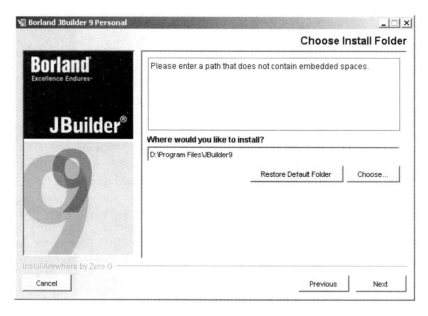

Figure 2.14 JBuilder installation.

3. Once installation is complete, the product needs to be registered with
    the vendor. A license activation file is sent automatically to the regis-
    tered email address. This should be saved to an appropriate location.

4. Enter the location of the activation file (Figure 2.15).

5. Once the activation location has been given, the IDE is now ready
    for use. However, the IDE is not quite ready for J2ME development.
    We need to also install the Mobile Set to give the option of working
    with J2ME capabilities as well as J2SE.

6. Execute `mobileset.exe` to commence installation. A prompt will
    appear to determine the installation type. The Full Install option also
    installs the RetroGuard obfuscator.

7. After setting the destination for the tool, installation should continue
    without further prompting.

2.3.2.2 Metrowerks CodeWarrior Wireless Studio 7

Overview

CodeWarrior is a commonly-used IDE that provides the developer with
all the tools required for MIDP application creation. A new version of the
tool is on its way, and it will integrate Java with native C++ development.

The Wireless Development Toolkit has been integrated into the IDE.
This means the default emulators are present. Device emulators such as

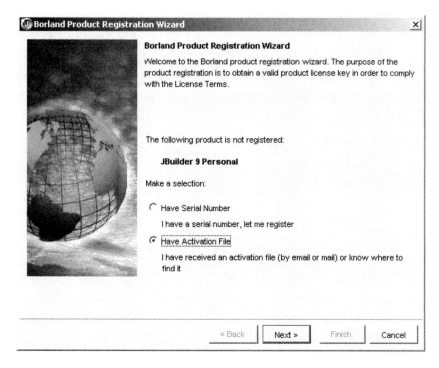

Figure 2.15 Registering the tool.

that for the Sony Ericsson P800 can, however, also be added to the IDE. Consequently, the packaging, pre-verification, compilation, and testing can all be carried out within one user interface. JAD files are also created automatically for the developer, while WYSIWYG drag and drop RAD tools supporting MIDP are also present.

CodeWarrior offers code obfuscation, just as JBuilder does. This is useful for two reasons. It provides a level of protection against pirating of software by mangling the source code; if the application is ever decompiled, the results will, hopefully, be confusing enough to prevent the code from being stolen. Obfuscation also provides shortened naming conventions within the output code. This is a known method for creating more efficient MIDP applications and will speed up performance.

Project management and team development are supported by version control and integrated management of targets, classes and source code. Remote debugging can also be carried out on JDWP-compliant virtual machines.

Installation
Metrowerks does not at present provide an online evaluation version of the software. This document will therefore give a brief overview of the installation of the full Professional Wireless Edition.

The minimum system requirements are as follows:

- Windows 98/2000/ME/NT 4.0 with Service Pack 4 or later
- Sun's Java SDK, v1.2 or later (JSDK 1.3.1 and JSDK 1.4.0 included)
- Pentium class or AMD-K6 class processor
- 64 MB RAM
- 250 MB hard disk space
- CD-ROM drive for installation
- an Internet connection for registration.

To install the IDE:

1. Insert the CodeWarrior CD-ROM. It should automatically display the setup menu. If it does not, locate and run Launch.exe. The user is welcomed to the installation process and warned that the installation process is about to begin.

2. A dialog asks the user to accept the licensing conditions and provides a brief introduction to the product.

3. The user is asked to specify the destination for the installation (Figure 2.16).

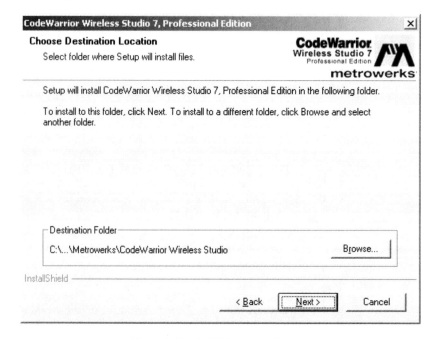

Figure 2.16   CodeWarrior installation.

4. The user is asked to name the shortcut for later use.

5. The user is given the chance to make file associations between the IDE and, amongst others, Java source files.

6. A summary of the installation information is displayed for confirmation. Upon acceptance, the installation process begins.

7. During this process, the option of installing PersonalJava is presented. If this is required, a separate installation process will be run before the CodeWarrior installation continues.

8. Next, the installation of the J2ME Wireless Toolkit is required. If this already resides on the PC this can be ignored. Otherwise proceed with its installation.

9. Select the Stand Alone installation type when prompted.

10. At the end of the process, the user will be asked if they wish to search for any updates and patches to the IDE software.

11. The registration process then needs to be followed (see Figure 2.17). Registration details are sent to Metrowerks and a temporary license is granted until the license request has been validated. An Internet connection is required for this. The permanent license will be sent via email and the instructions within the readme.txt file should be followed.

12. The user will be prompted to restart the PC. Make sure all necessary files are saved at this point.

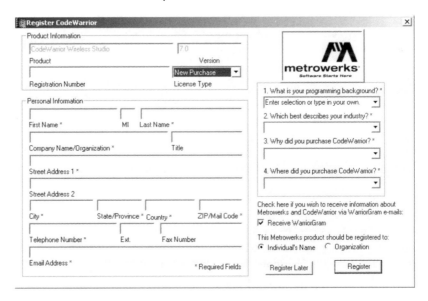

Figure 2.17 Registering CodeWarrior.

2.3.2.3   *Sun ONE Studio 4, Mobile Edition*

Overview

Sun ONE Studio 4 is widely used within the Java developer community. This IDE gives the developer all the usual source file editing, packaging, pre-verification and compilation processes. The Wireless Toolkit has been integrated with the IDE. It also comes with plenty of examples to get the developer started, both with the IDE and with MIDP development.

There is a free offering of the IDE from the Sun Java website at the following location: ***http://wwws.sun.com/software/sundev/jde/studio_me/index.html***). The free version can be used for non-commercial evaluation purposes. In the same way that JBuilder 9 can be integrated with the Nokia Developer's Suite, so can this IDE.

The text editor offers code completion and contextual shortcut menus to save the developer having to search for commands. A project navigator is also available, as is version control through its "VCS groups" and CVS functions.

While this book will be examining version 4 of the software, it should be noted that at the time of writing an early access edition of version 5.0 was being released. While this is not a full production release it is worth noting that it has the following features:

- J2ME Wireless Toolkit integration

- dual support for both J2ME MIDP 1.0 and 2.0 development

- MIDP 2.0 development features

- application signing utility to sign MIDlet suites

- Push Registry development

- over-the-air (OTA) testing

- J2ME Wireless Toolkit Project Import Wizard

- Wireless Connection Wizard for development of networked J2ME applications

- integration of third-party device SDKs through the emulator registry

- XML-file-based emulator configuration and integration

- sample MIDlets to get the developer started.

Installation

The IDE will run on the following systems:

- Solaris 8 and 9 operating environments

- Windows XP, NT 4.0 SP6, 2000 SP2, 98 (Community Edition only)

- Red Hat Linux 7.2 and Sun Linux 5.0

As a runtime environment, it requires J2SE at version 1.3.1, 1.4.0, or 1.4.1. It will compile code developed with JDK 1.0 or 1.1, or J2SE 1.2, 1.3, 1.3.1, 1.4.0, or 1.4.1.

The installation package can be obtained from the following location: ***http://wwws.sun.com/software/sundev/jde/studio_me/index.html***.

1. To begin the installation process, execute the file `ffj_me_win32.exe`. A welcome dialog is displayed to the user (Figure 2.18).

2. When the user accepts the terms and condition of using the software, a search for a suitable Java Virtual Machine starts. If one can be found then accept it, otherwise its location, if present on the PC, should be given to the installer.

3. Next, specify the destination for the IDE. On some PC operating system versions it may be wise to avoid locations with spaces. It may have a detrimental effect on the Wireless Toolkit.

4. A summary of the installation information gathered from the user is displayed. Also the choice is given to associate Sun ONE Studio with Java file types.

5. Press Next to begin the installation. Upon completion, the user will be told whether it was successful or not. Assuming the installation was fine, the IDE is now ready for use. However, some configuration issues will be asked for, such as the window mode of use for the IDE and some proxy settings. Set these as desired and then continue.

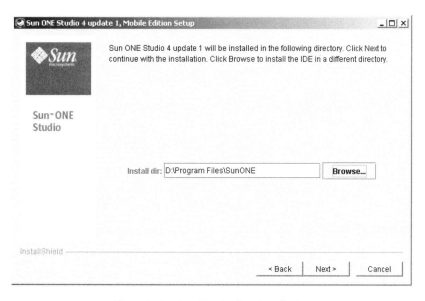

Figure 2.18 Sun ONE Studio 4 installation.

6. Registration then needs to be made with Sun's website. This requires the user to enter a username and password, which is the user details used to obtain the software in the first instance.

2.3.2.4 *Unified Emulator Interface*

As more device manufacturers create emulators for content developers, it becomes increasingly difficult for Integrated Development Environment (IDE) makers to support each emulator. Most emulators have different directory structures, different commands and different command-line arguments. A generic unified emulator interface (UEI) that all emulators support is needed. The UEI allows IDE manufacturers to write to a single interface and, with little or no effort, be able to support emulators from many different companies.

The UEI specification defines a directory structure for the emulator distribution unit (executables, documentation and library files), binary executables (emulator, etc.), names and command line execution arguments.

In the next release, Symbian will provide a compliant UEI implementation to facilitate easier and more standard integration of the MIDP emulator with existing IDEs such as JBuilder and Sun ONE Studio.

Symbian OS Version 8.0 will support launching a MIDlet in the emulator VM from within the IDE and provide options to start the VM in debug mode to enable debugging with your IDE. You develop and compile in your working folder. When you run the emulator, you would continue to develop in this way, using the IDE, and Symbian UEI takes care of packaging the classes, copying them to the emulator file space and launching the MIDlet.

The following example demonstrates how to integrate a UEI-compliant emulator with Sun ONE Studio.

Adding the Emulator to Sun ONE Studio

1. From the Explorer window, right-click on Installed Emulators and click on Add Emulator (Figure 2.19).

2. Browse to the directory that contains the distribution unit for the product/platform variant (Figure 2.20).

Setting the Default Emulator
In the explorer window (Figure 2.19), you should now see the Symbian UEI added to the list of installed emulators. Right-click on Default Emulators and click on Set Default Emulator. From the list of installed emulators, select one of the options (Figure 2.21).

Figure 2.19 Add emulator.

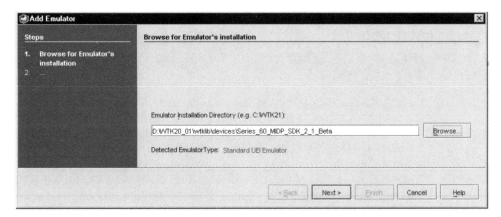

Figure 2.20 Browse for udeb.

Figure 2.21 Select Emulator.

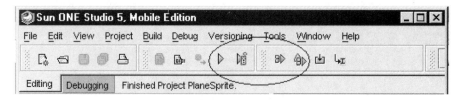

Figure 2.22 Run and debug toolbar.

Running and Debugging a MIDlet

This is done as with any other MIDlet within Sun ONE Studio, using the menus, the shortcuts or the Toolbar (Figure 2.22). The UEI will take care of creating the JAR file and copying it and the descriptor (JAD) file into the appropriate place in the emulator file system and then starting the VM in the required mode.

2.3.3 Device Emulators

2.3.3.1 UIQ SDK

Overview

The UIQ platform provides the basis for Symbian OS phones that use a pointing device as the means of user input. The UIQ SDK provides developers with the ability to test and develop MIDP 2.0 applications for devices such as the Sony Ericsson P900. The SDK provides classes and the emulator facilitates development of native Symbian, PersonalJava and MIDP 1.0 and 2.0 applications. Developers do not need to install the full SDK to develop MIDP 2.0 applications, as we shall demonstrate in the installation section below.

The SDK provides an environment that includes Symbian's CLDC 1.0-based VM, MIDP 2.0, including the Bluetooth and Wireless Messaging APIs.

Setting Up the SDK

In the first instance, some minor housekeeping needs to be carried out to ensure the tool will execute in a suitable way.

First, make sure the path C:\ is in the system path. The EPOCROOT environment variable must be set to the location of the UIQ tool installation. In this case we have used the SET command at the command prompt in Windows as follows:

```
D:\>SET EPOCROOT=<installation of UIQ>\UIQ_21_\
```

Also, the devices command should be used to check that the default device is the UIQ emulator. Assuming Perl is installed (this can be installed as part of the installation process), issuing the command `devices.exe` will return the following:

```
D:\>devices.pl
UIQ_21:com.symbian.UIQ - default
UIQ_21:com.symbian.UIQ-runtime
```

If this does not appear then the `devices.pl` command should be used to set the default command to the UIQ tool. This is done in the following way:

```
D:\>devices.exe -setdefault @ UIQ_21:com.symbian.UIQ
```

Once these have been set, the following command can be issued:

```
D:\>epoc.exe -wins -rel
```

This will execute the WinS release version of the emulator. Other versions such as a debug version can also be executed, although these are used for debugging native C++ applications. Once this command has been run, the UIQ 2.1 emulator will appear on the screen.

Installing a MIDP 2.0 Application on the Emulator

The MIDP packages can be placed in the emulator device's virtual drive, for example `<installation directory>\epoc32\wins\c`. This package can be installed from the emulator interface in the following way:

1. Navigate to the Launcher menu on the emulator and use the mouse to select Install (Figure 2.23).

2. A sub menu prompting the developer to locate the MIDP suite will appear (Figure 2.24). Press the Install button and the MIDlet will be installed.

3. It will appear as an icon on the emulator's desktop. In this case we have installed our Helloworld application from Section 2.2 (Figure 2.25).

Installation

The SDK can be downloaded from the Symbian Developer Network at ***www.symbian.com/developer/sdks_uiq21.asp***.

1. This download is delivered in the form of a ZIP file which needs to be extracted to a suitable temporary location.

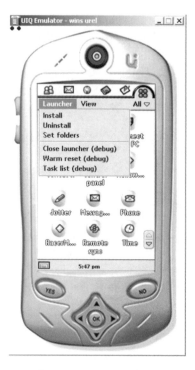

Figure 2.23   UIQ emulator.

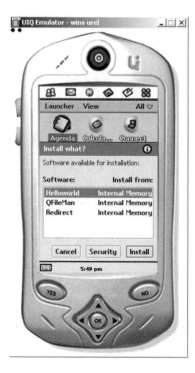

Figure 2.24   Install MIDlet.

2. Navigate to the extracted files and execute `Setup.exe`. The installation process will begin.

3. After accepting terms, conditions and the license agreement, a prompt for the destination of the SDK is given (Figure 2.26).

4. Once this has been selected, you will be prompted to select the components you wish to install (Figure 2.27). The rather greedy system requirement for disk space (Figure 2.26) can be ignored. It refers to the full Symbian "DevKit", which includes the full source code. The example installation was installed on a PC with modest available disk space. A figure of approximately 550 MB, depending upon the packages, example and documentation selected, is more accurate. As well as the packages forming the SDK itself, Perl and a Java Runtime are required. (This refers to the full Java Runtime Edition (JRE) version 1.3.1 and should not be confused with the MIDP 2.0 runtime.) If these are not present on the target PC, then select them as well. In this case it has been decided not to install them.

5. After a summary dialog, an installer kit is installed. This is the first stage of the installation. If Perl, which is required to run the emulator,

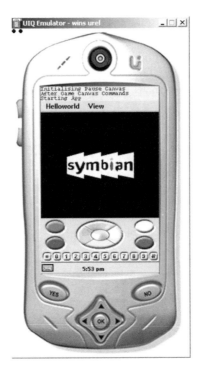

Figure 2.25 Helloworld.

and the Java Runtime have been selected, they will also be installed at this stage. This part can take some time.

6. The installer is now ready to install the required SDK packages (Figure 2.28).

7. The developer should now decide which packages to install. Figure 2.29 demonstrates how the developer can pick and choose what they want to be installed on the PC. In this case, we are only interested in the emulator, the MIDP package and the documentation, which might help us better understand the SDK. Note that UIQ 2.1 Java SDK has not been selected. This is, in fact, for PersonalJava and therefore we are not interested in installing it in this instance.

8. The installer gathers the packages together and displays the names of all the selected packages and the required disk space. Press Next to continue. Before installing, a prompt appears asking the user to accept the terms of the license. The SDK will then be installed. Once it has been successfully installed, Figure 2.30 appears.

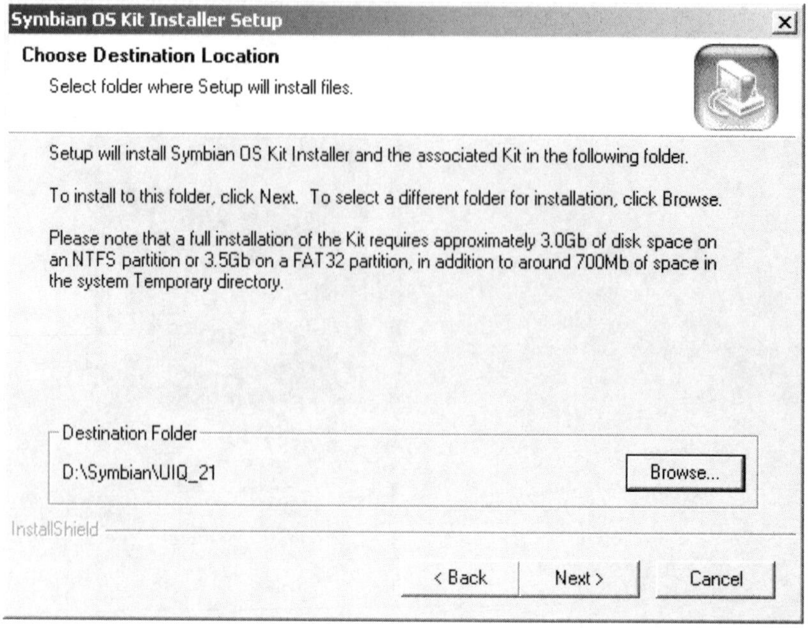

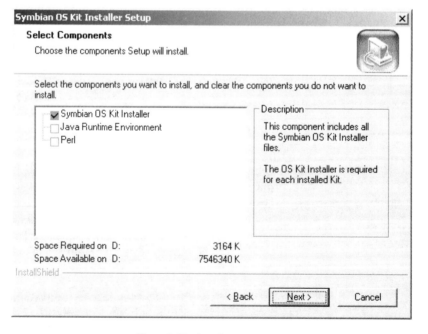

Figure 2.26   Symbian OS Kit Installer.

Figure 2.27   Install components.

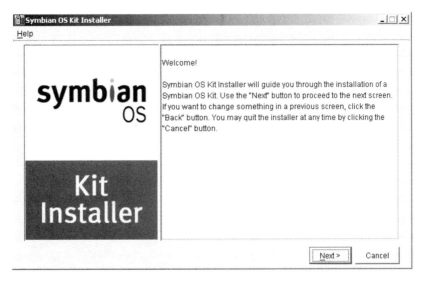

Figure 2.28 Ready to install SDK.

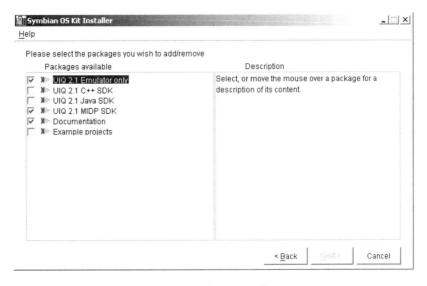

Figure 2.29 Choosing packages.

2.3.3.2 *Sony Ericsson P900 J2ME SDK*

Also available for UIQ developers is a Sony Ericsson MIDP 2.0 emulator that can be plugged into the Wireless Toolkit, version 2.1. This is a very useful tool for perfecting the user interface side of application development. However, the drawback is that the Java runtime is Sun's reference implementation, rather than the actual Symbian OS device

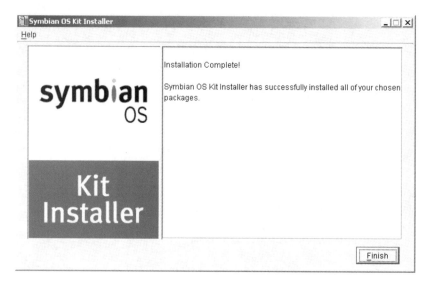

Figure 2.30   Installation complete.

implementation, which can be found within the UIQ SDK described in Section 2.3.3.1. The Symbian emulator device is based upon Symbian's source code and more evenly reflects the real device, where the binaries are optimized for the ARM processor rather than the x86.

The installation of the P900 emulator (Figure 2.31) for the Wireless Toolkit is fairly straightforward. The required files can be downloaded from the Sony Ericsson developer portal at: ***www.sonyericsson.com/developer/ user/ViewDocument.jsp?id=65090&name=java_midp2_p900.zip***.

All the emulator devices for the toolkit are stored in the directory `<installation location>\wtklib\devices\<emulator name>`. Once the ZIP file has been obtained, the files within the archive can be extracted to `SonyEricsson_P900`, a subdirectory under `device`. When the toolkit is next executed the new P900 device emulator will be available for selection.

2.4   Installing and Running a MIDlet

Now that we have created our first MIDP 2.0 application and tested it with the various emulators and toolkits described above, it is time to try it out on a real device. There are a number of ways to install the MIDlet suite. All have their own merits and conveniences. However, the developer shouldn't be reliant upon just one method.

During development, from time to time, you should try out a test run on the target device, rather than relying on the emulators. The latter may

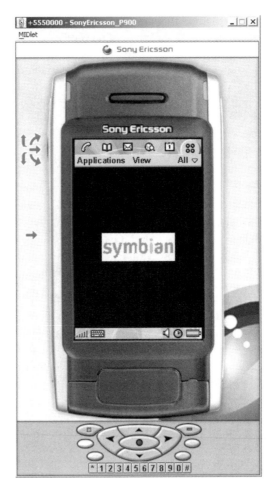

Figure 2.31 P900 Emulator.

not provide a true indication of application performance and usability. Emulator speeds can vary from the real devices and memory management may not be the same either. During development, Bluetooth or infrared deployment should be used. These are the easiest forms of installation and avoid the costs of installing the application over the air.

2.4.1 Transferring the MIDlet to a Device

2.4.1.1 Infrared Installation

On the device, in this case the Nokia 6600, locate the Connect menu and then the infrared command. Press Options > Open. This will activate the infrared functionality. Put the device in line with and within range of a laptop with an infrared port, or a PC with an infrared pod. The laptop will recognize that another computer is nearby. In this case, the "nearby computer" is in fact the Nokia 6600.

Navigate to the MIDlet JAR file and engage the shortcut menu. Select Send to > nearby computer. Assuming the mobile device is within range, the JAR file will be sent to the device. When the phone has received the JAR file, it will appear as if a message has arrived on the device. When the developer tries to open the message, the application manager software takes over and installs the MIDlet on the device. This installation process can be seen in more detail below.

2.4.1.2 Bluetooth

There are many Bluetooth accessories that can be added to laptops and desktops. In this case, we used a Smart Modular Technologies USB Adaptor and connected it to a laptop.

Assuming the software has been installed, the laptop has the ability to browse for other Bluetooth devices within its range. Transferring the file to the mobile phone is simple. The Smart software allows the developer to browse for and select the appropriate JAR file. The Bluetooth software searches for and compiles a list of available devices. When the Nokia 6600 realizes that it has been contacted, it prompts the user to give permission to accept contact. In return, the mobile device passes a password back to the laptop which has to be entered correctly before the conversation can continue. After validation, the JAR file is sent to the Nokia device. The JAR file arrives as a message and can be installed as demonstrated below.

The great advantage of this is that the laptop and the phone can be anywhere within 10 meters of each other and the connection is persistent, saving time for the developer.

2.4.1.3 Over the Air

Compared to the two methods described above, installing over the air (OTA) is a cumbersome way of installing an application on a device during development. However, it is an important mechanism for distributing finished MIDlets and should therefore be tested rigorously prior to distribution.

Whereas the infrared and Bluetooth methods do not require a JAD file to install, the OTA method does. The JAD file specification is part of the MIDP 2.0 specification and forms an extra layer of security between the device and the application. It provides information to the device as to what it is about to receive. The specification requires the information in the JAD file to be very precise and, if it is not, the MIDlet installation will be unsuccessful. It is therefore very important to test installation by this method to ensure the end-user can install and purchase the application. It is, after all, convenient for the user and is a way to maximize revenue streams if the application has been distributed to content providers and network operators to good effect.

To facilitate this, the developer will need to create the JAD file as described in Section 2.1.1.6. Next, a WML card, or XHTML mobile profile, needs to be created; it will be the target for the user to navigate to while they are browsing for an application to purchase. In reality, this card will be hosted by an operator or content aggregator.

This is a simple WML with a link to the JAD file:

```
<?xml version="1.0"?>
<!DOCTYPE wml PUBLIC "-// WAPFORUM// DTD WML 1.1// EN"
        "www.wapforum.org/DTD/wml_1.1.xml">
<wml>
    <card id="card1" title="Symbian Download Test">
        <p align="center">
            To download game click below:
        </p>
        <p>
            <a href="Helloworld.jad">Hello World Turbo</a>
        </p>
    </card>
</wml>
```

The XHTML file works in the same way as the WML file. The Nokia 6600 and Sony Ericsson P900 will recognize both XHTML and WML file formats.

```
<?xml version="1.0"?>
<!DOCTYPE html
 PUBLIC "-// W3C// DTD XHTML Basic 1.0// EN"
        "www.w3.org/TR/xhtml-basic/xhtml-basic10.dtd">
    <html xmlns="www.w3.org/1999/xhtml" xml:lang="en" lang="en">
    <head>
        <title>Symbian Download Test</title>
    </head>
    <body>
        <a href="Helloworld.jad">Hello World Turbo</a><br/>
    </body>
    </html>
```

Once the WML and XHTML files are loaded onto the webserver, there is one more configuration setting that needs to be checked. This tells the webserver to recognize the JAD and JAR file types as downloadable. The third line tells the webserver to serve the WML files as text.

```
AddType text/vnd.sun.j2me.app-descriptor jad
AddType application/java-archive jar
AddType text/vnd.wap.wml wml
```

Once the device has recognized and validated the JAD file information against the contents of the JAR file, download and installation will commence.

2.4.2 Installing the MIDlet

The previous section looked at how to physically put the MIDlet suite on the device. Once this has been achieved it needs to be installed by the application management software.

When the AMS detects that the user has either downloaded or transferred a MIDlet to the device, it will ask the user whether they wish to install the application. In this case we are installing the Helloworld application on a Nokia 6600 (Figure 2.32).

The softkeys display Yes and No options. Selecting No cancels the installation. Select Yes and you will be shown two options (Figure 2.33).

Selecting View Details displays information from the JAD file (Figure 2.34).

Figure 2.32   AMS checks that installation is required.

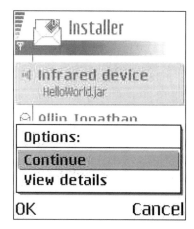

Figure 2.33   AMS gives user the option to view details.

Figure 2.34 JAD file information.

Figure 2.35 AMS checks that installation can continue.

After viewing this information, press OK to return to the previous prompt. Continue can then be selected. Another message appears (Figure 2.35).

Selecting No will cancel the installation. If installation is continued, Figure 2.36 may appear.

The AMS may detect that the MIDlet has been previously installed on the device. The user can choose to overwrite the previous version of the application or cancel the process. On the Nokia 6600, the user will then be prompted for a location for the MIDlet (Figure 2.37).

This allows the user to determine whether to install the MIDlet on the phone memory or the removable multimedia card. Use the joystick to choose one of the two options and press OK. Figure 2.38 illustrates what then appears.

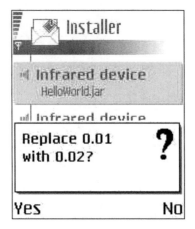

Figure 2.36 AMS detects that an existing application will be upgraded.

Figure 2.37 Specifying the location.

Figure 2.38 AMS checks whether to save existing data.

Selecting No overwrites the RMS data created by the previous installation of the MIDlet, if it existed. Selecting Yes leaves the current data
intact for use by the new MIDlet. After this, the new MIDlet is installed
on the device and an icon will appear in the Menu. Click the MIDlet
icon with the joystick, or select Options > Open, and the application will
be executed.

2.5   MIDP on Symbian OS Phones

All Symbian OS phones currently available in Western markets support
at least MIDP 1.0. The latest generation of Symbian OS phones, such as
the Nokia 6600 and Sony Ericsson P900 (and its localized variants) ship
with MIDP 2.0. The Nokia 6600 is based on the Series 60 Developer
Platform 2.0, itself built on top of Symbian OS Version 7.0s. The Sony
Ericsson P900 is built on Symbian's UIQ 2.1 touch screen reference
design. In addition to MIDP 2.0, both these devices also support a range
of additional optional APIs from the J2ME JSRs. Both phones support the
Wireless Messaging API (JSR 120), allowing phones to send and receive
SMS messages, and the Java API for Bluetooth Wireless Technology (JSR
82). In addition, the Nokia 6600 ships with an implementation of the
Mobile Media API (JSR 135). Chapters 3 and 4 cover programming these
phones, in detail.

2.6   Summary

In this chapter we have looked in greater depth at the MIDP 2.0 model.
We have looked at how a MIDlet is structured, the GUI, the Event model
and the MIDlet lifecycle. We have also looked at how to build, pre-verify
and package MIDlet suites. We have created a sample application and
shown how to put it onto a real device. We have also shown some of the
tools on offer to the developer, from basic toolkits and emulators to full
development environments.

In Chapter 3 we shall be looking in greater detail at MIDP 2.0, the
security model, the push registry and the Game API, to mention a few
topics. We shall also be examining some of the extra APIs falling under
the Java Technology for the Wireless Industry (JTWI) specification.

3

MIDP 2.0 and the JTWI

The Java Technology for the Wireless Industry (JTWI) initiative is part of the Java Community Process (JSR 185) and its expert group has as its goal the task of defining an industry-standard Java platform for mobile phones. By specifying a minimum set of Java APIs (as defined in the respective JSRs) that every JTWI-compliant device should support, it provides a lowest common denominator Java platform that developers and service providers can expect on future Java-enabled mobile phones.

In this chapter we will take a look at the JTWI and the JSRs that form part of Release 1. After introducing the JTWI, we will briefly review the CLDC on Symbian OS. Then we will take a detailed look at MIDP 2.0 and the optional APIs that are part of the JTWI roadmap.

3.1 Introduction to the JTWI

The main goal of the JTWI is to minimize API fragmentation of the wireless Java platform by reducing the need for proprietary APIs and providing a clear specification that phone manufacturers, network operators and developers can target. Release 1 of the JSR 185 specification received final approval in July 2003.

The JTWI specification concerns three main areas:

- it provides a minimum set of APIs (JSRs) that a compliant device should support

- it defines what optional features within these component JSRs must be implemented on a JTWI-compliant device

- it provides clarification of component JSR specifications, where appropriate.

Programming Java 2 Micro Edition on Symbian OS: A developer's guide to MIDP 2.0.   Martin de Jode
© 2004 Symbian Ltd   ISBN: 0-470-09223-8

3.1.1   Component JSRs of the JTWI

The JTWI defines three categories of JSR that fall under the specification: **mandatory, conditionally required** and **minimum configuration**.

The following mandatory JSRs must be implemented as part of a Java platform that is compliant with JTWI Release 1:

- MIDP 2.0 (JSR 118)
- Wireless Messaging API (JSR 120).

The Mobile Media API (JSR 135) is conditionally required in the JTWI Release 1. It must be present if the device exposes multimedia APIs (e.g. audio or video playback or recording) to Java applications.

The minimum configuration required for JTWI compliance is CLDC 1.0 (JSR 30). Since CLDC 1.1 is a superset of CLDC 1.0 it may be used instead, in which case it supersedes the requirement for CLDC 1.0.

3.1.2   JTWI Specification Requirements

As mentioned earlier, the JTWI specification makes additional requirements on the implementation of the component JSRs. A few selected examples of these are listed below. For full details of the requirements imposed on component JSRs consult the JTWI specification available from the Java Community Process (JCP) website (***http://jcp.org***).

CLDC 1.0/1.1

- must allow a MIDlet suite to create a minimum of ten running threads
- must support Unicode characters.

MIDP 2.0

- must allow creation of at least five independent recordstores
- must support the JPEG image format
- must provide a mechanism for selecting a phone number from the device's phonebook when the user is editing a `TextField` or `TextBox` with the `PHONENUMBER` constraint.

WMA

- GSM/UMTS phones must support SMS protocol push handling within `PushRegistry`

MMA

- must support MIDI playback
- must support `VolumeControl` for MIDI playback

- must support JPEG encoding for video snapshots
- must support Tone Sequence file format.

Security Policy for GSM/UMTS Compliant Devices
The JTWI specification provides a clarification of aspects of the MIDP 2.0 recommended security policy for GSM/UMTS devices relating to untrusted domains.

3.1.3 JTWI Deliverables

As well as defining the specification for the JTWI and providing a reference implementation (RI) and technology compatibility kit (TCK), JSR 185 also delivers a roadmap of candidate JSRs related to mobile phones that are likely to form part of future releases of JSR 185. The JTWI initiative does not discourage the adoption of additional JSRs to those defined in the specification or featured in the roadmap; it merely defines a minimum set of APIs that a JTWI-compliant device should support.

3.1.4 Symbian and the JTWI

Symbian supports and endorses the efforts of the JTWI and is a member of the JSR 185 expert group. At the time of writing, the current release of Symbian OS (Version 7.0s) provides implementations of the mandatory JSRs and minimum configuration required by JTWI Release 1: CLDC 1.0, MIDP 2.0 and Wireless Messaging API.

Current releases also provide an implementation of JSR 82, the Java APIs for Bluetooth Wireless Technology (see Chapter 4). The Nokia Series 60 Developer Platform Version 2.0 is built on Symbian OS Version 7.0s and, in addition to the JSRs already implemented, also provides Nokia's implementation of the Mobile Media API (JSR 135) as part of the Java platform.

Current Symbian MIDP 2.0-enabled phones support the following JSRs:

		Nokia 6600	**Sony Ericsson P900/P908**
UI Reference Design		Series 60 v 2	UIQ 2.1
CLDC 1.0	(JSR 30)	Yes	Yes
MIDP 2.0	(JSR 118)	Yes	Yes
WMA	(JSR 120)	Yes	Yes
MMA	(JSR 135)	Yes	No
JABWT	(JSR 82)	Yes	Yes

Because the final release of the JTWI specification postdated that of the MIDP 2.0 specification by some eight months, the current implementation

of Symbian's CLDC 1.0/MIDP 2.0 Java platform (and devices using it
such as the Nokia 6600 and the Sony Ericsson P900 and its localized
variants) is not fully compliant with all the requirements of the JTWI
specification. Future releases (and devices based upon them) will be
JTWI-compliant.

The following sections will cover the component APIs that are part of
JTWI Release 1.

3.2   The CLDC on Symbian OS

The Connected Limited Device Configuration (CLDC) was introduced in
Chapter 1. In this section we will briefly describe the implementations of
CLDC available on Symbian OS.

Symbian's MIDP 1.0 offering runs on top of a port of Sun's CLDC
1.0-based Virtual Machine (VM – also known as the KVM). Like early
desktop Java VMs, this CLDC 1.0 VM is a pure interpreter written in the
C programming language. Symbian OS supports a subset of the C STDLIB
(originally written to support the implementation of Symbian's first JDK
1.1.6-based Java offering in Symbian OS Version 5), making porting CLDC
1.0 a relatively straightforward task. Conscious of the performance overhead inherent in interpreted environments, Symbian integrated ARM's
VMA Technology Kit (VTK) into the CLDC 1.0 implementation. VTK
provides a number of optimizations for the ARM architecture, including
a re-write of the bytecode interpreter loop in ARM assembler (instead
of the original C code). These optimizations provide very significant
performance enhancements compared with standard KVM implementations, giving Symbian's CLDC 1.0/MIDP 1.0 implementation best-in-class
performance.

With the release of Symbian OS Version 7.0s, Symbian enhanced
its VM offering for MIDP 2.0 by providing a port of Sun's new CLDC
1.0 Hotspot Implementation VM (CLDC HI, also known by its code
name of Monty). CLDC HI is a highly optimized VM incorporat-
ing many advanced technologies previously only available in desktop
Java VMs, such as Dynamic Adaptive Compilation (DAC). CLDC HI
delivers nearly an order of magnitude better performance than the
standard KVM (see *The CLDC Hotspot Implementation Virtual Machine*
at ***http://java.sun.com***) while still retaining the small memory footprint
required by mobile phones. This gives Symbian's CLDC HI/MIDP 2.0
Java platform the performance to run demanding applications that take
full advantage of the additional functionality offered by MIDP 2.0 and
the additional optional APIs. The MIDP 2.0 implementation on the
Sony Ericsson P900/P908 and the Nokia 6600 runs on top of CLDC
1.0 HI.

In future releases, Symbian OS will provide an implementation of Sun's CLDC 1.1 HI VM. As well as offering further performance enhancements compared with CLDC 1.0 HI, this brings in floating point support (a standard part of the CLDC 1.1 specification).

3.3 MIDP 2.0

3.3.1 New Features in MIDP 2.0

MIDP 2.0 was introduced in the previous chapter. In this section we shall look in more detail at the features available in MIDP 2.0.

Although MIDP 1.0 can be regarded as a success story, with widespread adoption of the technology within the wireless industry, it was soon realized that MIDP 1.0 on its own was too restrictive. MIDP 1.0 was targeted at severely resource-constrained CLDC devices. The MIDP API set was targeted at the lowest common denominator of functionality likely to be available on mobile phones. For these highly-constrained devices, a lightweight security model was required. MIDP 1.0 adopted the sandbox security model: an application runs in a closed environment and can only access APIs defined in the configuration and profile (or any OEM-specific libraries that ship with the device).

The influence of Moore's Law is, however, felt in the wireless space. Once MIDP 1.0 was adopted as a standard for wireless devices, it was soon being ported to devices with far richer native functionality than the lowest common denominator phone that the MIDP 1.0 specification was originally designed for. For instance, Symbian OS provides a very rich native API set, the majority of which are not accessible to MIDlets.

The solution was the formation of the MIDP 2.0 expert group (with Symbian a member) and a proliferation of J2ME JSR expert groups defining optional APIs, in the majority of which Symbian participates. The MIDP 2.0 expert group released the final specification in November 2002, resulting in the following major additions to the profile:

- a more fine-grained security model

- extended networking

- a push registry

- user interface modifications

- the Game API

- the Media API.

We will now look at these additions in more detail.

3.3.2 Security Model

3.3.2.1 *Overview*

The MIDP 2.0 security model is built on two concepts: **trusted** MIDlet suites and **protected** APIs. Trusted MIDlet suites are those whose origin and integrity can be trusted by the device on the basis of some objective criterion. Protected APIs are APIs to which access is restricted, with the level of access being determined by the **permissions** (Allowed or User) allocated to the API. A protection domain defines a set of permissions which grant, or potentially grant, access to an associated set of protected APIs. An installed MIDlet suite is bound to a protection domain, thereby determining its access to protected APIs. A MIDP 2.0 device must support at least one protection domain, the **untrusted domain**, and may support several protection domains, although a given MIDlet suite can only be bound to one protection domain. The set of protection domains supported by an implementation defines the security policy.

If installed, an unsigned MIDlet suite is always bound to the untrusted domain, in which access to protected APIs may be denied or require explicit user permission. Since a requirement of the MIDP 2.0 specification is that a MIDlet suite written to the MIDP 1.0 specification runs unaltered in a MIDP 2.0 environment, MIDP 1.0 MIDlets are automatically treated as untrusted.

3.3.2.2 *Trusted MIDlet Suites*

The mechanism for identifying and verifying that a signed MIDlet suite should be bound to a trusted domain is not mandated by the MIDP 2.0 specification but is left to the manufacturer of the device and other stakeholders with an interest in the security of the device, for example, network operators in the case of mobile phones. The specification does, however, define how the X.509 Public Key Infrastructure (PKI) can be used to identify and verify a signed MIDlet suite.

3.3.2.3 *The X.509 PKI*

The Public Key Infrastructure is a system for managing the creation and distribution of digital certificates. At the heart of the PKI lies the system of public key cryptography. Public key cryptography involves the creation of a key pair consisting of a private key and a public key. The creator of the key pair keeps the private key secret, but can freely distribute the public key. Public and private key pairs have two principal uses: they enable secure communication using cryptography and authentication using digital signatures. In the first case, someone wishing to communicate with the holder of the private key uses the public key to encrypt the communication. The encrypted communication is secure since it can only be decrypted by the holder of the private key.

In the current context, however, we are more interested in the second use of public–private key pairs, enabling authentication using digital signatures. A digital signature is an electronic analogy of a conventional signature. It authenticates the source of document and verifies that the document has not been tampered with in transit. Signing a document is a two-stage process: a message digest is created that is a unique representation of the contents of the document; the message digest is then encrypted using the private key of the sender (see Figure 3.1).

The receiver of the document then uses the public key of the sender to decrypt the message digest, creates a digest of the received contents, and checks that it matches the decrypted digest that accompanied the document. Hence, a digital signature is used to verify that a document was actually sent by the holder of the private key, not some third party masquerading as the sender, and that the contents have not been tampered with in transit.

This raises the issue of key management and how the receiver of a public key can verify the source of the public key. For instance, if I receive a digitally signed JAR file I will need the public key of the signer to verify the signature, but how do I verify the source of the public key? The public key itself is just a series of numbers, with no clue as to the identity of the owner. I need to have confidence that a public key purporting to belong to a legitimate organization does in fact originate from that organization and has not been distributed by an impostor, enabling the impostor to masquerade as the legitimate organization, signing files using the private key of a bogus key pair. The solution is to distribute the public key in the form of a certificate from a trusted **certificate authority** (CA).

A certificate authority distributes a certificate that contains details of a person's or organization's identity, the public key belonging to that person or organization, and the identity of the issuing CA. The CA vouches that the public key contained in the certificate does indeed belong to the person or organization identified on the certificate. To verify that the certificate was issued by the CA, the certificate is digitally signed by

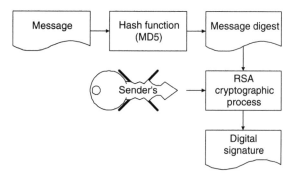

Figure 3.1 Creating a digital signature: create a message digest using the hash function and encrypt the digest using the sender's private key.

the CA using its private key. The format of certificates used in X509.PKI is known as the X509 format.

Of course, this raises the question of how the recipient of the certificate verifies the digital signature contained therein. This is resolved using **root certificates** or **root keys**. The root certificate contains details of the identity of the CA and the public key of the CA (the root key) and is signed by the CA itself (self-signed). For mobile phones which support one or more trusted protection domains, one or more certificates will ship with the device, placed on the phone by manufacturer or embedded in the WIM/SIM card by the network operator. Each certificate will be associated with a trusted protection domain, so that a signed MIDlet that is authenticated against a certificate will be bound to the protection domain associated with that certificate.

3.3.2.4 Certification Paths

In practice, the authentication of a signed file using the root certificate may be more involved than the simplified approach described above. The PKI allows for a hierarchy of certificate authorities (see Figure 3.2) whose validity can be traced back to a root certification authority, the uppermost CA in the hierarchy, also known as the **trust anchor**.

In this case the root certificate on the device (the **trust root**) belongs to the root certification authority in the hierarchy (the trust anchor) which directly or indirectly validates all the other CAs in the certification path. The certificate supplied with the signed JAR file does not need to be validated (signed) by the trust anchor whose certificate is supplied with the device, as long as a valid certification path can be established between the certificate accompanying the signed JAR file and the root CA.

It is not actually necessary for a device to have various self-signed top-level certificates from CAs, manufacturers and operators installed. In practice, it only needs access to one or more certificates which are known to be trustworthy, for example, because they are in ROM or secure storage on a WIM/SIM, or because the user has decided that they are. These certificates act as **trust roots**. If the authentication of an arbitrary certificate chains back to a trust root known to the device, and the trust root is also identified as being suitable for authenticating certificates being used for a given purpose, e.g., code-signing, web site identification, etc., then the arbitrary certificate is considered to have been authenticated.

3.3.2.5 Signing a MIDlet Suite

To sign a MIDlet suite, a supplier must create a public–private key pair and sign the MIDlet JAR file with the private key. The JAR file is signed using the RSA-SHA1 algorithm. The resulting signature is encoded in Base64 format and inserted into the application descriptor as the following attribute:

```
MIDlet-Jar-RSA-SHA1: <base64 encoding of Jar signature>
```

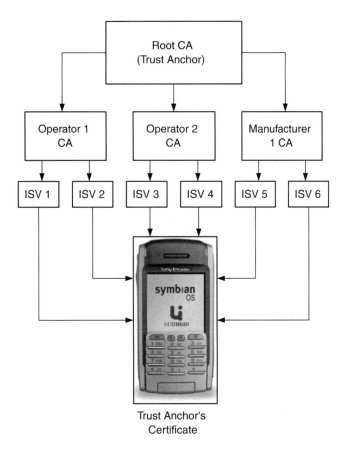

Figure 3.2 Applications from a variety of independent software vendors (ISVs) signed by various CAs and authenticated by a single trust root.

The supplier must obtain a suitable MIDlet suite/code-signing certificate from an appropriate source, e.g., the developer program of a device manufacturer or network operator containing the identity of the supplier and the supplier's public key. The certificate is incorporated into the MIDlet suite application descriptor (JAD) file.

In the case of a certification path, we need to include all the necessary certificates required to validate the JAR file. Furthermore, a MIDlet suite may include several certification paths in the application descriptor file (if, for example, the MIDlet suite supplier wishes to target several different device types, each with a different root certificate).

In Figure 3.3, we need to include certificates containing the public keys belonging to CA 1, CA 2 and the Supplier.

The root certification authority's certificate (the root certificate) is available on the device. Using the root certification authority's public key, we can validate CA 1's public key. This is then used to validate CA

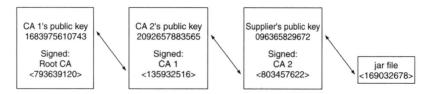

Figure 3.3 Using a certification path to authenticate a signed JAR file.

2's public key, which is then used to validate the Supplier's public key. The Supplier's public key is then used to verify the origin and integrity of the JAR file. The MIDP 2.0 specification defines an application descriptor attribute of the following format:

```
MIDlet-Certificate-<n>-<m>: <base64 encoding of a certificate>
```

Here `<n>` represents the certification path and has a value of 1 for the first certification path, with each additional certification path adding 1 to the previous value (e.g. 1, 2, 3, ...). There may be several certification paths, each leading to a different root CA. `<m>` has a value of 1 for the certificate belonging to the signer of the JAR file and a value 1 greater than the previous value for each intermediate certificate in the certification path.

For the example shown in Figure 3.3, with just one certification path the relevant descriptor attribute entries would have the following content:

```
MIDlet-Certificate-1-1: <base64 encoding of Supplier's certificate>
MIDlet-Certificate-1-2: <base64 encoding of CA 2's certificate>
MIDlet-Certificate-1-3: <base64 encoding of CA 1's certificate>
```

3.3.2.6 Authenticating a Signed MIDlet Suite

Before a MIDlet suite is installed, the Application Management Software (AMS) will check for the presence of the `MIDlet-Jar-RSA-SHA1` attribute in the application descriptor and, if it is present, attempt to authenticate the JAR file by verifying the signer certificate and the JAR file. If it is not possible to successfully authenticate a signed MIDlet suite, it will not be installed.

If the MIDlet suite descriptor file does not include the `MIDlet-Jar-RSA-SHA1` attribute then the MIDlet can only be installed as untrusted.

3.3.2.7 Authorization Model

A signed MIDlet suite containing MIDlets which access protected APIs must explicitly request the required permissions. The MIDP 2.0 specification defines two new attributes: `MIDlet-Permissions` and `MIDlet-Permissions-Opt` for this purpose. Permissions that are required for access to protected APIs that are essential to the operation of MIDlets (**critical permissions**) must be listed under the `MIDlet-Permissions` attribute. Permissions required to access protected APIs that are not essential to the operation of the MIDlets (in other words the MIDlets can run in a restricted mode without access to these APIs) are **non-critical permissions** and should be listed under the `MIDlet-Permissions-Opt` attribute.

The `MIDlet-Permissions` and `MIDlet-Permissions-Opt` attributes may appear in the JAD file or the manifest of a signed MIDlet suite, or in both, in which case their respective values in each must be identical, but only the values in the manifest are 'protected' by the signature of the JAR file.

It is important to note that a MIDlet suite that has been installed as trusted will not be granted any permission it has not explicitly requested in either the `MIDlet-Permissions` or `MIDlet-Permissions-Opt` attributes, irrespective of whether it would be granted were it to be requested.

The naming scheme for permissions is similar to that for Java package names. The exact name of a permission to access an API or function is defined in the specification for that API. For instance, the entry requesting permission to open HTTP and secure HTTP connections would be as follows:

```
MIDlet-Permissions: javax.microedition.io.Connector.http,
        javax.microedition.io.Connector.https
```

The successful authorization of a trusted MIDlet suite requires that the requested critical permissions are recognized by the device (for instance, in the case of optional APIs) and are granted, or potentially granted, in the protection domain to which the MIDlet suite would be bound, were it to be installed. If either of these requirements cannot be satisfied, the MIDlet suite will not be installed.

3.3.2.8 Protection Domains

A protection domain is a set of permissions determining access to protected APIs or functions. A permission is either Allowed, in which case MIDlets in MIDlet suites bound to this protection domain have automatic access to this API, or User, in which case permission to access the protected API or function is requested from the user, who can then either grant or deny access. In the case of User permissions there are three interaction modes:

- Blanket – as long as the MIDlet suite is installed, it has this permission unless the user explicitly revokes it

- Session – user authorization is requested the first time the API is invoked and it is in force while the MIDlet is running

- Oneshot – user authorization is requested each time the API is invoked.

The protection domains for a given device are defined in a security policy file. A sample security policy file is shown below:

```
alias: net_access
javax.microedition.io.Connector.http,
javax.microedition.io.Connector.https,
javax.microedition.io.Connector.datagram,
javax.microedition.io.Connector.datagramreceiver,
javax.microedition.io.Connector.socket,
javax.microedition.io.Connector.serversocket,
javax.microedition.io.Connector.ssl
domain: Untrusted
session (oneshot): net_access
oneshot (oneshot): javax.microedition.io.Connector.sms.send
oneshot (oneshot): javax.microedition.io.Connector.sms.receive
session (oneshot): javax.microedition.io.PushRegistry
domain: Symbian
allow: net_access
allow: javax.microedition.io.Connector.sms.send
allow: javax.microedition.io.Connector.sms.receive
allow: javax.microedition.io.PushRegistry
```

User permissions may offer several interaction modes, the user being able to select the level of access. For instance, the following line indicates that the API or functions defined under the net_access alias have User permission with either session or oneshot interaction modes, the latter being the default.

```
session (oneshot): net_access
```

3.3.2.9   The Security Model in Practice

In this section we go through the steps involved in producing a signed MIDlet suite. We shall illustrate this process using the tools provided by the Nokia Developer's Suite (NDS) for J2ME 2.0 – a set of tools aimed at developers developing for Nokia's MIDP phones, including Series 60 devices. The Sun J2ME Wireless Toolkit 2.0 offers similar capabilities. The basic steps in producing a signed MIDlet suite are listed below:

1. Obtain (or generate) a public–private key pair.

2. Associate the key pair with a code signing certificate from a recommended CA.

3. Sign the MIDlet suite and incorporate the certificate into the JAD file.

To sign a MIDlet suite the supplier of the suite needs to obtain a public–private key pair either by generating a new pair or importing an existing key pair. The NDS provides tools for doing this. These can be accessed by selecting the Sign Application Package option (Figure 3.4) from the main panel. Clicking the New Key Pair button brings up the panel shown in Figure 3.5.

To generate the key pair, enter the appropriate details and click the Create button. A new key pair will be generated and added to the NDS key store. The newly-generated public key is incorporated into a self-signed certificate. We use this to obtain a suitable MIDlet suite code-signing certificate from an appropriate source (such as a recommended Certification Authority) that can be authenticated by a root certificate that ships with the device or is contained in the WIM/SIM

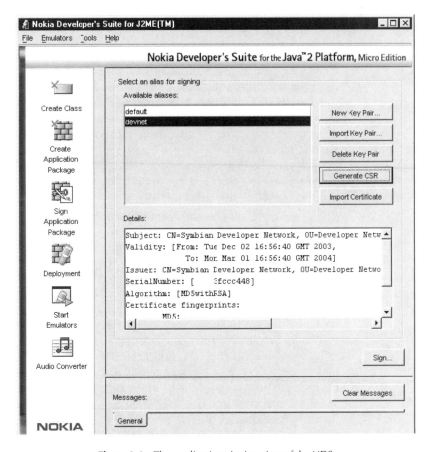

Figure 3.4   The application signing view of the NDS.

Figure 3.5   Creating a new public–private key pair in the NDS.

card. Application developers and suppliers should contact the relevant
developer program of the device manufacturer or network operator to
ascertain the appropriate CA. We can then generate a Certificate Signing
Request (CSR) using our self-signed certificate and the Generate CSR
option in the NDS (Figure 3.4). This generates a file containing the CSR
that can be saved to a convenient location. The contents of the CSR
can then be copied into an email to the recommended CA, requesting a
code-signing certificate.

When we have received the certificate from the recommended CA we
need to associate this with our key pair. The Import Certificate option
of the NDS associates the certificate with our key pair, identified by its
alias, and held in the key store. If the public key that we provided in the
CSR, and now contained in the certificate, matches the public key of the
key pair held in the key store we should be notified accordingly and are
now ready to sign our MIDlet suite. To sign the MIDlet suite we simply
select the Sign option (Figure 3.4) and choose the JAD file belonging
to the MIDlet suite we wish to sign. The MIDlet suite is now ready for
deployment on the target device. For further information on using the
NDS refer to the User's Guide contained in the NDS documentation.

As mentioned earlier, the Sun J2ME Wireless Toolkit 2.0 (WTK 2.0)
offers tools for creating and signing MIDlet suites. It also offers additional
functionality to test out signed MIDlet suites under emulation within the
WTK 2.0 environment. The WTK 2.0 provides a default trusted key pair
(and an associated certificate recognized by the emulator) that can be
used to install and bind a signed MIDlet suite to a trusted protection
domain within the emulator environment. This then allows MIDlets in the

signed suite to run within the WTK 2.0 environment as trusted without the cost and hassle of obtaining and importing a certificate from a CA. This feature is particularly useful for ensuring that the appropriate permissions to access protected APIs have been requested in the JAD file in order for the MIDlets within the signed MIDlet suite to install and run successfully as trusted MIDlets. It is important to remember that this feature of the WTK 2.0 only simulates a real signing event. It is, of course, necessary to obtain and sign your MIDlet suite with a valid certificate from a recommended CA before deploying your signed MIDlet suite onto a real device.

3.3.2.10   Untrusted MIDlets

An untrusted MIDlet suite is an unsigned MIDlet suite, i.e. one which does not include the `MIDlet-Jar-RSA-SHA1` attribute in its application descriptor (JAD), which has successfully been installed and bound to the untrusted protection domain. MIDlets in untrusted suites execute within a restricted environment where access to protected APIs or functions may be prohibited or allowed only with explicit user permission, depending on the security policy in force on the device. Unsigned MIDlet suites should not request permissions explicitly in either the application descriptor or the manifest. To ensure compatibility with MIDlets developed according to the MIDP 1.0 specification, the MIDP 2.0 specification demands that the untrusted domain must allow unrestricted access to the following APIs:

- `javax.microedition.rms`
- `javax.microedition.midlet`
- `javax.microedition.lcdui`
- `javax.microedition.lcdui.game`
- `javax.microedition.media`
- `javax.microedition.media.control`

Furthermore, the specification requires that the following APIs can be accessed with explicit permission of the user:

- `javax.microedition.io.HttpConnection`
- `javax.microedition.io.HttpsConnection`

The full list of permissions for the untrusted domain is device-specific however the MIDP 2.0 specification does provide a **Recommended Security Policy Document for GSM/UMTS Compliant Devices** as an addendum (with some clarifications added in the JTWI Release 1 **Security Policy for Untrusted MIDlet Suites**).

Finally, note that if a signed MIDlet fails authentication or authorization, it does not run as an untrusted MIDlet, but rather is not installed by the AMS. For more information on the MIDP 2.0 security model, including mechanisms for certificate revocation, see the MIDP 2.0 specification.

3.3.2.11 *Recommended Security Policy*

The MIDP 2.0 specification provides a framework for the MIDP 2.0 security model but does not itself mandate the device security policy in terms of specifying protection domains and permissions within those protection domains. The MIDP 2.0 specification does, however, supply an addendum to the specification that provides a recommended security policy (RSP) for GSM/UMTS compliant devices. It is not a mandatory part of the MIDP 2.0 specification, but GSM/UMTS compliant devices are expected to comply with it.

In addition to the untrusted domain, the RSP defines a set of three protection domains (Manufacturer, Operator and Trusted Third Party) to which trusted MIDlet suites can be bound (and that a compliant device may support).

For a trusted domain to be enabled there must be a certificate on the device, or a WIM/SIM, identified as a trust root for MIDlet suites in that domain, i.e. if a signed MIDlet suite can be authenticated using that trust root it will be bound to that domain.

For example, to enable the Manufacturer protection domain the manufacturer must place a certificate on the device. This is identified as the trust root for the Manufacturer domain.

A signed MIDlet suite will be bound to the Operator domain if it can be authenticated using a certificate found on the WIM/SIM and identified as a trust root for the Operator domain. A signed MIDlet suite will be bound to the Trusted Third Party protection domain if it can be authenticated using a certificate found on the device or on a WIM/SIM and identified as a trust root for the Trusted Third Party protection domain.

The RSP defines its policy in terms of function groups rather than individual permissions. A function group is a set of functionally related permissions, e.g. the Net Access function group contains all those permissions which relate to functionality that accesses the network, i.e. HTTP, HTTPS, datagram connection, secure socket and socket connections. The policy defines whether each function group is Allowed or User. User permission is requested in terms of the function group to which an individual permission belongs rather than the permission itself and the user's response applies to all permissions in that function group.

For more information on the **Recommended Security Policy for GSM/UMTS Compliant Devices** refer to the addendum contained in the MIDP 2.0 specification.

As already mentioned, the recommended security policy is not a mandatory requirement for a MIDP 2.0-compliant device. An implementation does not have to support the RSP in order to install signed MIDlet suites; it simply has to implement the MIDP 2.0 security model and support at least one trusted protection domain.

3.3.2.12   Security Model on Symbian OS Phones

At the time of writing the current MIDP 2.0 phones based on Symbian OS are the Sony Ericsson P900/P908 and the Nokia 6600. The Sony Ericsson P900/P908 (Organizer firmware versions R2B02 or later) provides support for a single trusted protection domain and therefore supports the installation of appropriately signed MIDlet suites. At the time of writing the available firmware (version 3.42.1) on the Nokia 6600 only supports the untrusted domain, although Nokia have indicated future firmware releases will bring in support for the Manufacturer and Trusted Third Party protection domains (see *Known Issues in the Nokia 6600 MIDP 2.0 Implementation* Version 1.2 at ***www.forum.nokia.com***).

With regard to the *Recommended Security Policy for GSM/UMTS Compliant Devices* Symbian's MIDP 2.0 implementation does not in itself implement the RSP, but instead provides the necessary framework for licensees to implement the security policy. To implement the RSP, the associated trusted protection domains (Manufacturer, Operator and Trusted Third Party) need to be associated with trust root certificates in the ROM or WIM/SIM card of the device. In addition, to be effective the MIDlet signing process needs to be associated with a certification scheme run by the relevant stakeholder's developer program. At the time of writing the infrastructure for the RSP is not yet fully in place, thus the current MIDP 2.0 phones based on Symbian OS are not fully compliant with the RSP. In the future this is likely to change as certification programs under development, such as the Java Verified Program for J2ME (***www.javaverified.com***), become established.

3.3.3   Over-the-Air Provisioning

The MIDP 1.0 specification provided a recommended practice for over-the-air (OTA) provisioning, but it was not a mandatory requirement that MIDP 1.0 implementations supported it. With the release of MIDP 2.0, support for user-initiated OTA provisioning became a mandatory part of the specification.

Symbian's MIDP implementation has provided the necessary support for OTA provisioning since MIDP 1.0. Therefore MIDP 1.0 devices such as the Nokia Series 60 N-Gage, 7650, 3650, 3660 and 3620 all support OTA provisioning, as does the Sony Ericsson P800. Naturally, Symbian OS-based MIDP 2.0 devices also support OTA provisioning.

3.3.4   Connection Framework

3.3.4.1   What's Optional and What's Not

The CLDC provides a Generic Connection Framework (GCF), which is an extensible framework that can be customized by a J2ME profile to support the necessary networking protocols required by that vertical device category. The MIDP 1.0 specification only required support (in other words, a concrete implementation) for the HTTP protocol. The MIDP 2.0 specification extends the support required for networking protocols to include mandatory support for HTTPS. The MIDP 2.0 specification also states that implementations should (where "should" implies a recommended practice that can be ignored only in exceptional circumstances) provide support for sockets, secure sockets, server sockets and datagrams. Support for serial port access via the CommConnection interface is optional under the MIDP 2.0 specification.

Symbian's implementation of MIDP 2.0 complies with the specification, providing implementations for all of the above except the optional serial port access. So, Symbian's MIDP 2.0 currently provides implementations of the following protocols:

- HTTP
- HTTPS
- sockets
- server sockets
- secure sockets
- datagrams.

In the following sections we will explore using these connections in a little more detail.

3.3.4.2   HTTP and HTTPS Support

HTTP connections have been supported since MIDP 1.0. To open an HTTP connection we use the Connector.open() method with a URL of the form www.myserver.com.

So code to open an HttpConnection and obtain an InputStream would look something like this.

```
try{
    String url = "www.myserver.com";
    HttpConnection conn = (HttpConnection)Connector.open(url);
    InputStream is = conn.openInputStream();
    ...
    conn.close()
}catch(IOException ioe){...}
```

Under the MIDP 2.0 security model, untrusted MIDlets can open an HTTP connection only with explicit user confirmation. Signed MIDlets that require access to an HTTP connection must explicitly request the `javax.microedition.io.Connector.http` permission in the `MIDlet-Permissions` attribute:

```
MIDlet-Permissions: javax.microedition.io.Connector.http, ...
```

The MIDP 2.0 specification adds the requirement that implementations must support the HTTPS protocol, which implements HTTP over a secure network connection via the Secure Sockets Layer (SSL). Opening an HTTPS connection follows the same pattern as a normal HTTP connection, with the exception that we pass in a connection URL of the form `https://www.mysecureserver.com` and cast the returned instance to an `HttpsConnection` object, as in the following example of code for interrogating a secure server for security information associated with the connection.

```
try{
    String url = "https://www.mysecureserver.com";
    HttpsConnection hc = (HttpsConnection)Connector.open(url);
    SecurityInfo info = hc.getSecurityInfo();

    String protocolName = info.getProtocolName();
    String protocolVersion = info.getProtocolVersion();
    String cipherSuite = info.getCipherSuite();
    Certificate c = info.getServerCertificate();
    String name = c.getIssuer();
    ...
}catch(IOException ioe){...}
```

The MIDP 2.0 specification requires that MIDlets in untrusted MIDlet suites be able to open HTTPS connections with User permission. A signed MIDlet suite which contains MIDlets that open HTTPS connections must explicitly request the `javax.microedition.io.Connector.https` permission in its `MIDlet-Permissions` attribute:

```
MIDlet-Permissions: javax.microedition.io.Connector.https, ...
```

3.3.4.3   *Socket and Server Socket Support*

Although support for socket connections was an optional part of the MIDP 1.0 specification, MIDP 2.0 now makes support for socket connections a recommended practice. Socket connections come in two forms: client connections in which a socket connection is opened to another host; and server connections in which the system listens on a particular port for incoming connections from other hosts. The connections are specified using Universal Resource Identifiers (URI).

You should be familiar with the syntax of a URI from Web browsing. They have the format `<string1>://<string2>` where `<string1>` identifies the communication protocol to be used (e.g. `http`) and `<string2>` provides specific details about the connection. The protocol may be one of those supported by the Generic Connection Framework (see Section 2.1.3.2).

To open a client socket connection to another host we pass a URI of the following form to the connector's `open()` method:

```
socket://www.symbian.com:80
```

The host may be specified as a fully qualified hostname or IPv4 address and the port number refers to the connection endpoint on the remote peer. Some sample code is shown below:

```
SocketConnection sc = null;
OutputStream out = null;
try{
    sc = (SocketConnection)Connector.open ("socket://localhost:79");
    ...
    out = c.openOutputStream();
    ...
}catch(IOException ioe){...}
```

A server socket connection is used for listening for inbound socket connections. To obtain a server socket connection we can pass a URI in either of the following forms to the connector's `open()` method:

```
socket://:79
socket://
```

In the first case the system listens for incoming connections on port 79 (of the local host). In the latter case, the system allocates an available port for the incoming connections.

```
ServerSocketConnection ssc = null;
InputStream is = null;
try{
    ssc = (ServerSocketConnection)Connector.open("socket://:1234");
    SocketConnection sc = (SocketConnection)ssc.acceptAndOpen();
    ...
    is = sc.openInputStream();
    ...
}catch(IOException ioe){...}
```

The ServerSocketConnection interface extends the StreamConnectionNotifier interface. To obtain a connection object for an incoming connection the acceptAndOpen() method must be called on the ServerSocketConnection instance. An inbound socket connection results in the call to the acceptAndOpen() method, returning a StreamConnection object which can be cast to a SocketConnection as desired.

The SocketConnection interface defines several useful methods including:

```
public void setSocketOption(byte option, int value)
```

This allows the developer to set several socket options using the following public static final byte constants defined in SocketConnection:

- DELAY
  A value of zero disables the use of Nagle's algorithm – written data is not buffered pending acknowledgement of previously written data. This may be desirable when sending and receiving small packets of data, for instance, in a peer-to-peer messenger application.

- LINGER
  A non-zero value represents the interval in seconds that the system will continue to try to process queued data after the close() method has been called. After the interval has elapsed the connection will be forcefully closed with a TCP RST. A value of zero disables linger on close.

- KEEPALIVE
  If enabled (by a non-zero value), a keepalive probe will be sent to the remote peer after an implementation-specific time interval (the default is two hours) if no other data has been sent or received on the socket during that time interval. The purpose of the probe is to detect if the peer has become unreachable. The peer can respond in one of three ways: a TCP ACK response indicating all is well – no action is taken; a TCP RST response indicating the peer has crashed and been rebooted in which case the socket is closed; no response from the remote peer – the socket is closed. A value of zero disables this feature.

- RCVBUF
  This option is used by the platform's networking code as a hint for the size at which to set the underlying network I/O receiving buffer.

- SNDBUF
  This option is used by the platform's networking code as a hint for the size to set the underlying network I/O sending buffer.

A signed MIDlet suite which contains MIDlets which open socket
connections must explicitly request the `javax.microedition.io.`
`Connector.socket` permission (needed to open client connections) and if required the `javax.microedition.io.Connector.`
`serversocket` permission (needed to open server connections), in its
`MIDlet-Permissions` attribute, for example:

```
MIDlet-Permissions: javax.microedition.io.Connector.socket, ...
```

or:

```
MIDlet-Permissions: javax.microedition.io.Connector.socket,
javax.microedition.io.Connector.serversocket, ...
```

If the protection domain to which the signed MIDlet suite would be
bound grants, or potentially grants, these permissions, then the MIDlet
suite will be installed and the MIDlets it contains will be able to open
socket connections, either automatically or with user permission, depending upon the security policy in effect on the device for the protection
domain to which the MIDlet suite has been bound.

Whether MIDlets in untrusted MIDlet suites can open socket connections depends on the security policy relating to the untrusted domain in
force on the device.

3.3.4.4 *Secure Socket Support*

Secure socket connections are client socket connections over SSL. To
open a secure socket connection we pass in a hostname (or IPv4 address)
and port number to the connector's `open()` method using the following
URI syntax:

```
ssl://hostname:port
```

We can then use the secure socket connection in the same manner as
a normal socket connection, for example:

```
try{
    SecureConnection sc = (SecureConnection)
            Connector.open("ssl://www.secureserver.com:443");
    ...
    OutputStream out = sc.openOutputStream();
    ...
    InputStream in = sc.openInputStream();
    ...
}catch(IOException ioe){...}
```

A signed MIDlet suite that contains MIDlets which open secure connections must explicitly request the `javax.microedition.io.Con-
nector.ssl` permission in its `MIDlet-Permissions` attribute, for
example:

```
MIDlet-Permissions: javax.microedition.io.Connector.ssl, ...
```

If the protection domain to which the signed MIDlet suite would be
bound grants, or potentially grants, this permission, the MIDlet suite can
be installed and the MIDlets it contains will be able to open secure
connections, either automatically or with user permission, depending on
the security policy in effect.

Whether MIDlets in untrusted MIDlet suites can open secure connections depends on the permissions granted in the untrusted protection
domain.

3.3.4.5 Datagram Support

Symbian's MIDP 2.0 implementation includes support for sending and
receiving UDP datagrams. A datagram connection can be opened in
client or server mode. Client mode is for sending datagrams to a remote
device. To open a client mode datagram connection we use the following
URI format:

```
datagram://localhost:1234
```

Here the port number indicates the port on the target device to
which the datagram will be sent. Sample code for sending a datagram is
shown below:

```
String message = "Hello!";
byte[] payload = message.toString();
try{
    UDPDatagramConnection conn = null;
    conn = (UDPDatagramConnection)
        Connector.open("datagram://localhost:1234");
    Datagram datagram = conn.newDatagram(payload, payload.length);
    conn.send(datagram);
}catch(IOException ioe){...}
```

Server mode connections are for receiving (and replying to) incoming
datagrams. To open a datagram connection in server mode we use a URI
of the following form:

```
datagram://:1234
```

The port number in this case refers to the port on which the local device is listening for incoming datagrams. Sample code for receiving incoming datagrams is given below:

```
try{
    UDPDatagramConnection dconn = null;
    dconn = (UDPDatagramConnection)Connector.open("datagram://:1234");
    Datagram dg = dconn.newDatagram(300);
    while(true){
        dconn.receive(dg);
        byte[] data = dg.getData();
        ...
    }
}catch(IOException ioe){...}
```

A signed MIDlet suite which contains MIDlets that open datagram connections must explicitly request the `javax.microedition.io.Connector.datagram` permission (needed to open client connections) and the `javax.microedition.io.Connector.datagramreceiver` permission (needed to open server connections) in its `MIDlet-Permissions` attribute, for example:

```
MIDlet-Permissions: javax.microedition.io.Connector.datagram, ...
```

or:

```
MIDlet-Permissions: javax.microedition.io.Connector.datagramreceiver,
...
```

or:

```
MIDlet-Permissions: javax.microedition.io.Connector.datagram,
javax.microedition.io.Connector.datagramreceiver, ...
```

If the protection domain to which the signed MIDlet suite would be bound grants, or potentially grants, the requested permissions, the MIDlet suite can be installed and the MIDlets it contains will be able to open datagram connections, either automatically or with user permission, depending on the security policy in effect.

Whether MIDlets in untrusted MIDlet suites can open datagram connections depends on permissions granted to MIDlet suites bound to the untrusted protection domain.

3.3.4.6   *Security Policy for Network Connections*

The connections discussed above are part of the Net Access function group (see the **Recommended Security Policy for GSM/UMTS Compliant**

Devices addendum to the MIDP 2.0 specification). On the Nokia 6600 and Sony Ericsson P900/P908, MIDlets in untrusted MIDlet suites can access the Net Access function group with User permission (explicit confirmation required from the user). On the Sony Ericsson P900/P908, the default User permission is set to session (and is not customizable by the user). On the Nokia 6600, the default User permission is set to oneshot, but can be changed by the user to session or disallowed.

The Sony Ericsson P900/P908 supports the trusted protection domain on Organizer firmware versions R2B02 or later. The security policy in effect for MIDlets in MIDlet suites bound to the trusted protection domain on the P900/P908 allows automatic access (Allowed permission) to the Net Access function group connections. At the time of writing, the available firmware release (3.42.1) on the Nokia 6600 only supported the untrusted domain, although future releases will add support for trusted protection domains.

3.3.4.7 Practical Networking using Wireless Networks

In the spirit of providing practical information, we shall now digress slightly into a discussion of networking on wireless data networks. The most common GSM networks at the time of writing are 2.5 G General Packet Radio Service (GPRS) networks. GPRS networks can be regarded as a private sub-network behind a gateway to the Internet. All current GPRS network providers operate their consumer networks behind Network Address Translation (NAT) gateways and dynamically allocate private IP addresses to mobile terminals on each PDP activation (data session).

This has important consequences for application developers wishing to use wireless networking. One consequence is that mobile terminals on a GPRS network typically are unable to receive inbound connections since their private IP addresses are not visible on the Internet. Another issue relates to connection-less communications protocols such as UDP. When a terminal on a GPRS network sends a UDP packet to a remote host on the Internet, the sender address is stripped out of the packet and replaced with the IP address of the gateway and a port number representing the terminal data session. How long this session information remains valid (enabling the remote host to reply to the sender) depends on the NAT gateway. After a limited period of time the gateway will re-allocate that port to another GPRS terminal. Some NAT policies allow for the session information (and thus the allocated port) to remain associated with the GPRS terminal as long as traffic flows through it. Such inactivity timeouts though, vary quite significantly between operators.

The most effective way of avoiding complications arising out of operating behind NAT gateways is for developers to use TCP-based protocols such as HTTP. As long as there is an active TCP session in place, the gateway port will remain allocated to that GPRS terminal by the NAT gateway, enabling two-way traffic between the GPRS terminal and the remote device.

3.3.4.8 Socket Demo MIDlet

We will finish this section with a simple example using TCP sockets to interrogate a web browser. The Socket Demo MIDlet sends an HTTP GET request to a web server over a client socket connection and then reads and displays the response. The Socket Demo MIDlet consists of two classes, `SocketMIDlet` extending `MIDlet` and the `ClientConnection` class. The source code for the `SocketMIDlet` class is shown below.

```java
import javax.microedition.midlet.*;
import javax.microedition.lcdui.*;
public class SocketMIDlet extends MIDlet implements CommandListener {
    private final static String defaultURL =
            "socket://www.symbian.com:80";
    private Command exitCommand, sendCommand;
    private Display display;
    public TextBox textBox;

    public SocketMIDlet() {
        display = Display.getDisplay(this);
        exitCommand = new Command("Exit", Command.EXIT, 2);
        sendCommand = new Command("Send request", Command.SCREEN, 1);
    }

    public void startApp() {
        textBox = new TextBox("Sockets Demo", defaultURL, 256,
                TextField.ANY);
        textBox.addCommand(exitCommand);
        textBox.addCommand(sendCommand);
        textBox.setCommandListener(this);
        display.setCurrent(textBox);
    }

    public void commandAction(Command c, Displayable s) {
        if (c == exitCommand) {
            notifyDestroyed();
        }
        else if (c == sendCommand) {
            ClientConnection socketConn = new ClientConnection(this);
            socketConn.sendMessage(textBox.getString());
            textBox.removeCommand(sendCommand);
        }
    }

    public void pauseApp() {
    }

    public void destroyApp(boolean unconditional) {
    }

}
```

SocketMIDlet sets up the UI and responds to the "Send request" Command by creating an instance of ClientConnection and invoking its sendMessage() method, passing in a String representing the URL of the required web server.

The main work is done in the ClientConnection class:

```java
import javax.microedition.io.*;
import java.io.*;
public class ClientConnection extends Thread {

    private final static String line1 = "GET /index.html\r\n";
    private final static String line2 = "Accept: */*\r\n";
    private final static String line3 = "Accept-Language: en-us\r\n";
    private final static String line4 =
            "Accept-Encoding: gzip, deflate\r\n";
    private final static String line5 =
        "User-Agent: Mozilla/4.0 (Compatible; MSIE 5.01; Windows NT)\r\n";

    private SocketMIDlet sM = null;
    private String url = null;
    private String request = null;

    public ClientConnection(SocketMIDlet sM) {
        this.sM = sM;
    }

    public void sendMessage(String url) {
        this.url = url;
        String host = url.substring(url.lastIndexOf('/') + 1);
        System.out.println("host is " + host);
        String hostLine = "Host: " + host + "\r\n";
        request = line1 + line2 + line3 + line4 + line5 + hostLine;
        start();
    }

    public void run() {
        try{
            SocketConnection conn =
                    (SocketConnection)Connector.open(url);
            DataOutputStream out = conn.openDataOutputStream();
            byte[] buf= request.getBytes();
            out.write(buf);
            out.flush();
            out.close();
            sM.textBox.insert("Finished request!\n" +
                    "Receiving response...\n", sM.textBox.size());

            DataInputStream in = conn.openDataInputStream();
            int ch;
            while ( (ch = in.read()) != -1 &&
                    sM.textBox.size() < sM.textBox.getMaxSize()) {
                String str = new Character((char) ch).toString();
                try {
                    sM.textBox.insert(str, sM.textBox.size());
                }catch(Exception e) {
                    e.printStackTrace();
                }
```

```
            }
            conn.close();
            conn = null;
        }catch(Exception e){
            e.printStackTrace();
        }
    }
}
```

The `url` parameter of the `sendMessage()` method has the following form:

```
socket://www.symbian.com:80
```

The `sendMessage()` method creates a GET request and then starts a new `Thread` to create the connection, send the request and read the response. Let us look at the contents of the thread's `run()` method in more detail.

```
SocketConnection conn = (SocketConnection)Connector.open(url);
DataOutputStream out = conn.openDataOutputStream();
byte[] buf= request.getBytes();
out.write(buf);
out.flush();
out.close();
```

A `SocketConnection` is opened using a URI of the form `socket://hostname:port` and the returned `SocketConnection` object is used to get a `DataOutputStream`. After converting the request to a byte array, this is written to the `DataOutputStream` using the `write()` method. The `flush()` method is then called on the `DataOutputStream` to ensure any buffered data is written to the connection endpoint. This last step is essential. Symbian's implementation of `OutputStream` buffers data internally and only writes it to the connection endpoint when the buffer is full, or when the buffer is flushed. Failing to call `flush()` may result in data never being written to the connection endpoint. Once we have finished with the `OutputStream` we can close it.

Having written the request we are now ready to read the response. We use our `SocketConnection` to get a `DataInputStream` and use the `read()` method to read from it in the standard manner.

```
DataInputStream in = conn.openDataInputStream();
int ch;
while ( (ch = in.read()) != -1 &&
     sM.textBox.size() < sM.textBox.getMaxSize()) {
    ...
}
```

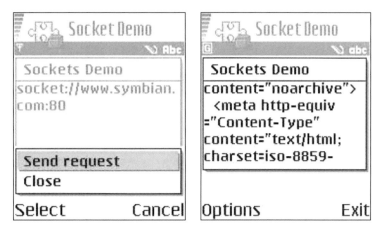

Figure 3.6   Socket Demo MIDlet running on a Nokia 6600.

The response from the web server should be a stream of raw HTML. We read the stream until our MIDlet's TextBox is full and then close the connection (reading the response in its entirety is likely to be a lengthy process for most web sites!).

The screenshots in Figure 3.6 show the Socket Demo MIDlet running on a Nokia 6600.

Note that the purpose of this sample code is to demonstrate how to use client TCP socket connections. Normally, to make requests to a HTTP server we would use an HttpConnection or HttpsConnection. Also, under the JTWI security policy for GSM/UMTS compliant devices, the implementation of SocketConnection using TCP sockets must throw a SecurityException when an untrusted MIDlet suite attempts to connect on ports 80, 8080 (HTTP) and 443 (HTTPS). Hence the above code is not future-proof for untrusted MIDlet suites.

3.3.5   The Push Registry

3.3.5.1   Introduction

One of the exciting new additions to MIDP 2.0 is the Push Registry API, which allows MIDlets to be launched in response to incoming network connections. Many applications, particularly messaging applications, need to be continuously listening for incoming messages. Previously, to achieve this a Java application would have had to be continually running in the background. Although the listening Java application may itself be small, it would still require an instance of the virtual machine to be running, thus appropriating some of the mobile phone's scarce resources. The JSR 118 recognized the need for an alternative, more resource-effective solution for MIDP 2.0 and so introduced the push registry.

3.3.5.2   *Using the Push Registry*

The Push Registry API is encapsulated in the `javax.microedition.io.PushRegistry` class. The push registry maintains a list of inbound connections that have been previously registered by installed MIDlets. A MIDlet registers an incoming connection with the push registry either statically at installation via an entry in the JAD file or dynamically (programmatically) via the `registerConnection()` method.

When a MIDlet is running, it handles all the incoming connections (whether registered with the push registry or not). If, however, the MIDlet is not running, the AMS listens for registered incoming connections and launches the MIDlet in response to an incoming connection previously registered by that MIDlet, by invoking the `startApp()` method. The AMS then hands off the connection to the MIDlet which is then responsible for opening the appropriate connection and handling the I/O.

In the case of static registration, the MIDlet registers its interest in incoming connections in the JAD file, in the following format:

```
MIDlet-Push-<n>: <ConnectionURL>, <MIDletClassName>, <AllowedSender>
```

The `<ConnectionURL>` field specifies the protocol and port for the connection end point in the same URI syntax used as the argument to the `Connector.open()` method that is used by the MIDlet to process the incoming connection. Examples of `<ConnectionURL>` entries might be:

```
sms://:1234
socket://:1234
```

The `<MIDletClassName>` field contains the package-qualified name of the class that extends `javax.microedition.midlet.MIDlet`. This would be the name of the MIDlet class as listed in the application descriptor or manifest file under the `MIDlet-<n>` entry.

The `<AllowedSender>` field acts as a filter indicating that the AMS should only respond to incoming connections from a specific sender. For the SMS protocol, the `<AllowedSender>` entry is the phone number of the required sender. For a server socket connection endpoint the `<AllowedSender>` entry would be an IP address (note in both cases that the sender port number is not included in the filter). The `<AllowedSender>` syntax supports two wildcard characters: * matches any string including an empty string and ? matches any character. Hence the following would be valid entries for the `<AllowedSender>` field:

```
*
129.70.40.*
129.70.40.23?
```

The first entry indicates any IP address, the second entry allows the last three digits of the IP address to take any value, while the last entry allows only the last digit to have any value.

So the full entry for the MIDlet-Push-<n> attribute in a JAD file may look something like this:

```
MIDlet-Push-1: sms://:1234, com.symbian.devnet.ChatMIDlet, *
MIDlet-Push-2: socket://:3000, com.symbian.devnet.ChatMIDlet,
        129.70.40.*
```

If the request for a static connection registration can not be fulfilled then the AMS must not install the MIDlet. Examples of when a registration request might fail include the requested protocol not being supported by the device, or the requested port number being already allocated to another application.

To register a dynamic connection with the AMS we use the static registerConnection() method of PushRegistry:

```
PushRegistry.registerConnection("sms://:1234",
        "com.symbian.devnet.ChatMIDlet", "*");
```

The arguments take precisely the same format as those used to make up the MIDlet-Push-<n> entry in a JAD or manifest. Upon registration, the dynamic connection behaves in an identical manner to a static connection registered via the application descriptor.

To un-register a dynamic connection the static boolean unregisterConnection() method of PushRegistry is used:

```
boolean result = PushRegistry.unregisterConnection(("sms://:1234");
```

If the dynamic connection was successfully unregistered a value of true is returned.

The AMS will respond to input activity on a registered connection by launching the corresponding MIDlet (assuming that the MIDlet is not already running). The MIDlet should then respond to the incoming connection by launching a thread to handle the incoming data in the startApp() method. Using a separate thread is the recommended practice for avoiding conflicts between blocking I/O operations and the normal user interaction events. For a MIDlet registered for incoming SMS messages, the startApp() method might look something like this:

```
public void startApp() {
    // List of active connections.
    String[] connections = PushRegistry.listConnections(true);
```

```
for (int i=0; i < connections.length; i++) {
    if(connections[i].equals("sms://:1234")){
        new Thread(){
            public void run(){
                Receiver.openReceiver();
            }
        }.start();
    }
}
...
}
```

One other use of the push registry should be mentioned before we leave this topic. The `PushRegistry` class provides the `register-Alarm()` method:

```
public static long registerAlarm(String midlet, long time)
```

This allows a running MIDlet to register itself or another MIDlet in the same suite for activation at a given time. The `midlet` argument is the class name of the MIDlet to be launched at the time specified by the `time` argument. The launch time is specified in milliseconds since January 1, 1970, 00:00:00 GMT. The push registry may contain only one outstanding activation time entry per MIDlet in each installed MIDlet suite. If a previous activation entry is registered, it will be replaced by the current invocation and the previous value returned. If no previous wakeup time has been set, a zero is returned.

3.3.5.3   The Push Registry and the Security Model

The `PushRegistry` is a protected API and, as such, a signed MIDlet suite which registers connections statically or contains MIDlets which register connections and/or alarms, must explicitly request the `javax.microedition.io.PushRegistry` permission in its `MIDlet-Permissions` attribute, for example:

```
MIDlet-Permissions: javax.microedition.io.PushRegistry, ...
```

Note that a signed MIDlet suite must also explicitly request the permissions necessary to open the connection types of any connections it wishes to register either statically or dynamically. If the protection domain to which the signed MIDlet suite would be bound grants, or potentially grants, the requested permission, the MIDlet suite can be installed and the MIDlets it contains will be able to register and deregister connections, and register alarms, either automatically, or with user permission, depending on the security policy in effect.

Untrusted MIDlets do not require a `MIDlet-Permissions` entry. Whether access is granted to the Push Registry API will depend on the security policy for the untrusted protection domain in effect on the device.

On the Sony Ericsson P900/P908 and Nokia 6600, MIDlets in untrusted MIDlet suites can use the Push Registry APIs (Application Auto-Invocation function group) with user permission. On both the 6600 and the P900/P908, the default user permission is set to session. On the Nokia 6600, the default value can be changed by the user to oneshot or disallowed. For the Sony Ericsson P900/P908, the security policy in effect for MIDlets in MIDlet suites bound to the trusted protection domain allows automatic access to the Push Registry API.

3.3.5.4 Symbian's Implementation

At the time of writing, the current version of Symbian OS, Version 7.0s, supports the following connection types in its implementation of the MIDP 2.0 push architecture:

- Server socket
- Datagram
- SMS.

In Symbian's implementation, all connections that can be registered as push connections are managed by the system AMS, even if they are not requested to be push-enabled by an application. In the case of server connections that spawn off a connected stream due to an incoming connection, the stream connections are also maintained through the system AMS.

Future releases of Symbian OS are likely to increase the types of connections supported by the push architecture to include Bluetooth, L2CAP and RFCOMM connections.

3.3.6 Additions to the LCDUI

3.3.6.1 A Quick Tour

The MIDP 2.0 specification introduces a number of new features to the LCDUI toolkit which are designed to give developers more control over their application's user interface. In this section we briefly look at some of them.

Display
MIDP 2.0 introduces two useful new methods to the `Display` class which allow MIDlets to control the screen backlight and the vibration of the phone:

```
public boolean flashBackLight(int duration)
public boolean vibrate(int duration)
```

The duration of the effect is specified by the `duration` parameter – a value of zero causes the action to stop. The return value is `false` if the relevant feature is not supported by the phone.

Form

MIDP 2.0 introduces a new layout algorithm for arranging items in a `Form`. The layout algorithm arranges items in rows according to a **layout direction** defined by the implementation for the language convention in use. For European and North American markets the default layout direction will be left to right. The layout algorithm then arranges items from left to right and starts a new row when there is insufficient space in the row to accommodate the next `Item`. The layout algorithm uses the concept of **current alignment**. For an implementation with a left to right layout direction the initial current alignment is `Item.LAYOUT_LEFT`. Other possible values for the current alignment are `Item.LAYOUT_RIGHT` and `Item.LAYOUT_CENTER`. The current alignment changes when the layout algorithm encounters an `Item` with a (horizontal) layout value other than the current setting (the layout directive for an `Item` is set using the `setLayout()` method). When this happens, the layout algorithm adds that `Item` on a new row and uses the new alignment value until an `Item` with a different horizontal directive is encountered.

Vertical layout directives provided are `Item.LAYOUT_TOP`, `Item.LAYOUT_BOTTOM` and `Item.LAYOUT_VCENTER`. These are used to indicate the required vertical alignment of an `Item` within the current row.

MIDP 2.0 added the `getPreferredWidth()`, `getPreferredHeight()`, `getMinimumWidth()` and `getMinimumHeight()` methods to the `Item` class. These are used by the form layout algorithm to position and size `Items` within rows. In addition a MIDlet can influence the size of an `Item` by using the `Item.LAYOUT_EXPAND`, `Item.LAYOUT_VEXPAND` and `Item.LAYOUT_SHRINK` and `Item.LAYOUT_VSHRINK` directives.

When filling a row, the layout algorithm first adds each `Item` according to its preferred width (or minimum width, if the `LAYOUT_SHRINK` directive is set). Once the row has been filled, any remaining space is proportionately distributed amongst the items by expanding their widths. Any `Item` with the `LAYOUT_SHRINK` directive set is expanded to no more than its preferred size and then any remaining space is taken up expanding `Items` with the `LAYOUT_EXPAND` directive set.

The height of a row is determined by the tallest `Item` in the row. The height of an `Item` is determined by its preferred height (unless the `LAYOUT_VSHRINK` directive has been set, in which case initially the minimum height is used). Once the height of the row has been determined, any `Item` shorter than the row height that has its `LAYOUT_VEXPAND` directive set is expanded to the height of the row. Any `Item` with its `LAYOUT_VSHRINK` directive set is expanded to its preferred size or the height of the row, whichever is shorter. Finally, any `Item` with vertical directives (`LAYOUT_TOP`, `LAYOUT_BOTTOM` or `LAYOUT_CENTER`) set is positioned accordingly in the row. Remaining items with no vertical directive are positioned at the bottom of the row.

It is possible to force a row break using `setLayout(Item.LAYOUT_NEWLINE_BEFORE)` and `setLayout(Item.LAYOUT_NEWLINE_AFTER)`. In the first case, the item will be added on a new row. In the second case, a row break will occur immediately after the item that called the method. Note that for backward compatibility with MIDP 1.0, `TextField`, `DateField`, `Gauge` and `ChoiceGroup` items are always positioned with a row to themselves unless the `Item.LAYOUT_2` directive has been set.

Item
MIDP 2.0 introduces new features into the `Item` class including:

* support for the new layout algorithm with new directives defined as `public static final int` (see above)
* the `addCommand()` method; an item can have commands associated with it
* the `setItemCommandListener()` method
* the `getMinimumHeight()`, `getMinimumWidth()`, `getPreferredHeight()` and `getPreferredWidth()` methods.

It also introduces new `public static final int` appearance modes:

* `BUTTON` indicates the item is to appear as a button
* `HYPERLINK` indicates the item is to appear as a hyperlink
* `PLAIN` indicates the item is to have a normal appearance.

CustomItem
This is a new class introduced in MIDP 2.0 that can be sub-classed to create new visual elements for use in `Forms`.

StringItem
MIDP 2.0 introduces a new constructor to the `StringItem` class that creates a `StringItem` with the indicated appearance mode: `PLAIN`, `BUTTON`, or `HYPERLINK`.

```
public StringItem(String label,String text,int appearanceMode)
```

ItemCommandListener
A listener type introduced in MIDP 2.0 for receiving notification of commands that have been invoked on Item objects.

Spacer
A new class introduced in MIDP 2.0 representing a blank Item with a settable minimum size whose primary purpose is to position other items.

Choice
New features introduced in MIDP 2.0 to the Choice interface include:

- static int POPUP

- static int TEXT_WRAP_DEFAULT

- static int TEXT_WRAP_OFF

- static int TEXT_WRAP_ON

- deleteAll()

- getFitPolicy()

- getFont()

- setFitPolicy(int fitPolicy)

- setFont(int elementNum, Font font).

3.3.6.2 Exploring the LCDUI: the KeyPad Example

Rather than exploring the new features of the LCDUI API by API, we will instead discuss an example MIDlet that illustrates some of the features. For a more thorough exposition of the LCDUI APIs, the reader is referred to Sun's MIDP 2.0 documentation.

We will use as the example a simple numeric keypad. Screenshots of our KeyPad MIDlet running on the Series 60 and UIQ reference designs are shown in Figure 3.7.

The KeyPad MIDlet consists of two classes: the KeyPad class extends MIDlet and provides the main UI in the guise of a Form instance; and the Button class extends CustomItem and models a simple button. The Button instances are appended to the Form to create our keypad.

First, let's consider the KeyPad class:

```
import javax.microedition.midlet.MIDlet;
import javax.microedition.lcdui.*;
public class KeyPad extends MIDlet implements CommandListener {
    private Display display;
    private Form container;
    private Command exit;
```

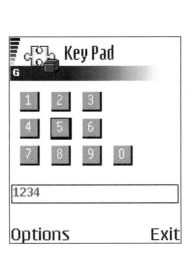
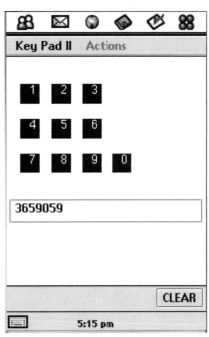

Figure 3.7   The KeyPad MIDlet on Series 60 and UIQ.

```
private Command clear;
private TextField field;

public KeyPad() {
    display = Display.getDisplay(this);
    container = new Form("");
    clear = new Command("CLEAR",Command.SCREEN,1);
    exit = new Command("EXIT",Command.EXIT,1);
    container.addCommand(exit);
    container.addCommand(clear);
    container.setCommandListener(this);

    Button one = new Button(this, "1");
    Button two = new Button(this, "2");
    Button three = new Button(this, "3");
    Button four = new Button(this, "4");
    Button five = new Button(this, "5");
    Button six = new Button(this, "6");
    Button seven = new Button(this, "7");
    Button eight = new Button(this, "8");
    Button nine = new Button(this, "9");
    Button zero = new Button(this, "0");

    field = new TextField(null,null,32,TextField.UNEDITABLE);

    int bheight = one.getPrefContentHeight(-1);
    int bwidth = one.getPrefContentWidth(-1);
```

```
    container.append(new Spacer
            (container.getWidth(),bheight/2));

    container.append(new Spacer (bwidth/2, bheight));
    container.append(one);
    container.append(new Spacer (bwidth/2, bheight));
    container.append(two);
    container.append(new Spacer (bwidth/2, bheight));
    container.append(three);

    container.append(new Spacer
            (container.getWidth(),bheight/4));

    container.append(new Spacer (bwidth/2, bheight));
    container.append(four);
    container.append(new Spacer (bwidth/2, bheight));
    container.append(five);
    container.append(new Spacer (bwidth/2, bheight));
    container.append(six);

    container.append(new Spacer
            (container.getWidth(),bheight/4));

    container.append(new Spacer (bwidth/2, bheight));
    container.append(seven);
    container.append(new Spacer (bwidth/2, bheight));
    container.append(eight);
    container.append(new Spacer (bwidth/2, bheight));
    container.append(nine);
    container.append(new Spacer (bwidth/2, bheight));
    container.append(zero);

    container.append(new Spacer
            (container.getWidth(),bheight/2));

    container.append(field);
}

public void setString(String s) {
    String current = field.getString();
    field.setString(current.concat(s));
}

public void commandAction(Command c, Displayable d) {
    if(c == exit) {
        notifyDestroyed();
    }
    else if(c == clear) {
        field.setString("");
    }
}

public void startApp() {
    display.setCurrent(container);
}

public void pauseApp() {
```

```
    }

    public void destroyApp(boolean unconditional) {
    }
}
```

The main work is done in the constructor. We create the Form, plus a couple of Command instances. We add the commands to the form and set the CommandListener. Then we create various instances of our Button and a TextField to display the output of the button presses. We append the Button instances to the Form, separated by instances of the Spacer class, plus the TextField instance. We implement a setString() callback method that is invoked by a Button instance, taking the button's label as its parameter. Finally, we implement the commandAction() method mandated by the CommandListener interface, which our KeyPad class implements.

Now let's look at the Button class:

```
import javax.microedition.lcdui.*;
public class Button extends CustomItem{
    private static final int HEIGHT = 20;
    private static final int WIDTH = 20;
    private static final int DELTA = 2;
    private String num;
    private KeyPad pad;

    public Button(KeyPad pad, String num){
        super("");
        this.pad = pad;
        this.num = num;
    }

    protected void paint(Graphics g, int w, int h){
        g.setColor(0, 0, 0);
        g.fillRect(0, 0, WIDTH+DELTA, HEIGHT+DELTA);
        g.setColor(128, 128, 128);
        g.fillRect(0, 0, WIDTH-DELTA, HEIGHT-DELTA);
        int xOffset = WIDTH/3;
        int yOffset = 2*HEIGHT/3;
        g.setColor(255, 255, 255);
        g.drawString(num, xOffset, yOffset,
                Graphics.BASELINE | Graphics.LEFT);
    }

    protected int getPrefContentHeight(int width) {
        return getMinContentWidth();
    }

    protected int getPrefContentWidth(int height) {
        return getMinContentHeight();
    }

    protected int getMinContentHeight() {
```

```
        return HEIGHT;
    }

    protected int getMinContentWidth() {
        return WIDTH;
    }

    protected void pointerPressed(int x, int y) {
        pad.setString(num);
    }

    public void keyPressed(int keyCode){
        int gameAction = getGameAction(keyCode);
        if (gameAction == Canvas.FIRE){
            pad.setString(num);
        }
    }
}
```

The constructor takes as arguments the `KeyPad` instance, to facilitate a callback, and a `String` acting as the button label. The `paint()` method must be implemented to render the `CustomItem`. In the example code above we have produced a minimal button, leaving it as an exercise to the reader to add the embellishments. We must also implement the `getPrefContentWidth()`, `getPrefContentHeight()`, `getMin-ContentWidth()` and `getMinContentHeight()` methods inherited from `CustomItem`; here we have provided trivial implementations. An attractive feature of `CustomItem` is the optional support for pointer input, via the protected `pointerPressed()`, `pointerDragged()` and `pointerReleased()` methods. The `Button` class redefines the `pointerPressed()` method to provide support for touch screen user interfaces such as Symbian's UIQ.

Of course, we could have adopted a simpler approach to our keypad. Instead of providing a custom `Button` class extending `CustomItem` we could have simply used `StringItem` instances with `appearanceMode` set to `Item.BUTTON`:

```
public StringItem (String label, String text, int appearanceMode)
```

We would then add a `Command` to the `StringItem` to take appropriate action when it is selected and implement an `ItemCommandListener` on each `StringItem` instance, as shown below:

```
public class KeyPad extends MIDlet implements CommandListener,
        ItemCommandListener{
    ...
    public KeyPad() {
        ...
        StringItem button1 = new StringItem(null, "1", Item.BUTTON);
```

```
        button1.setDefaultCommand(new Command("Select 1",
                Command.Item, 1));
        button1.setItemCommandListener(this);
        ...
        form.append(button1);
        ...
    }
    ...
    public void commandAction(Command command, Item item) {
        StringItem button = (StringItem)item;
        setString(button.getText());
    }
    ...
}
```

We adopted the `CustomItem` approach for our keypad example
for two reasons: it provides an opportunity to illustrate the use of
`CustomItem`, and its inherent support for touch screens; and the particular variant of `StringItem` shown above was subject to a defect
on the original Nokia 6600 firmware release (but should be fixed in
future upgrades).

3.3.7 The Game API

3.3.7.1 Introduction

The MIDP 1.0 specification, though limited in many respects, proved a
big hit with the gaming fraternity. The vast majority of MIDlets developed
so far are games.

As mentioned briefly in Chapter 2, the MIDP 2.0 specification extends
support for games developers with the introduction of the `javax.micro-
edition.lcdui.game` package. We will now discuss programming
this API in more detail. The aim of the API is to facilitate richer gaming
content by providing a set of APIs, targeted at games developers, that
map directly to native functionality, taking advantage of the performance
enhancements offered by native code and minimizing the amount of
work required in pure Java code.

The game package contains the following classes:

- `GameCanvas`

- `LayerManager`

- `Layer`

- `Sprite`

- `TiledLayer`.

In the next few sections we shall look at the functionality offered by these
classes, illustrating some of the key concepts with sample code.

3.3.7.2 *GameCanvas*

A basic game user interface class extending `javax.microedition.lcdui.Canvas`, `GameCanvas` provides an offscreen buffer as part of the implementation even if the underlying device doesn't support double buffering. The `Graphics` object obtained from the `getGraphics()` method is used to draw to the screen buffer. The contents of the screen buffer can then be rendered to the display synchronously by calling the `flushGraphics()` method.

The `GameCanvas` class also provides the ability to query key states and return an integer value in which each bit represents the state of a specific key on the device:

```
public int getKeyStates()
```

If the bit representing a key is set to 1 then this key is pressed or has been pressed at least once since the last invocation of the method. The returned integer can be ANDed against a set of predefined constants (shown below), each representing the appropriate bit for a specific key set to 1 (support for the last four values is optional).

```
public static final int UP_PRESSED
public static final int DOWN_PRESSED
public static final int LEFT_PRESSED
public static final int RIGHT_PRESSED
public static final int FIRE_PRESSED
public static final int GAME_A_PRESSED
public static final int GAME_B_PRESSED
public static final int GAME_C_PRESSED
public static final int GAME_D_PRESSED
```

We would use these values to ascertain the state of a key in the manner shown below.

```
if ( getKeyStates() & FIRE_PRESSED != 0 ) {
    // FIRE key is down or has been pressed
    // take appropriate action
}
```

3.3.7.3 *TiledLayer*

The abstract `Layer` class is the parent class of `TiledLayer` and `Sprite`.

A `TiledLayer` consists of a grid of cells each of which can be filled with an image tile. An instance of `TiledLayer` is created by invoking the constructor of the `TiledLayer` class:

```
public TiledLayer(int columns, int rows, Image image, int tileWidth,
        int tileHeight)
```

The `columns` and `rows` arguments represent the number of columns and rows in the grid. The `tileWidth` and `tileHeight` arguments represent the width and height of a single tile in pixels. The image argument represents the image used for creating the set of tiles that will be employed to populate the `TiledLayer`. Naturally, the dimension of the image in pixels must be an integral multiple of the dimension of an individual tile. The use of `TiledLayer` is best illustrated with an example.

The image in Figure 3.8 (taken with a Symbian OS phone) is a panoramic view of Prague. The dimensions of the image are 560×140 pixels and we will use it to provide the tile set for our `TiledLayer`. We will use a `TiledLayer` to pan through this view. To fit comfortably in the display of a phone we will display samples of the image on a `TiledLayer` of 140×140 pixels, consisting of a 7×7 grid, as shown in Figure 3.9.

Note that cells are identified by their column and row number, the top left cell having coordinates (0, 0) and the bottom right (7, 7). The dimensions of the `TiledLayer` and the number of cells it contains dictates that the individual tile dimensions are 20×20 pixels in this example and that the image can be treated as a 28×7 matrix of tiles (see Figure 3.10).

A given tile is specified by its tile index. Tile indices in this example run from 1 for the top left tile to 196 for the bottom right tile.

Figure 3.8   Basic image for use by a `TiledLayer`.

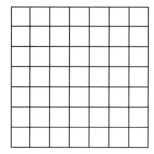

Figure 3.9   Example of a 7×7 `TiledLayer`.

Figure 3.10   Dividing our image into tiles.

Figure 3.11   Panning through a panoramic view using TiledLayer.

To pan through the whole image we simply shift each column of tiles one position left within the `TiledLayer`, as shown in Figure 3.11.

The source code for the `TiledLayerCanvas` class, which renders the panned view, is listed below:

```
import javax.microedition.lcdui.*;
import javax.microedition.lcdui.game.*;
import java.io.*;
public class TiledLayerCanvas extends Canvas implements Runnable {

    private Image image;
    private int x;
    private int y;
```

```
    private TiledLayer layer;
    public TiledLayerCanvas(String imageName)
            throws ApplicationException {
        //create the image
        try {
            image = Image.createImage(imageName);
            layer = new TiledLayer(7, 7, image, 20, 20);
            x = (getWidth() - layer.getHeight())/2;
            y = (getHeight() - layer.getWidth())/2;
            layer.setPosition(x, y);
        }catch(IOException ioe) {
            throw new ApplicationException("Unable to create image");
        }
    }

    public void paint(Graphics g) {
        layer.paint(g);
    }

    public void run() {
        int n = 0;
        while ( n <= 21) {
            for(int i = 0; i < 7; i++) {
                for(int j = 0; j < 7; j++) {
                    layer.setCell(i, j, (i + 1) + n +(j*28));
                }
            }
            repaint();

            try {
                Thread.sleep(100);
            }catch(InterruptedException ie) {}
            n++;
        }
    }
}
```

The `TiledLayerCanvas` constructor creates an instance of `Image` from a resource file containing the panoramic view. This is then used to create the `TiledLayer` instance:

```
layer = new TiledLayer(7, 7, image, 20, 20);
```

This consists of a 7 × 7 grid, to be populated with tiles of dimensions 20 × 20 pixels. The position of the `TiledLayer` relative to the containing `Canvas` is defined by the `setPosition()` method of the parent `Layer` class. To render the `TiledLayer`, we call its `paint()` method from the `Canvas` `paint()` method. We pan through the image using a `while` loop that increments a counter running from 0 to 21 for each new tile set. Each iteration of the `while` loop sets the tile set and then calls `repaint` (and increments the counter). The `TiledLayer` grid is populated with a tile set by multiple calls to `setCell` from within nested `for` loops:

```
for(int i = 0; i < 7; i++) {
    for(int j = 0; j < 7; j++) {
        layer.setCell(i, j, (i + 1) + n +(j*28));
    }
}
repaint();
```

The setCell() method of TiledLayer takes integers representing the row and column of the TiledLayer grid (which in this case run from 0 to 6 for a 7 × 7 grid) in which the tile is to be placed, and an integer representing the index of the tile within the image (which in this example runs from 1 to 196 for an image consisting of 28 × 7 tiles) as arguments.

```
public void setCell(int col, int row, int tileIndex)
```

The full source code and JAR and JAD files for the Panorama MIDlet can be downloaded from the Symbian website at **www.symbian.com/books**.

One of the principal uses of TiledLayer is the creation of large scrolling backgrounds from relatively few tiles. Consider the rather simplistic, but nonetheless illustrative, example in Figure 3.12.

We have built up a background TiledLayer from just four tiles. By changing the arrangement of the four tiles within the TiledLayer grid we can convey the impression of an infinite scrolling background. For more information on using TiledLayer to create backgrounds, including the use of animation, consult the MIDP 2.0 documentation which includes a comprehensive example.

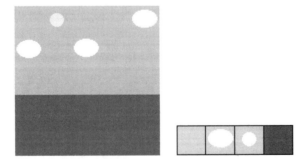

Figure 3.12   A simple background TiledLayer built up from four tiles.

3.3.7.4 *Sprite*

Sprite is a basic visual element suitable for creating animations. A Sprite consists of an image composed of several smaller images (frames). The Sprite can be rendered as one of the frames. By rendering

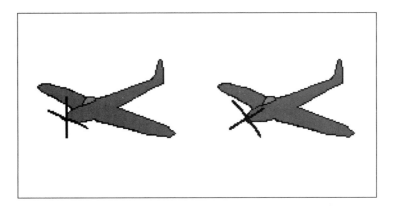

Figure 3.13 A `Sprite` image consisting of two frames.

different frames in a sequence, a `Sprite` provides animation. Let us
consider a simple example. Figure 3.13 consists of two frames, each of
the same width and height.

By displaying the frames in a sequence, we can produce an animation.
The following code shows how this can be achieved:

```
import javax.microedition.lcdui.*;
import javax.microedition.lcdui.game.*;
import java.io.*;
public class SpriteCanvas extends Canvas implements Runnable {
    private static final int SPRITE_WIDTH = 140;
    private static final int SPRITE_HEIGHT = 140;

    private Sprite plane;
    private int spritePositionX;
    private int spritePositionY;
    private boolean running = false;

    public SpriteCanvas(String imageName) throws
            ApplicationException {
        try {
            Image image = Image.createImage(imageName);
            plane = new Sprite(image, SPRITE_WIDTH, SPRITE_HEIGHT);
            spritePositionX = (getWidth() - SPRITE_WIDTH)/2;
            spritePositionY = (getHeight() - SPRITE_HEIGHT)/2;
            plane.setPosition(spritePositionX, spritePositionY);
        }catch(IOException ioe) {
            throw new ApplicationException("Unable to create image");
        }
    }

    public void paint(Graphics g) {
        g.setColor(255, 255, 255);
        g.fillRect(0, 0, getWidth(), getHeight());
//paint background white
        plane.paint(g);
    }
```

```
public void run() {
    running = true;
    while (running) {
        repaint();
        plane.nextFrame();
        try {
            Thread.sleep(50);
        } catch(InterruptedException ie){}
    }
}

public void stop() {
    running = false;
}
}
```

A new `Sprite` is created using the following constructor:

```
public Sprite(Image image, int frameWidth, int frameHeight)
```

The first argument is the image consisting of the sequence of frames. The second and third arguments indicate the width and height in pixels of the individual frames within the image. Note that the width and height of the image in pixels must be an integer multiple of the frame width and height.

The `setPosition()` method of `Sprite` is used to position the `Sprite` in the coordinate space of the containing object, a `Canvas` in this example.

```
plane.setPosition(spritePositionX, spritePositionY);
```

To render the `Sprite`, we call the `paint()` method. Here this is done within the `paint()` method of `SpriteCanvas`:

```
public void paint(Graphics g) {
    g.setColor(255, 255, 255);
    g.fillRect(0, 0, getWidth(), getHeight());
    plane.paint(g);
}
```

To animate the sprite we call the `nextFrame()` method of `Sprite` after a `repaint()`, as shown below:

```
while (running) {
    repaint();
    plane.nextFrame();
    ...
}
```

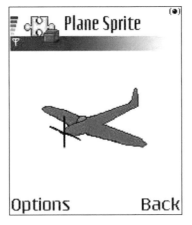 

Figure 3.14 `PlaneSprite` running on the Nokia 6600.

Figure 3.14 illustrates the `PlaneSprite` MIDlet running on a Nokia 6600. The full source code for the `PlaneSprite` MIDlet can be downloaded from Symbian's website at ***www.symbian.com/books***.

In addition to various transformations such as rotation and mirroring, the `Sprite` class also provides collision detection. Collision detection allows the developer to detect when the sprite collides with another element. The following three methods are available in the `Sprite` class:

```
public final boolean collidesWith(Image image, int x, int y,
     boolean pixelLevel)
public final boolean collidesWith(Sprite s, boolean pixelLevel)
public final boolean collidesWith(TiledLayer t, boolean pixelLevel)
```

The first method detects collisions between the invoking `Sprite` and the specified `Image`, while the second detects collisions with another `Sprite` and the last method detects collisions with the specified `Tiled-Layer`. If `pixelLevel` is set to `true`, collision detection is performed on a pixel by pixel basis; if it is `false` then collision detection is performed on the basis of the bounding rectangle of the sprite. The bounding rectangle of the sprite can be set using the method:

```
public void defineCollisionRectangle(int x, int y, int width,
     int height)
```

Otherwise, the default, bounding rectangle is located at (0,0) in the coordinate space of the sprite and is of the same dimensions as the sprite.

For more information on using sprites refer to the MIDP 2.0 documentation.

3.3.7.5 *Layer Manager*

As the name implies, the LayerManager manages a series of Layer objects. Sprite and TiledLayer both extend Layer. More specifically a LayerManager controls the rendering of Layer objects. The LayerManager maintains an ordered list so that they are rendered according to their z-values (in standard computer graphics terminology). We add a Layer to the list using the method:

```
public void append(Layer l)
```

The first layer appended has index zero and the lowest z-value, that is, it appears closest to the user (viewer). Subsequent layers have successively greater z-values and indices. Alternatively we can add a layer at a specific index using the method:

```
public void insert(Layer l, int index)
```

To remove a layer from the list we use the method:

```
public void remove(Layer l)
```

We position a layer in the LayerManager's coordinate system using the setPosition() method. The contents of LayerManager are not rendered in their entirety, instead a view window is rendered using the paint() method of the LayerManager:

```
public void paint(Graphics g, int x, int y)
```

The x and y arguments are used to position the view window on the Displayable object the Canvas or GameCanvas upon which the LayerManager is ultimately rendered and therefore the device's screen. The size of the view window is set using the method:

```
public void setViewWindow(int x, int y, int width, int height)
```

The x and y values determine the position of the top left corner of the rectangular view window in the coordinate system of the Layer-Manager. The width and height arguments determine the width and height of the view window and are usually set to a size appropriate for the device's screen. By varying the x and y coordinates we can pan through the contents of the LayerManager.

We shall illustrate using LayerManager to display our plane sprite against a simple moving background. The image used to make up the

Figure 3.15   The background image for the LayerManager Demo MIDlet.

background `TiledLayer` is shown in Figure 3.15 and consists of just one tile.

The source code for the `LayerManagerCanvas` class is listed below.

```java
import javax.microedition.lcdui.game.*;
import javax.microedition.lcdui.*;
import java.io.*;
public class LayerManagerCanvas extends Canvas implements Runnable {

    private static final int TILE_WIDTH = 140;
    private static final int TILE_HEIGHT = 140;
    private static final int SPRITE_WIDTH = 140;
    private static final int SPRITE_HEIGHT = 140;
    private static final int WINDOW_WIDTH = 140;
    private static final int WINDOW_HEIGHT = 140;

    private Sprite sprite;
    private TiledLayer backgroundLayer;
    private LayerManager layerManager;

    private boolean running = false;
    private int x;
    private int y;

    public LayerManagerCanvas(String spriteImageName,
            String backgroundImageName) throws ApplicationException {
        try {
            Image spriteImage = Image.createImage(spriteImageName);
            Image backgroundImage =
                Image.createImage(backgroundImageName);
            sprite = new Sprite(spriteImage, SPRITE_WIDTH,
                SPRITE_HEIGHT);
            backgroundLayer = new TiledLayer(2, 1, backgroundImage,
                TILE_WIDTH, TILE_HEIGHT);
            backgroundLayer.setCell(0,0,1);
            backgroundLayer.setCell(1,0,1);
            layerManager = new LayerManager();
            layerManager.append(sprite);
            layerManager.append(backgroundLayer);

            //set layer position relative to LayerManager origin
            // this is the default anyway
            sprite.setPosition(0, 0);
```

```
            //this is the default anyway
            backgroundLayer.setPosition(0, 0);

            //set view window size and position relative to
            //LayerManager's origin
            layerManager.setViewWindow(0, 0, WINDOW_WIDTH,
                    WINDOW_HEIGHT);

            //calculate coordinates to position view window in Canvas
            x = (getWidth() - WINDOW_WIDTH)/2;
            y = (getHeight() - WINDOW_HEIGHT)/2;
        }catch(IOException ioe) {
            throw new ApplicationException("Unable to create image");
        }
    }

    public void paint(Graphics g) {
        g.setColor(255, 255, 255);
        //paint Canvas background white
        g.fillRect(0, 0, getWidth(), getHeight());
        //position view window in Canvas and render
        layerManager.paint(g, x, y);
    }

    public void run() {
        running = true;
        int layerX = -TILE_WIDTH;

        while ( running) {
            if (layerX == 0) {
                layerX = -TILE_WIDTH;
            }
            backgroundLayer.setPosition(layerX, 0);
            sprite.nextFrame();
            repaint(x, y, TILE_WIDTH, TILE_HEIGHT);
            try {
                Thread.sleep(30);
            }catch(InterruptedException ie) {}
            layerX++;
        }
    }

    public void stop() {
        running = false;
    }
}
```

The class constructor first creates the `Sprite` and a `TiledLayer` for the background, as shown below.

```
Image spriteImage = Image.createImage(spriteImageName);
Image backgroundImage = Image.createImage(backgroundImageName);
sprite = new Sprite(spriteImage, SPRITE_WIDTH, SPRITE_HEIGHT);
backgroundLayer = new TiledLayer(2, 1, backgroundImage,
      TILE_HEIGHT);
```

Figure 3.16   The background `TiledLayer`.

```
backgroundLayer.setCell(0,0,1);
backgroundLayer.setCell(1,0,1);
```

Our background `TiledLayer` consists of a 2 × 1 grid of tiles (see Figure 3.16) sufficient to simulate an infinite scene.

Next a `LayerManager` is created and the sprite and background layers are appended:

```
layerManager = new LayerManager();
layerManager.append(sprite);
layerManager.append(backgroundLayer);
//this is the default anyway
sprite.setPosition(0, 0);
//this is the default anyway
backgroundLayer.setPosition(0, 0);
layerManager.setViewWindow(0, 0, WINDOW_WIDTH, WINDOW_HEIGHT);
x = (getWidth() - WINDOW_WIDTH)/2;
y = (getHeight() - WINDOW_HEIGHT)/2;
```

The layers are positioned relative to the `LayerManager`'s coordinate system using their `setPosition()` methods.

The `LayerManager`'s view window is rendered by the `paint()` method of `Canvas` as follows:

```
public void paint(Graphics g) {
    g.setColor(255, 255, 255);
    //paint Canvas background white
    g.fillRect(0, 0, getWidth(), getHeight());
    //position view window in Canvas and render
    layerManager.paint(g, x, y);
}
```

The animation of the MIDlet is handled in the `run()` method listed below.

```
public void run() {
    running = true;
    int layerX = -TILE_WIDTH;
```

```
while ( running) {
    if (layerX == 0) {
        layerX = -TILE_WIDTH;
    }
    backgroundLayer.setPosition(layerX, 0);
    sprite.nextFrame();
    repaint(x, y, TILE_WIDTH, TILE_HEIGHT);
    try {
        Thread.sleep(30);
    }catch(InterruptedException ie) {}
    layerX++;
    }
}
```

In this example, to generate the illusion of motion, instead of moving the sprite, we move the background layer relative to the coordinate system of the Canvas using the setPosition() method. The plane sprite remains stationary while alternating between its two frames on each cycle. The background layer is initially offset in a negative direction by an amount equal to TILE_WIDTH. On each cycle we move its position by one pixel in the positive direction until it has shifted by a total amount equal to TILE_WIDTH. We then reset the position of the background layer back to its initial position to avoid running out of scenery. Because of the symmetrical nature of the background image the effect is to simulate an infinitely scrolling background (see Figure 3.17).

To observe the full effect, download and run the example. The source code and JAR and JAD files for the LayerManagerDemo MIDlet are available from the Symbian website at *www.symbian.com/books*.

The DemoRacer case study, discussed in Chapter 5, provides a further detailed study of programming the Game API, including using collision detection.

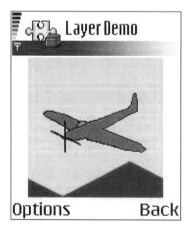 

Figure 3.17   The LayerManagerDemo MIDlet.

3.3.8   The Media API

As mentioned in Chapter 2, MIDP 2.0 introduces support for audio playback and sound generation in two new packages:

- `javax.microedition.media`
- `javax.microedition.media.control`.

Specifically, the Media API mandates support for tone generation and audio playback of WAV files. Support for other audio formats is optional. Symbian's MIDP 2.0 Media API implementation, at the time of writing, does not provide support for additional optional audio formats. However, licensee phones built on Symbian OS may provide support for additional audio formats, particularly if they provide implementations of the full Mobile Media API (JSR 135), such as found on the Series 60 Nokia 6600.

The MIDP 2.0 Media API is an audio-only building block subset of the Mobile Media API that is fully upward compatible with the Mobile Media API. The rationale behind providing only audio support in the Media API was that the MIDP 2.0 specification is targeted at the whole spectrum of mobile phones including mass-market low-end phones with no support for video rendering capabilities. In contrast, the optional Mobile Media API is targeted at high-end feature phones and PDAs with advanced sound and video capabilities.

Since the Media API is a proper subset of the Mobile Media API we shall leave a detailed discussion of programming tone generation and audio playback to later in the chapter where a section is devoted to the Mobile Media API.

3.3.9   Other New Features

3.3.9.1   *MIDlet Class*

MIDP 2.0 brings a couple of new methods into the `MIDlet` class including the `platformRequest()` method:

```
public final boolean platformRequest(String URL)
```

This method allows the `MIDlet` to bring certain native applications to the foreground and permits the user to interact with the context while the `MIDlet` continues running in the background. Forms of the `String` `URL` argument required by the MIDP 2.0 specification include:

```
platformRequest("www.symbian.com/mobile/MyMidlet.jad")
```

or:

```
platformRequest("tel:07940176427")
```

The former launches the installer to install the indicated `MIDlet` suite. The latter launches the native phone application, if supported by the device. If the platform cannot handle the specified URL request a `ConnectionNotFoundException` will be thrown. Note that at the time of writing `platformRequest()` was not supported on the current firmware release (3.42.1) available on the Nokia 6600. Later versions of the firmware will support this feature (see *Known Issues in the Nokia 6600 MIDP 2.0 Implementation* Version 1.2 at ***www.forum.nokia.com***).

Another new method introduced in MIDP 2.0 is the `checkPermission()` method.

```
public final int checkPermission(String permission)
```

This allows the `MIDlet` to check the permission of a particular API, passed in as the `permission` argument. For example, the code shown below would check the permission to open an SMS connection.

```
checkPermission("javax.microedition.io.Connector.sms")
```

The return value can be:

- 1 – if the permission is Allowed

- 0 – if the permission is denied (including when the API is not supported on the device)

- −1 – if the permission is unknown, including the case where the permission requires user interaction.

3.3.9.2 *Alpha Blending*

MIDP 2.0 adds functionality to the `Image` and `Graphics` classes to provide support for alpha blending. Alpha blending is a way of combining a semi-transparent mask image with a background image to create a blended image with the appearance of transparency. The degree of transparency depends on the alpha coefficient. The alpha coefficient can take a value ranging from 0, in which case the mask is totally transparent and the blended image is simply the background image, to 1 (FF) in which case the mask is completely opaque and therefore the blended image is the same as the mask image.

In particular, MIDP 2.0 provides the `createRGBImage()` method of the `Image` class, which allows an image to be created from an array of ARGB values:

```
public static Image createRGBImage(int[] rgb, int width, int height,
        boolean processAlpha)
```

Figure 3.18 Illustrating the drawRGB() method.

The rgb argument represents the image data consisting of an array of 32-bit values of the form 0xAARRGGBB. The high eight bits of each 32-bit value provide the value of the alpha coefficient and the remaining 24 bits represent the 8-bit RGB values. The alpha value is used in alpha blending. The width and height arguments represent the width and the height of the image in pixels. If the processAlpha argument is false, alpha blending is disabled and the image will appear totally opaque.

MIDP 2.0 also adds the drawRGB() method to the Graphics class:

```
public void drawRGB(int[] rgbData, int offset, int scanlength,
        int x, int y, int width, int height, boolean processAlpha)
```

The rgbData argument is presented in 0xAARRGGBB format, as previously. The offset argument represents the array index of the first value to be drawn and scanlength represents the relative offset in the rgbData array between corresponding pixels in consecutive rows. For instance, let us consider an array of 32 ARGB values representing an image 8 pixels wide and 4 pixels high. However, we only want to render pixels corresponding to a central strip of an image 4 pixels wide and 4 pixels high (see Figure 3.18).

In this case we would invoke the drawRGB() method with the offset value set to 2 and the scanlength equal to 8. The values for width and height are both equal to 4 in this case.

Let us now consider an example of alpha blending in action. The AlphaCanvas class shown below uses alpha blending to progressively render a semi-transparent red mask over a background image:

```
import javax.microedition.midlet.*;
import javax.microedition.lcdui.*;
import java.io.*;
public class AlphaCanvas extends Canvas implements Runnable {

    private Image backgroundImage;
    private int[] maskArray;
    private int imageWidth;
    private int imageHeight;
    private int x;
    private int y;
    private int maskHeight = 0;
    public AlphaCanvas(String imageName) {
```

```
    //create the background image
    try {
        backgroundImage = Image.createImage(imageName);
    }catch(IOException ioe) {
        ioe.printStackTrace() ;
    }
    imageWidth = backgroundImage.getWidth();
    imageHeight = backgroundImage.getHeight();

    //create a semi-transparent red mask to cover the
    //background image
    maskArray = new int[imageWidth*imageHeight];
    for (int i = 0; i < imageWidth*imageHeight; i++) {
        maskArray[i] = 0x80FF0000;
        //alpha coefficient set to 0.5
    }
    x = (getWidth() - imageWidth)/2;
    y = (getHeight() - imageHeight)/2;
}

public void paint(Graphics g) {
    g.drawImage(backgroundImage, x, y,
            Graphics.TOP|Graphics.LEFT);
    //render the semi-transparent mask
    if (maskHeight != 0){
        g.drawRGB(maskArray, 0, imageWidth, x, y, imageWidth,
            maskHeight, true);
    }
}

public void run() {
    for(int i = 1; i <= imageHeight; i++) {
        maskHeight = i;
        repaint();
        try {
            Thread.sleep(50);
        }catch(InterruptedException ie) {}
    }
}
}
```

A background image is created from a resource file in the Alpha-
Canvas constructor. We then create a data array containing a sufficient
number of values to completely mask the background image:

```
maskArray = new int[imageWidth*imageHeight];
for (int i = 0; i < imageWidth*imageHeight; i++) {
    maskArray[i] = 0x80FF0000;
    //alpha coefficient set to 0.5
}
```

In this case the alpha coefficient is set to 0.5 (0×80). The paint()
method first renders the background image and then the mask using the
drawRGB() method:

```
g.drawRGB(maskArray, 0, imageWidth, x, y, imageWidth, maskHeight,
        true);
```

Figure 3.19   Alpha blending on a Nokia 6600.

As we want to render over the full width of the background image, the `offset` value is set to 0 and the `scanlength` is equal to the width of the background image. By successively incrementing the mask height and calling `repaint()` we are able to gradually cover the background image with the transparency. Figure 3.19 displays screenshots of the AlphaBlending MIDlet running on a Nokia 6600.

The full source code for the AlphaBlending MIDlet can be downloaded from Symbian's website at **www.symbian.com/books**.

3.3.9.3   RMS Storage

The Record Management System (RMS) storage mechanism was introduced in Chapter 2. We will now investigate it in more detail. The RMS provides simple record-based persistent storage, with data stored as a record in the form of a byte array. The MIDP 1.0 specification required that a record store created by a MIDlet can only be accessed by a different MIDlet if both MIDlets belonged to the same MIDlet suite. The MIDP 2.0 specification has relaxed this restriction, allowing any MIDlet to access another MIDlet's record store provided that the MIDlet that created the record store has given authorization.

To use the RMS, we must first open a record store using one of the overloaded `openRecordStore()` methods:

```
public static RecordStore openRecordStore(String recordStoreName,
        boolean createIfNecessary)
public static RecordStore openRecordStore(String recordStoreName,
        boolean createIfNecessary, int authmode, boolean writable)
```

```
public static RecordStore openRecordStore(String recordStoreName,
        String vendorName, String suiteName)
```

The last two methods were added by the MIDP 2.0 specification. The second `openRecordStore()` method takes an `authmode` argument that can have one of two possible `public static final int` values: `AUTHMODE_ANY` and `AUTHMODE_PRIVATE`.

`AUTHMODE_ANY` allows the `RecordStore` to be accessed by any MIDlet in any MIDlet suite while `AUTHMODE_PRIVATE` restricts access only to MIDlets in the same suite as the creator of the `RecordStore`. If `writable` is `true`, MIDlets in other suites that have been granted access can write to this `RecordStore`.

The third `openRecordstore()` method is used to open a `RecordStore` associated with the MIDlet suite that is identified by the `suiteName` argument. If the `RecordStore` to be opened has `AUTHMODE_PRIVATE` access then the `vendorName` and `suiteName` arguments must match the respective attributes of the MIDlet suite as listed in the application descriptor or manifest file.

We shall illustrate sharing record stores between MIDlet suites with a simple example. The `RMSWriter` MIDlet creates an `Image` from a resource file and displays it. It then saves the image data into a recordstore. We shall then show how the image data can be retrieved from the recordstore by a different MIDlet suite using the `RMSReader` MIDlet example.

The source code for the `RMSWriter` class is listed below:

```
import javax.microedition.midlet.*;
import javax.microedition.lcdui.*;
import javax.microedition.rms.*;
import java.io.*;
public class RMSWriter extends MIDlet implements
        CommandListener {

    private static final String IMAGE_NAME = "/image.png";
    private static final int IMAGE_SIZE = 11222;

    private Display display;
    private Form form;

    private Command exitCommand;
    private Command startCommand;
    private Command saveCommand;

    private ImageCanvas imageCanvas;
    private byte[] data;

    public RMSWriter(){
        data = loadImage(IMAGE_NAME, IMAGE_SIZE);
        display = Display.getDisplay(this);
        Image image = Image.createImage(data, 0, data.length);
```

```java
    imageCanvas = new ImageCanvas(image);

    form = new Form("RMS Writing Demo");
    exitCommand = new Command("Exit", Command.EXIT, 2);
    startCommand = new Command("Start", Command.SCREEN, 1);
    saveCommand = new Command("Save image", Command.SCREEN, 1);
    form.addCommand(exitCommand);
    form.addCommand(startCommand);
    form.setCommandListener(this);
}

public void startApp() {
    display.setCurrent(form);
}

public byte[] loadImage(String imageName, int imageSize) {
    byte[] data = new byte[imageSize];
    try {
        Class c = this.getClass() ;
        InputStream is = c.getResourceAsStream(imageName);
        DataInputStream dis = new DataInputStream(is);
        dis.readFully(data);
        is.close();
    }catch(IOException ioe) {
        ioe.printStackTrace();
    }
    return data;
}

public int saveToStore(byte[] data) {
    int recordID = 0;
    try {
        RecordStore store =
                RecordStore.openRecordStore("ImageStore",
                true, RecordStore.AUTHMODE_ANY, true);
        recordID = store.addRecord(data, 0, data.length);
        store.closeRecordStore();
    }catch(RecordStoreException rse) {
        rse.printStackTrace();
    }
    return recordID;
}

public void commandAction(Command c, Displayable d) {
    if (c == exitCommand) {
        notifyDestroyed();
    }else if (c == startCommand) {
        display.setCurrent(imageCanvas);
        imageCanvas.addCommand(saveCommand);
        imageCanvas.setCommandListener(this);
    }else if (c == saveCommand) {
        int recordID = saveToStore(data);
        imageCanvas.removeCommand(saveCommand);
        display.setCurrent(form);
        form.append(new StringItem(null, "Image saved as record "
                + recordID));
    }
}
```

```
    public void pauseApp() {}
    public void destroyApp(boolean unconditional) {}
}
```

The image is loaded from the resources in the `loadImage()` method. This opens an input stream using the `getResourceAsStream()` method and stores the data in a byte array. This byte array is used to create the `Image` using one of the overloaded static `createImage()` methods. The image is then displayed in a `Canvas`. When the user selects the "Save image" option, the image data is saved into the record store by the `saveToStore()` method listed below:

```
public int saveToStore(byte[] data) {
    int recordID = 0;
    try {
        RecordStore store = RecordStore.openRecordStore("ImageStore",
                true, RecordStore.AUTHMODE_ANY, true);
        recordID = store.addRecord(data, 0, data.length);
        store.closeRecordStore();
    }catch(RecordStoreException rse) {
        rse.printStackTrace();
    }
    return recordID;
}
```

A `RecordStore` is opened with `AUTHMODE_ANY` permission. The data is saved to the `RecordStore` using the `addRecord()` method, which creates a new record and returns an integer identifying that record within the recordstore. The `RecordStore` is then closed using the `closeRecordStore()` method.

Figure 3.20 shows the `RMSWriter` MIDlet running on a Nokia 6600.

Figure 3.20 The `RMSWriter` MIDlet running on the Nokia 6600.

Now that we have created a `RecordStore`, we shall show how this can be accessed from a different MIDlet suite using the `RMSReader` MIDlet. The source code for the `RMSReader` class is listed below.

```java
import javax.microedition.midlet.*;
import javax.microedition.lcdui.*;
import javax.microedition.rms.*;
import java.io.*;
public class RMSReader extends MIDlet implements CommandListener {

    private Display display;
    private Form form;
    private Command exitCommand;
    private Command startCommand;
    private Command backCommand;
    private TextField storeName;
    private TextField recordNo;
    private ImageCanvas imageCanvas;

    public RMSReader() {
        display = Display.getDisplay(this);
        form = new Form("RMS Reading Demo");
        exitCommand = new Command("Exit", Command.EXIT, 2);
        startCommand = new Command("Load image", Command.SCREEN, 1);
        backCommand = new Command("Back", Command.BACK, 1);
        storeName = new TextField("Enter recordstore name",
            "ImageStore", 100, TextField.ANY);
        recordNo = new TextField("Enter record ID", "1", 10,
            TextField.NUMERIC);
        form.addCommand(exitCommand);
        form.addCommand(startCommand);
        form.append(storeName);
        form.append(recordNo);
        form.setCommandListener(this);
    }
    public void startApp() {
        display.setCurrent(form);
    }

    public byte[] loadFromStore(String storeName, int recordID) {
        byte[] data = null;

        try {
            RecordStore store =
                RecordStore.openRecordStore(storeName, false);
            data = store.getRecord(recordID);
            store.closeRecordStore();
        }catch(RecordStoreException rse) {
            rse.printStackTrace();
        }
        return data;
    }
    public Image constructImage() {
        Integer tempRecordID = Integer.valueOf(recordNo.getString());
        int recordID = tempRecordID.intValue();
        byte[] data = loadFromStore(storeName.getString(), recordID);
        Image image = null;
        if (data != null) {
```

```
        image = Image.createImage(data, 0, data.length);
    }
    return image;
}
public void commandAction(Command c, Displayable d) {
    if (c == exitCommand) {
        notifyDestroyed();
    }else if (c == startCommand) {
        Image image = constructImage();
        if (image != null) {
            imageCanvas = new ImageCanvas(image);
            display.setCurrent(imageCanvas);
            imageCanvas.addCommand(backCommand);
            imageCanvas.setCommandListener(this);
        }else {
            Alert alert = new Alert("Application error",
                    "Unable to create image.", null,
                    AlertType.ERROR);
            display.setCurrent(alert);
        }
    }else if (c == backCommand) {
        imageCanvas.removeCommand(backCommand);
        display.setCurrent(form);
    }
}
public void pauseApp() {}
public void destroyApp(boolean unconditional) {}
}
```

The image data is loaded from the `RecordStore` by the `loadFrom-Store()` method:

```
public byte[] loadFromStore(String storeName, int recordID) {
    byte[] data = null;
    try {
        RecordStore store = RecordStore.openRecordStore(storeName,
                false);
        data = store.getRecord(recordID);
        store.closeRecordStore();
    }catch(RecordStoreException rse) {
        rse.printStackTrace();
    }
    return data;
}
```

The `RecordStore` is opened and then the record is retrieved in the form of a byte array by the `getRecord()` method, using the record identifier. The `RecordStore` is then closed. The image data in the form of the byte array can then be used to create an `Image` and display it as before. Figure 3.21 shows the `RMSReader` MIDlet.

The full source code and JAR and JAD files for the RMSWriter and RMSReader MIDlets can be downloaded from the Symbian website at *www.symbian.com/books*.

Figure 3.21   RMSReader MIDlet running on a Nokia 6600.

The underlying operating system is responsible for maintaining the integrity of record stores throughout the normal use of the platform, however, the RMS store provides no support for locking records accessed by multiple threads; this is the responsibility of the developer. However, the `javax.microedition.rms` package does provide a `RecordListener` interface to assist the developer in synchronizing access to records. Since record IDs are lost when the MIDlet that created the records shuts down, the developer has to provide some process for searching through records and selecting the required one. The `javax.microedition.rms` package provides the `RecordComparator`, `RecordEnumerator` and `RecordFilter` interfaces to assist this process.

For more information on using the RMS APIs, consult the MIDP documentation. Further examples of using the RMS are presented in the case studies discussed in Chapter 5.

3.4   Optional J2ME APIs in the JTWI

In this section we consider the optional J2ME APIs that are indicated for a JTWI-compliant device. Note that these APIs do not themselves form part of the MIDP 2.0 specification, but have their own specifications derived from a Java Specification Request (JSR) presided over by an expert group.

3.4.1   Mobile Media API

As discussed in Chapter 2, one of the most commonly-cited limitations of MIDP 1.0 since it was launched in 2000 has been the level of support it provides for multimedia functionality. "Out of the box" there is no audio capability and limited graphics support only through the `Canvas` primitive. This was reasonable for the mainly monochrome devices with more limited capabilities at which MIDP was targeted, such as the pioneering Motorola i3000 phone and RIM BlackBerry 950 and 957 wireless handhelds. Given these limitations, it is perhaps remarkable how much media-rich content has yet made its way onto the first generation of MIDP 1.0-enabled mobile phones.

However, Symbian OS devices like the Psion netBook and the Nokia 9210 were already providing a PersonalJava Application Environment with AWT graphics, audio playback support and color screens. MIDP 1.0 was not sufficiently attractive to present itself as an alternative Java runtime environment for Symbian OS phones. It is interesting to note here that no Symbian OS phone has shipped without the MIDP 1.0 Java functionality being complemented either directly by additional multimedia functionality or else by inclusion of a PersonalJava Application Environment. Even the Nokia 7650, which provided one of the least feature-rich Java runtime environments among Symbian OS phones, extended the basic MIDP 1.0 specification with custom Nokia extension classes. A sound package allowed playing of several audio formats and a UI package provided API support for such multimedia enhancements as:

- full-screen display

- vibrator activation

- a number of graphics utilities.

And when the Nokia 3650 was released a few months later, the main enhancement to the programming environment it provided was in terms of MIDP multimedia functionality.

The limitations of MIDP have been systematically addressed over the last few years through the Java Community Process. From this have emerged a number of extensions that have been made to, or made available to, MIDP runtimes.

We note first in this regard the extensions made directly to MIDP 1.0 in its upgrade to MIDP 2.0, which have been discussed in Chapter 2 and Section 3.3. This upgrade included, for the first time, an audio API under the `javax.microedition.media` package. However, in recognition of the need for a J2ME-based framework supporting wider multimedia capabilities, such as tone generation, photo capture (given the ubiquity of camera phones) and video playback/capture, a Java Specification Request was initiated by Nokia under the Java Community Process. This was JSR 135, the Mobile Media API, which is the main subject of the present section. We shall follow here the convention introduced in the specification of referring to it as "MMAPI".

Given the wide scope that is encompassed by the concept of "multimedia", both in terms of the kind of content (e.g. video and audio) and of its encoding (e.g. JPEG and GIF), the authors of the multimedia API recognized a need for flexibility. As a result, MMAPI is highly modular; also, where a module is supported in an implementation there is a great degree of latitude as to which protocols or file formats are supported.

There are essentially three media types which can be handled within the framework. These are:

- audio

- video

- generated tones.

All of these or any non-zero subset may be supported in a particular MMAPI implementation, although it is unlikely that generated tones would be omitted given their mandatory status in MIDP 2.0. There is further modularity: three tasks can be performed in relation to audio and video:

- playing – stored video or audio content is recovered from a file at a specified URI (or perhaps stored locally) and displayed onscreen or sent to a speaker

- capturing – a video or audio stream is obtained directly from hardware (camera or microphone) associated with the device

- recording – video or audio content which is being played or captured is sent to a specified URI or else cached as a local `OutputStream` and is thus made available for "re-playing".

Because of the nature of tone generation, playing is the only task of relevance. Again, implementations are not required to support all three tasks, although clearly it is not possible to support recording without supporting either playing or capturing. Further, in the context of a mobile phone, there is little point in supporting capture without the ability to play. So the practical options for audio or video are:

- only playing is supported

- playing and capturing are supported, but not recording

- playing and recording are supported, but not capturing

- all three are supported.

As we shall see, Symbian OS phones typically provide the second option for video (recording not possible) and the fourth for audio (everything supported). There is further optionality in terms of supported formats and the ability to manipulate data streams or playback. We will return to this below.

3.4.1.1 MMAPI Architecture

At the heart of MMAPI is the concept of a media **player**. Players are obtained from a factory or **manager** which also serves to associate them with a particular media stream. While the player allows basic start/stop capability for the playback, fine-grained manipulation is achieved through various kinds of **control**, which are typically obtained from a player. Another task performed by controls is the recording of incoming media for later playback. Also of interest is the concept of a **player listener**. This allows you to track conveniently on multiple threads the progress of players being initialized, started or stopped. Since these events involve accessing (shared) hardware resources, they can take some time to complete, so you will typically not want your program to block while waiting.

The following classes or interfaces embody the above basic concepts:

- `Player`

- `Manager`

- `Control`

- `PlayerListener`.

These are the fundamental elements of the core package `javax.micro-edition.media`. In fact, of these only `Manager` is a concrete class; the others are all interfaces. The `Control` interface exists merely as a marker for the set of (more concrete) subinterfaces which are defined in the related package `javax.microedition.media.control`. The functionality provided by the latter is so diverse that nothing is in common, and the `Control` interface, remarkably, defines no methods!

The package `javax.microedition.media.protocol` is provided by MMAPI for users who wish to define new protocols for obtaining/downloading media content. This package provides data source functionality, introducing a common interface for handling content delivered by whatever protocol. Most MMAPI users will not have to work directly with data sources. Rather, `DataSource` objects will be marshaled on their behalf as a by-product of creating a player. But MMAPI does allow you the flexibility to define your own protocols for downloading/obtaining the media content to be played. This involves defining concrete implementations of the abstract `DataSource` class. As this is a specialist topic beyond the scope of this chapter, we shall not say anything further. The MMAPI specification document contains further details.

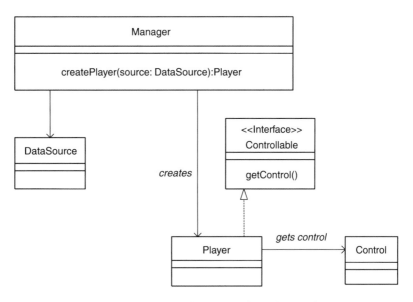

Figure 3.22   The basic architecture of the Mobile Media API.

3.4.1.2   Obtaining Media Content

The elements of the Mobile Media API work together as shown in Figure 3.22 (the `PlayerListener` has been omitted and we shall return to it in Section 3.4.1.3).

A `Player` is typically created using the `following` factory method of the `javax.microedition.media.Manager` class:

```
public static Player createPlayer(String locator)
```

The method's argument is a **media locator**, a `String` representing a URI that provides details about the media content being obtained. The details are specified using the well-documented BNF syntax (Augmented Backus–Naur Format). We'll look at some practical examples below.

In the context of MMAPI on Symbian OS, the only such communication protocol supported is HTTP (`http://`) but MMAPI also introduces a number of other protocol options, in particular:

- `capture://`
  This is used, as the name suggests, to capture live media from hardware such as an onboard camera (`capture://video`), microphone (`capture://audio`) or radio (`capture://radio`).

- `device://`
  This allows players to be configured for tone sequences (`device://tone`) or MIDI data (`device://midi`). These are defined as static

String members of the Manager class, denoted by TONE_DEVICE_
LOCATOR and MIDI_DEVICE_LOCATOR. The latter is not currently
supported on Symbian OS phones.

- rtp://
  The Real Time Protocol (RTP) allows for streaming media: playback
  begins without having to wait for all the media content to be down-
  loaded/buffered. This is not currently supported for any media type in
  the context of Symbian OS.

In summary, the following set of media locator formats are currently
supported on (at least some) Symbian OS phones:

- capture://audio

- capture://video

- device://midi

- device://tone

- http://

Specifying a URI is not the only way to create a Player. A second
variant of the Manager.createPlayer() method takes as arguments
an InputStream and a String representing a MIME type:

```
public static Player createPlayer(InputStream stream, String type)
```

This would be used, for example, to read a byte stream from the record
management system (RMS) as follows:

```
RecordStore rs;
int recordID;
   ...  // code to set up the recordstore.
try {
   InputStream is = new
          ByteArrayInputStream(rs.getRecord(recordID));
   Player p = Manager.createPlayer(is, "audio/X-wav");
   p.start();
} catch (IOException ioe) {
} catch (MediaException me) { }
```

A final variant of the Manager.createPlayer() method takes as
argument a custom data source deriving from the abstract DataSource
class and is used to handle proprietary or application-defined protocols:

```
Player p = Manager.createPlayer(customDataSource);
```

Note that all variants of `createPlayer` throw a `MediaException` if it is not possible to create a player of the correct type (perhaps due to that media type being unsupported). They also throw an `IOException` if there is a problem connecting to or reading from the source or stream.

We note in passing that an `IOException` would be expected to occur, if at all, only in the process of connecting to a `DataSource`, rather than in instantiating it. The connection is performed explicitly in client code *only* in the case of a custom `DataSource`, before it is passed as an argument to the `createPlayer()` method.

3.4.1.3 *Playing Media Content*

Because of the complexity of what a `Player` does, there are necessarily several stages (or states) it has to go through before it can do its playing. As we have just seen, the first stage is the creation of a `Player` object via the `Manager` factory class.

This involves the creation of a `DataSource` object, which provides a standard interface to the media content. The content is ultimately presented as a `SourceStream`, although this detail will not affect you unless you are designing a custom `DataSource`. The `DataSource` is created implicitly on your behalf when you instantiate the `Player`. However, if you are working with a custom `DataSource`, you will instantiate your `DataSource` explicitly.

Creating the `Player` object does not initialize the data transfer, which begins at the next stage. On creation, the `Player` will be in the `UNREALIZED` state. Its subsequent lifecycle is described in the state diagram in Figure 3.23.

Calling the `realize()` method causes the `Player` to initiate data transfer, e.g. communicating with a server or a file system. Peer classes to marshal the data on the native side will typically be instantiated at this point. When this method returns, the player is in the `REALIZED` state. Calling `prefetch()` causes the `Player` to acquire the scarce and exclusive resources it needs to play the media, such as access to the phone's audio device. It may have to wait for another application to release these resources before it can move to the `PREFETCHED` state. Once in this state, the `Player` is ready to start. A call to its `start()` method initiates playing and moves it on to the `STARTED` state. In order to interrogate the state of the `Player` the `getState()` method of the `Player` class is provided.

In many cases, of course, clients of MMAPI will not be interested in the fine distinctions of which resources are acquired by which methods. The good news is that you are free to ignore them if you wish: a call to `start()` on a `Player` in any state other than `CLOSED` will result in any intermediate calls needed to `realize()` or `prefetch()` being made implicitly on your behalf. Of course, the price you pay will be less fine-grained control of exception handling.

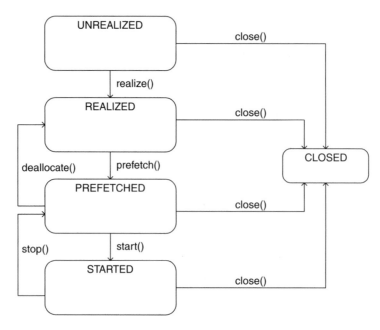

Figure 3.23   Lifecycle of a Player object.

The matching methods to stop the Player are close(), deallocate() and stop(). As with the start() method, the close() method encompasses the other two, so they need not be invoked on a Player directly. You should be aware, however, that reaching the end of the media results in the Player returning to the PREFETCHED state, as though the stop() method had been called. The good thing about this is that you can then conveniently replay the media by calling start() again.

However, you must ultimately call the close() method explicitly to recover all the resources associated with "realization" and "prefetching" and to set to null all references to your Player so the garbage collector can dispose of it. (You do want to dispose of it, since a closed Player cannot be reused!)

In playing media content it is often useful to work with one or more Control objects. These allow you to control media processing and are obtained from an implementer of the Controllable interface, in most cases a Player, using one of the following methods:

```
Control getControl(String controlType);
Control[] getControls();
```

DataSource also implements Controllable, thus providing custom DataSources with the flexibility to make available new ways to control playback. This approach to adding controls is necessary as there is no application-level API for making the availability of new controls known to the system-defined Players.

A media player of a given type may support a variety of `Controls`. The `String` passed in determines the name of the interface implemented by the `Control` returned, which will typically be one of the pre-defined types in the `javax.microedition.media.control` subpackage:

- `FramePositioningControl`
- `GUIControl`
- `MetaDataControl`
- `MIDIControl`
- `PitchControl`
- `RateControl`
- `TempoControl`
- `RecordControl`
- `StopTimeControl`
- `ToneControl`
- `VideoControl`
- `VolumeControl`.

If the type of `Control` you want is not available you will be returned a `null` value (which you should always check for!). You will also need to cast the `Control` appropriately before using it:

```
VolumeControl volC = (VolumeControl)
        player.getControl("VolumeControl");
if (volC != null)
    volC.setVolume(50);
```

Of these 12 controls, only the last five are currently supported on Symbian OS phones. The availability of support for the others depends on a number of factors, such as the media type and the phone model. Only `ToneControl` and `Volumecontrol` are available as part of the MIDP 2.0 audio subset. The remainder are specific to MMAPI.

An alternative approach to controls is the `getControls()` method, which returns an array containing all available controls. You can then use `instanceof` to ascertain whether the `Control` you want is available:

```
Control[] controls = player.getControls();
for (int i = 0; i < controls.length; i++)
{
```

```
  if (controls[i] instanceof VolumeControl) {
    VolumeControl volC = (VolumeControl) controls[i]
    volC.setVolume(50);
  }
  if (controls[i] instanceof VideoControl) {
    VideoControl vidC = (VideoControl) controls[i]
    vidC.setDisplayFullScreen(true);
  }
}
// allow controls to be garbage collected
controls = null;
```

Note that getControl() and getControls() cannot be invoked on a Player in the UNREALIZED or CLOSED states; doing so will cause an IllegalStateException to be thrown.

Aside from the use of Players, there is a further option to play simple tones or tone sequences directly using the static Manager.playTone() method. However, you will normally want the additional flexibility provided by working with a Player (configured for tones) and a ToneControl (see Section 3.4.1.7).

The final topic for this brief introduction to the Mobile Media API is the PlayerListener interface. This provides a playerUpdate() method for receiving asynchronous events from a Player. Any user-defined class may implement this interface and then register the PlayerListener using the addPlayerListener() method. The PlayerListener listens for a range of standard pre-defined events including STARTED, STOPPED and END_OF_MEDIA, with obvious meanings. For a listing of all the standard events refer to the MMAPI specification.

3.4.1.4 Working with Audio

In this section we shall demonstrate how to play audio files. We shall illustrate the section with code from a simple Audio Player MIDlet (see Figure 3.24).

 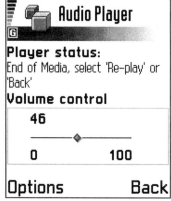

Figure 3.24 The Audio Player MIDlet running on a Nokia Series 60 phone.

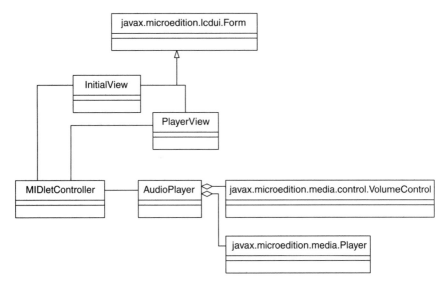

Figure 3.25 UML class diagram of the Audio Player MIDlet.

The Audio Player MIDlet consists of four classes: a controller, `MIDlet-Controller`; two views, `InitialView` and `PlayerView`; and the player, `AudioPlayer`. We shall look in detail only at the controller and the player, which contain all the information of interest from the viewpoint of MMAPI. A UML class diagram of the Audio Player MIDlet is shown in Figure 3.25.

The `AudioPlayer` Class
The `AudioPlayer` class performs the actual playing of the audio file and we shall consider it first. The key signatures are shown below:

```java
import javax.microedition.media.*;
import javax.microedition.media.control.*;
import java.io.*;
// Encapsulates the audio Player
public class AudioPlayer implements Runnable {

    private MIDletController controller;
    private Player player;
    private VolumeControl volumeControl;
    private String url;

    public AudioPlayer(MIDletController controller){...}

    public void initializeAudio(String url){...}

    public void run(){...}
```

```
    public void startPlayer(){...}

    public void stopPlayer(){...}

    public void closePlayer(){...}

}
```

We shall first look at the constructor.

```
public AudioPlayer(MIDletController controller){
    this.controller = controller;
}
```

This simply takes a reference to the `MIDletController` object, allowing the `AudioPlayer` to make callbacks to the controller.

We initialize the `Player` in a separate thread launched from the `initializeAudio()` method shown below. Generally it is good practice to put the (potentially time-consuming) initialization into a separate thread, performing it in the background to reduce latency.

```
public void initializeAudio(String url){
    this.url = url;
    Thread initializer = new Thread(this);
    initializer.start();
}
```

Another reason for performing the initialization in a separate thread is so that it is possible to update a progress gauge, giving the user valuable feedback as to how the audio acquisition is proceeding. The actual initialization takes place in the `run()` method mandated by the `Runnable` Interface.

```
public void run(){
    try {
        player = Manager.createPlayer(url);
        controller.updateProgressGauge();
        player.addPlayerListener(controller);
        player.realize();
        controller.updateProgressGauge();
        player.prefetch();
        controller.updateProgressGauge();
        volumeControl =
            (VolumeControl)player.getControl("VolumeControl");
        if (volumeControl != null) {
            volumeControl.setLevel(50);
        }
        else {
            controller.removeVolumeControl();
        }
```

```
        startPlayer();

    } catch (IOException ioe) {
        controller.showAlert("Unable to connect to resource",
                ioe.getMessage());
        closePlayer();
    } catch (MediaException me) {
        controller.showAlert("Unable to create player",
                me.getMessage());
        closePlayer();
    }
}
```

A `Player` is created and a `PlayerListener` registered with it. The `controller` reference serves two purposes: first to facilitate callbacks to the UI indicating the progress of the initialization; and, secondly, to act as the `PlayerListener` which will be notified of `Player` events. The `Player` is then moved through its states. In this example, we obtain a `VolumeControl` (providing the implementation supports this feature) although it is not essential for simple audio playback. Intuitively, a `VolumeControl` provides control over the audio playback volume, including a mute option. The volume range provided by a `VolumeControl` ranges from 0–100. Here we set the volume level midway. We then start the `Player`.

Our `AudioPlayer` class also contains some simple service methods. The `startPlayer()` method is used to start or re-start an initialized audio player.

```
public void replay(){
    try{
        player.start();
    } catch (MediaException me) {
        controller.showAlert("MediaException thrown",
                me.getMessage());
    }
}
```

The `setVolume()` method is used to change the volume level of the audio playback via the `VolumeControl`:

```
public void setVolume(int level){
    if (volumeControl != null) {
        volumeControl.setLevel(level);
    }
}
```

The `closePlayer()` method is called to release all resources associated with the audio `Player` by means of a call to `close()`. Additionally, the closePlayer() method sets to null the references to the Player and VideoControl instances to facilitate garbage collection.

```
public void closePlayer(){
    if (player != null){
        player.close();
    }
    player = null;
    volumeControl = null;
}
```

The MIDletController Class

The MIDletController sets up the instances of InitialView and PlayerView (see Figure 3.24). The InitialView instance provides a TextField for the audio file URL and a Gauge to indicate the progress of the audio player initialization, as well as controls to start playback or exit the application. The PlayerView instance provides a status StringItem and an interactive volume indicator (providing the implementation supports a VolumeControl), allowing the user to adjust the playback volume, plus controls to close the player or replay the audio content. The MIDletController constructs the AudioPlayer instance in response to user commands from the InitialView. The MIDletController receives callbacks from the AudioPlayer, via the playerUpdate() method of PlayerListener, and updates the InitialView progress gauge as the player moves through its initialization states. The MIDletController also receives callbacks from the PlayerView via the ItemStateChanged() method of ItemListener when the user adjusts the volume slider and passes these calls to the AudioPlayer. The key signatures of the MIDletController class are shown below:

```
import javax.microedition.lcdui.*;
import javax.microedition.midlet.*;
import javax.microedition.media.*;
import javax.microedition.media.control.*;
public class MIDletController extends MIDlet implements
        CommandListener, PlayerListener, ItemStateListener {
    private Display display;
    private Command exitCommand, playCommand, backCommand,
            replayCommand;
    private InitialView initialView;
    private PlayerView playerView;
    private AudioPlayer audioPlayer;

    public MIDletController() {...}

    public void startApp(){...}

    public void pauseApp(){...}

    public void destroyApp(boolean unconditional){...}
```

```
    public void commandAction(Command c, Displayable s){...}

    public void playerUpdate(Player p, String event,
            Object eventData) {...}

    public void itemStateChanged(Item item){...}

    public void updateProgressGauge(){...}

    public void removeVolumeControl() {...}

    public void showAlert(String title, String message){...}

    public void releaseResources() {...}
}
```

Let's first consider the `MIDletController` constructor:

```
public MIDletController() {
    display = Display.getDisplay(this);
    initialView = new InitialView(this);
    exitCommand = new Command("Exit", Command.EXIT, 2);
    playCommand = new Command("Play", Command.SCREEN, 1);
    initialView.addCommand(exitCommand);
    playerView = new PlayerView(this);
    audioPlayer = new AudioPlayer(this);
}
```

The constructor creates instances of the main UI classes `InitialView` and `PlayerView` plus their associated `Commands`. It also creates the `AudioPlayer` instance which encapsulates the audio `Player`.

Now let's look at the `MIDlet` lifecycle methods. The `startApp()` method sets `InitialView` as the current screen and adds the "Play" `Command` to it:

```
public void startApp(){
    display.setCurrent(initialView);
    initialView.addCommand(playCommand);
}
```

This latter measure is to ensure that the user can continue to use the application after resuming from the PAUSED state. If the `InitialView` already has a `playCommand` associated with it then `addCommand(playCommand)` does nothing.

The `pauseApp()` method releases all resources associated with the audio `Player` and removes the progress gauge (if any) from the `InitialView`:

```
public void pauseApp(){
    releaseResources();
```

```
        initialView.removeProgressGauge();
}
```

Again, this latter step is to ensure the MIDlet resumes from a pause in the correct state.

The `destroyApp()` method simply releases all resources associated with the audio `Player`:

```
public void destroyApp(boolean unconditional){
    releaseResources();
}
```

Now let's look at the `commandAction()` method mandated by the `CommandListener` interface:

```
public void commandAction(Command c, Displayable s){

    if(c == playCommand){
        initialView.removeCommand(playCommand);
        initialView.addProgressGauge();
        audioPlayer.initializePlayer(initialView.getURL());
    }
    else if(c == replayCommand){
        playerView.removeCommand(replayCommand);
        audioPlayer.startPlayer();
    }
    else if(c == backCommand){
        releaseResources();
        initialView.removeProgressGauge();
        display.setCurrent(initialView);
        initialView.addCommand(playCommand);
        playerView.removeCommand(replayCommand);
    }
    else if(c == exitCommand){
        releaseResources();
        notifyDestroyed();
    }
}
```

When the user selects the "Play" `Command`, the `initializePlayer()` method is called with the URL of the audio content (obtained from the `InitialView`) as an argument. In addition, a progress gauge is added to the `InitialView` to give visual feedback to the user as to how the audio acquisition is progressing. The "Play" `Command` is removed from the `InitialView` to avoid multiple `Players` being created.

The "Re-play" `Command` is used to replay a given audio file (for which a `Player` has already been created) once its end of media has been reached.

The "Back" `Command` allows the user to abandon the current `Player` session and return to the `InitialView`, either to play a different audio file, or quit the application.

Finally, when the user selects the "Exit" Command the MIDlet releases all resources associated with the Player and calls notifyDestroyed() to indicate to the AMS that it has moved into the DESTROYED state and can be reclaimed.

Now let us consider the playerUpdate() method mandated by the PlayerListener interface:

```
public void playerUpdate(Player p, String event, Object eventData) {
    if (event == PlayerListener.STARTED) {
        playerView.setStatus("Player started!");
        if(backCommand == null){
            backCommand = new Command("Back", Command.BACK, 1);
            playerView.addCommand(backCommand);
        }
        display.setCurrent(playerView);
    }

    //add "Replay" option when audio playback is finished
    else if (event == PlayerListener.END_OF_MEDIA){
        playerView.setStatus("End of Media, select 'Re-play' or 'Back'");
        if (replayCommand == null){
            replayCommand = new Command("Re-play", Command.SCREEN, 1);
        }
        playerView.addCommand(replayCommand);
    }

    else if (event == PlayerListener.VOLUME_CHANGED) {
        VolumeControl volumeControl = (VolumeControl)eventData;
        int currentLevel = volumeControl.getLevel();
        if (playerView.getVolumeLevel() != currentLevel) {
            playerView.setVolumeIndicator(currentLevel);
        }
    }
}
```

In this example, three types of PlayerListener event are processed: STARTED, END_OF_MEDIA and VOLUME_CHANGED. A STARTED event is broadcast in response to the Player starting. The PlayerView is made the current view, the "Back" Command is added to it and the status of PlayerView is set appropriately.

An END_OF_MEDIA event is generated when the Player reaches the end of the audio file. The "Re-play" Command is added to the PlayerView and the status set accordingly.

A VOLUME_CHANGED event is posted when the volume is changed using the VolumeControl. The eventData object is cast to a VolumeControl and used to get the current volume setting. The volume indicator Gauge owned by the PlayerView is adjusted accordingly, ensuring it correctly reflects the volume level of the VolumeControl.

The ItemStateChanged() method (listed below) is mandated by the ItemStateListener and listens for requests by the user to change the volume level via the interactive volume indicator Gauge of PlayerView.

```
public void itemStateChanged(Item item){
    if (item instanceof Gauge){
        Gauge volumeIndicator = (Gauge)item;
        int level = volumeIndicator.getValue();
        audioPlayer.setVolume(level);
    }
}
```

The itemStateChanged() method obtains the value requested by the user and invokes the setVolume() method to adjust the audio playback volume via the Player's VolumeControl.

The showAlert() method (see below) is called by the AudioPlayer instance in the event of an Exception being thrown at any stage of the Player lifecycle.

```
public void showAlert(String title, String message){
    Alert alert = new Alert(title, message, null, AlertType.ERROR);
    display.setCurrent(alert, initialView);
    initialView.removeProgressGauge();
    initialView.addCommand(playCommand);
}
```

After displaying an error Alert, the current Displayable is set to the InitialView allowing the user to try either the same URL again or a different URL.

The MIDletController class also provides a couple of callback methods: updateProgressGauge and removeVolumeControl. The first updates the InitialView progress gauge as the Player progresses through its lifecycle. The second removes the interactive volume indicator Gauge from the PlayerView in the event that the implementation of Player does not support a VolumeControl.

The full source code and JAR and JAD files for the Audio Player MIDlet can be downloaded from the Symbian website at ***www.symbian. com/books***.

3.4.1.5 *Working with Video*

We shall now illustrate how to play a video with code highlights taken from a simple Video Player MIDlet (see Figure 3.26).

The architecture of the Video Player MIDlet (see Figure 3.27) is very similar to that of the Audio Player.

The MIDlet contains four classes: MIDletController, InitialView, VideoPlayer and VideoCanvas. The VideoCanvas is used for rendering the video playback as well as providing controls similar to those found in the PlayerView of the Audio Player MIDlet. The other classes fulfill very similar roles to their equivalents in the Audio Player MIDlet.

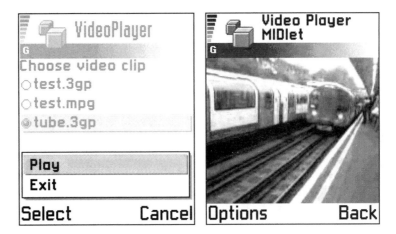

Figure 3.26   The Video Player MIDlet running on a Nokia Series 60 phone.

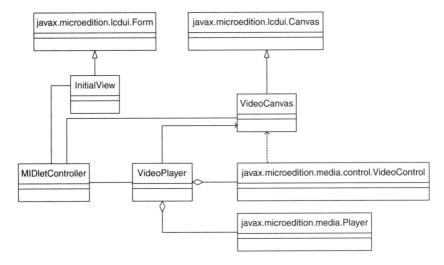

Figure 3.27   UML class diagram of the Video Player MIDlet.

The *VideoPlayer* Class
Let's first take a look at the key methods of the `VideoPlayer` class:

```
import javax.microedition.media.*;
import javax.microedition.media.control.*;
import java.io.*;
// Acquires the video content and renders it
public class VideoPlayer implements Runnable {

    private final static String THREE_GPP = "3gp";
    private final static String MPEG = "mpg";
```

```
    private final static String MIME_3GPP = "video/3gpp";
    private final static String MIME_MPEG = "video/mpeg";

    private MIDletController controller;
    private VideoCanvas canvas;
    private Player player;
    private VideoControl videoControl;
    private String resource;
    private String mimeType = THREE_GPP;
    private Thread initializer;

    public VideoPlayer(MIDletController controller,
            VideoCanvas canvas){...}

    public void initializeVideo(String resource){...}

    public void run(){...}

    public void startPlayer(){...}

    public void stopPlayer(){...}

    public void closePlayer(){...}
}
```

The constructor is shown below.

```
public VideoPlayer(MIDletController controller, VideoCanvas canvas){
    this.controller = controller;
    this.canvas = canvas;
}
```

It simply initializes the `controller` and `canvas` attributes with references to the `MIDletController` and the `VideoCanvas` respectively.

One difference between the Video Player and Audio Player MIDlets is that the Video Player obtains its content from resource files packaged in the MIDlet suite JAR file, rather than from a remote resource. The `initializeVideo()` method takes the name of the video file as a parameter.

```
public void initializeVideo(String resource){
    this.resource = resource;
    String fileExt =
            resource.substring(resource.lastIndexOf('.') + 1);
    if(fileExt.equals(THREE_GPP)) {
        mimeType = MIME_3GPP;
    }
    else if(fileExt.equals(MPEG)) {
        mimeType = MIME_MPEG;
    }
    initializer = new Thread(this);
    initializer.start();
}
```

The resource file name is tested to ascertain its format (MPEG for the Sun's J2ME Wireless Toolkit 2.0 emulator and 3GPP for real phones) and the appropriate MIME type set. A new thread is then launched to perform the essential initialization required to play the video content.

The `run()` method, mandated by the `Runnable` interface, contains the initialization of the `Player`.

```
public void run(){
    try {
        InputStream in = getClass().getResourceAsStream("/"
            + resource);
        player = Manager.createPlayer(in, mimeType);
        player.addPlayerListener(controller);
        player.realize();
        player.prefetch();
        videoControl =
            (VideoControl)player.getControl("VideoControl");
        if (videoControl != null) {
            videoControl.initDisplayMode(
                    videoControl.USE_DIRECT_VIDEO, canvas);
            int cHeight = canvas.getHeight();
            int cWidth = canvas.getWidth();
            videoControl.setDisplaySize(cWidth, cHeight);
            videoControl.setVisible(true);
            startPlayer();
        }
        else{
            controller.showAlert("Error!",
                    "Unable to get Video Control");
            closePlayer();
        }
    } catch (IOException ioe) {
        controller.showAlert("Unable to access resource",
                ioe.getMessage());
        closePlayer();
    } catch (MediaException me) {
        controller.showAlert("Unable to create player",
                me.getMessage());
        closePlayer();
    }
}
```

An `InputStream` is obtained from the resource file and used to create the `Player` instance. A `PlayerListener` (the `controller`) is registered with the `Player` in order to receive callbacks. The `prefetch` and `realize()` methods are then called on the `Player` instance.

Once the player is in the PREFETCHED state we are ready to render the video content. First we must obtain a `VideoControl` by calling `getControl` on the `Player`, and casting it down appropriately. Note that the MMAPI specification requires that a player for video media must support a `VideoControl`, unlike the case of a player for audio content, where support for `VolumeControl` is only a recommended practice.

The `initDisplayMode()` method is used to initialize the video mode that determines how the video is displayed. This method takes an integer mode value as its first argument with one of two predefined values: `USE_GUI_PRIMITIVE` or `USE_DIRECT_VIDEO`. In the case of MIDP implementations (supporting the LCDUI), `USE_GUI_PRIMITIVE` will result in an instance of a `javax.microedition.lcdui.Item` being returned:

```
Item display = control.initDisplayMode(control.USE_GUI_PRIMITIVE, null);
```

For CDC implementations supporting AWT, `USE_GUI_PRIMITIVE` will return an instance of `java.awt.Component`. For implementations that support both LCDUI and AWT, the required type must be specified by a `String` as the second argument:

```
Item display = control.initDisplayMode(control.USE_GUI_PRIMITIVE,
        "javax.microedition.lcdui.Item");
```

The `USE_DIRECT_VIDEO` mode can only be used with implementations that support the LCDUI (such as Symbian OS) and a second argument of type `javax.microedition.lcdui.Canvas` (or a subclass) must be supplied. This is the approach adopted in the example code above. Methods of `VideoControl` can be used to manipulate the size and the location of the video with respect to the `Canvas` where it will be displayed. Since we are using direct video as the display mode it is necessary to call `setVisible(true)` in order for the video to be displayed. (In the case of `USE_GUI_PRIMITIVE` the video is shown by default when the GUI primitive is displayed.) Finally, we start the rendering of the video with the `startPlayer()` method. If at any stage an `Exception` is thrown the `MIDletController.showAlert()` method is called and the resources acquired by the `Player` are released by calling the `closePlayer()` method.

The other methods of the `VideoPlayer` class are the same as their namesakes in the `AudioPlayer` class of the Audio Player MIDlet.

The MIDletController Class

The `MIDletController` class for the Video Player MIDlet is very similar to that of the Audio Player. The method signatures of the class are shown below.

```
import javax.microedition.midlet.*;
import javax.microedition.lcdui.*;
import javax.microedition.media.*;
// A simple video player MIDlet using JSR 135 - Mobile Media API
public class MIDletController extends MIDlet implements
```

```
        CommandListener, PlayerListener {

    private Command exitCommand, playCommand, backCommand,
            replayCommand;
    private Display display;
    private InitialView initialView;
    private VideoCanvas videoCanvas;
    private VideoPlayer videoPlayer;

    public MIDletController() {...}

    public void startApp(){...}

    public void pauseApp(){...}

    public void destroyApp(boolean unconditional){...}

    public void commandAction(Command c, Displayable s){...}

    public void playerUpdate(Player p, String event,
            Object eventData) {...}

    public void showAlert(String title, String message){...}

    public void releaseResources(){...}
}
```

The constructor is listed below:

```
public MIDletController() {
    int noOfVideos = Integer.parseInt(getAppProperty(
            "number-of-videos"));
    String[] videoNames = new String[noOfVideos];

    for (int i = 1; i <= noOfVideos; i++){
        videoNames[i-1] = getAppProperty("video-" + i);
    }

    initialView = new InitialView(this, videoNames);
    exitCommand = new Command("Exit", Command.EXIT, 2);
    playCommand = new Command("Play", Command.SCREEN, 1);
    initialView.addCommand(exitCommand);

    videoCanvas = new VideoCanvas(this);
    backCommand = new Command("Back", Command.BACK, 1);
    videoCanvas.addCommand(backCommand);

    videoPlayer = new VideoPlayer(this, videoCanvas);
    display = Display.getDisplay(this);
}
```

It first uses the MIDlet `getAppProperty()` method to retrieve user-defined attributes from the JAD file, namely the number of video files packaged in the JAR and their names. The names are then used to initialize the `InitialView`. The `VideoCanvas` and `VideoPlayer` instances are then created.

All the other methods in `MIDletController` are essentially the same as their Audio Player namesakes.

The `VideoCanvas` Class
We will briefly take a look at the (very simple) VideoCanvas class:

```
import javax.microedition.lcdui.*;
public class VideoCanvas extends Canvas{

    public VideoCanvas(MIDletController controller){
        setCommandListener(controller);
    }

    // Paints background color
    public void paint(Graphics g){
        g.setColor(128, 128, 128);
        g.fillRect(0, 0, getWidth(), getHeight());
    }
}
```

The important point to note is that the `paint()` method plays no part in rendering the video. This is performed directly by the `VideoControl`.

The full source code and JAR and JAD files for the Video Player MIDlet can be downloaded from the Symbian website at ***www.symbian. com/books***.

3.4.1.6   Capturing Images

Another use of VideoControl is to capture images from a camera. In this case, rather than specifying a file (and MIME type) as the data source, we specify `capture://video`. Other than that, the setting up of the video player and control proceeds pretty much as in the Video Player MIDlet above.

The Picture Puzzle MIDlet, included as a case study in Chapter 5, illustrates image capture. The following code which performs the necessary initialization of a video player and a control is reproduced from the `Capturer` class in that example.

```
// Creates a VideoPlayer and gets an associated VideoControl
public void createPlayer() throws ApplicationException {

    try {
        player = Manager.createPlayer("capture://video");
        player.realize();
        // Sets VideoControl to the current display.
        videoControl =
                (VideoControl)(player.getControl("VideoControl"));
        if (videoControl == null) {
            discardPlayer();
        } else {
```

```
        videoControl.initDisplayMode(VideoControl.USE_DIRECT_VIDEO,
                canvas);
    int cWidth = canvas.getWidth();
    int cHeight = canvas.getHeight();
    int dWidth = 160;
    int dHeight = 120;
    videoControl.setDisplaySize(dWidth, dHeight);
    videoControl.setDisplayLocation((cWidth - dWidth)/2,
            (cHeight - dHeight)/2);
}
```

By setting the Canvas to be the current one in the Display, we can use it as a "viewfinder" for the camera. When we are ready to take a picture, we simply call getSnapshot(null) on the VideoControl, as shown in the following code from the Picture Puzzle MIDlet:

```
public byte[] takeSnapshot() throws ApplicationException {
    byte[] pngImage = null;
    if (videoControl == null) {
        throw new ApplicationException("Unable to capture photo:
                VideoControl null");
    }
    try {
        pngImage = videoControl.getSnapshot(null);
    }catch(MediaException me) {
        throw new ApplicationException("Unable to capture photo",
                me);
    }

    return pngImage;
}
```

It should be noted that, if a security policy is in operation, user permission may be requested through an intermediate dialog, which may interfere with the photography!

3.4.1.7 *Generating Tones*

MMAPI also supports tone generation. Generating a single tone is simply achieved using the following method of the Manager class:

```
public static void playTone(int note, int duration, int volume)
        throws MediaException
```

The note is passed as an integer value in the range 0–127. ToneControl.C4 = 60 represents middle C. Adding or subtracting 1 increases or lowers the pitch by a semitone. The duration is specified in milliseconds and the volume is an integer value on the scale 0–100.

To play a sequence of tones it is more appropriate to create a Player and use it to obtain a ToneControl.

```
byte[] toneSequence = { ToneControl.C4, ToneControl.C4 + 2,
        ToneControl.c4 +4, ...};
try{
    Player player = Manager.createPlayer(Manager.TONE_DEVICE_LOCATOR);
    player.realize();
    ToneControl control = (ToneControl)player.getControl("ToneControl");
    control.setSequence(toneSequence);
    player.start();
} catch (IOException ioe) {
} catch (MediaException me) { //handle }
```

A tone sequence is specified as a list of tone–duration pairs and user-defined sequence blocks, using Augmented Backus–Naur form (ABNF) syntax (refer to the MMAPI specification for more detail). The list is packaged as a byte array and passed to the ToneControl using the setSequence() method. To play the sequence we simply invoke the start() method of the Player.

A more sophisticated example can be found in the documentation of ToneControl in the MMAPI specification.

3.4.2 MMAPI on Symbian OS Phones

We next look at the important question of which media capabilities are supported in practice on the various Symbian OS phones on the market. It is important to understand that when we talk about MMAPI on Symbian OS we are not talking about a single version but three, based on two distinct implementations. These are:

- Symbian MIDP 2.0 Audio subset (on Symbian OS Version 7.0)

- Series 60 Developer Platform 1.0 (on Symbian OS Version 6.1)

- Series 60 Developer Platform 2.0 (on Symbian OS Version 7.0s).

These MMAPI implementations will be discussed in turn.

MMAPI was first implemented on Symbian OS not by Symbian but by Nokia, for their Series 60 Developer Platform 1.0 (as embodied in the Series 60 MIDP SDK 1.2.1 for Symbian OS, Nokia edition, based on Symbian OS Version 6.1). This is available on all phones based on this platform, with the exception of the Nokia 7650 which was technically based on a precursor to the Series 60 Developer Platform 1.0, and provided multimedia capabilities only through custom Nokia APIs.

This implementation was extended by Nokia for the Series 60 Developer Platform 2.0 and Series 90 Developer Platform 1.0, both based on Symbian OS Version 7.0s. At the time of writing, the only announced phones based on these platforms are the Nokia 6600 and the Nokia 7700, based on Series 60 and Series 90 respectively.

As the number of phones based on these platforms continues to grow, the reader is referred to ***www.symbian.com/phones*** to ascertain the current list. Note that Nokia licenses its platforms to other mobile phone manufacturers, so the list is not restricted to Nokia phones.

At the same time, Symbian has separately implemented the audio subset ("building block") of MMAPI defined by MIDP 2.0, which became available with the release of Symbian OS Version 7.0s. Consequently, it is not available as standard on phones based on Symbian OS Version 7.0. However, the whole of MIDP 2.0 has been "backported" from Symbian OS Version 7.0s to Symbian OS Version 7.0 as part of the upgrade of the UIQ platform from UIQ 2.0 to UIQ 2.1. As a result, phones based on UIQ 2.1 (the first of which to be announced are the Sony Ericsson P900/P908 and the BenQ P30) support the audio subset.

Symbian is releasing a fully featured MMAPI implementation in the forthcoming Symbian OS Version 8.0, which will be available for all Symbian OS phones (see ***www.symbian.com/technology/standard-java.html***). This will certainly mean a closer match of the MMAPI capabilities of Symbian OS phones based on different UIs than at present.

3.4.2.1   *Symbian MIDP 2.0 Audio Subset*

The audio subset of MIDP 2.0 is described in the MIDP 2.0 specification document under `javax.microedition.media` and `javax.microedition.media.control`. Notably there is no `javax.microedition.media.protocol` package, since custom `DataSources` are not supported. The associated overridden version of `Manager.createPlayer()` is not, as a result, supported either. Only two controls are available, `VolumeControl` and `ToneControl`, both of which are fully supported by Symbian OS. There is no support for media recording or capture.

The following are the audio formats supported:

Format	File extension	MIME types
AU audio	.au	audio/basic
Wave audio	.wav	audio/wav, audio/x-wav
MP3	.mp3	audio/mp3
Tone sequence	n/a	audio/x-tone-seq

These can all, with the exception of tone sequences, be played via the various mechanisms described in Section 3.4.1.2. Tone sequences differ in that there is no file extension associated with them; they can only be created in a programmatic manner, in the context of a `ToneControl`.

The P900 adds additional support for the following audio types:

Format	File extension	MIME types
RMF (Beatnik)	.rmf	audio/rmf
iMelody	.imy	text/x-imelody, audio/x-imelody
MIDI	.mid	audio/midi, audio/x-midi

3.4.2.2 Series 60 Developer Platform 1.0

Nokia's implementation of MMAPI in Series 60 Developer Platform 1.0 supports playing of the following types of media:

Format	File extension	MIME types
Wave audio	.wav	audio/x-wav
AMR audio	.amr	audio/amr
Nokia ring tone	.rng	audio/x-nokia-rng
Tone sequence	n/a	audio/x-tone-seq
MIDI	.mid	audio/midi
Scalable Polyphonic MIDI	.mid	audio/sp-midi
3GPP video	.3gp	video/3gpp
NIM video	.nim	video/vnd.nokia.interleaved-multimedia

These all support `VolumeControl` and `StopTimeControl` (which allows you to specify in advance a stop time, rather than letting the media play to its end). In addition, tone sequences necessarily support `ToneControl` and videos support `VideoControl`. No other controls are supported.

It is worth noting that Nokia's MIDP implementation supports full-screen display of a Canvas, through a custom `FullCanvas` class. It is possible to play video full-screen using such a class as follows:

```
FullCanvas canvas
VideoControl videoControl;
Player player;
...
videoControl = (VideoControl)player.getControl("VideoControl");
videoControl.initDisplayMode(VideoControl.USE_DIRECT_VIDEO, canvas);
```

There are no recording capabilities. Nor is there support for audio capture. However, still images can be captured from the camera, using the protocol described in Section 3.4.1.2. The default encoding for the captured image on all Nokia phones is PNG. Alternatively you can specify one of the three supported formats:

- Portable Network Graphics (PNG)
- Bitmap (BMP)
- JPEG (JPG).

You do this by passing one of the strings encoding=png, encoding =bmp or encoding=jpeg as an argument to the getSnapshot() method of VideoControl. You can set the width and height in the same way. The default is 160 × 120 pixels. Be aware that if you change the aspect ratio in your specification, the image will be stretched rather than clipped. VideoControl is the only control which can be used in the context of video capture. Further details about the use of VideoControl can be found in *Camera MIDlet: A Mobile Media API Example* on Forum Nokia (***http://ncsp.forum.nokia.com/csp***).

Other points worth noting about Nokia's implementation are that:

- "mixing", in the sense of simultaneous playback by multiple players, is not supported; although the TimeBase concept is supported, it would not appear to be usable for its intended purpose of playback synchronization

- RTP streaming is not supported: the protocol itself is unsupported

- HTTP streaming is not supported; media data will be downloaded completely (during the "realization" phase) before "prefetching" and playing can begin (see Figure 3.23).

3.4.2.3   Series 60 Developer Platform 2.0

A number of modifications have been made to Nokia's MMAPI implementation for the Series 60 Developer Platform 2.0. The comments below can be expected to apply equally to the Series 90 Developer Platform 1.0 which is closely related.

The main differences are that support has been added for audio capture and recording, and there are changes to the set of supported content types. In particular, support for the proprietary Nokia audio and video file formats has been removed and support has been added for AU, Raw and AMR wideband audio formats and MP4 and Real Media video formats.

The following is the list of supported content types:

Format	File extension	MIME types
Wave audio	.wav	audio/wav, audio/x-wav
AMR audio	.amr	audio/amr
AMR wideband audio	.awb	audio/amr-wb
Raw audio	.raw	audio/basic
AU audio	.au	audio/au, audio/x-au
Tone sequence	n/a	audio/x-tone-seq
MIDI	.mid	audio/midi
Scalable Polyphonic MIDI	.mid	audio/sp-midi
3GPP video	.3gp	video/3gpp
MP4 video	.mp4	video/mp4
Real Media video	.rm	application/vnd.rn-realmedia

It might be observed here that a number of the file extensions have associated with them more than one MIME type. For media downloaded from a server this is not a problem; the server can specify the MIME type as part of the transaction. Where media is obtained from an `InputStream` rather than a URI (as will typically be the case for local data), a default MIME type will be assumed. In the case of AU and WAV files, the defaults are audio/au and audio/x-wav, respectively. With MIDI, the more powerful audio/sp-midi format will be assumed; if no prioritization of channels is specified (as will be the case for the generic MIDI format), but the number of requested channels exceeds the supported number, an arbitrary selection of channels is played.

Note that, although MP3 playback is supported on a number of Series 60 and Series 90 phones, it is not among the above-listed formats, so it is not supported through MMAPI. Again, although streaming video is supported on the Nokia 6600 and Nokia 7700, the restrictions on mixing and streaming media are the same as in Series 60 Developer Platform 1.0.

The support for controls is exactly the same as in Series 60 Developer Platform 1.0, with one exception. Because of the introduction of support for audio capture and recording, `RecordControl` is available for `audio/wav`, `audio/au` and `audio/amr`. Usage of `RecordControls` is illustrated in the following code sample reproduced from the MMAPI specification:

```
try {
    // Create a Player that captures live audio.
    Player p = Manager.createPlayer("capture://audio");
    p.realize();
    // Get the RecordControl, set the record stream,
    // start the Player and record for 5 seconds.
    RecordControl rc = (RecordControl)p.getControl("RecordControl");
```

```
    ByteArrayOutputStream output = new ByteArrayOutputStream();
    rc.setRecordStream(output);
    rc.startRecord();
    p.start();
    Thread.currentThread().sleep(5000);
    rc.commit();
    p.close();
} catch (IOException ioe) {
} catch (MediaException me) {
} catch (InterruptedException ie) { }
```

This will capture five seconds of audio input from the microphone. Notice here that the `commit()` method implies a call to `stopRecord` before ending the record session. The MIME type of the captured data can conveniently be ascertained using the `getContentType()` method of `RecordControl`. For the Nokia 6600, the default encoding is PCM. You can also, if you wish, specify the encoding to use for the recording. You should first ascertain which encodings are supported by the implementation (see Section 3.4.2.5). Then, if you wanted to ensure the audio stream was captured in WAV format, for example, you could specify `capture://audio&encoding=wav` as the argument to the `createPlayer()` method.

Similar code will allow recording from a remote URI providing audio data of one of the supported MIME types. The URI is passed in as an argument to the `setRecordLocation` of `RecordControl`. The server which delivers the audio content would specify the MIME type, which you can ascertain in the manner just discussed. Rather than causing the thread to sleep for a preset time, however, it would be better to arrange to `commit` the recording on receipt of an `END_OF_MEDIA` event. Clearly there is no important use case for recording local audio data since, by definition, a data `InputStream` would already exist which could be piped to an `OutputStream`.

3.4.2.4   Symbian OS Version 8.0

From Symbian OS Version 8.0, Symbian is providing a fully-featured MMAPI implementation as standard. Although at time of writing no phones have been announced based on this OS release, it is worth spending a little time reviewing some of the main features of this forthcoming implementation, to get a flavor of what is to come.

One of the main features is that the content types supported are not considered as a closed set but depend on what is implemented natively in the multimedia framework on the host phone. The capabilities will inevitably vary from phone to phone, so there is not so much value in discussing the details of Symbian's default implementation here. However, it is likely that playing MP3 files from Java will become possible for the first time on phones based on Symbian OS Version 8.0.

Another significant difference in the new implementation is that many more controls are supported than hitherto, and in more contexts. In fact, all 12 of the controls listed in Section 3.4.1.3 have been implemented. The details of which controls are supported for different players will be subject to some variation in practice, depending on the phone design. Perhaps the most important development in this regard is that Record-Control is supported in the context of both capture://audio and capture://video, opening up the possibility of recording video clips from Java for the first time!

Also device://midi is supported, and both tone generation and midi sound generation have PitchControl and RateControl available. Thus many more possibilities are presented.

3.4.2.5 *Working Out What Is Supported*

If you know which of the Symbian OS platforms you are targeting with a MIDlet, you will be able to craft your code to conform to the cited capabilities. However, in practice it is more likely that you will want to write portable code which can run on several or all of the above platforms, or indeed on non-Symbian OS phones with MMAPI capability. In this case you will need to be able to work out the supported capabilities dynamically and make use of what is available, or else fail gracefully (for example, by removing certain options from menus) if the capability you want is just not available.

This you can achieve by interrogating the javax.microedition.media.Manager class about the properties of interest. In particular, if you want to find out which content types are supported, you can do so with the following call:

```
String[] types = Manager.getSupportedContentTypes(null);
```

This will return an array of the MIME types as strings preceded by audio/ or video/. In the case of the Nokia 6600, the RealMedia MIME type is preceded by application/.

Correspondingly, to find out which protocols are supported, you can call:

```
String[] types = Manager.getSupportedProtocols(null);
```

This will return the appropriate selection of http, capture or device on Symbian OS phones. If you want to know which content types are available for a particular protocol, simply pass the relevant string returned by getSupportedProtocols(null) as the argument to getSupportedContentTypes(), instead of null. Similarly, if you want to know the protocols available for a particular content type, pass the content type to getSupportedProtocols().

In addition, there are a number of system properties which can be used to work out what multimedia capabilities are supported for a particular implementation. These are described in full in the overview of the MMAPI specification. They can be recovered as strings with the usual `System.getProperty()` method. The following properties are of particular use:

- `supports.mixing` – returns false on all Symbian OS phones
- `supports.audio.capture` – returns true on Nokia 6600 (Series 60 v2.0) and in the Symbian OS Version 8.0 implementation
- `supports.video.capture` – returns true on all Symbian OS phones, indicating that snapshots are possible
- `supports.recording` – returns true on Nokia 6600 (Series 60 v2.0) and in the Symbian OS Version 8.0 implementation
- `audio.encodings` – returns a list of encodings depending on the implementation
- `video.encodings` – returns non-null values on only the Symbian OS Version 8.0 implementation, which is the first to support video recording (the default is `encoding=video/msvideo`)
- `video.snapshot.encodings` – returns the default `encoding=png` for Series 60 v2.0; returns a list of all supported encodings for Series 60 v1.2 and Symbian OS Version 8.0 (for which the default is the first value in the list)
- `streamable.contents` – returns `null` on all Symbian OS phones.

3.4.3 MMAPI and the MIDP 2.0 Security Model

For reasons of privacy the following Mobile Media API calls are restricted under the MIDP 2.0 security model (see *Mobile Media API Specification 1.1 Maintenance Release* at ***http://jcp.org***.)

- `RecordControl.setRecordLocation(String locator)`
- `RecordControl.setRecordStream(OutputStream stream)`
- `VideoControl.getSnapshot(String type)`.

Under the MIDP 2.0 security model, a signed MIDlet suite which contains MIDlets that make use of these APIs must explicitly request the appropriate permission in its `MIDlet-Permissions` attribute. The required `MIDlet-Permissions` attribute entries in the JAD file or manifest are as follows:

```
MIDlet-Permissions: javax.microedition.media.control.RecordControl, ...
```

or:

```
MIDlet-Permissions:
        javax.microedition.media.control.VideoControl.getSnapshot, ...
```

These protected APIs are part of the Multimedia Recording function group as defined by the *Recommended Security Policy for GSM/UMTS Compliant Devices* addendum to the MIDP 2.0 specification.

It must also be remembered that if a MIDlet in a signed MIDlet suite makes use of a protected API of the `javax.microedition.io` package, for instance to fetch media content over HTTP, then explicit permission to access that API must be requested in the `MIDlet-Permissions` attribute. This is the case even if it is fetched implicitly, perhaps by calling:

```
Manager.createPlayer("www.myserver.com/video.3gp")
```

Whether MIDlets in untrusted MIDlet suites can use the protected APIs of the MMAPI depends on the security policy relating to the untrusted domain in force on the device. Under the JTWI Release 1 *Security Policy for GSM/UMTS Compliant Devices*, MIDlets in untrusted MIDlet suites can access the Multimedia Recording function group APIs with explicit permission from the user. The default user permission setting is oneshot ("Ask every time").

Current devices based on the MIDP 2.0-enabled Series 60 Developer Platform 2.0, such as the Nokia 6600, support both audio recording and capturing snapshots. The security policy for the untrusted domain on this device complies with the JTWI Release 1 requirements. Note that on the Nokia 6600, the user may change the default user permission from oneshot to session ("Ask first time") in the following manner (see Figure 3.28):

1. Navigate to the main menu.

2. Select the Application Manager.

3. Highlight the appropriate MIDlet from the list of applications.

4. Select Options > Settings > Multimedia.

5. Select "Ask first time".

Devices based on the MIDP 1.0-enabled Series 60 Developer Platform 1.x, such as the Nokia 3650, only support the capture of snapshots. Obviously such devices are not subject to the MIDP 2.0 security requirements. Taking photos using the `getSnapshot()` method of the `VideoControl` does not require explicit user permission on these devices.

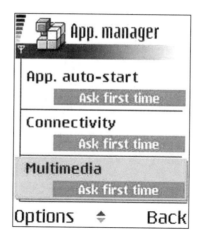

Figure 3.28 Changing the default user permission on the Nokia 6600.

3.4.4 Wireless Messaging API

3.4.4.1 Introduction

The Wireless Messaging API (JSR 120) is an optional API targeted at devices supporting the Generic Connection Framework defined in the CLDC. The Wireless Messaging API (WMA) specification defines APIs for sending and receiving SMS messages and receiving CBS messages. At the time of writing the current release of the Wireless Messaging API is version 1.1. This contains minor modifications to the 1.0 specification to enable the API to be compatible with MIDP 2.0.

The WMA is a compact API containing just two packages:

- `javax.microedition.io`

- `javax.wireless.messaging`.

The first package contains the platform network interfaces modified for use on platforms supporting wireless messaging connection, in particular an implementation of the `Connector` class for creating new `MessageConnection` objects. The second package defines APIs which allow applications to send and receive wireless messages. It defines a base interface `Message` from which `BinaryMessage` and `TextMessage` both derive. It also defines a `MessageConnection` interface, which provides the basic functionality for sending and receiving messages, and a `MessageListener` interface for listening to incoming messages.

In this section we shall consider sending and receiving SMS messages. We shall then go on to show how to use the Push Registry API of MIDP 2.0 to register an incoming SMS connection with a MIDlet.

3.4.4.2 *Sending Messages*

Sending an SMS message using the WMA could not be simpler, as the code paragraph below shows:

```
String address = "sms://+447111222333";
MessageConnection smsconn = null;
try {
    smsconn = (MessageConnection)Connector.open(address);
    TextMessage txtMessage =
         (TextMessage)smsconn.newMessage(MessageConnection.TEXT_MESSAGE);
    txtmessage.setPayloadText("Hello World");
    smsconn.send(txtMessage);
    smsconn.close();
} catch (Exception e) {
    //handle
}
```

First we obtain a `MessageConnection` instance by invoking the `Connector.open()` method with an address of the appropriate syntax. A `MessageConnection` can operate in client or server mode depending on the URL syntax of the address passed to the `open()` method. For a client mode connection (as used in the code listed above), messages can only be sent. The URL address syntax for a client mode connection has the following possible formats:

- `sms://+447111222333`

- `sms://+447111222333:1234`

The first format (as in the example above) is used to open a connection for sending a normal SMS message, which will be received in the end-user's inbox. The second format is used to open a connection to send an SMS message to a particular Java application listening on the specified port.

The `MessageConnector` instance is then used to create a `Message` instance using the method:

```
public Message newMessage(String type)
```

The `MessageConnection` interface defines two `public static final String` variables `BINARY_MESSAGE` and `TEXT_MESSAGE`. If type is equal to `BINARY_MESSAGE` an instance of `BinaryMessage` is returned, whereas if type equals `TEXT_MESSAGE` an instance of a `TextMessage` is returned. Both `BinaryMessage` and `TextMessage` implement the `Message` interface. In the above code we specify a type equal to `TEXT_MESSAGE` and cast the returned instance appropriately.

Now that we have a `TextMessage` object we use the following method to set the message text:

```
public void setPayloadText(String data)
```

We are now ready to send the message. This is achieved by invoking the `send` method of the `MessageConnection` class:

```
public void send(Message msg)
```

Finally, when we no longer need the connection we should close it using the `close()` method inherited from the `Connection` class.

3.4.4.3 Receiving Messages

Receiving a message is, again, straightforward and is illustrated with the code paragraph below.

```
MessageConnection smsconn = null;
Message msg = null;
String receivedMessage = null;
String senderAddress = null;

try {
    conn = (MessageConnection) Connector.open(("sms://:1234");
    msg = smsconn.receive();
    ...
    //get sender's address for replying
    senderAddress = msg.getAddress();
    if (msg instanceof TextMessage) {
        //extract text message
        receivedMessage = ((TextMessage)msg).getPayloadText();
        //do something with message
        ...
    }
}catch (IOException ioe) {
    ioe.printStackTrace();
}
```

We open a server mode `MessageConnection` by passing in a URL of the following syntax:

```
sms://:1234
```

We retrieve the message by invoking the following method on the `MessageConnection` instance.

```
public Message receive()
```

The address of the message sender can be obtained using the following method of the `Message` interface:

```
public String getAddress()
```

A server mode connection can be used to reply to incoming messages, by making use of the `setAddress()` method of the `Message` interface. In the case of a text message, we cast the `Message` object appropriately and then retrieve its contents with the `TextMessage` interface, using the method below.

```
public String getPayloadText()
```

If the `Message` is an instance of `BinaryMessage` then the corresponding `getPayloadData()` method returns a byte array.

In practice, of course, we need the receiving application to listen for incoming messages and then invoke the `receive()` method upon receipt. We achieve this by implementing a `MessageListener` interface for notification of incoming messages. The `MessageListener` mandates one method, below, which is called on registered listeners by the system when an incoming message arrives.

```
public void notifyIncomingMessage(MessageConnection conn)
```

The `MessageConnection` interface supplies the following to register a listener on `MessageConnection`:

```
public void setMessageListener(MessageListener l)
```

Only one listener can be registered on a given `MessageConnection` at a given time. A call to `setMessageListener(l)` will replace a previously registered `MessageListener` with l. To de-register a `MessageListener` on a `MessageConnection` we call `setMessageListener(null)`.

Note that the `notifyIncomingMessage()` method must return quickly to avoid blocking the event dispatcher. The method should not, therefore, handle the incoming message directly but hand off the processing to a new thread.

3.4.4.4   *WMA in MIDP 2.0*

The Wireless Messaging API can be implemented on either MIDP 1.0 or MIDP 2.0 platforms. When implemented in conjunction with MIDP 2.0, the Wireless Messaging API can take advantage of the push registry technology. A MIDlet suite lists the server connections it wishes to register in its JAD file, or manifest, by specifying the protocol and port for the connection end point. The entry has the following format:

```
MIDlet-Push-<n>: <ConnectionURL>, <MIDletClassName>, <AllowedSender>
```

In this example, the entry in the JAD file would be as follows:

```
MIDlet-Push-1: sms://:1234, SMSMIDlet, *
```

The <AllowedSender> field acts as a filter indicating that the AMS should only respond to incoming connections from a specific sender. For the SMS protocol the <AllowedSender> entry is the phone number of the required sender (note the sender port number is not included in the filter). Here the wildcard character ''*'' indicates respond to any sender.

The AMS will respond to an incoming SMS directed to the specified MessageConnection by launching the corresponding MIDlet (assuming it is not already running). The MIDlet should then respond by immediately handling the incoming message in the startApp() method. As before, the message should be processed in a separate thread to avoid conflicts between blocking I/O operations and the normal user interaction events.

3.4.4.5   *The SMS ChatMIDlet Sample Code*

We shall illustrate the WMA APIs just discussed using a simple SMS ChatMIDlet. The ChatMIDlet allows a user to send and receive SMS messages and displays the ongoing conversation in a TextBox. The ChatMIDlet also makes use of the push registry so that the MIDlet will be launched in response to an incoming SMS targeted at the application. Let's first consider the main controller ChatMIDlet class.

```
package com.symbian.devnet.chatmidlet;
import javax.microedition.midlet.*;
import javax.microedition.lcdui.*;
import javax.microedition.wireless.messaging.*;
import javax.microedition.io.*;
import java.io.*;
public class ChatMIDlet extends MIDlet implements CommandListener,
        MessageListener{
    private Sender sender;
    private Receiver receiver;
    private MessageConnection smsconn;

    //Widgets for the UI for entering and reading the msgs
    private ChatView chatBox;
    private MessageView messageView;
    private Display display;

    private String smsPort;//The port on which we send SMS messages

    private final static int SENT = 1;
    private final static int RECEIVED = 2;
    private final static int ERROR = 3;

    public ChatMIDlet() {
        display = Display.getDisplay(this);
```

```
        smsPort = getAppProperty("SMS-Port");
        receiver = new Receiver(this);
        sender = new Sender(smsPort);
        chatBox = new ChatView(this);
        messageView = new MessageView(this);
}
public void startApp() {
    smsconn = receiver.open(smsPort);
    if (smsconn != null) {
        String[] connections =PushRegistry.listConnections(true);
        if (connections.length > 0) {
            for(int i = 0; i < connections.length; i++) {
                if (connections[i].equals("sms://:" + smsPort)) {
                    receiver.handleMessage(smsconn);
                }
            }
        }
        display.setCurrent(chatBox);
    }else {
        //handle
    }
}
public void notifyIncomingMessage(MessageConnection conn) {
    if (conn == smsconn) {
        receiver.handleMessage(conn);
    }
}

public void pauseApp() {
    if (smsconn != null) {
        receiver.close(smsconn);
        smsconn = null; // make eligible for garbage collection
    }
}

public void destroyApp(boolean unconditional) {
    if (smsconn != null) {
        receiver.close(smsconn);
    }
}

public void commandAction(Command command,
        Displayable displayable) {
    if(command.getLabel().equals("Send")) {
        display.setCurrent(messageView);
    }
    else if(command.getLabel().equals("Exit")) {
        if (smsconn != null) {
            receiver.close(smsconn);
        }
        notifyDestroyed();
    }
    else if(command.getLabel().equals("OK")) {
        String message = messageView.getMessage();
        String phoneNumber = messageView.getPhoneNumber();
        sender.connectAndSend(message, phoneNumber);
        chatBox.addMsg(ChatMIDlet.SENT, message);
        display.setCurrent(chatBox);
```

```
        }
    }

    public Display getDisplay() {
        return display;
    }

    public void msgTypeError(String error) {
        chatBox.addMsg(ChatMIDlet.ERROR,error);
    }

    public void processMsg(String message, String destinationAddress) {
        chatBox.addMsg(ChatMIDlet.RECEIVED,message);
        messageView.setPhoneNumber(destinationAddress);
    }
}
```

The `ChatMIDlet` constructor creates instances of the `Sender` and `Receiver` classes which encapsulate functionality for sending and receiving SMS messages, and the `ChatView` and `MessageView` UI classes. The `startApp()` method sets up the `Receiver` for handling incoming SMS messages by calling `open()` on the `Receiver` instance:

```
public void startApp() {
    smsconn = receiver.open(smsPort);
    if (smsconn != null) {
        String[] connections = PushRegistry.listConnections(true);
        if (connections.length > 0) {
            for(int i = 0; i < connections.length; i++) {
                if (connections[i].equals("sms://:" + smsPort)) {
                    receiver.handleMessage(smsconn);
                }
            }
        }
        display.setCurrent(chatBox);
    }else {
        //handle
    }
}
```

As will be shown later, in addition to opening a connection, this also registers the ChatMIDlet as a `MessageListener` on the receiver connection. The `startApp()` method also checks to see if it was invoked in response to an incoming message via the push registry and, if so, immediately handles the message.

Since the `ChatMidlet` class implements the `MessageListener` interface it must implement the `notifyIncomingMessage` interface:

```
public void notifyIncomingMessage(MessageConnection conn) {
    if (conn == smsconn) {
        receiver.handleMessage(conn);
    }
}
```

This checks that the incoming connection bearing the SMS message belongs to this application and if so calls the `handleMessage()` method of `Receiver` to process the message in a separate `Thread`.

The `pauseApp()` method, in line with good practice, releases resources by closing the `Receiver`.

Now let's look at the `Receiver` class:

```
package com.symbian.devnet.chatmidlet;
import javax.wireless.messaging.*;
import java.io.*;
import javax.microedition.io.*;
// Opens and closes a connection for receiving SMS messages.
public class Receiver implements Runnable {

    private ChatMIDlet chat;
    private MessageConnection smsconn;
    private boolean listening = false;
    private int messageWaiting = 0;

    public Receiver(ChatMIDlet chat) {
        this.chat = chat;
    }
    public MessageConnection open(String smsPort) {
        String smsAddress = "sms://:" + smsPort;
        MessageConnection conn = null;
        try {
            conn = (MessageConnection) Connector.open(smsAddress);
            conn.setMessageListener(chat);
            receiverThread.start();
            listening = true;
        }catch (IOException ioe) {
            ioe.printStackTrace();
        }
        return conn;
    }

    public synchronized void handleMessage(MessageConnection conn) {
        messageWaiting++;
        smsconn = conn;
        notify();
    }

    public void run() {
        while (listening) {
            synchronized(this) {
                while (listening && messageWaiting == 0 ) {
                    try {
                        wait();
                    } catch (InterruptedException ie) {
                        // Handle interruption
                    }
                }
                if (messageWaiting != 0) {
                    receiveMessage();
                    messageWaiting--;
                }
            }
```

```
        }
    }

    public void receiveMessage() {
        Message msg = null;
        String senderAddress = null;
        String receivedMessage = null;
        try {
            msg = smsconn.receive();
            if (msg != null) {
                senderAddress = msg.getAddress();
                if (msg instanceof TextMessage) {
                    receivedMessage =
                             ((TextMessage)msg).getPayloadText();
                    chat.processMsg(receivedMessage, senderAddress)
                } else {
                    chat.msgTypeError("Error whilst receiving.");
                }
            }
        } catch (IOException ioe) {
            ioe.printStackTrace();
        }
    }

    public synchronized void close(MessageConnection conn) {
        listening = false;
        notify();
        if (conn != null) {
            try {
                conn.setMessageListener(null);
                conn.close();
            }catch(IOException ioe) {
                ioe.printStackTrace();
            }
        }
    }
}
```

The `open()` method opens a message connection, registers a `Mes-sageListener` (the `ChatMIDlet` instance) on this connection and starts a new thread for handling incoming messages. This is performed by the `run()` method:

```
public void run() {
    while (listening) {
        synchronized(this) {
            while (listening && messageWaiting == 0 ) {
                try {
                    wait();
                } catch (InterruptedException ie) {
                    // Handle interruption
                }
            }
            if (messageWaiting != 0) {
                receiveMessage();
                messageWaiting--;
```

```
            }
        }
    }
}
```

This processes incoming messages in a while loop. When there are no messages waiting the thread is paused. When awoken by a notification from the handleMessage() method, the thread checks that there is a message waiting and if so processes it by calling the receiveMessage() method.

Functionality for sending messages is encapsulated in the Sender class:

```
package com.symbian.devnet.chatmidlet;
import javax.microedition.io.*;
import javax.microedition.lcdui.*;
import javax.wireless.messaging.*;
import java.io.IOException;
// Sends an SMS message
public class Sender implements Runnable {
    private String smsReceiverPort;
    private String message;
    private String phoneNumber;

    public Sender(String smsReceiverPort) {
        this.smsReceiverPort = smsReceiverPort;
    }

    public void run() {
        String address = "sms://" + phoneNumber + ":" +
                smsReceiverPort;
        MessageConnection smsconn = null;
        try {
            smsconn = (MessageConnection)Connector.open(address);
            TextMessage txtmessage = (TextMessage)
                    smsconn.newMessage(MessageConnection.TEXT_MESSAGE);
            txtmessage.setPayloadText(message);
            smsconn.send(txtmessage);
        }
        catch (Exception e) {
            e.printStackTrace();
        }

        if (smsconn != null) {
            try {
                smsconn.close();
            }
            catch (IOException ioe) {
                ioe.printStackTrace();
            }
        }
    }

    public void connectAndSend(String message, String phoneNumber) {
        this.message = message;
        this.phoneNumber = phoneNumber;
```

```
        Thread t = new Thread(this);
        t.start();
    }
}
```

The `connectAndSend()` method takes a message and a phone number and creates a new `Thread` to send the message. The actual sending is performed by the `run()` method which opens a connection, sends the message and then closes the connection.

The application descriptor for the ChatMIDlet is listed below.

```
MIDlet-1: SMS Chat, , com.symbian.devnet.chatmidlet.ChatMIDlet
MIDlet-Data-Size: 0
MIDlet-Description: This midlet demonstrates SMS chatting
MIDlet-Jar-Size: 6476
MIDlet-Jar-URL: SMSChat.jar
MIDlet-Name: SMS Chat
MIDlet-Push-1: sms://:1234, com.symbian.devnet.chatmidlet.ChatMIDlet, *
MIDlet-Vendor: Symbian Ltd.
MIDlet-Version: 2.0
MicroEdition-Configuration: CLDC-1.0
MicroEdition-Profile: MIDP-2.0
```

Note that the `MIDlet-push-1` entry (shown below) is required to register a push registry connection:

```
MIDlet-Push-1: sms://:1234, com.symbian.devnet.chatmidlet.ChatMIDlet, *
```

Screenshots of the ChatMIDlet running on a Nokia 6600 are shown in Figure 3.29. The full source code and JAR and JAD files for the ChatMIDlet can be downloaded from the Symbian website at ***www.symbian.com/ books***.

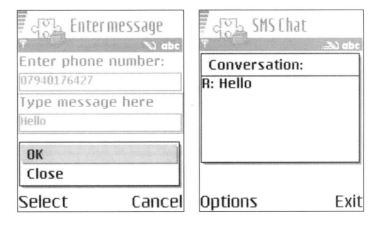

Figure 3.29 The SMS ChatMIDlet running on a Nokia 6600.

3.4.4.6 *WMA and the MIDP 2.0 Security Model*

A signed MIDlet suite that contains MIDlets which open and use SMS connections must explicitly request the following permissions as appropriate in its `MIDlet-Permissions` attribute:

- `javax.microedition.io.Connector.sms` – needed to open an SMS connection

- `javax.wireless.messaging.sms.send` – needed to send an SMS

- `javax.wireless.messaging.sms.receive` – needed to receive an SMS

```
MIDlet-Permissions: javax.microedition.io.Connector.sms,
        javax.wireless.messaging.sms.send
```

or:

```
MIDlet-Permissions: javax.microedition.io.Connector.sms,
        javax.wireless.messaging.sms.send,
        javax.wireless.messaging.sms.receive
```

If the protection domain to which the signed MIDlet suite would be bound grants, or potentially grants, the requested permissions, the MIDlet suite can be installed and the MIDlets it contains will be able to open SMS connections and send and receive SMS messages, either automatically or with explicit user permission, depending upon the security policy in effect.

Whether MIDlets in untrusted MIDlet suites can access the WMA depends on the security policy relating to the untrusted domain in force on the device. On the Nokia 6600 and Sony Ericsson P900/P908, MIDlets in untrusted MIDlet suites can access the Messaging function group APIs with User permission. On both devices, the User permission to access the Messaging function group is set to oneshot (and cannot be changed by the user, except to deny permission to that MIDlet suite altogether on the Nokia 6600). In line with the *Recommended Security Policy for GSM/UMTS Compliant Devices* addendum to the MIDP 2.0 specification and the JTWI *Security Policy for GSM/UMTS Compliant Devices* a Messaging function group permission of oneshot requires explicit user permission to send an SMS message, but allows blanket permission (permission is granted until the MIDlet suite is uninstalled or the user changes the function group permission) to receive SMS messages.

The security policy in effect on the Sony Ericsson P900/P908 for MIDlets in MIDlet suites bound to the trusted protection domain is the same as that for untrusted MIDlet suites detailed above. At the time of writing, the available firmware version (3.42.1) on the Nokia 6600 did not support the trusted protection domain (although this will be rectified in a future release).

3.4.4.7 *WMA on Symbian OS Phones*

The first implementation of the Wireless Messaging API on Symbian OS shipped as part of Nokia's Series 60 v1.x platform. This WMA implementation supplemented the MIDP 1.0 environment available on this platform. The first phone to support this implementation of the WMA was the Nokia 3650.

More recently, a MIDP 2.0-compatible version of the WMA shipped as part of Symbian OS Version 7.0s which forms the basis for Nokia's Series 60 v2.0 platform. The first mobile phone employing this platform, and therefore supporting WMA in conjunction with the push registry technology, was the Nokia 6600.

Symbian also back-ported its WMA implementation compatible with MIDP 2.0 to the UIQ 2.1 reference design based on Symbian OS Version 7.0. The first device released using this platform was the Sony Ericsson P900/P908.

Note that Symbian's implementation of the WMA currently does not support receiving CBS.

3.5 MIDP 2.0 and Symbian OS Phones

At the time of writing, two MIDP 2.0 phones based on Symbian OS have been released: the Nokia 6600 and Sony Ericsson P900/P908. Both phones implement the mandatory APIs and the minimum configuration required by the JTWI.

The Nokia 6600 (Figure 3.30) is a Series 60 Version 2.0 phone based on Symbian OS Version 7.0s. It runs the CLDC 1.0 HI (Monty) VM and, in addition to MIDP 2.0, includes the Wireless Messaging, Mobile Media APIs and also the Java Bluetooth APIs (which are not currently part of the JTWI and will be discussed in Chapter 4).

The Sony Ericsson P900/P908 (Figure 3.31) is based on Symbian OS Version 7.0 running UIQ 2.1 reference design. Symbian back-ported the CLDC 1.0 HI (Monty) VM, MIDP 2.0, the Wireless Messaging and Bluetooth APIs to the UIQ platform. An interesting feature of the P900/P908 is that it allows the user to install firmware upgrades downloaded from Sony Ericsson's website via a PC. It is therefore easy for users to ensure they are running the latest available firmware, including the latest bug fixes to the Java implementation.

Future MIDP 2.0-enabled phones in the pipeline include the Nokia 6620, 7700, BenQ P30, Panasonic X700 and Motorola A1000.

Figure 3.30   Nokia 6600 phone.

Figure 3.31   The Sony Ericsson P900 phone.

3.6   Summary

In this chapter we have discussed the JTWI and its component APIs with particular reference to their implementation on Symbian OS-based phones. First we briefly looked at the CLDC 1.0 and its various manifestations on Symbian OS. We then embarked on an in-depth discussion of MIDP 2.0 and its new features. Finally, we moved on to discuss the optional APIs required by the JTWI, namely the Wireless Messaging and

Mobile Media APIs. Throughout the chapter the emphasis has been on providing code examples that have been tested on real Symbian OS-based MIDP 2.0 phones.

In the next chapter we will look at another optional API, the Java API for Bluetooth Wireless Technology, that is supported by the latest generation of Symbian OS phones, but which does not currently fall under the JTWI.

4

Java APIs for Bluetooth Wireless Technology

In the last chapter we considered MIDP 2.0 and the optional APIs that form part of the current release (Release 1) of the Java Technology for the Wireless Industry initiative (JTWI). In this chapter we will consider an optional API that is also part of Symbian's current J2ME offering, but is not yet part of the JTWI: the Java API for Bluetooth Wireless Technology (JSR 82).

4.1 Introduction to Bluetooth

Bluetooth is an important emerging standard for wireless communication between small devices such as mobile phones. The original research on Bluetooth was performed by Ericsson and the name derives from the tenth century Danish King Harald Blätand who united Denmark and Norway. Ericsson decided to make Bluetooth an open standard by inviting other industry leaders to participate in the establishment of the Bluetooth Special Interest Group (SIG) in 1997. Today the Bluetooth SIG has over 2000 members.

Bluetooth is a short-range radio-based protocol operating in the 2.4 GHz band of the RF spectrum. Bluetooth is designed for connecting small, battery-powered devices at ranges of up to 10 m and at a data transfer rate of 1 Mb/s. By comparison with 802.11b (WiFi) technology, which also operates in the 2.4 GHZ band, Bluetooth has a shorter range (10 m compared to 100 m), lower data transfer rates (1 Mb/s compared to 10 Mb/s), but consumes much less power, making it a more suitable technology for battery-powered devices.

Symbian OS has provided native support for Bluetooth since Symbian OS Version 6.1.

Programming Java 2 Micro Edition on Symbian OS: A developer's guide to MIDP 2.0. Martin de Jode
© 2004 Symbian Ltd ISBN: 0-470-09223-8

4.2   Introduction to the Bluetooth APIs

The aim of JSR 82 was to provide a standard set of Java APIs to allow Java-enabled devices to integrate into a Bluetooth environment. The JSR 82 expert group was formed in November 2000, with Symbian a member, and produced a final release of the specification in March 2002.

The Bluetooth specification created and released by the Bluetooth SIG runs to more than 1500 pages and continues to grow as new profiles are added. It covers many layers and profiles and it is not the intention of JSR 82 to include them all. Rather, the Java API implements a core subset of the Bluetooth specification providing support for generic profiles (e.g. the Serial Port profile). It is the general intention that higher-level Bluetooth profiles can be built on top of this API using Java.

4.2.1   Bluetooth Protocol Stack

For a device to support Bluetooth, naturally it must provide both the necessary hardware support (an RF transmitter, etc.) and the necessary software support to implement the Bluetooth protocol and control the Bluetooth hardware programmatically. This software is known as the **Bluetooth protocol stack**. The Bluetooth protocol stack is directly analogous with other familiar communication protocol stacks, such as HTTP or WAP. Figure 4.1 shows a simplified diagram of the Bluetooth protocol stack.

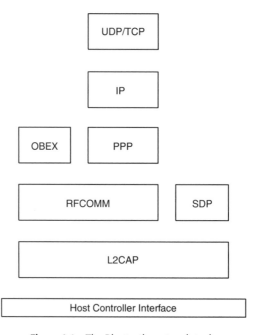

Figure 4.1   The Bluetooth protocol stack.

Some of the protocols are specific to Bluetooth, such as the Logical Link Control and Adaptation Protocol (L2CAP); others are adopted protocols, such as OBEX, PPP, IP, UDP and TCP. The Host Controller Interface (HCI) is the interface between software and hardware. Everything below the HCI is implemented in hardware, everything above is implemented in software.

L2CAP is the lowest protocol of the Bluetooth stack and it handles all data transmission from the upper layers. It is responsible for segmenting data into packets for transmission and re-assembling received data packets. The RFCOMM layer simulates the functionality of a standard serial communication port and is a cable replacement protocol. The service discovery protocol (SDP) is used for discovering Bluetooth services offered by remote devices.

4.2.2 Profiles

Profiles are defined by the Bluetooth SIG to enable Bluetooth devices to interoperate. Each profile specifies a set of functionality to achieve a particular task. It goes onto to define how this functionality is implemented using the layers of the protocol stack. Profiles range from low-level generic profiles, such as the Generic Access profile which is used by all other profiles for basic establishment of connections, to highly specific high-level profiles, such as the Headset profile, designed to enable Bluetooth devices to connect to cordless Bluetooth-enabled headsets.

Since there are hundreds of Bluetooth profiles, with new ones being added all the time, it was not the intention of the expert group for JSR 82 to attempt to provide support directly for high-level profiles. It supports only the generic profiles, which can then be used to implement higher-level profiles in Java.

4.2.3 Requirements of JSR 82

JSR 82 is an optional API targeted at J2ME devices. More specifically, it is aimed at any device that supports the Connected Limited Device Configuration (CLDC, see Chapter 1) and the Generic Connection Framework (or a superset of them, such as the CDC).

To implement the Java APIs for Bluetooth Wireless Technology, the underlying Bluetooth system must support the following layers and generic profiles in the Bluetooth stack:

- L2CAP

- RFCOMM

- SDP

- Service Discovery Application Profile

- Serial Port profile.

The specification for JSR 82 also requires that the system supply a nebulous entity known as the Bluetooth Control Center (BCC). The BCC is a "Control Panel"-like application that provides various functions amongst which are configuration options including allowing the user to specify security settings for Bluetooth connections as well as maintaining a list of known devices. On Symbian OS the BCC functionality is already provided by the underlying native Bluetooth system.

The current specification of JSR 82 was targeted at Version 1.1 of the Bluetooth specification as defined by the Bluetooth SIG. The intention is, however, that JSR 82 should be interoperable with stacks or hardware based on earlier or subsequent versions of the Bluetooth specification.

4.2.4   The Java Bluetooth Packages

JSR 82 specifies two packages:

- `javax.obex`
- `javax.bluetooth.`

The Object Exchange Protocol (OBEX) is a communication protocol originally defined by the Infrared Data Association (IrDA) that has been adopted by the Bluetooth SIG. Since OBEX is an independent protocol, it is supplied in a separate package. Applications may use the OBEX API independently of the Bluetooth API.

The Java Bluetooth API is intended to provide support for the following capabilities:

- registering services
- discovering devices and services
- establishing connections using RFCOMM, L2CAP and OBEX
- providing support for secure connections.

Symbian's current implementation of JSR 82 does not provide an implementation of the OBEX API and hence it does not have a `javax.obex` package.

4.3   Programming the Bluetooth APIs

4.3.1   Service Registration

4.3.1.1   Basic Steps

When we, as users, make a Bluetooth connection to a remote device to perform some task such as sending a file, what we are in fact doing is accessing a service offered by the remote device. To someone new to Bluetooth it is not immediately obvious that making Bluetooth connections is ultimately about connecting to services rather than devices. Before a Bluetooth host device can communicate with a remote Bluetooth peer, a service must be registered and offered by the remote device.

As application developers wishing to register a service, we need to perform the following steps:

- create a service record
- add a service record to the server's Service Discovery Database
- set security measures associated with connections to clients
- accept connections from clients that request service.

4.3.1.2   Service Records

The Service Discovery Database (SDDB) maintains a repository of service records corresponding to the services offered by the host device. A service record provides sufficient information to allow a client to connect to the Bluetooth service being offered by the server. Service discovery is the province of the Service Discovery Application Protocol (SDAP) which itself uses the Service Discovery Protocol layer in the Bluetooth stack. The APIs for creating a service record and adding it to the SDDB are Java wrappers around functionality defined in the SDAP and SDP.

The Java APIs provide an abstraction of the Bluetooth Service Record in the `javax.bluetooth.ServiceRecord` interface. A `ServiceRecord` contains information about the service in a set of attributes in the form of (ID, value) pairs, where the ID is a 16-bit unsigned integer, and the value is an instance of a `javax.bluetooth.DataElement`.

A `ServiceRecord` may contain many attributes to fully describe the service being offered. However, only two attributes are required to be present in a `ServiceRecord`, the `ServiceRecordHandle` and the `ServiceClassIDList`.

Some key attributes contained in a `ServiceRecord`:

Attribute Name	Attribute ID	Attribute Value Type
ServiceRecordHandle	0x0000	32-bit unsigned integer
ServiceClassIDList	0x0001	Sequence of UUIDs
ServiceRecordState	0x0002	32-bit unsigned integer
ServiceID	0x0003	UUID

Each Bluetooth device offering a service represents an instance of an SDP server. The `ServiceRecordHandle` identifies this `ServiceRecord` within the current instance of an SDP server. Otherwise identical service records running in different SDP instances will have different values for the `ServiceRecordHandle`.

The `ServiceClassIDList` is a list of UUIDs that represent the type of service being offered. For instance, a printing service being offered via the Serial Port profile may contain the following (16-bit) UUIDs: 0x11019 Serial Port and 0x1121 Basic Printing. The `ServiceClassIDList` must contain at least one service class UUID. We will discuss UUIDs in more detail in the next section.

The `ServiceRecordState` is used by the SDP server to maintain a cache of service attributes. The value of the `ServiceRecordState` attribute will change every time an attribute is added, deleted or changed within the service record.

The `ServiceID` is a UUID that uniquely and universally identifies the service instance being described by this record. It is particularly useful if the same service is offered by many SDP servers, but a particular instance needs to be identified.

Other useful attributes include:

Mnemonic for String ID	Attribute ID (relative)
ServiceName	0x0000
ServiceDescription	0x0001
ProviderName	0x0002

These attribute ID values must be added to the base offset (given by the `LanguageBaseAttributeIDList` with attribute ID 0x0006) which has the value of 0x0100 for the primary language.

For more information on service attributes refer to the Java Bluetooth API documentation or the SDP specification at the Bluetooth SIG (***www.bluetooth.org***).

The Java API provides methods in the `ServiceRecord` interface to set and retrieve attribute values.

```
public DataElement getAttributeValue(int attrID)
public boolean setAttributeValue(int attrID, DataElement attrValue)
```

The `getAttributeValue()` method returns the attribute specified by the `attrID` in the form of a `DataElement`. The `setAttributeValue()` method sets an attribute specified by `attrID` with a value represented by the `DataElement`, `attrValue`. To update a `ServiceRecord` already added in the SDDB we use the `updateRecord()` method of `LocalDevice`. Otherwise the `ServiceRecord` will be updated when we first add it to the SDDB (when `acceptAndOpen()` is called, see Section 4.3.1.4).

All attributes are stored in the `ServiceRecord` in the form of a `DataElement`. A `DataElement` can encapsulate data of the following types by using one of the overloaded constructors of the `DataElement` class:

- `UUID`
- `String`
- `integer`
- `boolean`
- sequences of any one of the above types.

Another useful method of `ServiceRecord` is:

```
public void setDeviceServiceClasses(int classes)
```

This is used to set the major service class in the `ServiceRecord` of this service (e.g. rendering, audio, telephony, etc.). This information is used to create a `DeviceClass` object which encapsulates information about the types of service offered by this device and is used in device inquiry to find suitable devices (see Section 4.3.2).

4.3.1.3 UUIDs

Universally Unique Identifiers (UUIDs) are 128-bit values that uniquely identify a Bluetooth service. For convenience the SDP allows the use of 16-bit or 32-bit alias ("short") UUIDs, with the Bluetooth specification providing an algorithm describing how a 16-bit or 32-bit alias can be promoted to the actual 128-bit UUID for comparison.

Every service, including generic low-level protocols and profiles, has a UUID. For regular protocols and profiles the UUIDs are pre-defined and, for convenience, are normally represented by their 16-bit (or 32-bit) aliases (see *Assigned Numbers* at ***www.bluetooth.org***). Some of the 16-bit UUIDs for Bluetooth protocols and profiles are listed below.

Protocol	UUID
L2CAP	0x0100
RFCOMM	0x0003
SDP	0x0001
OBEX	0x0008

Profile	UUID
Serial Port	0x1101
Basic Printing	0x1122
Fax	0x1111

To convert a 16-bit or 32-bit alias to the actual 128-bit UUID the following prescription is used:

```
128_bit_value = 16_bit_value * 2⁹⁶ + Bluetooth_Base_UUID
128_bit_value = 32_bit_value * 2⁹⁶ + Bluetooth_Base_UUID
```

Where the `Bluetooth_Base_UUID` has the value of:

```
0x0000000000001000800000805F9B34FB
```

However, Java developers do not have to worry about these conversions as the Java APIs for Bluetooth provide the `javax.bluetooth.UUID` class to create and manipulate UUIDs. To create an actual (long) 128-bit UUID we use the following constructor.

```
public UUID(long uuidValue)
```

The constructor takes a 16-bit or 32-bit alias as the `uuidValue` argument and returns a `UUID` instance representing the 128-bit value.

We can also create UUID instances from a `String` representing a 16-bit or 32-bit alias using an alternative constructor:

```
public UUID(String uuidValue, boolean shortUUID)
```

If `shortUUID` is `true`, the constructor will create an instance representing a 16- or 32-bit UUID depending on the length of the `String` representation of the UUID alias passed in as `uuidValue` (i.e. four characters for a 16-bit alias or eight characters for a 32-bit alias). If `shortUUID` is `false` then a 128-bit UUID will be returned, provided a 32 character `String` representation of a 128-bit value was passed in as `uuidValue`.

4.3.1.4 *Creating the Server*

Having introduced some of the concepts and classes necessary for registering a server, we shall now have a look at how this is realized in code using the APIs. The code for setting up a simple server to accept stream connections using the Serial Port profile is shown below.

```
private static final String uuidString =
"00112233445566778899AABBCCDDEEFF";
...
UUID uuid = new uuid(uuidString, false);
...
try {
    LocaDevice device = LocalDevice.getLocalDevice();
```

```
    //make generally discoverable
    device.setDiscoverable(DiscoveryAgent.GIAC);
    StreamConnectionNotifier service = (StreamConnectionNotifier)
          Connector.open("btspp://localhost:" +
          uuid.toString() + ";name=serialconn");

    StreamConnection conn = service.acceptAndOpen();
    InputStream input = conn.openInputStream();
    ...
    input.close();
    conn.close();
} catch(BluetoothStateException bse) {
    bse.printStackTrace();
}catch(InputOutputException ioe){
    ioe.printStackTrace();
}
```

Let's look at this code in more detail. First, we create a UUID to uniquely identify this service. Here we use a string representing a 128-bit UUID to create a UUID instance using the appropriate constructor:

```
private final String uuidString = "00112233445566778899AABBCCDDEEFF";
UUID uuid = new uuid(uuidString, false);
```

Note that we pass in false as the second argument as we are creating a long UUID. Next we use the static factory method getLocalDevice() to obtain an instance of the LocalDevice representing the host device.

```
LocaDevice device = LocalDevice.getLocalDevice();
device.setDiscoverable(DiscoveryAgent.GIAC);
```

We make the Bluetooth device discoverable using the setDiscoverable() method. The pre-defined public static final int GIAC value represents a General/Unlimited Inquiry Access Code, meaning there are no restrictions placed on which remote devices may discover the host.

To establish an RFCOMM connection using the SPP we use the open() method as follows:

```
StreamConnectionNotifier service =
      (StreamConnectionNotifier)Connector.open("btspp://localhost:" +
      uuid.toString() + ";name=serialconn");
```

The localhost identifier refers to the host device and is the RFCOMM server channel identifier. This is added to the ServiceRecord as the ProtocolDescriptorList attribute. It is also necessary to append a String representation of the UUID. This is added to the ServiceRecord in the ServiceClassIDList. An optional name for the service can also be appended to the URL which is added to the ServiceRecord as the ServiceName attribute.

The open() method returns an object of type StreamConnec-tionNotifier. Calling acceptAndOpen() on the StreamConnec-tionNotifier indicates the server is ready to accept client connections and adds the ServiceRecord to the SDDB.

```
StreamConnection conn = service.acceptAndOpen();
```

The acceptAndOpen() method blocks until the server accepts a connection request, returning a StreamConnection object to enable communication between the client and server.

4.3.2 Device Discovery

In the previous section, we saw how we can use the Java APIs to set up a server offering a Bluetooth service. In the next few sections we shall see how clients can locate and access this service. This is generally a two-stage process involving discovering active Bluetooth devices in the vicinity, then searching discovered devices for the required service. This section deals with device discovery.

Device discovery is in fact very simple. First we need to implement a DiscoveryListener. The javax.bluetooth.DiscoveryListe-ner interface mandates the four callback methods shown below.

```
public void deviceDiscovered(RemoteDevice btDevice, DeviceClass cod)
public void inquiryCompleted(int discType)
public void servicesDiscovered(int transID, ServiceRecord[] servRecord)
public void serviceSearchCompleted(int transID, int respCode)
```

To implement a device DiscoveryListener we need to provide non-trivial implementations for the first two methods.

The deviceDiscovered() method is called by the implementation when a device is discovered. It may be called many times. The implementation passes in a RemoteDevice instance representing the remote device just discovered and also a DeviceClass instance that provides information about the type of device just discovered, allowing filtering of unwanted devices.

The inquiryCompleted() method is called by the implementation when the device inquiry has completed. discType can have one of three values predefined in the DiscoveryListener interface:

- public static int INQUIRY_COMPLETED – which indicates that the inquiry terminated normally

- public static int INQUIRY_TERMINATED – which indicates that the inquiry was terminated by the application (via the can-celInquiry() method of DiscoveryAgent)

- `public static int INQUIRY_ERROR` – which indicates that the inquiry failed to complete normally, but was not terminated.

To initiate a device inquiry we need to obtain a `DiscoveryAgent` using the `getDiscoveryAgent()` method of the `LocalDevice` and invoke the following method on it:

```
public boolean startInquiry(int accessCode, DiscoveryListener listener)
```

The `startInquiry()` method takes an appropriately implemented `DiscoveryListener` and also an `accessCode` that can have one of two values pre-defined in the `DiscoveryAgent` class.

```
public static final GIAC
public static final LIAC
```

The General/Unlimited Inquiry Access Code (`GIAC`) indicates an unlimited search returning all devices found in the vicinity. Using the Limited Dedicated Inquiry Access Code (`LIAC`) discovers only remote devices in LIAC mode. Both values are defined in the Bluetooth GAP specification (***www.bluetooth.org***). Use `GIAC` for general inquiries.

We shall illustrate the APIs just discussed with a concrete example:

```
import java.io.*;
import javax.bluetooth.*;
import java.util.*;
public class DeviceDiscoverer implements DiscoveryListener {
    private BluetoothUI btUI;
    public Vector remoteDevices = new Vector();
    private LocalDevice localDevice;
    private DiscoveryAgent agent;

    public DeviceDiscoverer(BluetoothUI btUI) {
        this.btUI = btUI;

        try {
            localDevice = LocalDevice.getLocalDevice();
        }
        catch(BluetoothStateException bse){ //handle}
        agent = localDevice.getDiscoveryAgent();
    }

    public void startDeviceSearch() {
        try {
            agent.startInquiry(DiscoveryAgent.GIAC, this);
        } catch(BluetoothStateException bse){ //handle}
    }

    public void servicesDiscovered(int transID, ServiceRecord[] servRecord){}

    public void serviceSearchCompleted(int transID, int respCode) {}
```

```java
public void deviceDiscovered(RemoteDevice btDevice, DeviceClass cod) {
    // The major device class of 0x600 is an imaging device
    if ((cod.getMajorDeviceClass() == 0x600) {
        // The minor device class of 0x80 is a printer
        if ((cod.getMinorDeviceClass() & 0x80) != 0) {
            // The service class of 0x40000 is a rendering service
            if ((cod.getServiceClasses() & 0x40000) != 0) {
                remoteDevices.addElement(btDevice);
            }
        }
    }
}

public void inquiryCompleted(int discType) {
    if(discType == DiscoveryListener.INQUIRY_COMPLETED) {
        btUI.displayDevices(remoteDevices);
    }
    else{
        //take appropriate action
    }
}
}
```

Our `DeviceDiscoverer` class implements the `DiscoveryLis-tener` interface. We obtain a `LocalDevice` instance and use that to get a `DiscoveryAgent`, with which we start an inquiry using the general discoverable mode:

```java
public void startDeviceSearch() {
    try {
        agent.startInquiry(DiscoveryAgent.GIAC, this);
    } catch(BluetoothStateException bse) {//handle}
}
```

Note that the `startInquiry()` method is non-blocking.

Every time a device is discovered the `deviceDiscovered()` method is called. There may be many devices in range and we may not be interested in them all so we can use the `cod` value to filter out unwanted devices (as shown below).

```java
public void deviceDiscovered(RemoteDevice btDevice, DeviceClass cod) {
    // The major device class of 0x600 is an imaging device
    if ((cod.getMajorDeviceClass() == 0x600) {
        // The minor device class of 0x80 is a printer
        if ((cod.getMinorDeviceClass() & 0x80) != 0) {
            // The service class of 0x40000 is a rendering service
            if ((cod.getServiceClasses() & 0x40000) != 0) {
                remoteDevices.addElement(btDevice);
            }
        }
    }
}
```

The DeviceClass provides an abstraction of the Class of Device/Service (CoD) record, as defined in the Bluetooth specification *Assigned Numbers* document (***https://www.bluetooth.org/foundry/assignnumb/document/baseband***). The CoD record is a 24-bit number, formatted as shown in Figure 4.2.

Note that CoD records and the associated service class and device class values are unrelated to service UUIDs. CoDs classify the device (printer, phone, etc.), whereas UUIDs specify the service that may be offered by a device.

The getMajorDevice() method returns the major device class value. A device may have only one value for the major device class. For imaging, the bits are set in the CoD record representing a value of 0x600 (see Figure 4.3).

A device can have several values for the minor device class. So we use the printer bit mask to do an AND with the value returned by getMinorDevice and check the result is non-zero (see Figure 4.4).

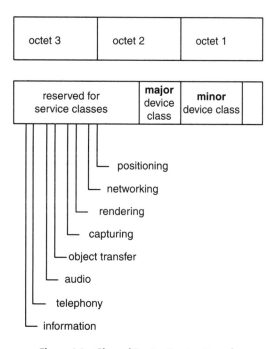

Figure 4.2   Class of Device/Service Record.

	12	11	10	9	8
	0	0	1	1	0

Figure 4.3   Major device bit values for imaging.

7	6	5	4
1	x	x	x

Figure 4.4 Minor device class bit mask for a printer.

Similarly, the major service class can have multiple values so we check that the rendering bit (bit 18) has been set. A device that has passed through all the filters is then added to the `remoteDevices Vector`.

When the inquiry is finished, the `inquiryCompleted()` method is called.

```
public void inquiryCompleted(int discType) {
    if(discType == DiscoveryListener.INQUIRY_COMPLETED) {
        btUI.displayDevices(remoteDevices);
    }
    else{
        //take appropriate action
    }
}
```

Assuming the inquiry completed successfully, we return our filtered `remoteDevices Vector` for further processing.

4.3.3 Service Discovery

Once we have located suitable devices in the vicinity we can search them for the required service. The process is similar to that for device inquiry. First we implement a service search `DiscoveryListener`. This requires supplying non-trivial implementations for the following methods:

```
public void servicesDiscovered(int transID, ServiceRecord[] servRecord)
public void serviceSearchCompleted(int transID, int respCode)
```

The `servicesDiscovered()` method is invoked by the implementation when the requested services are discovered. The implementation provides a transaction ID identifying the request that initiated the service search and an array of `ServiceRecords`, each identifying a service discovered in response to the request.

The `serviceSearchCompleted()` method is invoked by the implementation when a service search is completed or terminates. As well as the transaction ID, the implementation also supplies a `public static final int` code with the following values defined in the `DiscoveryListener` interface:

• `SERVICE_SEARCH_COMPLETED` indicates that the search completed normally

- `SERVICE_SEARCH_TERMINATED` means that the service search was terminated by the application calling the `DiscoveryAgent` `cancelServiceSearch()` method

- `SERVICE_SEARCH_ERROR` indicates the service search terminated with an error

- `SERVICE_SEARCH_NO_RECORDS` indicates that the remote device being searched holds no service records

- `SERVICE_SEARCH_NOT_REACHABLE` indicates that the remote device to be searched is not reachable (not in range anymore).

Before we can start a service search we have to get an instance of the `LocalDevice` and use it to obtain a `DiscoveryAgent` as before. To request a search we then invoke the following method on the `DiscoveryAgent`:

```
public int searchServices(int[] attrSet, UUID[] uuidSet, RemoteDevice btDev,
    DiscoveryListener discListener)
```

We have to pass in the `RemoteDevice` we wish to search (which we have retrieved previously from a device inquiry) and an appropriately implemented `DiscoveryListener`. We must also pass in an array of UUIDs corresponding to those offered by the service required. Note that for a successful service search the UUIDs contained in the `UUID[]` argument must match those contained in the `ServiceClassIDList` attribute of the `ServiceRecord` in the SDDB running on the remote device. Hence, we must know in advance the UUIDs of the service we are searching for.

We also pass in an array corresponding to the attributes we want to retrieve from the `ServiceRecord` of the service found. If `attrSet` is `null` a default list of attributes will be retrieved (`ServiceRecordHandle`, `ServiceClassIDList`, `ServiceRecordState`, `ServiceID` and `ProtocolDescriptorList`, with attribute IDs 0x0000 to 0x0004).

The integer value returned by the `searchServices()` method, corresponding to the transaction ID, can be used later to cancel the search if required. Note that `searchServices` is a non-blocking method.

Let's see how this all fits together in practice. The `ServiceDiscoverer` class listed below implements a `DiscoveryListener` for service search:

```
import javax.bluetooth.*;
import java.io.*;
public class ServiceDiscoverer implements DiscoveryListener {
    private BluetoothUI btUI;
    private LocalDevice localDevice;
```

```java
private DiscoveryAgent agent;
private ServiceRecord[] serviceRecord;

public ServiceDiscoverer(BluetoothUI btUI) {
    this.btUI = btUI;

    try {
        localDevice = LocalDevice.getLocalDevice();
    }
    catch(BluetoothStateException bse){ //handle }

    agent = localDevice.getDiscoveryAgent();
}

public void startServiceSearch(RemoteDevice btDevice) {
    UUID[] uuidSet = {new UUID("00112233445566778899AABBCCDDEEFF",
            false)};
    try {
        agent.searchServices(null, uuidSet, btDevice, this);
    }
    catch(BluetoothStateException bse) { //handle }
}

public void servicesDiscovered(int transID,
        ServiceRecord[] servRecord) {
    serviceRecord = servRecord;
}

public void serviceSearchCompleted(int transID, int respCode) {
    String message = null;
    if(respCode ==
            DiscoveryListener.SERVICE_SEARCH_DEVICE_NOT_REACHABLE) {
        message = "Device not reachable";
    } else if(respCode ==
            DiscoveryListener.SERVICE_SEARCH_NO_RECORDS) {
        message = "Service not available";
    } else if (respCode ==
            DiscoveryListener.SERVICE_SEARCH_COMPLETED) {
        message = "Service search completed";
        if (serviceRecord[0] != null) {
            btUI.serviceFound(serviceRecord);
        }
    } else if(respCode ==
            DiscoveryListener.SERVICE_SEARCH_TERMINATED) {
        message = "Service search terminated";
    } else if(respCode == DiscoveryListener.SERVICE_SEARCH_ERROR)
        message = "Service search error";
    }
    btUI.setStatus(message);
}

public void inquiryCompleted(int discType){}

public void deviceDiscovered(RemoteDevice btDevice, DeviceClass cod){}
}
```

Let's look at the code above in more detail. First, we obtain a
DiscoveryAgent and use it to start a service search, as follows.

```
public void startServiceSearch(RemoteDevice btDevice) {
    UUID[] uuidSet = {new UUID("00112233445566778899AABBCCDDEEFF", false)};
    try {
        agent.searchServices(null, uuidSet, btDevice, this);
    } catch(BluetoothStateException bse) { //handle }
}
```

We create a long representation of the UUID of the service for which we are searching, which in this is example is the single element in our UUID[] uuidSet. In this example, the default attribute set of the service record will suffice, so we pass in null for the attrSet argument.

If the required service is found, the servicesDiscovered() method will be invoked by the implementation and we cache the service records for all services offered by the device that correspond to our requirements. In the case of a search for generic services, such as SPP, there may be more than one instance offered by the device.

```
public void servicesDiscovered(int transID, ServiceRecord[] servRecord) {
    serviceRecord = servRecord;
}
```

When the service search is complete (whether successful or not) the searchCompleted() method is invoked. We can interrogate the respCode value to ascertain the success of search, as shown below.

```
public void serviceSearchCompleted(int transID, int respCode) {
String message = null;
if(respCode == DiscoveryListener.SERVICE_SEARCH_DEVICE_NOT_REACHABLE) {
        message = "Device not reachable";
    } else if(respCode == DiscoveryListener.SERVICE_SEARCH_NO_RECORDS) {
        message = "Service not available";
    } else if (respCode == DiscoveryListener.SERVICE_SEARCH_COMPLETED) {
        message = "Service search completed";
        if (serviceRecord[0] != null) {
            btUI.serviceFound(serviceRecord);
        }
    } else if(respCode == DiscoveryListener.SERVICE_SEARCH_TERMINATED)
        message = "Service search terminated";
    } else if(respCode == DiscoveryListener.SERVICE_SEARCH_ERROR) {
        message = "Service search error";
    }
    btUI.setStatus(message);
}
```

Assuming we successfully discovered our service, we pass on its ServiceRecord[] to enable a connection to be established with it.

4.3.4 Connecting to a Service

Once we have obtained the service record relating to our required service we have everything we need to connect to the service. We use the `getConnectionURL()` method of the `ServiceRecord` to obtain a `String` encapsulating the necessary information (protocol, Bluetooth address of device providing the service, RFCOMM server channel identifier, etc.) to connect to the service.

```
public String getConnectionURL(int requiredSecurity, boolean mustBeMaster)
```

The `requiredSecurity` argument specifies the level of security for the connection and can have one of three values defined in `ServiceRecord`:

```
public static final int NOAUTHENTICATE_NOENCRYPT
public static final int AUTHENTICATE_NOENCRYPT
public static final int AUTHENTICATE_ENCRYPT
```

The `mustBeMaster` argument indicates whether the local device must be master in connections to this service. If `false` the local device is willing to be master or slave in the relationship. The **master–slave** role relates to the frequency hopping pattern used in RF communications between two Bluetooth devices. The master device initiates the connection and determines the frequency hopping pattern used. The slaves hop in unison to the master's pattern. The role (master or slave) that a device assumes relates to low-level communication and is generally irrelevant to higher level protocols. The current implementation of JSR 82 on Symbian OS supports only a value of `false` for the `mustBeMaster` parameter (`true` will result in an exception being thrown by the `open()` method).

Once we have the connection URL we use it to open a `Connection`. In the case of connections using the SPP, the returned object is cast as a `StreamConnection`, as shown below.

```
String url =
   serviceRecord.getConnectionURL(ServiceRecord. NOAUTHENTICATE_NOENCRYPT,
      false);
StreamConnection conn = (StreamConnection)Connector.open(url);
OutputStream output = conn.openOutputStream();
```

4.3.5 Connecting to a Service: the Quick and Dirty Way

In the previous section we described how to access services robustly. We do a device enquiry then search the returned devices for the required services and, if found, open a connection using the returned `ServiceRecord`.

There is an alternative, quicker way of connecting to a service using the `selectService()` method of the `DiscoveryAgent` class:

```
public String selectService(UUID uuid, int security, boolean master)
```

This method simply takes the `UUID` of the service required; an `int` indicating the level of security for the connection; and the master/slave `boolean` indicator. The method will search for the service denoted by the `UUID` on any devices in range. If the service is found, a `String` representing the URL to be used to connect to the service via the `open()` method is returned. If no service is found a value of `null` is returned.

Note that when using this method it is not necessary to implement a `DiscoveryListener`. Nor does it require a `RemoteDevice` object to be specified. It simply searches all devices in the vicinity and, if one of them offers the required service, returns a connection URL. If there are many devices in the area offering the required service, a connection URL may be returned to any one of them (it is not possible to specify which). For these reasons, plus the fact that this method takes only a single UUID, it is best used to search for specific UUIDs created to denote a specific service (rather than pre-defined UUIDs representing generic services such as the SPP, which may be offered by many devices).

4.3.6   Retrieving a Cached Device

Before we leave this section we should discuss one other relevant method provided by the Java APIs for Bluetooth Wireless Technology. This is the `retrieveDevices()` method of the `DiscoveryAgent` class:

```
public RemoteDevice[] retrieveDevices(int option)
```

This takes an integer `option` argument that can have one of two values pre-defined in the `DiscoveryAgent` class:

```
public static final int CACHED
public static final int PREKNOWN
```

- `CACHED` means that the method will return an array of `RemoteDevices` that have been discovered by previous inquiries and cached by the implementation; if no devices have been cached, a `null` value will be returned

- PREKNOWN indicates a higher level of intimacy, referring to devices that the local device communicates with often ("paired devices"); the current implementation of JSR 82 on Symbian OS does not support the PREKNOWN option, so a call to retrieveDevices using the PREKNOWN option will return null.

The retrieveDevices() method will block the current thread until it returns; it should generally be launched in a new Thread.

4.4 L2CAP Protocol

4.4.1 Introduction

The discussion in the previous sections used Serial Port profile connections running over RFCOMM to illustrate opening connections. In this section we shall look at the other connection protocol currently offered by Symbian OS, L2CAP.

RFCOMM is a higher-level protocol that runs on top of L2CAP. Unlike SPP over RFCOMM, which is a stream-based protocol, L2CAP is packet-based. This makes it more suitable for certain types of non-stream communication, particularly those that route individual packets to different destinations, methods or classes. In addition, a lower level, datagram-like protocol such as L2CAP can confer performance advantages over RFCOMM by avoiding the latency and overheads involved in establishing and maintaining a stream connection.

4.4.2 Maximum Transmission Unit

Remember that L2CAP is a packet-based protocol. The maximum transmission unit (MTU) is the maximum size of a packet of data that can be sent over the L2CAP link. By default this size is set to 672 bytes. However, the Java API does give us the option to specify different values as part of the connection URL passed into the open() method (as will seen in later sections). MTUs can be specified for transmitting and receiving data. Specifying MTU values when opening a connection does not mean that communication (whether sending or receiving) will take place at that value. Instead, when a connection between a client and server is opened, a negotiation takes place to agree on acceptable MTUs for communications in both directions. The agreed MTU will be the lowest common denominator value that both parties can handle. For instance, if a server can transmit a packet size of 4096 bytes but the client can only receive a maximum packet size of 512 bytes, then the negotiated MTU will be 512 bytes.

It is possible to find out the maximum ReceiveMTU that the local device will support using the following code:

```
localDevice.getProperty("bluetooth.l2cap.receiveMTU.max");
```

On Symbian OS Version 7.0s, the maximum values for TransmitMTU and ReceiveMTU are both 672 bytes (the default values). We can also find out the negotiated values for ReceiveMTU and TransmitMTU using the following methods of L2CAPConnection:

```
public int getTransmitMTU()
public int getReceiveMTU()
```

For a more detailed discussion of MTUs see the JSR 82 specification.

4.4.3   Setting up an L2CAP Server

Setting up a server for L2CAP is very similar to our earlier example using the SPP, except that an L2CAPConnection is opened in response to incoming client requests.

```
L2CAPConnectionNotifier notifier =
        (L2CAPConnectionNotifier)Connector.open(url);
L2CAPConnection conn = notifier.acceptAndOpen();
```

Here url may have the following form:

```
"btl2cap://localhost:00112233445566778899AABBCCDDEEFF;name=l2capServer"
```

The name=l2capServer field is optional. Other optional fields include ReceiveMTU and TransmitMTU (see the JSR 82 specification for a full list of options). The open() method returns an instance of L2CAPConnectionNotifier. Calling the acceptAndOpen() method on the L2CAPConnectionNotifier object indicates the server is ready to accept client connections. It also adds the ServiceRecord to the SDDB. The acceptAndOpen() method blocks until the server accepts a connection request, returning an L2CAPConnection object enabling communication to take place.

4.4.4   Establishing a Client Connection

To obtain a connection to an L2CAP server, the process is very similar to that presented in earlier discussions using RFCOMM. We can use a ServiceRecord obtained by a service search to get the connection URL via the getConnectionURL() method. We then use this in the open() method to obtain an L2CAPConnection, as shown below.

```
String url =
        serviceRecord.getConnectionURL(ServiceRecord.NOAUTHENTICATE_NOENCRYPT,
        false);
L2CAPConnection conn = (L2CAPConnection)Connector.open(url);
```

The url will have the general form:

```
"btl2cap://0050CD00321B:1001;ReceiveMTU=512;TransmitMTU=512"
```

Where 0050CD00321B is the Bluetooth address of the server and 1001 is the Protocol Service Multiplexor value for the service which identifies the L2CAP service running on the device and allows the client to connect to the service.

Again, there are various possible options for the url (check out the JSR 82 specification for more details). Note that if we wish to change the ReceiveMTU or TransmitMTU we would have to edit the connection URL before passing it to the open() method.

Once we have obtained an L2CAPConnection we send a packet using the send() method, where byte[] data contains the packet to be sent:

```
public void send(byte[] data)
```

The size of data can have any value. However, if it exceeds the value of TransmitMTU, any additional data will be discarded.

To read a packet of data from an L2CAPConnection we call:

```
public int receive(byte[] inBuf)
```

The packet will be read into the inBuf byte array. The size of inBuf should at least be equal to ReceiveMTU to avoid loss of data. L2CAPConnection also provides the ready() method:

```
public boolean ready()
```

If ready() returns true, a packet of data is available to be received and we can call receive without blocking.

4.5 Security

Security is an important aspect of Bluetooth communication. JSR 82 provides various security options to prevent unauthorized access to a Bluetooth device and to provide secure communication between devices using data encryption.

4.5.1 Authentication

Authentication refers to the process of verifying the identity of a remote device. The authentication mechanism in Bluetooth is based on a PIN number shared between devices.

A Bluetooth server can require client authentication by adding the optional `authenticate=true` parameter to the connection URL, as shown below.

```
String url =
    "btspp://localhost:000011112222333344445555566667777;authenticate=true"
StreamConnectionNotifier service =
        (StreamConnectionNotifier)Connector.open(url);
```

Similarly, clients can request server authentication in the connection URL. In the absence of the `authenticate=true` parameter, either client or server can, at any time after establishing an connection, request remote device authentication via the `authenticate()` method of `RemoteDevice`.

On Symbian OS, if authentication of a remote device is requested the system will display a pop-up dialog on the local device requesting the user to enter a PIN number (see Figure 4.5) that is shared with the

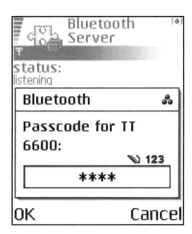

Figure 4.5 Bluetooth authentication on the Nokia 6600.

user of the remote device. The remote device will prompt its user for the shared PIN, and only if the PIN codes on both devices match will the authentication process succeed. Note that the PIN number itself is not transmitted between devices, instead a 128-bit key derived from the PIN number is used.

A device may determine if a remote device has been authenticated by invoking the `isAuthenticated()` method of `RemoteDevice`. A return value of `true` indicates that the remote device has previously been authenticated. Note that authentication is not specific to a particular connection. The remote device may have been authenticated by a previous connection or even another application.

4.5.2   Authorization

Bluetooth authorization is the process by which a server device grants a specific client access to a specific service it offers. A server can require that clients be authorized by adding the `authorize=true` parameter to the connection URL. Note that authorization also requires authentication so some parameter combinations (e.g. `authenticate=false;authorize=true`) are forbidden and will result in a `BluetoothConnectionException`.

If authorization was not requested in the connection URL, the server can request client authorization via the `authorize()` method of the `RemoteDevice`.

On Symbian OS, dynamic authorization is granted to a specific remote device by the user for each connection request. A dialog box prompts the user to accept or reject the connection (see Figure 4.6).

In addition, current Symbian OS devices allow static authorization by the user of a **paired** remote device via the system Bluetooth control panel

Figure 4.6   Bluetooth authorization on the Nokia 6600.

(the BCC, in JSR terminology). The remote device becomes trusted and all incoming connections from it are authorized until the static authorization is revoked via the Bluetooth control panel.

A server device can determine if a remote device has previously been authorized by invoking the `isAuthorized()` method of the `RemoteDevice`. A return value of `true` indicates the server side connection to the remote device has been authorized.

4.5.3   Encryption

Encryption is used in Bluetooth communication to protect sensitive data from eavesdropping. Either client or server can require that a connection is encrypted by adding the `encrypt=true` parameter to the connection URL. Note that encryption requires the previous authentication of the remote device so some parameter combinations (e.g. `authenticate=false;encrypt=true`) are forbidden and will result in a `BluetoothConnectionException`.

After establishing an unencrypted connection, it is possible to require further communication to be encrypted by using the `encrypt()` method of the `RemoteDevice`. Encryption is performed transparently by the implementation using a symmetric encryption algorithm.

A device can determine whether communication with a remote device is currently encrypted by invoking the `isEncrypted()` method of the `RemoteDevice`. A return value of `true` indicates that data exchange with the remote device is encrypted. Note that encryption of the data link with a remote device is not specific to a particular connection and may have enabled by a previous connection or even application.

4.6   Java Bluetooth API and the MIDP 2.0 Security Model

A signed MIDlet suite which contains MIDlets that open Bluetooth connections must explicitly request the appropriate permission in its `MIDlet-Permissions` attribute. To make outgoing (client) connections the MIDlet suite must request the `javax.microedition.io.Connector.bluetooth.client` permission. To accept incoming (server) connections the MIDlet suite must request the `javax.microedition.io.Connector.bluetooth.server` permission. For example, the `MIDlet-Permissions` attribute entry in the JAD file may be as follows.

```
MIDlet-Permissions: javax.microedition.io.Connector.bluetooth.client,
        javax.microedition.io.Connector.bluetooth.server
```

If the protection domain to which the signed MIDlet suite would be bound grants, or potentially grants, the requested permissions, the MIDlet suite can be installed and the MIDlets it contains will be able to open

Bluetooth client and server connections, either automatically or with explicit user permission, depending upon the security policy in effect.

The Bluetooth protected APIs form part of the Local Connectivity function group as defined in the *Recommended Security Policy for GSM/UMTS Compliant Devices* addendum to the MIDP 2.0 specification. The Sony Ericsson P900/P908 supports the trusted protection domain (on Organiser firmware versions R2B02 or later). The security policy in effect for MIDlets in MIDlet suites bound to the trusted protection domain on the P900/P908 allows automatic access to the Local Connectivity function group. At the time of writing, the available firmware release (3.42.1) on the Nokia 6600 only supports the untrusted domain, although future releases will add support for trusted protection domains.

Whether MIDlets in untrusted MIDlet suites can open Bluetooth connections depends on the security policy relating to the Local Connectivity function group for the untrusted domain in force on the device. On the Nokia 6600 and the Sony Ericsson P900/P908, untrusted MIDlets can access these APIs with User permission, the default being session. On the Nokia 6600, the user can change the default setting for this function group to *Blanket* (every invocation succeeds) or to disallow access altogether.

4.7   Sample Code

In this section we shall consider a small peer-to-peer application that transmits an image between two Bluetooth devices using the Serial Port profile over RFCOMM. First we consider a MIDlet that offers a service to receive and display an image. The classes making up the BT Demo Server MIDlet are depicted in Figure 4.7.

Figure 4.7   A UML class diagram of the BT Demo Server MIDlet.

The BTDemoServer code is listed below.

```
import javax.microedition.midlet.*;
import javax.microedition.lcdui.*;
import javax.microedition.io.*;
import javax.bluetooth.*;
import java.io.*;
public class BTDemoServer extends MIDlet implements CommandListener,
        Runnable {

   private static final int IMAGE_SIZE = 11222;

   private ImageCanvas canvas;
```

```
private Display display;
private Form displayForm;
private StringItem status = new StringItem("status: ", "Off");
private Command exitCommand = new Command("Exit", Command.EXIT, 1);
private Command startCommand = new Command("Start", Command.SCREEN,
    1);
private Command stopCommand = new Command("Stop", Command.SCREEN, 1);
private Command clearCommand = new Command("Clear", Command.SCREEN,
    1);

private final String uuid = "00112233445566778899AABBCCDDEEFF";
private LocalDevice device;
private byte[] data;
private boolean running = false;
private StreamConnection conn;

public BTDemoServer() {
    data = new byte[IMAGE_SIZE];
    display = Display.getDisplay(this);
}

public void commandAction(Command c, Displayable d) {
    if (c == exitCommand) {
        destroyApp(true);
        notifyDestroyed();
    } else if (c == startCommand) {
        running = true;
        startServer();
        displayForm.removeCommand(startCommand);
        displayForm.removeCommand(exitCommand);
        displayForm.addCommand(stopCommand);
        status.setText("listening");
    } else if (c == stopCommand) {
        running = false;
        displayForm.addCommand(exitCommand);
        displayForm.addCommand(startCommand);
        displayForm.removeCommand(stopCommand);
        status.setText("Off");
    } else if (c == clearCommand) {
        display.setCurrent(displayForm);
        canvas.removeCommand(clearCommand);
        canvas.setCommandListener(null);
        canvas = null;
    }
}

public void startApp() {
    displayForm = new Form("Bluetooth Server");
    displayForm.setCommandListener(this);
    displayForm.addCommand(exitCommand);
    displayForm.addCommand(startCommand);
    display.setCurrent(displayForm);
    displayForm.append(status);
}

public void startServer() {
    try {
        device = LocalDevice.getLocalDevice();
```

```
                device.setDiscoverable(DiscoveryAgent.GIAC);
                Thread btServer = new Thread(this);
                btServer.start();
        } catch(BluetoothStateException bse) {
            status.setText("BSException: " + bse.toString());
        }
    }

    public void run() {
        try {
            StreamConnectionNotifier notifier =
              (StreamConnectionNotifier)Connector.open("btspp://localhost:"
                    + uuid + ";name=serialconn");
            ServiceRecord record = device.getRecord(notifier);
            record.setDeviceServiceClasses(0x40000);//SERVICE_RENDERING

            while (running) {
                conn = notifier.acceptAndOpen();
                //record is saved to the SDDB on this call
                DataInputStream input = conn.openDataInputStream();
                input.readFully(data);
                input.close();

                DataOutputStream output = conn.openDataOutputStream();
                output.writeInt(-1);
                output.flush();
                output.close();
                conn.close();
                conn = null;

                Image image = Image.createImage(data, 0, IMAGE_SIZE);
                canvas = new ImageCanvas(image);
                canvas.addCommand(clearCommand);
                canvas.setCommandListener(this);
                display.setCurrent(canvas);
            }

        } catch(IOException ioe) {
            status.setText("IOException " + ioe.toString());
        } catch(Exception e) {
            status.setText("Exception: " + e.toString());
        }
    }

    public void destroyApp(boolean unconditionally) {
        try{
            if(conn != null)
                conn.close();
        }catch(IOException ioe){
            status.setText("IOException: " + ioe.toString());
        }
    }

    public void pauseApp() {
    }
}
```

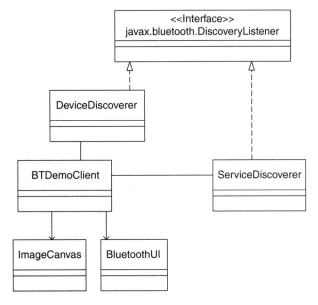

Figure 4.8 A UML class diagram of the BT Demo Client MIDlet.

Here we use a specific UUID of 00112233445566778899AABBC-
CDDEEFF to uniquely represent our service. In the run() method, we
launch the server in a new Thread listening for incoming connections.
When a remote device connects to the service an InputStream is
opened to read the data, then an Image is constructed from the data
and displayed.

The classes that make up the BT Demo Client MIDlet are depicted in
Figure 4.8.

The BTDemoClient class is listed below and acts as the controller for
the client MIDlet.

```java
import javax.microedition.midlet.*;
import javax.microedition.lcdui.*;
import javax.microedition.io.*;
import javax.bluetooth.*;
import java.io.*;
public class BTDemoClient extends MIDlet implements CommandListener {

    private static final String IMAGE_NAME = "/image.png";
    private static final int IMAGE_SIZE = 11222;
    private byte[] imageData;

    private Display display;
    private Command exitCommand = new Command("Exit", Command.EXIT, 1);
    private Command startCommand = new Command("Start", Command.SCREEN,
            1);
    private Command sendCommand = new Command("Send", Command.SCREEN, 1);
```

```java
private ImageCanvas imageCanvas;
private BluetoothUI btUI;

private DeviceDiscoverer deviceDiscoverer;
private ServiceDiscoverer serviceDiscoverer;
private RemoteDevice[] remoteDevices;
private ServiceRecord serviceRecord;
private StreamConnection conn;

public BTDemoClient() {
    display = Display.getDisplay(this);
    imageData = loadImage(IMAGE_NAME, IMAGE_SIZE);
    Image image = Image.createImage(imageData, 0, imageData.length);
    imageCanvas = new ImageCanvas(image);
    imageCanvas.addCommand(startCommand);
    imageCanvas.setCommandListener(this);
    btUI = new BluetoothUI();
    deviceDiscoverer = new DeviceDiscoverer(this);
    serviceDiscoverer = new ServiceDiscoverer(this);
}

public byte[] loadImage(String imageName, int imageSize) {
    byte[] data = new byte[imageSize];
    try {
        Class c = this.getClass() ;
        InputStream is = c.getResourceAsStream(imageName);
        DataInputStream dis = new DataInputStream(is);
        dis.readFully(data);
        is.close();
    }catch(IOException ioe) {
        btUI.setStatus("IOException: " + ioe.toString());
    }
    return data;
}

public void startServiceSearch(int index) {
    btUI.setStatus("Starting service search");
    serviceDiscoverer.startServiceSearch(remoteDevices[index]);
}

//Called from ServiceDiscoverer.serviceSearchCompleted
// when service search is complete.
public void searchCompleted(ServiceRecord servRecord,
        String message) {
    this.serviceRecord = servRecord;
    //cache the service record for future use
    btUI.setStatus(message);
    new Thread() {
        public void run() {
            sendImage(serviceRecord);
        }
    }.start();
}

//Called from ServiceDiscoverer.inqiryCompleted
// when device inquiry is complete.
public void inquiryCompleted(RemoteDevice[] devices, String message) {
```

```
        this.remoteDevices = devices;
        String[] names = new String[devices.length];

        for(int i = 0; i < devices.length; i++) {
            try {
                String name = devices[i].getFriendlyName(false);
                names[i] = name;
            }catch(IOException ioe){
                btUI.setStatus("IOException: " + ioe.toString());
            }
        }

        btUI.populateList(names);
        btUI.addCommand(sendCommand);
        btUI.setStatus(message);
}

public void sendImage(ServiceRecord serviceRecord) {
    try {
        String url =
serviceRecord.getConnectionURL(ServiceRecord.NOAUTHENTICATE_NOENCRYPT,
                false);
        conn = (StreamConnection)Connector.open(url);
        DataOutputStream dataOutputStream =
                conn.openDataOutputStream();

        btUI.setStatus("connected");
        dataOutputStream.write(imageData);
        dataOutputStream.flush();
        dataOutputStream.close();

        DataInputStream dataInputStream = conn.openDataInputStream();
        int eof = dataInputStream.readInt();
        if(eof == -1) {
            dataInputStream.close();
            conn.close();
            conn = null;
            btUI.setStatus("closed connection");
        }
    } catch(IOException ioe) {
        btUI.setStatus("IOException: " + ioe.toString());
    }
}

public void commandAction(Command c, Displayable d) {
    if (c == exitCommand) {
        destroyApp(true);
    notifyDestroyed();
    } else if (c == startCommand) {
        imageCanvas.removeCommand(exitCommand);
        imageCanvas.removeCommand(startCommand);
        imageCanvas.setCommandListener(null);
        btUI.addCommand(exitCommand);
        btUI.setCommandListener(this);
        display.setCurrent(btUI);
        deviceDiscoverer.startDeviceSearch();
        btUI.setStatus("Searching for Bluetooth devices");
    } else if (c == sendCommand) {
```

```
                    int index = btUI.getSelectedDevice();
                    startServiceSearch(index);
                    btUI.removeCommand(sendCommand);
            }
    }

    public void startApp() {
        display.setCurrent(imageCanvas);
    }

    public void destroyApp(boolean unconditionally) {
        try {
            if(conn != null)
                conn.close();
        }catch(IOException ioe) {
            btUI.setStatus("IOException: " + ioe.toString());
        }
    }

    public void pauseApp() {
    }

}
```

The class creates the `Image` from a resource file and displays it in a `Canvas`. Selecting the Start command starts a device inquiry using the `DeviceDiscoverer` class, listed below.

```
import javax.bluetooth.*;
import java.util.*;
public class DeviceDiscoverer implements DiscoveryListener {

    private BTDemoClient btClient;
    private Vector remoteDevices = new Vector();
    private DiscoveryAgent agent;

    public DeviceDiscoverer(BTDemoClient btClient) {
        this.btClient = btClient;
        try {
            LocalDevice localDevice = LocalDevice.getLocalDevice();
            agent = localDevice.getDiscoveryAgent();
        }
        catch(BluetoothStateException bse) {
            bse.printStackTrace();
        }
    }

    public void startDeviceSearch() {
        try {
            agent.startInquiry(DiscoveryAgent.GIAC, this); //non-blocking
        }
        catch(BluetoothStateException bse){
            bse.printStackTrace();
        }
    }
```

```
public void servicesDiscovered(int transID,
        ServiceRecord[] servRecord){}

public void serviceSearchCompleted(int transID, int respCode) {}

public void deviceDiscovered(RemoteDevice btDevice, DeviceClass cod) {
    // The minor device class of 0x40000 is a rendering service
    if ((cod.getServiceClasses() & 0x40000) != 0)
        remoteDevices.addElement(btDevice);
}

public void inquiryCompleted(int discType) {
    String message = null;
    RemoteDevice[] devices = null;

    if (discType == INQUIRY_COMPLETED) {
        message = "Inquiry completed";
        devices = new RemoteDevice[remoteDevices.size()];
        for(int i = 0; i < remoteDevices.size(); i++) {
            devices[i] = (RemoteDevice)remoteDevices.elementAt(i);
        }
    } else if (discType == INQUIRY_TERMINATED) {
        message = "Inquiry terminated";
    } else if (discType == INQUIRY_ERROR) {
        message = "Inquiry error";
    }
    btClient.inquiryCompleted(devices, message);
}
}
```

The `deviceDiscovered()` method filters the device inquiry for devices of the Rendering major service class.

When the inquiry is completed the system invokes the `inquiryCompleted()` method mandated by the `DiscoveryListener` Interface. This returns control to the `BTDemoClient` instance by calling its `inquiryCompleted()` method, passing back an array of `RemoteDevices` and a message indicating the success (or otherwise) of the inquiry.

The `BTDemoClient` class then instigates a service search using the `ServiceDiscoverer` class, listed below, which also implements the `DiscoveryListener` Interface.

```
import javax.bluetooth.*;
import java.io.*;
public class ServiceDiscoverer implements DiscoveryListener {

    private static final UUID[] uuidSet =
            {new UUID("00112233445566778899AABBCCDDEEFF", false)};
    private static final String SERVICE_NAME = "serialconn";
    //return service name attribute
    private static final int[] attrSet = {0x0100};

    private BTDemoClient btClient;
```

```java
private ServiceRecord serviceRecord;
private String message;

private DiscoveryAgent agent;

public ServiceDiscoverer(BTDemoClient btClient) {
    this.btClient = btClient;
    try {
        LocalDevice localDevice = LocalDevice.getLocalDevice();
        agent = localDevice.getDiscoveryAgent();
    }
    catch(BluetoothStateException bse) {
        bse.printStackTrace();
    }
}

public void startServiceSearch(RemoteDevice remoteDevice) {
    try {
        String device = remoteDevice.getFriendlyName(true);
    }catch(IOException ioe) {
        ioe.printStackTrace();
    }

    try {
        //non-blocking
        agent.searchServices(attrSet, uuidSet, remoteDevice, this);
    } catch(BluetoothStateException bse) {
        bse.printStackTrace();
    }
}

public void servicesDiscovered(int transID,
        ServiceRecord[] servRecord) {

    for(int i = 0; i < servRecord.length; i++) {
        DataElement serviceNameElement =
                servRecord[i].getAttributeValue(0x0100);
        //get the Service Name
        String serviceName = (String)serviceNameElement.getValue();

        if(serviceName.equals(SERVICE_NAME)){
            serviceRecord = servRecord[i];
        }
    }
}

public void serviceSearchCompleted(int transID, int respCode) {
    if (respCode ==
            DiscoveryListener.SERVICE_SEARCH_DEVICE_NOT_REACHABLE) {
        message = "Device not reachable";
    }
    else if(respCode == DiscoveryListener.SERVICE_SEARCH_NO_RECORDS) {
        message = "Service not available";
    }
    else if (respCode == DiscoveryListener.SERVICE_SEARCH_COMPLETED) {
        message = "Service search completed";
    }
```

```
        else if(respCode == DiscoveryListener.SERVICE_SEARCH_TERMINATED) {
            message = "Service search terminated";
        }
        else if (respCode == DiscoveryListener.SERVICE_SEARCH_ERROR) {
            message = "Service search error";
        }
        btClient.searchCompleted(serviceRecord, message);
    }

    public void inquiryCompleted(int discType){}

    public void deviceDiscovered(RemoteDevice btDevice, DeviceClass cod){}
}
```

When we call the following method to start the service search:

```
agent.searchServices(attrSet, uuidSet, remoteDevice, this);
```

we specify a non-null `attrSet` argument:

```
private static final int[] attrSet = {0x0100};
```

The value 0x0100 indicates the service name attribute (in the primary language) so this attribute will be retrieved from discovered service records in addition to the default attribute list. The system invokes the `servicesDiscovered()` method when a service is discovered. We filter the discovered services to find the one with name "serialconn" which is then cached.

When the service search is completed the system invokes the `serviceSearchCompleted()` method mandated by the `DiscoveryListener` Interface. This returns control to the `BTDemoClient` instance by calling its `searchCompleted()` method, passing back the cached `ServiceRecord` and a `message` reporting the success of the search.

The `BTDemoClient` can then use the discovered `ServiceRecord` to open a connection to the SPP server service using the `sendImage()` method:

```
public void sendImage(ServiceRecord serviceRecord) {
    try {
        String url = serviceRecord.getConnectionURL(
                ServiceRecord.NOAUTHENTICATE_NOENCRYPT, false);
        conn = (StreamConnection)Connector.open(url);
        DataOutputStream dataOutputStream = conn.openDataOutputStream();

        btUI.setStatus("connected");
        dataOutputStream.write(imageData);
        dataOutputStream.flush();
        dataOutputStream.close();
```

```
        DataInputStream dataInputStream = conn.openDataInputStream();
        int eof = dataInputStream.readInt();
        if(eof == -1) {
            dataInputStream.close();
            conn.close();
            conn = null;
            btUI.setStatus("closed connection");
        }
    } catch(IOException ioe) {
        btUI.setStatus("IOException: " + ioe.toString());
    }
}
```

Figure 4.9 shows screenshots from the sample application.

The full source code and JAR and JAD files for the BT Demo Server and BT Demo Client MIDlets can be downloaded from the Symbian website at *www.symbian.com/books*.

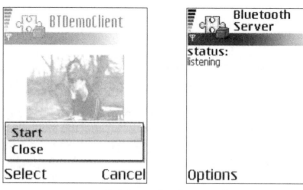

a. Before starting the search

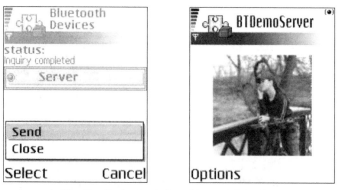

b. Sending the image to the discovered server

Figure 4.9   The Bluetooth application running on Nokia 6600 phones; the client is on the left and the server on the right.

4.8   Development Tools

In this section we shall consider some of the tools that are available to assist developers in building applications using the Java APIs for Bluetooth Wireless Technology (JSR 82). Tools for developing with JSR 82 come in two forms: those that interface to real Bluetooth devices (dongles) attached to the development platform; and those that simulate the Bluetooth hardware and interactions entirely in software. In this section we will look at tools that adopt both approaches.

4.8.1   Rococo Impronto Simulator

The Impronto Simulator from Rococo Software is an ideal way for developers new to JSR 82 to explore the APIs and for more experienced developers to produce prototypes of Java Bluetooth applications.

The Impronto Simulator runs Java Bluetooth applications in a simulated Bluetooth environment, allowing developers to easily test and configure applications before deploying them on Bluetooth devices. Since the Impronto Simulator provides total software emulation, developers can start programming JSR 82 without the hassle of acquiring and configuring multiple Bluetooth devices within their development environment.

At the time of writing, the Impronto Simulator integrates with both the Java 2 SE JDK 1.3.1 and the Java 2 ME Sun Wireless Toolkit 1.0.4 and is available for both Windows and Linux (Red Hat) platforms. The Impronto Simulator provides a virtual Bluetooth stack that processes JSR 82 API calls and routes the messages between virtual devices (such as instances of the WTK emulator) via localhost socket connections. The simulator also provides a Discovery Daemon allowing the virtual devices to locate each other. A Simulator Manager GUI allows developers to monitor the interaction of virtual devices and create and configure virtual devices non-programmatically. Figure 4.10 shows a simple Bluetooth client–server application running on Sun's Wireless Toolkit in Impronto.

The contents of the server's `ServiceRecord` are displayed in the bottom left frame of the Manager console and the control panel in the right hand frame allows the configuration of virtual devices.

For more information on the Impronto Simulator go to ***www.rococo-soft.com***.

4.8.2   Nokia Developer's Suite for J2ME 2.0

The Nokia Developer's Suite for J2ME 2.0 (NDS 2.0) is a development environment for Nokia's range of MIDP-enabled phones, including Series 60 MIDP 2.0 devices such as the Nokia 6600. Windows and Linux variants of the NDS 2.0 can be downloaded from Forum Nokia (***forum.nokia.com***). It can be integrated with industry standard IDEs

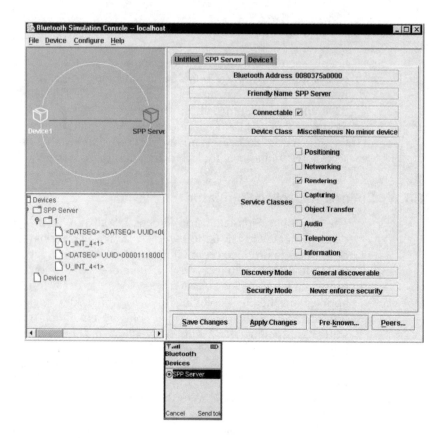

Figure 4.10   Using Impronto Simulator with Sun's Wireless Toolkit.

such as Borland's JBuilder and Sun ONE Studio Mobile Edition, or run in a standalone mode.

NDS 2.0 supports development using the Java Bluetooth APIs and takes a similar approach to Impronto Simulator in providing emulation of Bluetooth devices in software.

The default settings for Bluetooth emulation allow multiple instances of the emulator running on the same computer to communicate over the loopback address. The NDS 2.0 can also be configured to allow multiple instances of the emulator running on different host machines to communicate over UDP.

4.8.3   Symbian SDKs and Bluetooth

Both the Series 60 MIDP SDK 1.2.1 for Symbian OS, Nokia Edition and the UIQ 2.1 SDK provide implementations of the Java Bluetooth APIs. In both cases, they provide a testing environment that integrates with

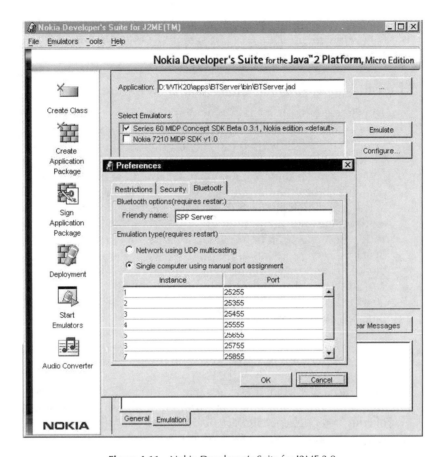

Figure 4.11 Nokia Developer's Suite for J2ME 2.0.

real Bluetooth devices rather than using software simulation as employed by the previously discussed tools. However, in each case only a limited range of Bluetooth devices is supported.

The Series 60 MIDP SDK 1.2.1 for Symbian OS, Nokia Edition is available from Forum Nokia. To use Bluetooth, the SDK should be installed on a laptop running Windows 2000. The SDK currently only supports either the Nokia Connectivity Card DTL-4 or the Socket Bluetooth CF Card. The Bluetooth card must be installed as a COM port using the Serial Communications Driver in Windows 2000 (rather than installing the proprietary drivers). For full installation instructions refer to *Setting Up and Using the Bluetooth Testing Environment for Series 60 Platform*, available from Forum Nokia.

The UIQ 2.1 SDK is available from ***www.symbian.com***. This SDK provides implementations of MIDP 2.0, WMA and the Java Bluetooth APIs. In terms of Bluetooth hardware, the UIQ 2.1 SDK currently only supports the Casira serial pod (see ***www.csr.com***). For installation and configuration instructions see the documentation that comes with the SDK, *How to configure comms settings / Configuring the UIQ emulator for Bluetooth connection.*

4.8.4 Choosing Tools for Java Bluetooth Development

The choice of tools for Java Bluetooth development falls into two categories: those that provide a virtual simulation of Bluetooth devices entirely in software; and those that provide integration with Bluetooth hardware. Currently, the support for Bluetooth hardware by developer tools is too limited to make these solutions attractive unless one already owns the particular Bluetooth device supported (particularly bearing in mind that at least two Bluetooth devices are likely to be required for any serious JSR 82 development).

The best approach at present, particularly for small third-party developers, is to employ one of the software simulation options provided by the Rococo Impronto Simulator or the Nokia Developer's Suite for J2ME 2.0, and then move straight to testing on the target phone. However, it is likely the situation will improve in the near future as the range of actual Bluetooth hardware supported by SDKs improves.

4.9 Java Bluetooth APIs and Symbian OS

At the time of writing, the latest release of Symbian OS is Version 7.0s. This is the first full release containing JSR 82 as part of Symbian's Java offering, although the UIQ 2.1 platform also offers the Java Bluetooth API as a backport to Symbian OS Version 7.0. Devices shipping with this API include Nokia 6600 (a Series 60 phone based on Symbian OS Version 7.0s) and Sony Ericsson P900 (based on UIQ 2.1).

As mentioned earlier, Version 7.0s and UIQ 2.1 implement the `javax.bluetooth` APIs but not the `javax.obex` package. Hence, Symbian OS currently provides no implementation for the Object exchange protocol (OBEX) or the related Generic Object Exchange Profile (GOEP). There is therefore no implementation for the `Connector.open(btgoep://...)` URI syntax. In addition, Bluetooth connections are not currently supported by the push registry implementation. It is intended that implementation of the `javax.obex` package will be added in future releases, along with push registry support for incoming L2CAP and RFCOMM connections.

4.10 Summary

In this chapter we have looked at programming the Java APIs for Bluetooth Wireless Technology (JSR 82). First we introduced Bluetooth as a technology and the Java APIs. Next we looked at programming these APIs: how to set up a Bluetooth Serial Port profile service over RFCOMM, discover the service and connect to it. We also looked at the equivalent procedure for establishing and connecting to L2CAP services. In the following section we discussed a simple client–server sample application, building on the material covered in the earlier sections. Finally, we reviewed some of tools available to programmers interested in working with JSR 82. In Chapter 5 we will look in depth at some MIDP case studies.

5

MIDP 2.0 Case Studies

5.1 Introduction

Case Study 1

This case study describes the design and creation of an expense claim application. Aimed at the enterprise market, this is an early prototype of an actual application designed for use by Symbian staff on the move with a Sony Ericsson P900 or Nokia 6600.

Case Study 2

This case study demonstrates how the Game API can be used to develop rich gaming content. We take you to the Symbian-sponsored speedway track to learn to manage a complex composite scene of background layers and sprites and to demonstrate the use of collision detection.

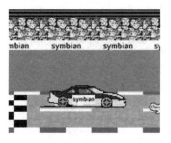

Programming Java 2 Micro Edition on Symbian OS: A developer's guide to MIDP 2.0.   Martin de Jode
© 2004 Symbian Ltd   ISBN: 0-470-09223-8

Case Study 3

This case study demonstrates the application of the Mobile Media API, the RMS and the TiledLayer class from the Game API. The Picture Puzzle MIDlet is a variation on the familiar Mix Pix native application that ships on Nokia Series 60 phones.

5.2   The Expense Application

This application uses a wide range of technologies including custom items for the user interface, record stores for persistent information and XML coupled with sockets for communication between the wireless devices and a central server. It also provides information regarding the J2ME development environment and practical considerations when creating applications for Series 60 and UIQ devices.

The design of this application was based upon two central themes:

- to demonstrate that viable services can be created on wireless devices using MIDP 2.0

- to create a useful prototype of an expense claim application in order to provoke a discussion within Symbian on the requirements for a system that could be made available to all staff and enable improvements in efficiency over the existing expense processing system.

The requirements for the expense application prototype are reasonably clear: as with all organizations, expenses must be approved by a manager or budget holder prior to payment. The expense application allows users, or claimants, to create and submit expenses on their wireless device. Budget holders receive a copy of the expense claim on their device and can either approve or reject it. In order for the approval mechanism to work, the wireless devices synchronize expense information with a central server.

5.2.1 The Development Environment

The expense application was developed using Sun's Wireless Toolkit (WTK) in conjunction with Sun's Java Developer Kit 1.4. Detailed discussion in this chapter will be limited to the WTK. WTK provides a comprehensive solution to the needs of the MIDlet developer, with numerous emulator skins and many parameters for restricting, monitoring and profiling MIDlets. It's worth spending some time understanding the WTK's capabilities, as this will pay dividends during development.

Nokia also provides a wireless toolkit that is downloadable from *http://forum.nokia.com*. This provides the same basic tooling as the WTK but with emulators for Series 60 devices. Sony Ericsson provides an emulator skin for the P900 and UIQ devices that plugs into the WTK. This can be downloaded from *http://developer.sonyericsson.com*.

The Symbian OS Toolkit can also be used when developing MIDlets. Although Symbian's toolkit is not designed specifically for MIDlet development, the emulator environment provides a close match to the actual device on which the MIDlet will run. The Symbian OS Toolkit should be downloaded from the manufacturer of the device that you wish to emulate. Each version is slightly different so that it accurately represents the capabilities of the individual devices.

5.2.2 Requirements Overview

Before discussing how MIDP 2.0 is used for the expense application, a more thorough overview of the application requirements must first be provided. The high-level requirements for the application included the following functions:

- claimants must be able to create, edit, view and delete expenses, subject to the current expense state

- budget holders must be able to approve or reject expenses and request additional information prior to approving or rejecting an expense

- all expenses should be synchronized with a central server

- expense information on the server should be able to be viewed on a website.

The high-level requirements do a good job of describing what must be achieved, but provide very little information regarding the detailed solution. Most of these requirements speak for themselves and do not require further explanation. What will be discussed further is the workflow of an

expense claim from creation to approval or rejection, the application's
user roles and synchronization of client device with server.

5.2.2.1 Workflow

The state of an expense claim reflects its current location on the path
from creation by a claimant to approval or rejection by a budget holder.
An expense claim can be in one of five states (see Figure 5.1).

5.2.2.2 User Roles

The application has two user roles: claimant and budget holder. The
claimant role provides the basic application functions, such as the creation
and submission of expenses and the viewing of retained expenses that
have been approved or rejected by a budget holder.

The budget holder role has a superset of the claimant's functions,
including the ability to review and either approve or reject a claimant's
expenses. Budget holders can use the application in claimant mode,
which allows them to create and submit their personal expenses.

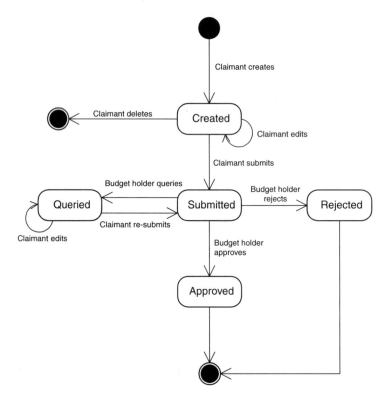

Figure 5.1 Expense claim state diagram.

5.2.2.3 *Synchronization*

A synchronization process is used to exchange expense claim and user information between the wireless device and the server. When an expense claim is updated or moves from one state to another, it will be sent to the server when the next synchronization occurs. If the server has any expense claims that must be sent to the device these will also be exchanged, for example when a budget holder receives a claimant's expenses for approval.

If the same expense claim is updated by two users who then synchronize, a conflict can occur. Under these circumstances it may be difficult, or impossible, to determine which expense information is correct and should be retained. Resolving such conflicts is a non-trivial problem that would normally become an administrative function of the application.

For the expense application, each claim must be treated as an inviolable financial transaction. Fortunately, it makes little sense for two users to be able to update an expense claim at the same time. Every state transition results in another user being responsible for the claim. Following a transition, the expense becomes read-only on the device where the transition occurred. When the next synchronization occurs the expense will be available for the user who is responsible for its continued progression towards approval or rejection.

The server also provides a website that allows expense information to be viewed. The site does not allow expenses to be modified or created; doing so would again raise the issue of synchronization conflicts. Keeping the business logic on the device also strengthens the demonstration of the technology. A production version of the application would deal with potential conflicts and allow the website to fulfill a view and amend role.

5.2.3 The Expense MIDlet

The expense application's MIDlet class is implemented in `midlet.view.ExpenseMidlet`, which is derived from `javax.microedition.midlet.MIDlet`. Unlike most MIDlets, the `ExpenseMidlet` does not implement any part of the application view, deferring this to a class derived from `javax.microedition.lcdui.Form`. The separation helps when implementing the different user interfaces required for UIQ and Series 60 devices. This is discussed further in Section 5.2.4.4.

The MIDlet object is important not only for managing the run state of the application, but also when using many MIDP APIs. The ability to retrieve the MIDlet's instance from other parts of the application is useful. The expense application MIDlet permits this by keeping an instance reference in a static member that is available using a static `getter()` method. The MIDlet's constructor is explicitly called from the MIDP implementation, which ensures there is only ever a single instance of the object. The basic MIDlet code is as follows:

```
public class ExpenseMIDlet extends MIDlet {
    public static ExpenseMIDlet getInstance() {
        return instance;
    }

    protected ExpenseMIDlet() {
        instance = this;
    }
    // instance of this MIDlet
    private static ExpenseMIDlet instance = null;
}
```

A commonly-used object `javax.microedition.lcdui.Display` can only be obtained using an instance of a MIDlet. The `Display` object is used to retrieve the attributes of a device's screen and display new `Displayable` objects, such as a `Form` or `Canvas`. There is a single `Display` instance per MIDlet.

The expense application uses MIDP forms extensively with custom items to make the user experience more agreeable. When a form needs to be displayed, the `Display.setCurrent()` method is used to replace the currently displayed object. Some additional methods were added to the expense MIDlet in order to simplify display handling, including a method to display the application's main form, when needed:

```
public Display getDisplay() {
    return Display.getDisplay(this);
}

public void displayMainForm() {
    Display.getDisplay(this).setCurrent(mainForm);
}

public void display(Displayable disp) {
    Display.getDisplay(this).setCurrent(disp);
}
```

The following code shows an example of how to use the helper methods to display a new form:

```
SettingsForm form = new SettingsForm(settings);
ExpenseMIDlet.getInstance().display(form);
```

The main form of the expense application is derived from `javax.microedition.lcdui.Form`. The `Form` contains a number of items and commands that are all initialized in the class's constructor. A number of listener interfaces are also implemented to handle command and item events. See the sample code for the details.

The main `Form` implements the Singleton pattern. Therefore, it has a private constructor and holds a static instance reference with a `getter` method. There will only ever be one instance of the main form and it exists for the duration of the MIDlet's execution. Implementing the form as a Singleton enforces this and provides a simple method of getting a reference to the main form as needed.

5.2.4 Custom Items

5.2.4.1 Overview

When development began on the expense application it became apparent that a form-based application was the best solution. Forms would make the display and editing of expense claim and application settings reasonably trivial. The only issue was how to create a main form with a list of expenses that allowed easy navigation between months. The work during the user interface prototyping suggested an interface that was just not possible using the standard high-level LCDUI components.

The solution was to use a new MIDP 2.0 feature called `CustomItem`. `CustomItem` allows the creation of new `Items` and gives the developer complete control over the look and feel within the bounding rectangle. As always, with great power comes great responsibility. In order to gain this level of freedom the developer must perform all paint operations, event handling and calculation of the currently visible rectangle if the item size exceeds the screen size.

Figures 5.2, 5.3 and 5.4 show the user interface prototype for the main form of the expense application, based loosely on the UIQ user interface, and its eventual implementation on the Nokia 6600, a Series 60 phone, and the Sony Ericsson P900, a UIQ device.

Two custom items were created for the expense MIDlet: the selector item that can be used to select the month and a multi-column list that shows the expenses for the month.

The selector item can be seen near the top in Figures 5.3 and 5.4. It has a secondary mode that allows ordinal selection, e.g. *2 of 6*, between a minimum and maximum value. Left and right arrows are drawn when it is possible to change the selection in that direction. On a Series 60 device, the selection change occurs when the joystick is pushed left or right.

The UIQ version of the selector allows additional buttons to be added, such as the Create button in Figure 5.4. The left and right arrows were also re-engineered to be treated as buttons. Each button has its own hotspot region to simplify pen tap logic. When a pen tap occurs the event handler enumerates the buttons, searching for a hit.

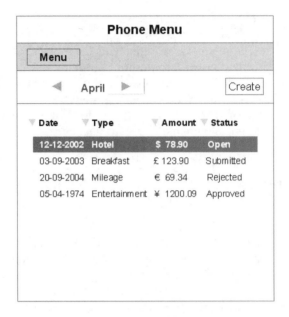

Figure 5.2 User Interface Prototype.

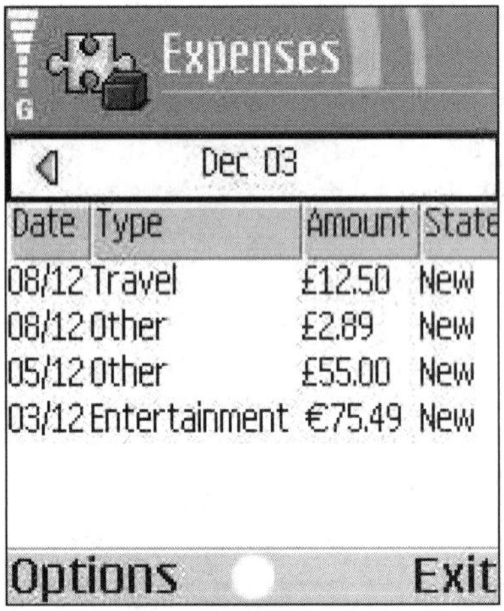

Figure 5.3 Series 60 Implementation on Nokia 6600.

The Series 60 implementation of the selector item is implemented in a single class, `midlet.uitools.SelectorItem`. The UIQ version is implemented using two classes and one interface (see Figure 5.5).

The multi-column list can be seen in the lower half of the screen in Figures 5.3 and 5.4. Users can move the current row selection up and down using the joystick or jog wheel and select a row to ''drill down'' and see detailed information about the expense item.

Figure 5.4   UIQ Implementation on Sony Ericsson P900.

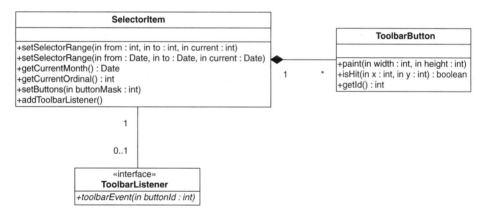

Figure 5.5   UIQ selection item class diagram.

The list item allows columns to be dynamically added, removed and re-sized. In the more complex, UIQ version, column headers can be tapped with the pen to change the sort order of the list. As the number of rows in the list grows so does the length of the list, until eventually it is longer than the screen. Under these circumstances the list item provides the currently selected row's bounding rectangle to the underlying form implementation so that MIDP can scroll the item and ensure the row is always visible on the screen (this is covered in detail later).

The Series 60 and UIQ implementations are different. The UIQ version is more complex because it supports changes in the sort order of the list. Both versions of the item have the same three basic classes (see Figure 5.6):

- a `midlet.uitools.ListItem` class which implements the custom item

- an abstract class `midlet.uitools.ListModel` which encapsulates the data that the list contains in a similar fashion to the Java Standard Edition `javax.swing.ListModel` interface

- a `midlet.uitools.ListColumn` class which represents individual columns and is responsible for painting the column header in the list item.

The UIQ version has an additional interface and class. The `midlet.utils.Comparator` interface provides a method that allows two instances of a class to be compared. It is used in conjunction with the `midlet.utils.Sorter` class, which sorts a `Vector` using a simple bubble sort algorithm. Java 2 Standard Edition (J2SE) has numerous utility classes for sorting and comparing. Unfortunately, due to size constraints, these are not included in J2ME and developers must re-implement them as needed.

5.2.4.2   Implementation

To create a custom item you must derive a class from the abstract `javax.microedition.lcdui.CustomItem` class. The abstract methods that must be implemented fulfill the form's most basic requirements: the dimensions of the custom item and how it should be painted.

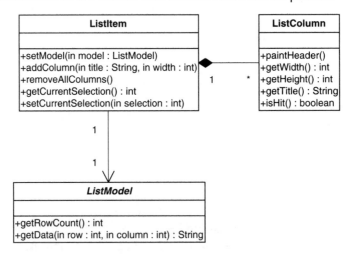

Figure 5.6 Class diagram for the list.

Item Size

The custom item's dimensions are handled by four methods, get-MinContentWidth(), getMinContentHeight(), getPrefContentWidth() and getPrefContentHeight(). The form and base custom item implementations use these methods when calculating the layout of the form that surrounds the custom item.

The selector and list custom items developed for the expense MIDlet have the minimum and preferred width set as the width of the display. The selector item has a fixed height that is set at design time and never changes. The list item must be of variable height to allow for differing numbers of rows. Initially, the list has a small height that allows the list header and up two rows to be shown. The preferred height is set to a large value that allows the list to grow as required, eventually to several times the screen length if needed.

Item Painting

Painting of the item is handled in the paint() method. It is passed a javax.microedition.lcdui.Graphics object and the width and height of the item's area. The top right (0,0) of the paint area corresponds to the top right position of the item on the screen; the underlying implementation takes care of transforming the drawing commands to the correct location on the physical screen.

If the custom item is larger than the physical screen size, the height and width passed to paint() reflect the item size, not the screen size. When painting a custom item the simplest approach is to draw everything whenever paint() is called. This method is used for the items in the expense application: neither has a sufficiently complex paint operation as to cause a noticeable flicker during painting. Various techniques exist to optimize painting by painting only the areas that have changed; discussion of these techniques is outside the scope of this chapter.

The following code shows the paint() method of the Series 60 selector item. The code has been pared down slightly by removing the ordinal mode painting. The paint() method breaks down into a series of simple operations. Firstly, the stage is set by painting the item's background color white using the fillRect() method followed by a drawRect() call to draw a single line border around the item. Next the text that will be displayed is formatted and its size and x and y offsets within the item calculated so that the text can be centrally aligned, horizontally and vertically. drawString is used to render the text. Finally, the item's current selection is compared to the upper and lower bounds of the item's range to determine whether we need to paint the left and right arrows using drawImage.

```
// Series 60 Selector Custom Item paint() method.
protected void paint(Graphics g, int width, int height) {
```

```
// blank canvas
int oldCol = g.getColor();
g.setColor(0xffffff);          // white
g.fillRect(0, 0, width, height);

// paint toolbar border
g.setColor(thisDisplay.getColor(Display.COLOR_BORDER));
g.drawRect(0, 0, width - 1, height - 1);
g.setColor(oldCol);
// format display text
int yr = currentSelection / 12;
String selectText = months[currentSelection % 12] + " " +
        ((yr < 10) ? "0" : "") + yr;

// work out some draw metrics
Font font = g.getFont();
Display thisDisplay = ExpenseMIDlet.getInstance().getDisplay();
int selectTextY = (height - font.getHeight()) / 2;
int xOfs = (width - font.stringWidth(selectText)) / 2;
g.drawString(selectText, xOfs, selectTextY,
        Graphics.TOP | Graphics.LEFT);

// draw left / right arrows if needed
if (currentSelection != selectFrom) {
    g.drawImage(leftSelect, SELECTOR_SPACER,
            ((SELECTOR_HEIGHT - leftSelect.getHeight()) / 2),
            Graphics.TOP | Graphics.LEFT);
}

if (currentSelection != selectTo) {
    g.drawImage(rightSelect,
            width - SELECTOR_SPACER - rightSelect.getWidth(),
            ((SELECTOR_HEIGHT - rightSelect.getHeight()) / 2),
            Graphics.TOP | Graphics.LEFT);
}
}
```

The code for painting the list item is slightly more complex in that we need to paint columns and rows and ensure that the current selection is highlighted. The list item has a list of columns and a model that represents the data within the list. The painting of the column headers is delegated to the individual column objects and a loop iterates through the model and draws the individual rows.

5.2.4.3   Event handling

Once the basic custom item methods have been implemented, it is time to consider how the item will interact with the user. Events are triggered when the keypad, joystick or pen are used. How the events are handled determines the nature of the interaction between the user and the custom item.

When discussing how to handle keypad events we must consider traversal. When there are several form items only one has the focus at any time; as the user navigates the form, different items gain and lose the focus. The developer does not have any code to write to make this happen, the underlying form takes care of all the details. In MIDP this is known as traversal: as users navigate around a form, they are traversing between form items.

Some form items, such as `javax.microedition.lcdui.TextField`, support internal traversal. While the item has focus, moving left and right moves the cursor position within the text. It does not change the focus to another form item. Internal traversal allows an item to specify a rectangle that should be currently visible on the screen: this is useful for items such as the list item created for the expense application which may become longer than the physical screen. By specifying the rectangle of the current row, the underlying implementation will ensure that the item is scrolled so that the current row is visible.

Key events can be handled in two ways: the first uses traversal to trap the directional buttons by overriding the `traverse()` method; the second overrides the `keyPressed()`, `keyReleased()` and `keyRepeated()` methods. If `traverse()` is not overridden then it is not possible to handle the directional keys: they will be used to change the form's current focus item.

The selector item uses `traverse()` to handle the left and right keys so that the currently selected month can be changed. The list item overrides both `keyPressed()` and `traverse()`. `keyPressed()` is used to view an expense claim in the details form. `traverse()` is used to change the current row selection and ensure that the current row is always visible on the screen.

The following code shows the implementation of `keyPressed()` for the list item. Only the joystick press is trapped; any registered state listeners (in this case, the parent form) are notified that a row has been selected and the expense detail form should be shown.

```
// Series 60 List Custom Item keyPressed() method
protected void keyPressed(int key) {
    // trap the joystick press for the item selection
    if (key == JOYSTICK_PRESS) {
        notifyStateChanged();
    }
}
```

The implementation of the `traverse()` method in the list item is certainly a great deal longer. The method returns a `boolean` that signifies whether the item is currently performing internal traversal. While internal traversal is occurring, the item will retain the focus.

The `traverse()` method takes four parameters:

- `direction` is the key code of the button that was pressed; only the left, right, up and down buttons are sent to the `traverse()` method

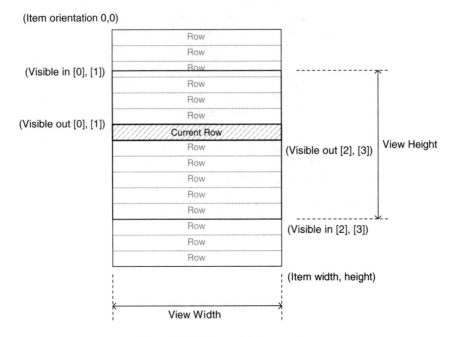

Figure 5.7   List item visible rectangles.

- `viewHeight` and `viewWidth` specify the size of the region that the item is currently painting into and is constrained by the size of the screen

- `visRect_inout` is the array that defines the currently visible region of the item (see Figure 5.7): `visRect_inout[0]` and `visRect_inout[1]` are the x and y coordinates of the top right corner and `visRect_inout[2]` and `visRect_inout[3]` are the width and height of the region.

`visRect_inout` must be updated to reflect the currently visible region of the item. It comes into play when the item size is larger than the screen. In the case of the list item, `visRect_inout` is set to the bounding rectangle of the currently selected row in the list. The selector item, which will always be visible on the screen, leaves the contents of `visRect_inout` unchanged.

Below is the `traverse()` method of the list item. The first section of code checks if the item is currently being traversed internally, if not then the current selection is set based on the direction from which the item was traversed into. If the item is currently traversing internally then a switch statement is used to update the current row selection based on the direction. If the current selection is no longer within the list, for example less than 0 or greater than the row count, then the user is traversing out of the list item; `false` is returned and the neighboring form item gets the focus. Finally, if the item is still traversing internally, the currently visible region is calculated and a `repaint()` call is made to ensure that the highlighted row has a chance to be painted; `true` is returned to ensure that the item retains focus.

```
// Series 60 List Custom Item traverse() method
protected boolean traverse(int direction, int viewWidth, int viewHeight,
        int[] visRect_inout) {
    // is this the current item, i.e. we are traversing inside currently??
    if (!isCurrentItem) {
        isCurrentItem = true;
        // set the current selected row
        if (direction == Canvas.DOWN)
            currentSelection = 0;
        else if (direction == Canvas.UP)
            currentSelection = model.getRowCount() - 1;
    } else {
        // we are currently traversing so handle the keypress
        switch (direction) {
            case Canvas.UP :
                currentSelection--;
                if (currentSelection < 0) {
                    currentSelection = 0;
                    return false; // traverse out
                }
                break;
            case Canvas.DOWN :
                currentSelection++;
                if (currentSelection >= model.getRowCount()) {
                    return false; // traverse out
                }
                break;
        }
    }
    // set the visible rectangle, i.e. just the current item, allow the
    // implementation to do the screen management
    int currentItemTopY = headerHeight + (rowHeight * currentSelection);
    visRect_inout[1] = currentItemTopY;
    visRect_inout[3] = rowHeight;
    repaint();
    return true;
}
```

There are three methods that can be overridden to handle pointer events: `pointerPressed()`, `pointerReleased()` and `pointer-Dragged()`. Each method is passed an x and y parameter that represents the position of the pointer event relative to the top right corner of the item that received the event.

When the pointer taps on a specific area of a custom item it is generally better to handle it with the `pointerReleased()` method rather than `pointerPressed()`, as it gives a more natural feel to the interaction. If the user decides not to perform the action, dragging the pointer away from the hotspot will avoid it triggering; and if the screen is redrawn as part of the pointer event, the pointer is not touching a new hotspot.

When a pointer event occurs it is necessary to determine what it actually means to the application, for example the list item must determine if a tap is to signal a change in sorting or to select a row. As the complexity of the custom item grows, so does the complexity of the logic to determine what the pointer event means.

The following code shows an example from the UIQ version of the list item. The code initially determines if the hit was in the list header; if so, the columns in the list are enumerated and each is checked to determine which was hit and the sort order updated. If the hit is not in the list header then the row hit is calculated using the y hit position divided by the row height.

```
// UIQ List Custom Item pointerReleased() method
protected void pointerReleased(int x, int y) {
    // is the hit within the header??
    if (y <= headerHeight) {
        // within header, enum and work out which one...
        Enumeration enum = columnList.elements();
        int colNum = 0;
        while (enum.hasMoreElements()) {
            ListColumn col = (ListColumn)enum.nextElement();
            if (col.isHit(x, y)) {
                // found our hit, update sort order
                ...
                break;
            }
            colNum++;
        }
    } else {
        // within the body of the list, work out which entry was selected
        currentSelection = 1 + ((y - headerHeight) / rowHeight);
        notifyStateChanged();
    }
}
```

5.2.4.4 *Designing Custom Items for Series 60 and UIQ*

As the user interface evolved during the development of the expense application it became apparent from an early stage that the UIQ and Series 60 user interfaces have sufficient differences that each MIDlet must be tailored specifically to the device. The differences are only skin-deep; all other application code remains identical.

This section aims to highlight the differences between the user interface metaphors and suggest a few considerations that can help simplify the implementation of device-specific versions of a MIDlet.

Device Look and Feel

The most notable difference between UIQ and Series 60 is that UIQ uses a pen and a jog dial as the primary input methods and Series 60 has a keypad and a joystick. Each interface has its own unique look and feel; users interact differently and expect different responses from them.

When creating a user interface the strengths of each interface metaphor should be used to provide an interface that is consistent, or at least fits broadly, with the expected characteristics of the device. For UIQ, this means regions to tap with the pen; for Series 60, longer menus and simple screen layouts.

A good example of how the user interface must be adapted for a device is the implementation of the list item on Series 60. The item is navigable using only the joystick. The column sort order cannot be modified as it is not easy to fit this into the user interface – it would require lengthy menu options that would only be available when the list item has the focus. While context-sensitive commands are available in MIDP, they may confuse the user. Menu options should generally remain as consistent as possible, no matter what the currently selected item, to aid application usability.

Conversely, the UIQ version of the list item allows rows to be selected using the pen or jog wheel. Changing the sort order on the columns can be achieved by tapping a column header. This is intuitive and consistent with how a user might expect a UIQ application to work. Similar differences exist between the different versions of the selector custom item.

Separation of Business Logic and Presentation Code

If the business logic and the presentation layer code are intertwined then updating the user interface inevitably has effects on the business logic and errors could be introduced. Of more concern is that you would have to maintain a different version of the business logic for each device. It also makes the both the business logic and UI code more difficult to understand.

To avoid this, there should be a clear separation of the user interface and the business logic. Most developers understand this need for separation; the model–view–controller (MVC) pattern is a good example of how this separation can be achieved when creating a user interface.

In the expense application, we have already seen separation in action with the definition of the MIDlet object itself. For different versions of the application there are different versions of the main form. Keeping these two objects separate allows the MIDlet code to remain the same while the code that produces the form changes independently.

Code Management

Separating the code into layers does not prevent us from having to keep multiple branches of the application source code, one for each device platform. Layer separation allows us to target our customization for each user interface more precisely. If the business logic is changed, or a bug found, the fixes can easily be applied to all versions.

The custom items created for the expense application look similar and share a lot of common code. It would be possible to create a single heavyweight custom item that works on both interfaces effectively; however, such an item places an unfair burden on the device by increasing the memory footprint of the application, which is not desirable. A more practical approach is to branch the code once a device-specific version of the custom item is close to completion, allowing as much code to be re-used as possible.

5.2.5   Record Store

The expense application must keep expense and claimant information as well as application settings on the device. This is achieved using the Record Management System (RMS) API. The RMS API allows an application to persist information as a series of records within a record store and each record has its own unique ID that is assigned by the underlying implementation. Several record stores can be maintained by an application.

In the expense application there are three record stores, one each for expenses, user information and application settings. Access to each record store is encapsulated in an individual object, a data access object (DAO). Encapsulating the persistence in this way allows its implementation to be abstracted away from the business logic; should the underlying persistence mechanism change, the updates are confined solely to the DAOs.

The expense application uses a single instance of each DAO for all persistence operations. Making the DAO a Singleton enforces that only one instance is created, ensuring that memory consumption is kept to a minimum. Additionally, opening a record store is a lengthy operation. By performing this operation once at application start-up we ensure that the rest of the application responds well. If there were ever a good reason for a splash screen in a MIDlet, opening several record stores is it.

5.2.5.1   Opening a Record Store

The DAO is created and opened in the `ExpenseMidlet` class; the following code shows the portion of the `startApp()` method where this occurs.

```
// make sure we have instances of the DAOs created and ready
ExpenseDAO.getInstance().openRecordStore();
PersonDAO.getInstance().openRecordStore();
SettingsDAO.getInstance().openRecordStore();
```

The `openRecordStore()` method opens a record store using the RMS. The following code shows the implementation of the `ExpenseDAO` object. DAOException is used to wrap any exceptions that occur in the DAOs.

```
// ExpenseDAO openRecordStore() method
public void openRecordStore() throws DAOException {
    try {
        if (rs != null)
            rs = RecordStore.openRecordStore(EXPENSE_RMS_NAME, true);
    } catch (Exception e) {
        // handling for RecordStoreException
        //              RecordStoreNotFound
        //              RecordStoreFullException
        //              IllegalArgumentException
        throw new DAOException("Failed to open the Expense RMS, reason: \n" +
                e);
    }
}
```

Each record has a unique ID, which allows individual records to be retrieved and without which deletions and updates cannot take place. When reading a record from the RMS, the record's unique ID is retrieved and stored in case the record needs to be updated or deleted. The following code shows the implementation of the get() method in the ExpenseDAO, which gets a record using its unique ID. The conversion of the record into a usable object is discussed in the next section.

```
// ExpenseDAO get expense method
public Expense get(int id) throws DAOException {
    try {
        // get the expense and parse into an Expense object
        byte[] expenseBytes = rs.getRecord(id);
        Expense expense = Expense.bytesToExpense(expenseBytes);
        expense.setRmsId(id);
        return expense;
    } catch (Exception e) {
        throw new DAOException("Failed to read record, cause\n" + e);
    }
}
```

The DAOs also provide functions to allow records to be updated, deleted and enumerated. See the source code for examples of how these functions are implemented.

5.2.5.2 Encoding Records

A single record is made up of a variable length array of bytes. In order to use the record store, an application must encode its information to and decode from a byte array. MIDP has implementations of the java.io. ByteArrayInputStream and java.io.ByteArrayOutputStream classes, which provide an excellent solution for this.

When interacting with the DAOs, the application uses objects that represent an expense, a person or the application settings. Each of these objects is responsible for encoding their data into a byte array ready for persistence, which ensures that any modifications to the underlying information do not affect the DAO. The following method shows how an expense claim is encoded ready for persistence. The `expense-ToBytes()` method in the `midlet.model.Expense` class uses a `java.io.ByteArrayOutputStream` object in combination with a `java.io.DataOutputStream` to encode an expense claim and return an array of bytes:

```
// Expense objects expenseToBytes() method
public byte[] expenseToBytes() throws IOException {
    byte[] bytes = null;
    ByteArrayOutputStream baos = null;
    DataOutputStream dos = null;
    try {
        // open streams that will do the work
        baos = new ByteArrayOutputStream();
        dos = new DataOutputStream(baos);
        // write information to the output stream
        dos.writeShort(getOwnerId());
        dos.writeByte(getState());
        ...
        dos.writeUTF(getBhNotes());
        // convert byte output stream to byte array
        bytes = baos.toByteArray();
    } finally {
        // tidy
        if (dos != null)
            dos.close();
    }
    // return bytes to caller
    return bytes;
}
```

The decoding operation is similar to the encoding operation but uses input streams and returns an `Expense` object. The fields must be encoded and decoded in the same order. If a field is added then we must ensure that both methods are updated; failure to do so would result in fields being populated with the wrong data.

```
// Expense objects bytesToExpense() method
public static Expense bytesToExpense(byte[] expenseBytes)
        throws IOException {
    DataInputStream dis = null;
    try {
        // get at bytes via data stream
        dis = new DataInputStream(new ByteArrayInputStream(expenseBytes));
        // create empty expense object
        Expense expense = new Expense();
        // load the expense information from the byte array
```

```
    expense.setOwnerId(dis.readShort());
    expense.setState(dis.readByte());
    ...
    expense.setBhNotes(dis.readUTF());
    // give the caller back their expense
    return expense;
} finally {
    // tidy
    if (dis != null)
        dis.close();
}
}
```

If changes to the underlying object require changes to the record encoding, perhaps due to a new version of the application, then reading old records from an existing record store would inevitably result in errors. To ensure that future changes to the record format can be dealt with, an object version number can be inserted into each record to allow alternate decoding for legacy record versions. The expense application we are discussing here does not handle different record versions as it is a demonstration application.

5.2.5.3 Enumerating Records

The RMS permits the enumeration of records within a record store. During enumeration, the records returned can be filtered by passing an object that implements the `javax.microedition.rms.RecordFilter` interface or sorted by passing an object that implements the `javax.microedition.rms.RecordComparator` interface.

The expense application implements filtering using the `ExpenseFilter` class, which implements the `matches()` method from the `RecordFilter` interface. Each record in the store is passed in turn to `matches()`, which returns `true` if the record should be included in the enumeration. `ExpenseFilter` allows filtering on a number of different expense attributes, each of which is checked during the `matches()` call:

```
// ExpenseFilter's matches() method
public boolean matches(byte[] expenseBytes) {
    boolean matchFound = true;
    // do we have any search clauses? if not then let all records through
    if ((personId == 0) && (monthCal == null)
            && (changedAfterSyncId == -1) && (createdDate == null))
        return true;
    Expense expense;
    try {
        // get the information from the record and filter
        expense = Expense.bytesToExpense(expenseBytes);
    } catch (IOException e) {
        // we need to filter but cannot read this record,
```

```
        // we assume no match
        System.err.println("Failed to read expense in ExpenseFilter: "
                + e);
        return false;
    }
    // test for owner match up
    if (personId != 0)
        matchFound = (isOwner)
                ? (expense.getOwnerId() == personId)
                : (expense.getOwnerId() != personId);
    // test for month match up only if owner check still means its useful
    if ((matchFound) && (monthCal != null)) {
        // get everything set up for compare...
        Calendar receiptCal = Calendar.getInstance();
        receiptCal.setTime(expense.getReceiptDate());
        // check month and year on calendars
        matchFound =
                ((monthCal.get(Calendar.MONTH)
                    == receiptCal.get(Calendar.MONTH))
                && (monthCal.get(Calendar.YEAR)
                    == receiptCal.get(Calendar.YEAR)));
    }
    // test for last change match up only if owner check still useful
    if ((matchFound) && (changedAfterSyncId >= 0)) {
        matchFound = (expense.getLastSyncId() > changedAfterSyncId);
    }
    // test for created date match
    if ((matchFound) && (createdDate != null)) {
        matchFound =
            (createdDate.getTime() == expense.getCreatedDate().getTime());
    }
    return matchFound;
}
```

A record enumeration can return either the unique record ID or the record itself; the DAO must fetch both. The following code enumerates the unique record IDs and explicitly retrieves each expense record before placing it into a `Vector` ready to be returned to the caller.

```
// ExpenseDAO enumerateExpenses() method
private Vector enumerateExpenses(ExpenseFilter filter)
    throws DAOException {
    Vector expenseList = new Vector();
    try {
        // create an enumeration of the records that we need
        RecordEnumeration enum = rs.enumerateRecords(filter, null, false);

        // enumerate the record ids and use them to retrieve the expenses
        while (enum.hasNextElement()) {
            Expense expense = get(enum.nextRecordId());
            expenseList.addElement(expense);
        }
    } catch (Exception e) {
        // failed to enumerate records...
        throw new DAOException("Failed to enumerate expenses, cause " + e);
```

```
    }
    return expenseList;
}
```

5.2.6 Synchronization

At the heart of the expense MIDlet is the exchange of information between the client device and the server. Without synchronization, expenses could not advance through the workflow from creation to approval or rejection. Prior to using the expense MIDlet for the first time a user must enter the synchronization server details; this allows the first synchronization to take place so any existing expenses can be retrieved and the user's role is known.

The synchronization occurs when the Synchronize command is selected from the menu. A form is displayed with some animation to show progress while a worker thread is created to undertake the synchronization process.

5.2.6.1 Animation of Synchronization Form

The synchronization form is simple, as can be seen in Figure 5.8. The animation is achieved by scheduling a `java.util.TimerTask` that updates the current image in the form. The timer task is implemented as an anonymous inner class.

When the form is created the `startSync()` method, starts the worker thread and schedules the timer task. The timer task has two purposes: to animate the image on the form by cycling through a set of images loaded during the form creation and to check if the worker thread has terminated. Once the thread has terminated, its status is checked to determine the success or failure of the operation. The animation timer task is scheduled

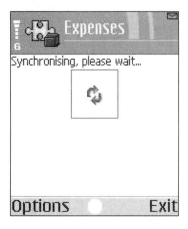

Figure 5.8 Synchronization form.

to trigger after $\frac{1}{2}$ second and then every $\frac{1}{2}$ second after that. This can be seen at the end of the method where the timing parameters appear after the inner class definition.

```
// SynchronizeForm startSync() method
private void startSync() {
    timer = new Timer();
    // start sync thread
    Synchronizer = new SynchronizeThread(settings);
    workerThread = new Thread(Synchronizer);
    workerThread.start();
    //schedule a timer for animation and to check if sync complete
    timer.schedule(new TimerTask() {
        public void run() {
            // animate
            currentImage = (currentImage + 1) % syncImages.length;
            syncAnimation.setImage(syncImages[currentImage]);
            // is sync operation complete??
            if (!workerThread.isAlive()) {
                timer.cancel();
                // inform the user of the sync result, use the next
                // displayable param to go back to the main form.
                // so was there a problem?
                if (Synchronizer.getErrorMessage() != null) {
                    // let the user know about the problem
                    ExpenseMIDlet.alert(
                            "Failed to Synchronize: "
                            + Synchronizer.getErrorMessage(),
                            AlertType.ERROR,
                            MainForm.getInstance());
                } else {
                    // update the last sync date information
                    settings.syncCompleted(Synchronizer.getSyncId());
                    ExpenseMIDlet.alert(
                            "Synchronization complete!",
                            AlertType.INFO,
                            MainForm.getInstance());
                }
            }
        }
    }, 500, 500);
}
```

5.2.6.2   Synchronization Worker Thread

The synchronization thread implements the `java.lang.Runnable` interface; the implementation of the `run()` method has been included below. Synchronization has three steps: check for change of user or server, synchronize information and remove unneeded expenses from the device.

```
// SynchronizationThread run() method
public void run() {
    try {
```

```
            // are we changing user (sync required set)?
            // sync expenses before clearing followed by normal sync of user
            // & expenses from sync id of 0
            if (settings.isNeedToSync()) {
                // sync the expense information
                SynchronizeExpense();
                // remove all expenses from phone
                ExpenseDAO.getInstance().removeAll();
                // reset sync id to ensure complete info sent
                syncId = oldSyncId = 0;
            }
            // Synchronize the person information
            SynchronizePerson();
            // sync the expense information
            SynchronizeExpense();
            // remove all expenses that are no longer required.
            // i.e. if we are not the owner & state != SUBMITTED then remove!
            Vector expenseList =
                    ExpenseDAO.getInstance().getExpenses(null, false, null);
            for (int i = expenseList.size() - 1; i >= 0; i--) {
                Expense expense = (Expense)expenseList.elementAt(i);
                if ((expense.getOwnerId() != settings.getUserId())
                        && (expense.getState() != Expense.STATE_SUBMITTED)) {
                    // remove this expense as we no longer need it!!
                    ExpenseDAO.getInstance().remove(expense);
                }
            }
        } catch (Exception e) {
            // set error code
            errorMessage = e.getMessage();
        }
    }
```

If the current user or synchronization server address has changed then a complete synchronization must occur. Any updated expenses on the device should be uploaded and the device's record store purged in preparation for new information that will be received from a complete synchronization. As complete and partial synchronization use the same code, a synchronization ID is used to differentiate between the two operations. During a complete synchronization the last synchronization ID is set to 0; in a partial synchronization a unique ID received from the server during the last synchronization is used so that only the updated information is exchanged. In the run() method the isNeedToSync call is used to determine whether a complete synchronization is required.

The exchange of information takes place in the SynchronizePerson and SynchronizeExpense() method calls. Each method packages and submits the information to the server, each request sent starts with the current user ID and the last synchronization ID. The server response includes a new globally unique synchronization ID for use during the next synchronization. The code that handles the request and response is discussed later.

The final operation in the synchronization is to remove all expenses that are no longer needed on the device; these include other users' expenses that have been approved or rejected by the current user acting in the budget holder role.

The synchronization thread communicates with the server using the HTTP protocol. XML formatted requests that contain all the information that the device wishes to exchange are sent. After processing the request, the server formats an XML response containing updates.

XML is space inefficient; many additional bytes are required to encode information. So why use XML in an environment where memory is at a premium and the network connections are slow? XML is convenient, it is easy to validate and there are many existing tools and APIs to simplify its use, allowing the expense application prototype to be created in the minimum of time.

The `javax.microedition.io.HttpConnection` class is used for the server communication. Requests to the server use a utility method, `sendMessageToServer()`, that has a single parameter containing the XML request to be sent. An `HttpConnection` is opened to the server URL and the XML request sent via the connection's `OutputStream`.

The response is read into a `StringBuffer` before being returned to the caller. If there is an error then an exception is thrown that will eventually find its way back to the synchronization form to be presented to the user.

```java
// SynchronizationThread sendMessageToServer() method
private String sendMessageToServer(String message)
    throws IOException, ServerCommException {
    StringBuffer sb = new StringBuffer();
    HttpConnection connection = null;
    InputStream is = null;
    // open connection
    connection = (HttpConnection)Connector.open(settings.getSyncServer());
    // send message to server
    OutputStream os = connection.openOutputStream();
    os.write(message.getBytes());
    os.close();
    // make sure we got a good response code, i.e. >= 200 && < 300
    if ((connection.getResponseCode() >= 200)
            && (connection.getResponseCode() < 300)) {
        is = connection.openInputStream();
        byte[] buffer = new byte[512];
        int bytesRead = 0;
        while (-1 != (bytesRead = is.read(buffer, 0, 512))) {
            sb.append(new String(buffer, 0, bytesRead));
        }
    } else {
        // error of some kind
        throw new ServerCommException(
                "Server communications error: "
            + connection.getResponseCode()
            + ", "
            + connection.getResponseMessage());
    }
    // close connection.
```

```
    connection.close();
    return sb.toString();
}
```

5.2.6.3 Format of Synchronization Message

An XML schema was created for the interaction between the client device and the server. This allowed the XML to be validated as well as allowing the server side parsing code to be generated using JAXB, the Java API for XML Binding. The schema is shown below.

```xml
<xsd:schema xmlns:xsd="www.w3.org/2001/XMLSchema">
    <xsd:element name="etsync" type="ExpenseTrackerSync"/>
    <xsd:complexType name="ExpenseTrackerSync">
        <xsd:sequence>
            <xsd:element name="req" type="ExpenseTrackerRequest"
                    minOccurs="0" />
            <xsd:element name="resp" type="ExpenseTrackerResponse"
                    minOccurs="0" />
        </xsd:sequence>
    </xsd:complexType>
    <xsd:complexType name="ExpenseTrackerRequest">
        <xsd:sequence>
            <xsd:element name="userupdate" type="UpdateUser" minOccurs="0"
                    maxOccurs="1" />
            <xsd:element name="expense" type="PhoneExpense" minOccurs="0"
                    maxOccurs="unbounded" />
        </xsd:sequence>
        <xsd:attribute name="lastSyncId" type="xsd:integer" />
        <xsd:attribute name="userId" type="xsd:integer" />
    </xsd:complexType>
    <xsd:complexType name="ExpenseTrackerResponse">
        <xsd:sequence>
            <xsd:element name="mainuser" type="User" minOccurs="0"
                    maxOccurs="1" />
            <xsd:element name="subord" type="User" minOccurs="0"
                    maxOccurs="unbounded"/>
            <xsd:element name="expense" type="PhoneExpense" minOccurs="0"
                    maxOccurs="unbounded"/>
        </xsd:sequence>
        <xsd:attribute name="sid" type="xsd:integer" />
    </xsd:complexType>
    <xsd:complexType name="UpdateUser">
        <xsd:attribute name="name" type="xsd:string" use="required"/>
    </xsd:complexType>
    <xsd:complexType name="PhoneExpense">
        <xsd:sequence>
            <xsd:element name="owner" type="xsd:integer" minOccurs="1"
                    maxOccurs="1" />
            <xsd:element name="state" type="xsd:integer" minOccurs="1"
                    maxOccurs="1" />
            <xsd:element name="type" type="xsd:integer" minOccurs="1"
                    maxOccurs="1" />
            <xsd:element name="receiptdate" type="xsd:date" minOccurs="1"
                    maxOccurs="1" />
            <xsd:element name="amount" type="xsd:integer" minOccurs="1"
```

```
                          maxOccurs="1" />
            <xsd:element name="currency" type="xsd:string" minOccurs="1"
                  maxOccurs="1" />
            <xsd:element name="vatpercentage" type="xsd:integer"
                  minOccurs="1" maxOccurs="1"/>
            <xsd:element name="project" type="xsd:integer" minOccurs="1"
                  maxOccurs="1" />
            <xsd:element name="dept" type="xsd:integer" minOccurs="1"
                  maxOccurs="1" />
            <xsd:element name="createdate" type="xsd:dateTime"
                  minOccurs="1" maxOccurs="1" />
            <xsd:element name="lastsyncid" type="xsd:integer"
                  minOccurs="1" maxOccurs="1"/>
            <xsd:element name="ownernotes" type="xsd:string" minOccurs="1"
                  maxOccurs="1" />
            <xsd:element name="bhnotes" type="xsd:string" minOccurs="1"
                  maxOccurs="1" />
        </xsd:sequence>
    </xsd:complexType>
    <xsd:complexType name="User">
        <xsd:attribute name="id" type="xsd:int" use="required"/>
        <xsd:attribute name="name" type="xsd:string" use="required"/>
    </xsd:complexType>
</xsd:schema>
```

On the device, XML requests are encoded by appending to a string buffer. There is no need to use an XML library: it overcomplicates the process and increases memory overhead. The kXML library was used to parse the XML responses on the device. It is designed to run under MIDP and has a small memory footprint. The library can be downloaded from *http://xmlpull.org*.

5.2.6.4   Parsing XML using kXML

The kXML parser is simple to use, once an `InputStream` has been set. Parsing involves iterating through events in the XML stream. An event includes beginning and end tags, elements and attributes. While parsing, `getName` gets the tag name and `getAttributeValue` gets a named attribute from the current tag. For tags that have text between a start and end tag, the `getNext()` method must be used – the text is considered another event.

The code below shows the kXML parser in action. In this example all information is made up of attributes within tags, so the parser's `getNext()` method is not used for retrieving text (see `processExpenseResponse` in the `midlet.sync.SynchronizeThread` class for an example of its usage).

```
// SynchronizationThread processPersonResponse() method
private void processPersonResponse(String reply)
    throws IOException, XmlPullParserException, DAOException {
    KXmlParser parser = new KXmlParser();
```

```
// turn the reply into a input stream for the xml parser...
ByteArrayInputStream bais = new ByteArrayInputStream(reply.getBytes());
parser.setInput(bais, null);
int eventType = parser.getEventType();
while (eventType != KXmlParser.END_DOCUMENT) {
    if (eventType == KXmlParser.START_TAG) {
        // the information we want is always in the attributes, parsing
        // is simple: if it's a tag we are interested in then get
        // the information, otherwise ignore!
        int tagId = 0;        // id == 1 for main user, 2 == subordinate

        if (parser.getName().equals(TAG_PERSON_MAIN)) {
            // main user, ensure they are the first person
            tagId = 1;
        } else if (parser.getName().equals(TAG_PERSON_SUBORD)) {
            // subordinate person, ensure they are in the RMS
            tagId = 2;
        } else if (parser.getName().equals(TAG_RESPONSE)) {
            syncId = Long.parseLong(parser.getAttributeValue("",
                    TAG_RESPONSE_SYNCID));
        }

        // are we doing some processing??
        if (tagId != 0) {
            // get the attributes and do some more work
            String name = parser.getAttributeValue("", TAG_PERSON_NAME);
            short id = Short.parseShort(parser.getAttributeValue("",
                    TAG_PERSON_ID));
            short bhId = -1;

            if (tagId == 1) {
                // remove current users
                ...
            } else {
                // sub ord instead of main user.
                bhId = settings.getUserId();
            }
            // ensure the RMS is update to date...
            ...
        }
    }

    eventType = parser.next();
}
bais.close();
}
```

5.2.6.5 Message Exchange Example

An example of the XML request and response messages from a synchro-nization operation now follows.

The first request and response is for a user that is using a device for the first time. The request includes the name the user entered into the application settings and the response includes the user's unique ID and any claimants, of which there are none in this instance.

```
<etsync>
    <req lastSyncId="0" userId="0">
        <userupdate name="Yossarian" />
    </req>
</etsync>
<?xml version="1.0" encoding="UTF-8" standalone="yes"?>
<etsync>
    <resp sid="424">
        <mainuser name="Yossarian" id="2">
        </mainuser>
    </resp>
</etsync>
```

The next exchange retrieves the expenses that already exist for the
user. Note how the last sync ID remains 0 for the request to ensure that
all expenses are exchanged:

```
<etsync>
    <req lastSyncId="0" userId="2">
    </req></etsync>
<?xml version="1.0" encoding="UTF-8" standalone="yes"?>
<etsync>
    <resp sid="425">
        <expense>
            <owner>2</owner>
            <state>4</state>
            <type>0</type>
            <receiptdate>2003-06-09+00:00</receiptdate>
            <amount>1299</amount>
            <currency>&#163; </currency>
            <vatpercentage>1750</vatpercentage>
            <project>3</project>
            <dept>2</dept>
            <createdate>2003-06-11T19:52:46.000+00:00</createdate>
            <lastsyncid>367</lastsyncid>
            <ownernotes>one</ownernotes>
            <bhnotes></bhnotes>
        </expense>
        <expense>
            <owner>2</owner>
            <state>2</state>
            <type>2</type>
            <receiptdate>2003-06-16+00:00</receiptdate>
            <amount>2197</amount>
            <currency>$ </currency>
            <vatpercentage>1750</vatpercentage>
            <project>0</project>
            <dept>0</dept>
            <createdate>2003-06-16T08:55:21.000+00:00</createdate>
            <lastsyncid>381</lastsyncid>
            <ownernotes></ownernotes>
            <bhnotes></bhnotes>
        </expense>
    </resp>
</etsync>
```

The final XML request shows a new expense claim being submitted to the server:

```
<etsync>
    <req lastSyncId="436" userId="2">
        <expense>
            <owner>2</owner>
            <state>2</state>
            <type>0</type>
            <receiptdate>2003-12-09</receiptdate>
            <amount>1299</amount>
            <currency>&#xA3;</currency>
            <vatpercentage>1750</vatpercentage>
            <project>0</project>
            <dept>0</dept>
            <createdate>2003-12-09T11:22:20</createdate>
            <lastsyncid>437</lastsyncid>
            <ownernotes>hello world</ownernotes>
            <bhnotes></bhnotes>
        </expense>
    </req>
</etsync>
```

A discussion of how the requests are processed on the server takes place in the next section.

5.2.7   Implementation of the Web Server Components

Apache Tomcat is used to provide the server functionality for the expense application. Java Server Pages (JSP) are used in conjunction with JavaBeans to provide a view of existing expenses. A servlet is used for the synchronization process. This section gives an overview of the web application.

Figures 5.9 and 5.10 are examples of the main web pages for the expense application. The first image shows all the expenses in the system for a single user, the second shows the full details of an expense item.

The web application uses a relational database management system (RDBMS) to store the expenses and user information. The schema for the database has just three tables. A homegrown library is used to simplify the database code, allowing a simple mapping of a database table to a Java class. See the source code on the support website at ***www.symbian.com/books*** for more information.

The most complex part of the server is the synchronization servlet. All XML parsing uses the Java API for XML Binding (JAXB). JAXB was used to create a class hierarchy from the XML schema: if the schema changes the classes can be automatically regenerated as part of the build process to ensure that they always correctly map to the XML stream.

When the servlet receives a synchronization request, JAXB is used to unmarshal the information into an object hierarchy that is used to process

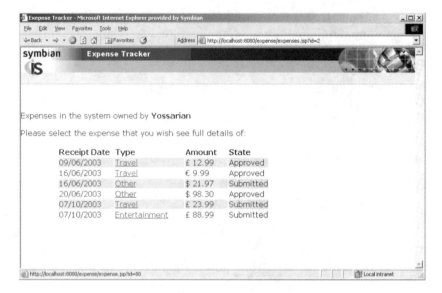

Figure 5.9 Expenses list for a user.

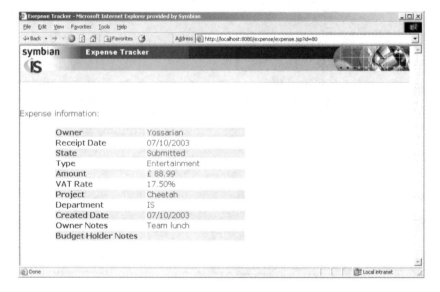

Figure 5.10 Expense item details.

the request. A response is built by creating an object hierarchy from classes generated by JAXB. Once processing is complete, the response hierarchy is marshaled into an XML stream and sent back to the device. The synchronization servlet does not handle any XML directly.

JAXB is available from Sun as part of the Java Web Services Toolkit.

5.2.8   Building the MIDlet

This next section details the build and run scripts that were used during the development. The scripts are modified versions of batch files that are included with Sun's Wireless Toolkit.

5.2.8.1   Build Script

The build script performs the following operations:

1. It builds the Java source into class files.

2. It packages the classes into a Java archive (JAR).

3. It reduces the application size using obfuscation.

4. It pre-verifies the application ready for deployment.

5. It updates the Java application descriptor (JAD) file with the correct application JAR file size.

Building the Class Files

Sun's Java Development Kit (JDK) is used to build the class files from the Java source files. The `javac` command line is fairly standard apart from an additional parameter to specify that the J2ME libraries should be used to provide the bootstrap classes:

```
javac -bootclasspath %WTK_HOME%\lib/midpapi.zip -d build\classes
      -classpath build\classes src/java/org/xmlpull/v1/*.java
      src/java/org/kxml2/io/*.java src/java/midlet/utils/*.java
      src/java/midlet/model/*.java src/java/midlet/view/*.java
      src/java/midlet/uitools/*.java src/java/midlet/sync/*.java
```

Packaging into a Java Archive

An application JAR file is created from the classes. The obfuscation process requires separate input and output JAR files. For this reason an intermediate filename of `ExpenseTrackerTemp.jar` is used for the initial packaging operation.

```
jar cmf src\meta\MANIFEST.MF build\ExpenseTrackerTemp.jar
      -C build\classes .
```

Obfuscating

Obfuscation must be performed prior to pre-verification. If pre-verification is performed first, the obfuscation process invalidates the pre-verification checksums and the MIDlet will not run.

Sun's Wireless Toolkit ships with the Proguard obfuscation library (see ***http://proguard.sourceforge.net***). To use Proguard, a configuration file must be created that contains the options for the obfuscation process. The file is passed to Proguard as a command line parameter, as follows. If obfuscation is not required, the command should be commented out of the build script.

```
java -jar lib\proguard.jar @proguard.txt
```

The contents of the configuration file, `proguard.txt`, follow:

```
-libraryjars /wtk20/lib/midpapi.zip
-injars build/ExpenseTrackerTemp.jar
-outjar build/ExpenseTracker.jar
-keep public class * extends javax.microedition.midlet.MIDlet
```

Pre-verifying the Application
The standard Java runtime performs verification of classes prior to launching a Java application, to ensure that class files are well-formed and do not contain any malicious code. MIDP specifies that a MIDlet should be pre-verified prior to deployment, allowing the MIDP implementation on the wireless device to be reduced in size. Sun's Wireless Toolkit is supplied with a tool to perform pre-verification; the following command line shows this operation in the build script:

```
%WTK_HOME%\bin\preverify -classpath
%WTK_HOME%\lib\midpapi.zip;build\tmpclasses build\ExpenseTracker.jar
```

Updating the JAD File
The final step in creating a deployable MIDlet is to update the JAD file with the size of the application JAR. The JAD file contains configuration information that a device requires for installing, managing and running a MIDlet, such as the MIDlet's main class and vendor information. A small Java program was created to embed the size into a template file and write out the expense application's JAD. The command in the build script is as follows:

```
java -cp . SizeEncoder build\ExpenseTracker.jar
```

The JAD template file is as follows (the `$size$` token is replaced with the size of the JAR file when the template is used):

```
MIDlet-1: Expenses,,midlet.view.ExpenseMidlet
MIDlet-Jar-Size: $size$
MIDlet-Jar-URL: ExpenseTracker.jar
MIDlet-Name: Expenses
```

```
MIDlet-Vendor: Symbian IS
MIDlet-Version: 1.0
MicroEdition-Configuration: CLDC-1.0
MicroEdition-Profile: MIDP-2.0
```

5.2.8.2 Run Script

The run script has only one line of real interest: the line that launches the expense MIDlet in Sun's emulator. There are a number of useful parameters available when using the emulator; for example, `-Xheapsize` sets the maximum heap size and allows a MIDlet to be tested in different memory conditions. The emulator skin can be set using the `-Xdevice` parameter; the skin name should mirror the directory name of the skin in the Wireless Toolkit's `wtklib` directory. In the following example, the Sony Ericsson P900 skin would be used. Default values are used for any parameters not set on the command line but they can be changed using the Preferences application in the toolkit.

```
%WTK_HOME%\bin\emulator -classpath build\ExpenseTracker.jar -
Xdescriptor:build\ExpenseTracker.jad -Xheapsize:192k -
Xdevice:SonyEricsson_P900
```

Sun's emulator makes output from the `System.out` and `System.err` streams visible on the console when running a MIDlet, providing a good source of debugging information. On the device this output is not generally available. Fortunately, the behavior of the device is usually consistent with the emulator. Several bugs found on a device when developing the expense application were reproducible using the emulator.

To run an application on a wireless device, the MIDlet must first be installed. The documentation for each device must be consulted for the correct installation instructions.

5.2.9 Summary

We have demonstrated how an expense claim application can be written and have shown some of the techniques that are essential to the success of MIDlets.

As the number of devices that ship with MIDP 2.0 increases, it will become a compelling platform. The inclusion of key features such as custom items and enhanced networking now means that MIDP is ready for the creation of enterprise applications in addition to the games that are currently common.

Full source code for this application can be downloaded from ***www. symbian.com/books***.

5.3 The Demo Racer Game

In this case study we will look at a sample application using the Game API. The Demo Racer MIDlet demonstrates how the Game API can be used to build rich gaming content (see Figure 5.11).

This sample application illustrates the use of `LayerManager` to manage a complex composite scene of layers (a `TiledLayer` background and `Sprites`) and also demonstrates the use of collision detection between the sprites (the car with the puddle and the car with the start–finish line). A UML class diagram of the application is shown in Figure 5.12.

We will discuss the application class by class, starting with the layers that make up the scene.

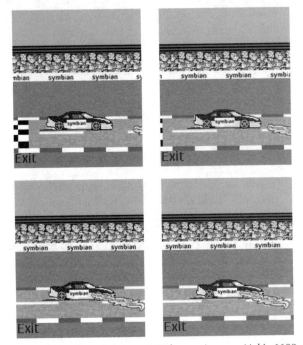

Figure 5.11   The Demo Racer MIDlet running on a Nokia 6600.

5.3.1 The `Background` Class

```
package demoracer;

import javax.microedition.lcdui.game.*;
import javax.microedition.lcdui.*;
public class Background extends TiledLayer  {

    static final int WIDTH = 5;
    static final int HEIGHT = 5;
    static final int TILE_WIDTH = 60;
```

```
static final int TILE_HEIGHT = 47;
static int xMove = -2;
static int yMove = 0;

public Background(int columns, int rows, Image image, int tileWidth,
        int tileHeight) {
    super(columns, rows, image, tileWidth, tileHeight);

    // the array which is the tile map for the tiledlayer
    int[] map = {
        4,4,4,4,4,
        5,5,5,5,5,
        3,3,3,3,3,
        1,2,1,2,1,
        3,3,3,3,3
    };

    // insert the tiles into the tiled layer using the setCell() method
    for (int i = 0; i < map.length; i++) {
        int column = i % WIDTH;
        int row = (i - column) / WIDTH;
        setCell(column, row, map[i]);
    }
}

public void tick(){
    move(xMove,yMove);
    if (this.getX() == (this.getCellWidth() * -2)) {
        setPosition(0, 0);
    }
}
}
```

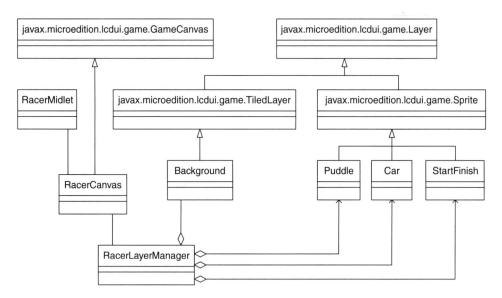

Figure 5.12 UML class diagram of the Demo Racer MIDlet.

Figure 5.13   The image used to build up the background layer.

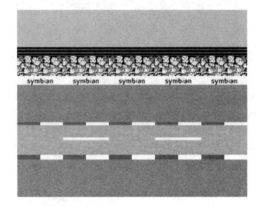

Figure 5.14   The background layer.

The constructor takes the image shown in Figure 5.13, consisting of five tiles, each of 60 × 47 pixels.

This is then used to construct the background layer (Figure 5.14), which consists of a grid of 5 × 5 cells.

For each application redraw cycle, the tick() method is called to move the position of the TiledLayer two pixels to the left (i.e. −2) relative to the co-ordinate system of the object upon which it is ultimately rendered (in this case the GameCanvas). When the TiledLayer has been offset by an amount equal to the width of two cells of the background grid (120 pixels requiring 60 redraw cycles – enough for the pattern to repeat itself), the position of the TiledLayer is re-set to the origin of the co-ordinate system of the rendering object.

5.3.2   The Puddle Class

A Puddle is an instance of Sprite to facilitate easy collision detection. The Puddle Sprite is created from an image consisting of just one frame (Figure 5.15).

Figure 5.15   The image used to build up the puddle Sprite.

```
package demoracer;
import javax.microedition.lcdui.Image;
import javax.microedition.lcdui.game.Sprite;
public class Puddle extends Sprite {

    static final int FRAME_COLS = 1;
    static final int FRAME_WIDTH = 1;
    private int xInitial;
    private int yInitial;
    private int repPeriod

    public Puddle(Image image, int width, int height, int x, int y) {
        super(image, width, height);
        setPosition(x, y);
        xInitial = x;
        yInitial = y;
        repPeriod = 2*Background.TILE_WIDTH;
    }

    public void tick() {
        if (repPeriod == 0) {
            setPosition(xInitial, yInitial);
            repPeriod = 2*Background.TILE_WIDTH;
        } else{
            move(Background.xMove, Background.yMove);
        }

        // set visible to false if it is off screen
        if(getX() + getWidth() <= 0) {//definitely outside Canvas clip area
            setVisible(false);
        } else {
            if( !isVisible() ) {
                setVisible(true);
            }
        }

        repPeriod--;
    }

}
```

The `tick()` method, called by the application clock, moves the puddle `Sprite` in step with the background layer, so that the puddles appear to remain stationary on the race track. The cycle length of 120 (`repPeriod = 2*Background.CELL_WIDTH`) is half that required to complete a lap, so the puddle appears twice per lap. At the end of the cycle the puddle is repositioned with `setPosition(xInitial, yInitial)` (remember `setPosition` positions the `Sprite` in the co-ordinate system of the painting object, here a `GameCanvas`). When the puddle `Sprite` is definitely outside the clip area displayed by the `Canvas`, its visibility is set to `false`.

Figure 5.16   The image used to build the Sprite for the start–finish line.

5.3.3   The `StartFinish` Class

This is similar to `Puddle`, again extending `Sprite` to facilitate ease of collision detection. Once more, the `Sprite` is created from an image consisting of a single frame (Figure 5.16).

```
package demoracer;
import javax.microedition.lcdui.Image;
import javax.microedition.lcdui.game.Sprite;
public class StartFinish extends Sprite {
    static final int FRAME_COLS = 1;
    static final int FRAME_WIDTH = 1;
    private int xInitial;
    private int yInitial;
    private int repPeriod;
    private boolean lapComplete = false;

    public StartFinish(Image image, int width, int height, int x, int y) {
        super(image,width,height);
        this.setPosition(x,y);
        xInitial = x;
        yInitial = y;
        repPeriod = 4*Background.TILE_WIDTH;
    }

    public boolean getLapComplete(){return lapComplete;}
    public void setLapComplete(boolean bln){lapComplete = bln;}

    public void tick() {
        if (repPeriod == 0) {
            setPosition(xInitial, yInitial);
            repPeriod = 4*Background.TILE_WIDTH;
        } else{
            move(Background.xMove, Background.yMove);
        }

        // set to invisible if the sprite is off screen.
        if(getX() + getWidth() <= 0) {//definitely outside Canvas clip area
            setVisible(false);
        } else {
            if( !isVisible() ) {
                setVisible(true);
            }
        }

        repPeriod--;
    }

}
```

A `tick()` method is called by the application clock to keep the position of the start finish line in step with the background layer (and thus appear to remain stationary on the race track). The cycle length of 240 (`repPeriod = 4*Background.CELL_WIDTH`) defines the length of a lap.

5.3.4 The `Car` class

```
package demoracer;
import javax.microedition.lcdui.Image;
import javax.microedition.lcdui.game.Sprite;
public class Car extends Sprite {
    static final int RAW_FRAMES = 4;
    static final int DRIVE_NORMAL = 0;
    static final int DRIVE_WET = 1;
    private int frameOrder[][] = {{0, 1}, {2, 3}};
    private StartFinish startFinish;
    private Puddle puddle;
    private RacerLayerManager layerManager;
    private int puddleCount;
    private boolean wet = false;

    public Car(Image image, int width, int height, int x, int y,
            RacerLayerManager layerManager) {
        super(image, width, height);
        setFrameSequence(frameOrder[DRIVE_NORMAL]);
        setPosition(x, y);
        defineCollisionRectangle(getWidth()-1,0,1,getHeight());
        layerManager = layerManager;
        puddle = layerManager.getPuddle();
        startFinish = layerManager.getStartFinish();
    }

    public void tick() {
        checkCollisions();
        nextFrame();
    }

    public void checkCollisions() {
        if(startFinish.isVisible()) {
            if (this.collidesWith(startFinish, true)) {
                startFinish.setLapComplete(true);
            } else {
                startFinish.setLapComplete(false);
            }
        }
        if(puddle.isVisible()) {
            if (!wet && this.collidesWith(puddle, true)) {
                setFrameSequence(frameOrder[DRIVE_WET]);
                puddleCount = puddle.getWidth()/2;
                wet = true;
            } else if (--puddleCount == 0) {
                setFrameSequence(frameOrder[DRIVE_NORMAL]);
                wet = false;
            }
        }
    }
}
```

Figure 5.17   The image used to build up the car Sprite.

The constructor creates the `Sprite` from an image consisting of four frames (Figure 5.17).

The top two frames generate the car moving in the dry. The bottom two frames generate the car in the wet (as it moves through the puddle).

On each application cycle, the `tick()` method is invoked to check for collisions with the `Puddle` and the `StartFinish` sprites. If the car is in collision with the puddle the set of frames used to generate the moving car is switched from the dry to the wet. If the car intersects with the start–finish line, a flag is set. Collision detection is on a pixel level basis, e.g. `collidesWith(puddle, true)`. If opaque pixels within the collision rectangle of the `Sprite` (by default the dimensions of the `Sprite` unless explicitly set) collide with opaque pixels of the target `Sprite` then a collision is detected.

5.3.5   The `RacerLayerManager` Class

Now that we have introduced the `Layers` that make up the application, let's look at the `RacerLayerManager` class that manages the rendering of the composite scene.

```
package demoracer;
import javax.microedition.lcdui.game.*;
import javax.microedition.lcdui.*;
import java.io.IOException;
public class RacerLayerManager extends LayerManager {

    private Background backGround;
    private Car car;
    private Puddle puddle;
    private StartFinish startFinish;
    private int xWindow;
    private int yWindow;
    private RacerGameCanvas gameCanvas;
    private final String LAP_COMPLETE = "Lap Complete";
    private final String PAUSED = "PAUSED";
    private int yOffset = 0;
    private int xOffset = 0;
    private Font font = Font.getFont(Font.FACE_PROPORTIONAL,
            Font.STYLE_BOLD, Font.SIZE_LARGE);

    public RacerLayerManager(RacerGameCanvas gameCanvas)
            throws IOException {
        // get the GameCanvas and set it to full screen mode
        this.gameCanvas = gameCanvas;
```

```java
        gameCanvas.setFullScreenMode(true);
        // create the sprites and then add them to the layer manager
        backGround = createBackground();
        startFinish = createStartFinishSprite();
        puddle = createPuddleSprite();
        car = createCarSprite();
        append(car);
        append(puddle);
        append(startFinish);
        append(backGround);
    }

    // move the sprite objects on to the next frame.
    public void tick() {
        backGround.tick();
        car.tick();
        puddle.tick();
        startFinish.tick();
    }

    public Puddle getPuddle(){return puddle;}
    public StartFinish getStartFinish(){return startFinish;}

    // this draws all the Sprites to the display
    public void draw(Graphics g) {
        g.setClip(0,0,gameCanvas.getWidth(),gameCanvas.getHeight());
        paint(g, xOffset, yOffset);
        drawMessage(g);
    }

    private void drawMessage(Graphics g) {
        int x;
        int y;
        g.setFont(font);
        // draw a "lap complete" message on screen according to the
        // toggle.
        if(startFinish.getLapComplete()) {
            g.setColor(200,0,0);
            x = gameCanvas.getWidth()/2;
            y = gameCanvas.getHeight()/2;
            g.setClip(0,y, gameCanvas.getWidth(), font.getHeight());
            g.drawString(LAP_COMPLETE,x,y,Graphics.TOP|Graphics.HCENTER);
        }

        if(!gameCanvas.isRunning()) {
            g.setColor(200,0,0);
            x = gameCanvas.getWidth()/2;
            y = gameCanvas.getHeight() / 2;
            g.drawString(PAUSED, x, y, Graphics.TOP | Graphics.HCENTER);
        }

        // draw the "Exit" button on the screen
        x = 0;
        g.setColor(0,0,0);
        y = gameCanvas.getHeight()-font.getHeight();
        g.setClip(0,y, gameCanvas.getWidth(), font.getHeight());
        g.drawString("Exit",2,y,Graphics.TOP|Graphics.LEFT);
```

```
        y = 20;
        g.setClip(0,y, gameCanvas.getWidth(), font.getHeight());
    }

    private Background createBackground() throws IOException {
        Image image = Image.createImage("/background.png");
        return new Background(Background.WIDTH, Background.HEIGHT, image,
                Background.TILE_WIDTH, Background.TILE_HEIGHT);
    }

    private Car createCarSprite() throws IOException {
        Image image = Image.createImage("/car.png");
        int width = image.getWidth() / 2;
        int height = image.getHeight() / 2;
        int x = gameCanvas.getWidth()/5;
        int y = backGround.getCellHeight()*4-(int)(height*2);
        return new Car(image, width, height, x, y, this);
    }

    public StartFinish createStartFinishSprite() throws IOException {
        Image image = Image.createImage("/startfinish.png");
        int width = image.getWidth() / StartFinish.FRAME_COLS;
        int height = image.getHeight() / StartFinish.FRAME_WIDTH;
        int x = backGround.getCellWidth() * 4;
        int y = backGround.getCellHeight() * 3;
        return new StartFinish(image, width, height, x, y);
    }

    public Puddle createPuddleSprite() throws IOException {
        Image image = Image.createImage("/puddle.png");
        int width = image.getWidth() / Puddle.FRAME_COLS;
        int height = image.getHeight() / Puddle.FRAME_WIDTH;
        int x = backGround.getCellWidth() * 3;
        int y = backGround.getCellHeight() * 3;
        return new Puddle(image, width, height, x, y);
    }
}
```

The `RacerLayerManager` constructor creates the `Background` instance, and instances of the `Car`, `Puddle` and `StartFinish` sprites. These are appended to the `RacerLayerManager` instance, with the `Car` Sprite being appended first (lowest z-value) and the `Background` last (highest z-value).

The `tick()` method, invoked by the application clock, simply invokes the corresponding `tick()` methods of the managed layers. The other major function of the `RacerLayerManager` is to render the view of the composite scene. This is performed in the `draw()` method:

```
public void draw(Graphics g) {
    g.setClip(0,0,gameCanvas.getWidth(),gameCanvas.getHeight());
    paint(g, xOffset, yOffset);
    drawMessage(g);
}
```

This takes a `Graphics` object, g (from the `RacerGameCanvas`) and uses it to set the clip area equal to the dimensions of the `Canvas`. To render the composite view, the `paint()` method of `LayerManager` is invoked. Additionally, the `drawMessage()` method is called to add the "Lap Complete" message to the scene when a lap has been completed.

The scene is rendered to screen in the `RacerGameCanvas` class:

```java
package demoracer;
import javax.microedition.lcdui.game.*;
import javax.microedition.lcdui.*;
import java.io.IOException;
public class RacerGameCanvas extends GameCanvas implements Runnable {
    private RacerMidlet midlet;
    private RacerLayerManager layerManager;
    private Thread thread;
    private boolean running;
    private final int SLEEP = 0;

    public RacerGameCanvas(RacerMidlet midlet) throws IOException {
        super(false);
        this.midlet = midlet;
        layerManager = new RacerLayerManager(this);
    }

    public boolean isRunning(){return running;}

    synchronized void start() {
        running = true;
        thread = new Thread(this);
        thread.start();
    }

    public void run() {
        Graphics graphics = getGraphics();
        try {
            while (running) {//repaints at equal time intervals
                long start = System.currentTimeMillis();
                // draw the current frame for each Sprite on screen
                paint(graphics);
                flushGraphics();
                // set the next frame to be displayed.
                layerManager.tick();
                long end = System.currentTimeMillis();
                long snooze = SLEEP-(end-start);
                if (snooze > 0) {
                    Thread.sleep(snooze);
                }
            }
        }catch(InterruptedException ie) {
            System.out.println(ie.toString());
        }
    }

    synchronized void stop() {
        running = false;
    }
```

```
public void paint(Graphics g) {
    layerManager.draw(g);
}

public void keyPressed(int keyCode) {
    if(keyCode == -6) {
        midlet.releaseResource();
        midlet.notifyDestroyed();
    }
}
}
```

This class extends `GameCanvas` and hence renders the game onto a `Canvas` using double buffering. The class renders the game in a new `Thread` using the `run()` method. Each cycle renders the graphics and then calls the `tick()` method of `RacerLayerManager` to move on to the next frame of the scene. The way in which the `while` loop is written ensures that the graphics are rendered at equal time intervals so that the game speed does not depend on how long individual `paint()`, `flushGraphics()` or `tick()` methods take to complete.

The implementation of the `GameCanvas` `paint()` method simply calls the `draw()` method of `LayerManager`, passing in the `Graphics` object.

The `RacerGameCanvas` also accepts user input via the `keyPressed()` method of `GameCanvas` to exit the application.

5.3.6   The `RacerMIDlet` Class

```
package demoracer;
import javax.microedition.lcdui.*;
import javax.microedition.midlet.*;
import java.io.IOException;
public class RacerMidlet extends MIDlet{

    private RacerGameCanvas gameCanvas;
    private Display display;
    private Displayable displayable;

    public RacerMidlet() {
        // get the current display context.
        display = Display.getDisplay(this);
    }

    protected void startApp() {
        // get the Canvas and then set it as the current display
        try {
            getCanvasDisplay();
            display.setCurrent(displayable);
        }catch(Exception e) {
            Alert alert = new Alert("Error", e.getMessage(), null,
```

```
                    AlertType.ERROR);
            display.setCurrent(alert);
            try {
                Thread.sleep(2000);
            }catch (InterruptedException ie) {

            }
            notifyDestroyed();
        }
    }

    protected void pauseApp() {
        if(displayable != null) {
            display.setCurrent(displayable);
        }
        releaseResource();
    }

    protected void destroyApp(boolean unconditional) {
        releaseResource();
    }

    public void releaseResource() {
        if(gameCanvas != null) {
            gameCanvas.stop();
        }
    }

    private void getCanvasDisplay() throws Exception{
        try{
            // if there is no canvas then create one
            if(gameCanvas == null) {
                gameCanvas = new RacerGameCanvas(this);
            }
            // if the canvas is not running then start it
            if(!gameCanvas.isRunning()) {
                gameCanvas.start();
            }
            //set the canvas as the "global" displayable object
            displayable = gameCanvas;
        }catch(IOException ioe) {
            throw new Exception("Unable to load image!!");
        }
    }
}
```

This implements the MIDlet lifecycle methods in such a way as to release resources (notably stopping the `RacerGameCanvas` clock thread) when the AMS causes the MIDlet to move into the PAUSED state. Similarly, calling `startApp` will cause the `MIDlet` to resume where it left off if it was previously put into the PAUSED state by a call to `pauseApp`.

The full source code for the Demo Racer MIDlet is available to download from Symbian's website at *www.symbian.com/books*.

5.4   The Picture Puzzle

This case study describes a simple game that uses the Mobile Media API to take photographs using a camera phone. The sample MIDlet also illustrates using the RMS store to save, load and delete persistent records and makes use of a `TiledLayer` from the Game API.

The Picture Puzzle MIDlet is a variation on the familiar Mix Pix native application that ships on Nokia Series 60 phones. In this sample MIDlet we use the on-board camera to capture a snapshot that acts as the original image. The MIDlet automatically displays this as a scrambled 4 × 4 grid (Figure 5.18). The user has to unscramble the image by re-arranging the tiles to complete the game (Figure 5.19).

The MIDlet stores newly captured images in the RMS record store so that they are available for subsequent games, as shown in Figure 5.20. The Picture Puzzle MIDlet comprises the classes shown in Figure 5.21.

Figure 5.18   The Picture Puzzle MIDlet running on a Nokia 6600.

Figure 5.19   The completed Picture Puzzle game.

Figure 5.20 Starting a new game: the user can create a new image or load an existing image from the RMS.

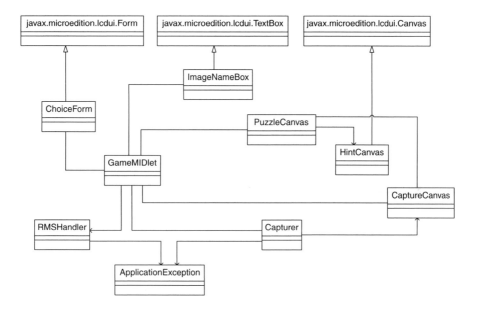

Figure 5.21 A UML class diagram of the Picture Puzzle MIDlet.

5.4.1 The `GameMIDlet` Class

```
package picturepuzzle;
import javax.microedition.midlet.MIDlet ;
import javax.microedition.lcdui.* ;
import java.io.* ;
```

```
public class GameMIDlet extends MIDlet {
    private Display display;
    private ChoiceForm choiceForm;
    private CaptureCanvas captureCanvas;
    private PuzzleCanvas puzzleCanvas;
    private Capturer capturer;
    private RMSHandler rms;

    public GameMIDlet() {
        rms = new RMSHandler();
        display = Display.getDisplay(this);
        choiceForm = new ChoiceForm(this);
    }

    public void startApp() {
        Displayable current = display.getCurrent();
        try{
            rms.openRecordStore();
        }catch(ApplicationException ae){
            showAlert(ae);
        }

        if (current == null) {
            // first call
            displayChoiceForm();
        }else {
            //called after a pause
            display.setCurrent(current);
            //player will have been discarded so recreate.
            try{
                capturer.createPlayer();
            }catch(ApplicationException ae) {
                showAlert(ae);
            }
        }
    }

    public void pauseApp() {
        try{
            rms.closeRecordStore();
        }catch(ApplicationException ae){}
        if(capturer != null){
            capturer.discardPlayer();
        }
    }

    public void destroyApp(boolean unconditional) {
        try{
            rms.closeRecordStore();
        }catch(ApplicationException ae){}
        if(capturer != null){
            capturer.discardPlayer();
        }
    }

    public void displayChoiceForm() {
        try {
```

```
            String[] imageNames = loadImageNames();
            choiceForm.setImageNames(imageNames);
     }catch(ApplicationException ae) {
         showAlert(ae);
     }
     display.setCurrent(choiceForm);
}

public void displayHintCanvas(Image image){
     HintCanvas hintCanvas = new HintCanvas(image);
     display.setCurrent(hintCanvas);
     try {
         Thread.sleep(1500);
     }catch (InterruptedException ie) {}
     display.setCurrent(puzzleCanvas);
}

public void displayCaptureCanvas() {
     if (captureCanvas == null) {
         //create CaptureCanvas and associated player (Capturer)
         captureCanvas = new CaptureCanvas(this);
         try{
             capturer = new Capturer(this, captureCanvas);
             capturer.startPlayer();
             display.setCurrent(captureCanvas);
         }catch(final ApplicationException ae){
             //set to null if unable to create player
             captureCanvas = null;
             showAlert(ae);
         }
     } else {
         //CaptureCanvas and associated player (Capturer) already exist
         display.setCurrent(captureCanvas);
     }
}

public void displayPuzzleCanvas(byte[] imageData) {
     Image image = Image.createImage(imageData, 0, imageData.length);
     puzzleCanvas = new PuzzleCanvas(this, image);
     display.setCurrent(puzzleCanvas);
}

public void takePhoto(){
     try {
         byte[] data = capturer.takeSnapshot();
         capturer.stopPlayer();
         ImageNameBox imageNameBox = new ImageNameBox(this, data);
         display.setCurrent(imageNameBox);
     }catch(final ApplicationException ae) {
         showAlert(ae);
     }
}

public void loadAndDisplayImage(String imageName){
     try{
         byte[] imageData = rms.retrieveImageFromStore(imageName);
         displayPuzzleCanvas(imageData);
     }catch(ApplicationException ae){
```

```
            showAlert(ae);
        }
    }

    public String[] loadImageNames() throws ApplicationException {
        String[] images = rms.retrieveStoredImageNames();
        return images;
    }

    public void saveImage(String imageName, byte[] data) {
        try {
            rms.addImageToStore(imageName, data);
        }catch(ApplicationException ae) {
            showAlert(ae);
        }
    }

    public void deleteImage(String imageName) {
        try{
            rms.deleteImageFromStore(imageName);
        }catch(ApplicationException ae){
            showAlert(ae);
        }
    }

    public void showAlert(final ApplicationException ae){
        new Thread() {
            public void run() {
                Alert alert = new Alert(ae.getExceptionType(),
                        ae.getMessage(), null, AlertType.ERROR);
                alert.setTimeout(1500);
                display.setCurrent(alert);
            }
        }.start();
    }

    public void exit(){
        try{
            rms.closeRecordStore();
        }catch(ApplicationException ae){}
        if(capturer != null){
            capturer.discardPlayer();
        }
        notifyDestroyed();
    }
}
```

The GameMidlet class extends MIDlet and provides implementations for the MIDlet lifecycle methods. The startApp() and pause-App() methods are worth looking at in more detail.

When the MIDlet is requested to move into the PAUSED state, the pauseApp() method (listed below) closes the RMS record store and releases any resources associated with the VideoPlayer used to capture photos by calling the discardPlayer() method of the Capturer class. This is important since no other application can access the camera while the MIDlet holds the VideoPlayer.

```
public void pauseApp() {
    try{
        rms.closeRecordStore();
    }catch(ApplicationException ae){}
    if(capturer != null){
        capturer.discardPlayer();
    }
}
```

The `startApp()` method (listed below) opens the record store and then determines whether the current invocation is the first call to `startApp()`, in which case it displays the first application screen by calling `displayChoiceForm`. If, on the other hand, `startApp()` has been invoked after a previous call to `pauseApp()`, it sets the display to the last `Displayable` that was shown prior to the MIDlet moving into the PAUSED state. In addition, it recreates the `VideoPlayer` that was discarded when the MIDlet moved into the PAUSED state.

```
public void startApp() {
    Displayable current = display.getCurrent();
    try{
        rms.openRecordStore();
    }catch(ApplicationException ae){
        showAlert(ae);
    }

    if (current == null) {
        // first call
        displayChoiceForm();
    }else {
        //called after a pause
        display.setCurrent(current);
        //player will have been discarded so recreate.
        try{
            capturer.createPlayer();
        }catch(ApplicationException ae) {
            showAlert(ae);
        }
    }
}
```

The `GameMIDlet` class also acts as the application controller. It provides a number of callback methods that are invoked by the application's user interface objects in response to user interaction. This helps to isolate the UI objects from tasks that are not related to the user interface, such as accessing the RMS record store. The `GameMIDlet` class handles the flow of control of the application using the following methods:

```
public void displayChoiceForm() {...}

public void displayHintCanvas(Image image){...}
```

```
public void displayCaptureCanvas() {...}

public void displayPuzzleCanvas(Image image) {...}

public void takePhoto(){...}

public void loadAndDisplayImage(String imageName){...}

public String[] loadImageNames() throws ApplicationException {...}

public void saveImage(String imageName, byte[] data) {...}

public void deleteImage(String imageName) {...}

public void showAlert(final ApplicationException ae){...}

public void exit(){...}
```

5.4.2 The `ChoiceForm` Class

The first action performed by the `GameMIDlet` when it starts is to call the `displayChoiceForm()` method:

```
public void displayChoiceForm() {
    try {
        String[] imageNames = loadImageNames();
        choiceForm.setImageNames(imageNames);
    }catch(ApplicationException ae) {
        showAlert(ae);
    }
    display.setCurrent(choiceForm);
}
```

This loads the names of any stored images and displays them in an instance of `ChoiceForm`. The user has the option of creating a new image or using a previous image stored in the RMS (if any exist). The source code for `ChoiceForm` is listed below.

```
package picturepuzzle;
import javax.microedition.lcdui.*;
import java.io.*;
/**
 * Displays names of images stored in the record store and provides the
 * user with the option to create a new image.
 */
public class ChoiceForm extends Form implements CommandListener {

    private GameMIDlet midlet;
    private ChoiceGroup cg;
    private Command startCommand;
    private Command deleteCommand;
    private Command exitCommand;
```

```
    // Creates the ChoiceForm. Adds Commands and a ChoiceGroup.
    public ChoiceForm(GameMIDlet midlet){
        super("Saved Images");
        this.midlet = midlet;
        startCommand = new Command("Start" , Command.SCREEN , 2);
        deleteCommand = new Command("Delete" , Command.SCREEN , 3);
        exitCommand = new Command("Exit", Command.EXIT, 1);
        addCommand(exitCommand);
        addCommand(startCommand);
        setCommandListener(this);
        cg = new ChoiceGroup("Choose image option:",
                ChoiceGroup.EXCLUSIVE);
        append(cg);
        cg.append("Create new image", null);
    }

    //Adds the names of the stored images to the ChoiceGroup.
    public void setImageNames(String[] imageNames) {
        while( cg.size() > 1 ){
            cg.delete(1);
        }
        cg.setSelectedIndex(0, true);
        if (imageNames != null) {
            for (int i = 0 ; i < imageNames.length ; i++) {
                cg.append(imageNames[i] , null);
            }
            addCommand(deleteCommand);
        }
    }

    public void commandAction(Command command , Displayable displayable) {
        if (command == exitCommand) {
            midlet.exit();
        } else if(command == startCommand) {
            if (cg.getSelectedIndex() == 0) {
                midlet.displayCaptureCanvas();
            }else {
                String imageName = cg.getString(cg.getSelectedIndex());
                midlet.loadAndDisplayImage(imageName);
            }
        }else if(command == deleteCommand) {
            int index = cg.getSelectedIndex();
            if(index > 0) {
                String imageName = cg.getString(index);
                cg.setSelectedIndex(index - 1, true);
                cg.delete(index);
                midlet.deleteImage(imageName);
            }
            if(cg.size() == 1) {
                removeCommand(deleteCommand);
            }
        }
    }
}
```

This uses a ChoiceGroup to display the names of any previous images stored by the user or allows the user to capture a new image.

If the user selects the "Create new image" option the ChoiceForm instance calls the displayCaptureCanvas() method of GameMI-Dlet (listed below).

```
public void displayCaptureCanvas() {
      if (captureCanvas == null) {
          //create CaptureCanvas and associated player
          captureCanvas = new CaptureCanvas(this);
          try{
              capturer = new Capturer(this, captureCanvas);
              capturer.startPlayer();
              display.setCurrent(captureCanvas);
          }catch(final ApplicationException ae){
              //set to null if unable to create player
              captureCanvas = null;
              showAlert(ae);
          }
      } else {
          //CaptureCanvas and associated player already exist
          display.setCurrent(captureCanvas);
      }
   }
```

This creates an instance of the Capturer class encapsulating a Video-Player and an associated Canvas to display the output. It then calls the startPlayer() method of the Capturer class to start the Video-Player which renders the output of the phone's camera to the Canvas.

5.4.3 The Capturer Class

```
package picturepuzzle;
import javax.microedition.media.*;
import javax.microedition.media.control.*;
import java.io.IOException;

// Creates the VideoPlayer used to capture a photo.
public class Capturer {

    private GameMIDlet midlet;
    private CaptureCanvas canvas;
    private Player player = null;
    private VideoControl videoControl = null;
    private boolean active = false;

     // Performs initialization and creates the VideoPlayer instance.
    public Capturer(GameMIDlet midlet, CaptureCanvas canvas)
        throws ApplicationException {
        this.midlet = midlet;
        this.canvas = canvas;
        createPlayer();
    }

// Creates a VideoPlayer and gets an associated VideoControl
    public void createPlayer() throws ApplicationException {
```

```
    try {
        player = Manager.createPlayer("capture://video");
        player.realize();
        // Sets VideoControl to the current display.
        videoControl =
                (VideoControl)(player.getControl("VideoControl"));
        if (videoControl == null) {
            discardPlayer();
        } else {
            videoControl.initDisplayMode(VideoControl.USE_DIRECT_VIDEO,
                    canvas);
            int cWidth = canvas.getWidth();
            int cHeight = canvas.getHeight();
            int dWidth = 160;
            int dHeight = 120;
            videoControl.setDisplaySize(dWidth, dHeight);
            videoControl.setDisplayLocation((cWidth - dWidth)/2,
                    (cHeight - dHeight)/2);
        }
    } catch (IOException ioe) {
        discardPlayer();
        throw new ApplicationException("Unable to access camera",
                ioe);
    } catch (MediaException me) {
        discardPlayer();
        throw new ApplicationException("Unable to access camera", me);
    } catch(SecurityException se) {
        discardPlayer();
        throw new ApplicationException("Unable to access camera", se);
    }
}

public byte[] takeSnapshot() throws ApplicationException {
    byte[] pngImage = null;
    if (videoControl == null) {
        throw new ApplicationException(
                "Unable to capture photo: VideoControl null");
    }
    try {
        pngImage = videoControl.getSnapshot(null);
    }catch(MediaException me) {
        throw new ApplicationException("Unable to capture photo", me);
    }

    return pngImage;
}

public void discardPlayer() {
    if(player != null) {
        player.close();
        player = null;
    }
    videoControl = null;
}

public void startPlayer() throws ApplicationException {
    if ((player != null) && !active) {
```

```
        try {
            player.start();
            videoControl.setVisible(true);
        } catch(MediaException me) {
            throw new ApplicationException(
                    "Unable to start video player", me);
        } catch(SecurityException se) {
            throw new ApplicationException(
                    "Unable to start video player", se);
        }
        active = true;
    }
}

public void stopPlayer() throws ApplicationException {
    if ((player != null) && active) {
        try {
            videoControl.setVisible(false);
            player.stop();
        } catch (MediaException me) {
            throw new ApplicationException(
                    "Unable to stop video player", me);
        }
        active = false;
    }
}
}
```

The creation and initialization of the `VideoPlayer` takes place in the `createPlayer()` method. We use the static `createPlayer()` method of `Manager` to create the `VideoPlayer` instance using the `capture://video` URI to indicate that the data source is the phone's camera. Next we call the `realize()` method to move the player to the REALIZED state. We then get a `VideoControl` and initialize it with our `CaptureCanvas` instance.

The photo is taken using the `takeSnapshot()` method. It calls the `VideoControl.getSnapshot()` method which takes a snapshot of the current contents of the display and returns it as a PNG image. The `takeSnapshot()` method is called from the `CaptureCanvas` object.

5.4.4 The `CaptureCanvas` Class

```
package picturepuzzle;
import javax.microedition.lcdui.*;
/**
 * A Canvas for rendering the output of the VideoPlayer. Also handles the
 * user interaction to take the snapshot.
 */
public class CaptureCanvas extends Canvas implements CommandListener{

    private Command captureCommand;
    private GameMIDlet midlet;
```

```
//Creates the CaptureCanvas. Adds a "Capture" command.
public CaptureCanvas(GameMIDlet midlet){
    this.midlet = midlet;
    captureCommand = new Command("Capture", Command.SCREEN, 1);
    addCommand(captureCommand);
    setCommandListener(this);
}

// Paints a yellow background.
public void paint(Graphics g) {
    g.setColor(0x00FFFF00); // yellow
    g.fillRect(0, 0, getWidth(), getHeight());
}

//Responds to the "Capture" command and takes the photo.
public void commandAction(Command command , Displayable displayable) {
    if(command == captureCommand){
        midlet.takePhoto();
    }
}

//Responds to the Joystick being pressed and takes the photo.
public void keyPressed(int keyCode) {
    int key = getGameAction(keyCode);
    if (key == Canvas.FIRE) {
        midlet.takePhoto();
    }
}
}
```

The `CaptureCanvas` class provides the `Canvas` onto which the output of the camera is rendered. When the user is satisfied with the scene, the snapshot is taken by selecting the "Capture" `Command`. The `commandAction()` method makes a call back to the `GameMIDlet` `takePhoto()` method:

```
public void takePhoto(){
    try {
        byte[] data = capturer.takeSnapshot();
        capturer.stopPlayer();
        ImageNameBox imageNameBox = new ImageNameBox(this, data);
        display.setCurrent(imageNameBox);
    }catch(final ApplicationException ae) {
        showAlert(ae);
    }
}
```

This calls the `takeSnapshot()` method of the `Capturer`, which returns the captured image data. Once the photo has been taken the `VideoPlayer` is then stopped using the `stopPlayer()` method. An instance of `ImageNameBox` is created to enable the user to associate a name with the new image.

5.4.5   The `ImageNameBox` Class

`ImageNameBox` extends `TextBox` and provides an area into which the user can enter a name for the new image.

```
package picturepuzzle;
import javax.microedition.lcdui.*;
public class ImageNameBox extends TextBox implements CommandListener {

    private GameMIDlet midlet;
    private byte[] data;
    private Command saveCommand;

    public ImageNameBox(GameMIDlet midlet, byte[] data) {
        super("Enter image name", "", 20, TextField.ANY);
        this.midlet = midlet;
        this.data = data;
        saveCommand = new Command("Save" , Command.SCREEN , 2);
        setCommandListener(this);
        addCommand(saveCommand);
    }

    public void commandAction(Command command , Displayable displayable) {
        if (command == saveCommand) {
            midlet.saveImage(getString(), data);
            midlet.displayPuzzleCanvas(image);
        }
    }
}
```

When the user selects the "Save" command, the image data and name are saved to the RMS store via a call to the `GameMIDlet saveImage()` method. The `GameMIDlet displayPuzzleCanvas()` method is invoked to display the image.

```
public void displayPuzzleCanvas(byte[] imageData) {
    Image image = Image.createImage(imageData, 0, imageData.length);
    puzzleCanvas = new PuzzleCanvas(this, image);
    display.setCurrent(puzzleCanvas);
}
```

The `displayPuzzleCanvas()` method creates the `Image` and a new `PuzzleCanvas` instance and displays it.

5.4.6   The `PuzzleCanvas` Class

The game logic is encapsulated in the `PuzzleCanvas` Class:

```
package picturepuzzle;
import javax.microedition.lcdui.*;
import javax.microedition.lcdui.game.*;
import java.util.*;
```

```
/**
 * The game Canvas. Displays the randomized image as a 4x4 grid of
 * tiles. Allows the user to re-arrange the tiles. Indicates when the
 * correct arrangement has been arrived at and the game is over.
 */
public class PuzzleCanvas extends Canvas implements CommandListener {

    static final int IMAGE_WIDTH = 160;
    static final int IMAGE_HEIGHT = 120;
    static final int COLS = 4;
    static final int ROWS = 4;
    private TiledLayer imageLayer;
    private Image image;
    private int cursorX, cursorY;//position coordinates of cursor
    private GameMIDlet midlet;
    private boolean doublePaired;
    private Command exitCommand;
    private Command hintCommand;
    private Command newCommand;
    private int firstBlock = 0;
    private int secondBlock = 0;
    private int firstCol = 0;
    private int firstRow = 0;
    private int secondCol = 0;
    private int secondRow = 0;

    // Creates the scrambled puzzle from an image.
    public PuzzleCanvas(GameMIDlet midlet, Image image) {
        super();
        this.midlet = midlet;
        this.image = image;
        exitCommand = new Command("Exit", Command.EXIT, 1);
        hintCommand = new Command("Hint", Command.SCREEN, 2) ;
        newCommand = new Command("New game", Command.SCREEN, 2);
        addCommand(exitCommand);
        addCommand(hintCommand);
        setCommandListener(this);
        createBoard();
        cursorX = getWidthDiff() / 2;
        cursorY = getHeightDiff() / 2;
        imageLayer.setPosition(getWidthDiff() / 2, getHeightDiff() / 2);
        doublePaired = true;
    }
    public int getWidthDiff() {
        return getWidth() - IMAGE_WIDTH;
    }
    public int getHeightDiff() {
        return getHeight() - IMAGE_HEIGHT;
    }
    // randomize the order of tiles in the image layer.
    private void createBoard() {
        imageLayer = new TiledLayer(COLS, ROWS, image, IMAGE_WIDTH/COLS,
                IMAGE_HEIGHT/ROWS);
        Random ran = new Random();
        Vector v = new Vector(ROWS*COLS);
        boolean b = true;
        int i;
        // get integer numbers from 1 to ROWS*COLS in random order
```

```
        while (b) {
            i = ran.nextInt()%(ROWS*COLS)+1;
            if (i > 0 && i <= (ROWS*COLS)) {
                if ( !v.contains(new Integer(i)) ) {
                    v.addElement(new Integer(i));
                }
                if (v.size() == ROWS*COLS) {
                    b = false;
                }
            }
        }
        for (int m = 0; m < ROWS*COLS; m++) {
            int integer = ( (Integer) v.elementAt(m)).intValue();
            imageLayer.setCell( m/ROWS ,m%ROWS, integer);
        }
    }
// Paints the current TiledLayer arrangement and draws the cursor.
// Also indicates "Game over" when the game is completed.
public void paint(Graphics g) {
    g.setColor(255, 255, 255);// Paint a white background
    g.fillRect(0, 0, getWidth(), getHeight());
    imageLayer.paint(g);
    g.setColor(255, 0, 0);
    drawFrame(cursorX, cursorY, g);
    if (isWinning()){
        g.setFont(Font.getFont(Font.FACE_MONOSPACE, Font.STYLE_BOLD,
                Font.SIZE_LARGE));
        g.drawString("Game Over!!", getWidth() / 2, getHeight() / 2,
                Graphics.HCENTER | Graphics.TOP);
    }
}
// Responds to movement of the Joystick.
public void keyPressed(int keyCode) {
    int key = getGameAction(keyCode);
    if (key == LEFT) {
        moveLeft();
    } else if (key == RIGHT) {
        moveRight();
    } else if (key == UP) {
        moveUp();
    } else if (key == DOWN) {
        moveDown();
    } else if (key == FIRE && !doublePaired) {
        setSecondBlock();
        if (isWinning()) {
            addCommand(newCommand);
        }
    } else if (key == FIRE && doublePaired) {
        setFirstBlock();
    }
    repaint();
}
// Ascertains whether the current arrangement of tiles is equal to the
//original image and hence the game has been successfully completed.
public boolean isWinning() {
    int count = 1 ;
    for (int row = 0 ; row < imageLayer.getRows() ; row++) {
        for (int col = 0 ; col < imageLayer.getColumns() ; col++) {
```

```
                if (imageLayer.getCell(col, row) != count) {
                    return false ;
                }
                count++;
            }
        }
        return true;
}


// Draws cursor.
private void drawFrame(int x, int y, Graphics g) {
    g.drawRect(x, y, imageLayer.getCellWidth(),
            imageLayer.getCellHeight());
}
// Moves cursor one tile up.
public void moveUp() {
    cursorY = cursorY - imageLayer.getCellHeight();
    if (cursorY < getHeightDiff() / 2) {
        cursorY = getHeightDiff() / 2;
    }
}
// Moves cursor one tile down.
public void moveDown() {
    cursorY = cursorY + imageLayer.getCellHeight();
    int yMax = IMAGE_HEIGHT + getHeightDiff()/2 -
            imageLayer.getCellHeight();
    if (cursorY > yMax) {
        cursorY = yMax;
    }
}
// Moves cursor one tile left */
public void moveLeft() {
    cursorX = cursorX - imageLayer.getCellWidth();
    if (cursorX < getWidthDiff() / 2) {
        cursorX = getWidthDiff() / 2;
    }
}


// Moves cursor one tile right.
public void moveRight() {
    cursorX = cursorX + imageLayer.getCellWidth();
    if ( cursorX > IMAGE_WIDTH + getWidthDiff() / 2 -
            imageLayer.getCellWidth()) {
        cursorX = IMAGE_WIDTH + getWidthDiff() / 2 -
                imageLayer.getCellWidth();
    }
}
// Gets the initial tile that the user has selected for transposition.
public void setFirstBlock() {
    firstCol = (cursorX - getWidthDiff() / 2) /
            imageLayer.getCellWidth();
    firstRow = (cursorY - getHeightDiff() / 2) /
            imageLayer.getCellHeight();
    firstBlock = imageLayer.getCell(firstCol, firstRow);
    doublePaired = false;
}


// Gets the destination tile selected by the user.
```

```
// Then interchanges the initial and destination tiles.
public void setSecondBlock() {
    secondCol = (cursorX - getWidthDiff() / 2) /
            imageLayer.getCellWidth();
    secondRow = (cursorY - getHeightDiff() / 2) /
            imageLayer.getCellHeight();
    secondBlock = imageLayer.getCell(secondCol, secondRow);
    // interchange two cells
    imageLayer.setCell(firstCol, firstRow, secondBlock);
    imageLayer.setCell(secondCol, secondRow, firstBlock);
    doublePaired = true;
}
public void commandAction(Command command, Displayable displayable) {
    if (command == exitCommand) {
        midlet.exit();
    } else if (command == hintCommand){
        new Thread() {//to avoid blocking despatcher
            public void run(){
                midlet.displayHintCanvas(image);
            }
        }.start();
    } else if (command == newCommand) {
        midlet.displayChoiceForm();
        image = null;
        midlet = null;
    }
}
}
}
```

The createBoard() method takes the captured image and re-arranges it. It uses the image to create a 4 × 4 TiledLayer. Re-arranging the image then simply becomes a matter of successively calling the set-Cell() method of the TiledLayer. The PuzzleCanvas handles all user interaction itself either in the keyPressed() method (inherited from Canvas) or the commandAction() method mandated by the CommandListener interface which PuzzleCanvas implements. The keyPressed() method listens for arrow key (or joystick, in the case of the Nokia 6600) events and moves the cursor appropriately.

In response to FIRE key events (choosing "Select" in the Wireless Toolkit or depressing the joystick on the Nokia 6600), the application selects the tile from the first FIRE event and transposes it with the one from the second FIRE event.

The commandAction() method provides options to exit the application, start a new game (upon successful completion of the current game) and display a hint screen.

The hint option calls the GameMIDlet method displayHintCanvas(), which creates a HintCanvas instance displaying the original (unscrambled) image as a hint to the user. Note that this method should be called from within a new Thread so that the commandAction() method can return quickly and avoid blocking the single VM event dispatcher Thread.

The exitCommand option calls the exit() method of GameMIDlet:

```
public void exit(){
    try{
        rms.closeRecordStore();
    }catch(ApplicationException ae){}
    if(capturer != null){
        capturer.discardPlayer();
    }
    notifyDestroyed();
}
```

This closes the record store and discards the player, releasing its resources, then calls notifyDestroyed() to indicate to the AMS that the MIDlet has moved into the DESTROYED state and can be reclaimed.

5.4.7 The RMSHandler Class

The last class we should describe is the RMSHandler (shown below) which handles loading previous images from storage, saving a new image to storage and deleting images from storage.

```
package picturepuzzle;
import javax.microedition.rms.*;
import java.io.*;
import java.util.*;
// Used to store images in RMS storage.
// Stores images in the IMAGE RecordStore. Creates an INDEX record store
// to store the name of the image and its record id for easy retrieval.
public class RMSHandler {

    //Name of record store for storing images
    public static final String IMAGE_RECORD_STORE = "IMAGES";

    //Name of record store for storing index entries
    public static final String INDEX_RECORD_STORE = "KEYS";

    private RecordStore indexRecordStore;
    private RecordStore imageRecordStore;
    private Hashtable hashTable;

    public RMSHandler(){
        hashTable = new Hashtable();
    }

    //Opens IMAGE and INDEX record stores
    public void openRecordStore() throws ApplicationException {
        try {
            imageRecordStore =
                    RecordStore.openRecordStore(IMAGE_RECORD_STORE, true);
            indexRecordStore =
                    RecordStore.openRecordStore(INDEX_RECORD_STORE, true);
        } catch (RecordStoreException rse) {
```

```
              throw new ApplicationException("Unable to open record store",
                  rse);
      }
}

//Closes IMAGE and INDEX record stores.
public void closeRecordStore() throws ApplicationException {
    try {
        imageRecordStore.closeRecordStore();
        indexRecordStore.closeRecordStore();
    } catch (RecordStoreException rse) {
        throw new ApplicationException("Unable to close record store",
                rse);
    }
}

//Adds an entry to the INDEX store
private int addKey(String name, int recordID) throws
        ApplicationException {
    try {
        ByteArrayOutputStream baos = new ByteArrayOutputStream();
        DataOutputStream dos = new DataOutputStream(baos);
        dos.writeUTF(name);
        dos.writeInt(recordID);
        byte[] data = baos.toByteArray();
        int keyID = indexRecordStore.addRecord(data, 0, data.length);
        return keyID;
    } catch (IOException ioe) {
        throw new ApplicationException(
                "Unable to add key to record store", ioe);
    } catch (RecordStoreException rse) {
        throw new ApplicationException(
                "Unable to add key to record store", rse);
    }
}

//Deletes the index entry from the INDEX record store.
private void deleteKey(int keyID) throws ApplicationException {
    try {
        indexRecordStore.deleteRecord(keyID);
    } catch (RecordStoreException rse) {
        throw new ApplicationException(
                "Unable to delete key from record store", rse);
    }
}

//Adds Image data to IMAGE RecordStore.
private int addImageRecord(byte[] data) throws ApplicationException {
    try {
        int recordID = imageRecordStore.addRecord(data, 0,
                data.length);
        return  recordID;
    } catch (RecordStoreException rse) {
        throw new ApplicationException(
                "Unable to add record to record store", rse);
    }
}
```

```java
//Deletes Image data from IMAGE RecordStore.
private void deleteImageRecord(int recordID) throws
        ApplicationException {
    try {
        imageRecordStore.deleteRecord(recordID);
        return;
    } catch (RecordStoreException rse) {
        throw new ApplicationException(
                "Unable to delete record from record store", rse);
    }
}

 //Adds an Image to the IMAGE RecordStore and its name and record ID
 //to the INDEX record store.
public void addImageToStore(String name, byte[] imageData)
        throws ApplicationException {
    int[] recordIndices = new int[2];
    recordIndices[0] = addImageRecord(imageData);
    recordIndices[1] = addKey(name, recordIndices[0]);
    hashTable.put(name, recordIndices);
}

//Deletes image from IMAGE store and associated entry in INDEX store
public void deleteImageFromStore(String name)
        throws ApplicationException {
    int[] recordIndices = (int[])hashTable.get(name);
    if (recordIndices != null) {
        deleteImageRecord(recordIndices[0]);
        deleteKey(recordIndices[1]);
        hashTable.remove(name);
    }
}

//Retrieves an Image from the IMAGE RecordStore.
public byte[] retrieveImageFromStore(String name)
        throws ApplicationException {
    int[] recordIndices = (int[])hashTable.get(name);
    byte[] imageData = null;
    if (recordIndices != null) {
        try {
            imageData = imageRecordStore.getRecord(recordIndices[0]);
        }catch(RecordStoreException rse) {
            throw new ApplicationException(
                    "Unable to retrieve record from record store",
                    rse);
        }
    }
    return imageData;
}

//Retrieves the names of images stored in the record store.
public String[] retrieveStoredImageNames()
        throws ApplicationException {
    String[] entries = null;
    try {
        if (indexRecordStore.getNumRecords() == 0) {
```

```
        return null;
    }
    RecordEnumeration records =
        indexRecordStore.enumerateRecords(null, null, false);
    int numOfRecords = records.numRecords();
    int[][] recordIndices = new int[numOfRecords][2];
    entries = new String[numOfRecords];
    for (int i = 0; i < numOfRecords; i++) {
        int keyID = records.nextRecordId();
        byte[] data = indexRecordStore.getRecord(keyID);
        ByteArrayInputStream bais =
                new ByteArrayInputStream(data);
        DataInputStream dis = new DataInputStream(bais);
        String imageName = dis.readUTF();
        int recordID = dis.readInt();
        recordIndices[i][0] = recordID;
        recordIndices[i][1] = keyID;
        entries[i] = imageName;
        hashTable.put(imageName, recordIndices[i]);
    }
    return entries;
} catch (IOException ioe) {
    throw new ApplicationException(
            "Unable to read from record store", ioe);
} catch (RecordStoreException rse) {
    throw new ApplicationException(
            "Unable to read from record store", rse);
    }
  }
}
```

The RMS record store provides persistent storage of data in the form of records within a `RecordStore`. In this example, we create two `RecordStores`, one for storing the image data (the IMAGE `Record-Store`) and a lightweight INDEX `RecordStore`. Why do we use a separate INDEX record store? When we create a new record and save it in a `RecordStore` with the `addRecord()` method, an integer record ID is returned that uniquely identifies that record within the `RecordStore`. This value can be cached by the MIDlet and used to retrieve the record while the MIDlet is running. However, as soon as the MIDlet is shut down the value of the record ID will be lost, unless, as we do here, we also save the record ID in another `RecordStore`. By creating a lightweight INDEX record store, which contains small records each consisting only of the name of the saved image and the record ID of the saved image, we can quickly retrieve the names (and record IDs) of the saved images without having to enumerate through the large `RecordStore` of image data.

As we saw earlier, when the `GameMIDlet` starts, it calls the `display-ChoiceForm`, the first action of which is to call the `loadImageNames()` method:

```
public String[] loadImageNames() throws ApplicationException {
    String[] images = rms.retrieveStoredImageNames();
    return images;
}
```

This calls the `retrieveStoredImageNames()` method of the `RMSHandler`, which enumerates through the INDEX record store and caches the image names, their record IDs and the ID of the respective INDEX entry in a hashtable for use during the lifetime of the application.

To retrieve an image from the record store we invoke the `retrieveImageFromStore()` method, which takes the name of the required image as a parameter and uses it as the key to the hashtable, retrieving the cached record indices. It uses the record ID of the image data to retrieve the data from the IMAGE `RecordStore`.

To delete a record we use the `deleteImageFromStore()` method, which takes the name of the image to be deleted as a parameter. It retrieves the record indices from the hashtable and uses them to delete the image data from the IMAGE `RecordStore` and the key entry from the INDEX `RecordStore`. Finally, it removes the relevant entry from the hashtable.

The `addImageToStore()` method takes the image name and image data as parameters and adds the image data to the IMAGE `RecordStore`. The returned record ID and the image name are then stored in the INDEX `RecordStore`. The returned index entry record ID and the image record ID are cached in the hashtable as an integer array using the image name as the hash key.

5.4.8 Summary

The Picture Puzzle MIDlet is a fully working example, however, note that it was written primarily for pedagogic purposes, with clarity of code regarded as a higher priority than efficiency or richness of features. Adding extra bells and whistles, perhaps including a peer-to-peer mode in which a newly captured and scrambled photo is transmitted over Bluetooth (using JSR 82) for a friend to unscramble, is left as an exercise for the reader.

The full source code for the Picture Puzzle can be downloaded from Symbian's website at ***www.symbian.com/books***.

Section 2

Writing Quality Code for Smartphones

6

Making Java Code Portable

6.1 Introduction

In this chapter and the next, we shall examine how to make applications as portable as possible and how to write efficient code. Although Java (particularly wireless Java) is not "write once, run anywhere", porting Java MIDlets to different wireless devices is generally straightforward. The problems associated with portability are due to the wide variation in mobile phones: variations in heap memory, persistent storage, screen size and resolution, and user input methods all contribute to an application's inability to execute consistently across a range of devices. Some devices have optional APIs and there are network considerations specific to each operator, such as permissible JAR file sizes.

This chapter will investigate how to develop MIDlets that are portable across as wide a range of mobile phones as possible. We will look at how we can use design patterns and coding guidelines to assist in portability, enabling developers to maximize revenue-earning opportunities from their endeavors.

The value of creating portable code is magnified by the number of Java devices in the marketplace. Many of them are similar; for example, the Series 60 Platform provides a way of creating applications for a broad range of devices. Even among Series 60 devices, however, differences exist in the development environment. Some phones include the Wireless Messaging API (JSR 120) and Java APIs for Bluetooth (JSR 82). Newer Series 60 devices, such as the Nokia 6600, have MIDP 2.0, while earlier ones, such as the Nokia 3650, have MIDP 1.0. Symbian OS devices have diverse user interfaces. Screen sizes vary and, more significantly, so do user input methods: the Sony Ericsson P900 uses a large touch screen with a jog dial, whereas Series 60 phones have a smaller screen and use a keypad and a four-way joystick.

Programming Java 2 Micro Edition on Symbian OS: A developer's guide to MIDP 2.0. Martin de Jode
© 2004 Symbian Ltd   ISBN: 0-470-09223-8

These variations do not, however, mean that an application has to be totally rewritten to run on all these devices. Whether our application uses high-level components, such as `Forms`, `TextFields` and `Lists`, or does its own drawing and event handling using a `Canvas` (or indeed uses a combination of these techniques), we can still do much to make our MIDlet portable.

At the very least, the core application should remain the same across devices and any differences should be expressed principally through variations in the user interface. For example, graphics may have to be adapted to cope with a smaller screen, or alternative menus may have to be created for different methods of capturing user input. Making the core application invariant requires separating it from the UI, based on a suitable model.

As well as creating a portable architecture, the developer may have to cater for individual device capabilities. This requires knowing which APIs are supported by the device and adapting the MIDlet appropriately, either at runtime or by creating different variations.

While examining programming models we shall also look at the differences among Symbian OS devices and see how this will affect application implementation.

6.2   Design Patterns

There are many types of structural design that can be adopted when programming with an object-orientated language such as Java, and these can be used to facilitate portable code. While we shall not be examining the design theory in great detail, it is worth considering the broader concepts for MIDlet development in general. These designs are traditionally associated with desktop or server-based application development; however, they will become more important for wireless applications as these become more sophisticated and memory and processing power become less of a constraint. Two useful design patterns are listed in the following sections.

6.2.1   Model–View–Controller Design Pattern

This is an architecture commonly used for GUI applications. It breaks the application into three specialized entities: a Model, a View and a Controller. Each entity is reliant upon the others, but is self-contained. The Model–View–Controller (MVC) pattern traces its roots to the UI paradigm used in the Smalltalk programming language. The three entities are as follows:

- the Model: also known (perhaps more appropriately) as the Engine The model holds the application's data. It processes instructions from the controller to change the data. It has a relationship with the views, notifying them when its data has changed, thus ensuring the latest state of the data is reflected in the views. It responds to queries about its state from the views. In short, it provides the core business logic for the application.

- the View
The view is responsible for presenting the data to the user. In response to a notification from the model, the view gets the current state of the data and renders it to the screen. It also provides the interface for accepting input from the user.

- the Controller
The controller is responsible for managing the flow of the application. It responds to captured user input from the views, processing the input and issuing instructions to the model to change its data state accordingly.

A UML class diagram of a basic MVC implementation is shown in Figure 6.1 and the interaction between the objects is shown in a UML sequence diagram (Figure 6.2).

One of the ideas behind the MVC pattern is to promote loose coupling between the components of the application. It allows the presentation of the data (the views) to be decoupled from the engine and its data (the model). It also allows for multiple (and simultaneous) views of the same model (for instance, the same data might be presented as both a table and a pie chart). In practice, implementations of the MVC pattern are more complicated than the simplistic example shown in Figure 6.1, involving multiple concrete `View` classes (all deriving from an abstract `View` class), possibly each with an associated concrete `Controller` (deriving from an abstract `Controller`).

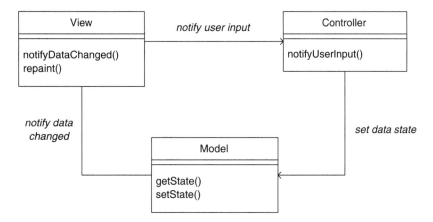

Figure 6.1   A simple example of the MVC pattern.

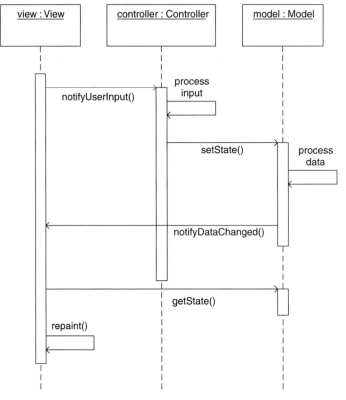

Figure 6.2   The interaction of objects in the MVC pattern.

6.2.2   Model–View Design Pattern

The Model–View design pattern (MV) is a simplified version of the MVC pattern. The MV pattern is a specific variant of the Observer pattern (also known as the Publisher–Subscriber). In the MV pattern, the `View` class combines the functionality of the `View` and `Controller` classes in the MVC pattern. The `View` class in the MV paradigm will be familiar to desktop Java GUI programmers (even if they don't realize it), as typical application UIs make use of it. For example, the UI class shown below is essentially a `View` class in the MV pattern:

```
public class MyCanvas implements MouseListener, KeyListener {

    public MyCanvas() {
        ...
        addMouseListener(this);
        addKeyListener(this);
    }
    ...
}
```

Under the MV pattern, application classes may be classified into one of the two component groups:

- the Model
  The model manages the application's data. It responds to queries from the views regarding its state and updates its state when requested to do so by the views. It notifies the views when the state of the data has changed.

- the View.
  The view presents a view of the model data. It responds to user input, instructing the model to update its data accordingly. On notification of changes to the model data, it retrieves the new model state and renders a view of the latest state of the data.

This simpler pattern is perhaps more appropriate to simpler MIDlet applications. It does not overcomplicate the class structure, and the application software (and, indeed, the developers working on the application) may be organized into two distinct groups, one responsible for the UI and the other for the core application logic. It also means that porting the application between different MIDP devices that may utilize completely different UI paradigms (for example, from a touch screen-based Sony Ericsson P900 to a keypad-driven Nokia 6600) can be achieved without having to touch the Model classes.

A UML class diagram for part of a hypothetical MV-based application supporting a pointer-based view and a keypad-based view is shown in Figure 6.3.

6.2.3 Practical Application of Design Patterns

The reality is that these design techniques should be applied cautiously to wireless Java development. Limitations such as the overall application size may restrict the purest implementation. Even the smallest class can create an overhead of around 200 bytes and this will ultimately lead to a larger JAR file; class abstraction may need to be reduced to keep JAR file sizes realistic. However, the theories and approaches are definitely valid and will become more so as devices become less resource-constrained.

A cursory look at Symbian OS devices based on MIDP 2.0 reveals two user interface types. Phones such as the Series 60 Nokia 6600 offer a keypad interface, whereas the UIQ-based Sony Ericsson P900 offers a stylus-driven UI. In addition, the two phones also have different screen sizes: 176×208 pixels for the Series 60 phone and 208×253 for the UIQ phone. So porting an application from one device to the other may involve changing the application code. By making use of the high-level API, developers may be able to let the MIDP implementation itself take

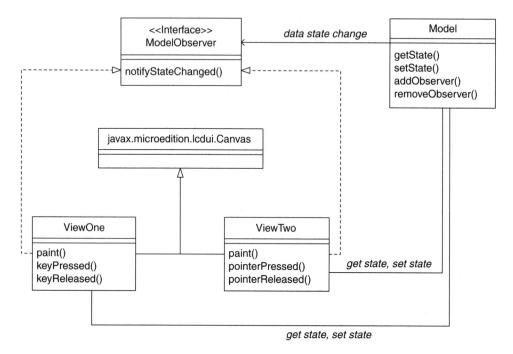

Figure 6.3 Multiple views supported by the Model–View design pattern.

care of the UI for some applications. Once the developer ventures into the realm of action games, however, it is a different matter altogether.

Gaming applications generally require the use of low-level APIs, as they give pixel-level control to the developer. Objects such as sprites and layers give the developer the ability to create animations that represent the virtual world to the user. However, the underlying image files need to be optimized for screen size and resolution. Other changes may be necessary as well. For example, a level-based game ported to a device with a smaller screen may need to have smaller levels and less complexity.

Another issue with games is the capture of user input. Touch screen devices, such as the UIQ-based P900, handle this differently from those with a keypad. As well as being captured by different methods (for example, in the `Canvas` class, by `pointerPressed` rather than `keyPressed`), user input may need to be processed differently to ensure the game still works correctly. In terms of design patterns this may require an abstraction layer, such as the Controller in the MVC pattern, acting as an intermediary between the UI (the View) and the application game logic (the Model), ensuring that user input is processed appropriately regardless of the UI type. Whatever design approach is adopted, it is important that the user interface is separated from the core logic of the application, allowing the game logic to remain the same across different platforms and UIs.

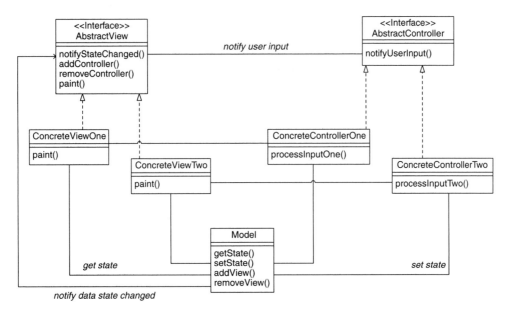

Figure 6.4 Separating the UI from the engine using abstraction.

This yields a model where the development team in charge of creating the user interface can concentrate on recreating the UI for a new device without having to understand the underlying game logic. They can repurpose sprite graphics and make changes to user interaction classes while leaving the core game classes untouched. Separating the UI can be more easily approached with an abstraction of certain core classes (for instance an abstract `View` and an abstract `Controller` in the MVC design pattern). This provides a standard set of interfaces for the other classes within the application model to use. Extended classes then provide the implementation; for example, concrete `View` classes, possibly each with a dedicated concrete `Controller` (see Figure 6.4).

This approach creates a set of reusable components that can be implemented across a range of devices without having to rewrite the application on a grand scale.

6.2.4 Summary

In this section, we have seen how applications may be designed using architectures derived from established design patterns. These patterns are largely used for server and desktop applications; however, the principles still apply in the wireless world, although some of the roles may be compressed to suit the constrained nature of the environment. While we want to make sure we are not overcrowding the JAR file with unused class abstractions, we need to make our MIDlets as portable as possible.

6.3   Portability Issues

This section looks at a number of specific portability issues associated with the UI (both low-level graphics and higher-level UI components), optional and proprietary APIs, and download size limitations.

To create a MIDlet that will run on a wide range of devices with different form factors and functionality, it can be useful to identify the device's characteristics either when the MIDlet is run, so that it can adapt its behavior dynamically, or when the MIDlet is provisioned, so that the server can deliver an appropriately tailored JAR file.

Runtime support for device identification is fairly limited: we can use `System.getProperty()` to identify the JTWI or MIDP version, and we can identify the display characteristics using `Canvas.getHeight()`, `Canvas.getWidth()`, `Canvas.isDoubleBuffered`, `Display.isColor()` and `Display.numColors()`.

Currently, when downloading an application, it is generally left to the user to click on the link appropriate to their phone (e.g. ''BoyRacer for Sony Ericsson P800/P900'' or ''BoyRacer for Nokia 6600 or Series 60''). However, in every HTTP transaction, devices identify themselves in the User Agent field (e.g. ''Sony Ericsson P900'' or ''Nokia 6600''), and this can be used by the provisioning server to deliver the correctly packaged application. The Composite Capability/Preference Profiles (CC/PP, see ***www.w3.org/Mobile/CCPP***) UAProf standard for device identification is slowly becoming established and will enable the provisioning server to identify a phone's characteristics in more detail.

The HTTP transaction includes a URI that points to details of the phone, but can also include a set of differences that identify how the individual's phone may have been modified from the factory standard. This potentially enables the provisioning server to dynamically create a JAR file tailored for a specific phone.

In general, check out any style guides for target devices and try to conform to the guides. Even though developers may implement whatever GUI they wish in the low-level APIs, it is easier for the user to use a familiar interface. So, in deference to the host device, try to emulate the nomenclature of menus and commands as far as possible. Some devices impose certain styles to provide the user with a consistent UI. On Nokia phones, for example, the right soft key is generally used for ''negative'' commands, such as Exit, Back and Cancel, and the left soft key for ''positive'' commands, such as OK, Select and Connect.

6.3.1   Low-Level Graphical Content

The graphical content in gaming applications forms the basis of the user experience.

Although in a gaming environment the central character sprites can usually remain the same size, this may not be true for the background images. The background forms the backdrop to the game "world" and has to vary in size with the size of the screen. For example, the Nokia 6600 display is 176 × 208 pixels, while the Sony Ericsson P900 display is 208 × 253, reduced to 208 × 173 when the soft keypad is visible.

When the UI is initiated, it needs to query the width and height of the device's screen using `Canvas.getHeight()` and `Canvas.getWidth()`. This gives it enough information to create the background image. Using `TiledLayer` we can do one of two things:

- we can change the size of the tiles to reflect the screen size
  This minimizes the impact on the MIDlet, though it puts a burden on the graphic designer. More importantly, the tiles may now be out of proportion to the rest of the game world.

- we can make the `TiledLayer` intelligent enough to query the device for its screen dimensions on initialization and make the appropriate changes to the background.
  The new dimensions of the tiled background depend on the individual tile and screen dimensions. This is a better approach that allows us to adjust the viewport to reflect the differing screen dimensions, giving the MIDlet user on a bigger device a larger view of the game world. For example, a maze game would show more of the maze. The LifeTime MIDlet in Section 7.14 takes this approach, showing more of the playing field on devices with a larger screen.

The images used to construct the game usually have to be tailored to the screen characteristics of the target phones, and possibly also to the memory and performance characteristics of the phone. They may even have to be adapted to cope with operator restrictions on download JAR size. So we need small black and white images on some phones, but can (and should) use larger color images for more capable phones with color screens. It is generally necessary to create a JAR package for each target device, or family of devices.

One of the more useful additions to MIDP 2.0 is the Game API. It allows a `Sprite` to be created with one graphics file containing all the frames for that character or screen object. In the Demo Racer MIDlet in Chapter 5, we supplied a four-frame strip which encapsulated all the frames required for animation.

The `Sprite` subclass is initiated with the PNG file and creates the frames for itself by knowing its own dimensions. This means that if the size of the screen changes and the number of frames remains the same, we can change the frame strip rather than making code changes and the sprite will remain in proportion.

We have talked about the need to adjust graphics to suit the device, but the characteristics of the sprites may also need to be changed. If the `Sprite` classes are intelligent enough to determine their own size then all well and good. They may move differently, however, and this means changing the movement methods. Collisions between sprites may change. For example, a smaller image may require a smaller collision area. In some cases using the whole image for collision detection is too expensive on the processor, so we define a smaller area using `defineCollisionRectangle()`. A change in sprite size may mean a related change to this collision area.

A change in screen size may also require fewer copies of certain sprites. There may be less room for enemy characters, or the frequency with which they are to appear on the screen may drop. In the classic Space Invaders game, for example, smaller screen dimensions may mean fewer invaders attacking the player character. Do you allow them to shoot as many bullets as on a larger screen? Do you ask the MIDlet to work out at initialization time how many can comfortably fit on the screen without compromising the game difficulty? Should there be fewer or smaller barriers to hide behind? Some of these values may have been hard-coded in the `Sprite` class members. Is it wiser to create a resource bundle to supply these values, or perhaps add them to the JAD file and then ask the MIDlet to query those properties at startup?

Use `GameActions` as far as possible. These provide a mapping between commonly used gaming actions, such as Fire, Up, Down, Left, and Right, and easily selectable buttons on a keypad, such as 2, 8, 4 and 6. A keypad with a different layout, such as that of the Siemens SX-1, a MIDP 1.0 phone, may map these actions to different keys. Even though the Sony Ericsson P900 is mainly a pointer-based device, the jog dial facility can be used for Up and Down game actions. The game design may have to be simplified, or it may be possible to make selections such as game menus into scrollable choice lists.

Some devices provide the ability to poll a key to determine its state, which can either be "depressed" or "released". Polling a key to check whether it is currently depressed means we can give the user "rapid fire" functionality. Not all devices have this capability, so it is something to watch for.

6.3.2   Variations in Input Methods

Developers need to be aware of the different input methods on different devices. At the very least, they need to code defensively to allow for variations. It may be wise to test for the presence of a pointer device or keypad entry. If a MIDlet is being ported to the Sony Ericsson P900, for instance, buttons may need to be put onto the screen, or graphics may need to be expanded to make it easier for the user to select an item. On keypad devices, such as the Nokia 6600, the user relies on the joystick to navigate between items and the selection occurs automatically.

The Sony Ericsson P900 provides a soft keyboard to compensate for the missing keys. How will this affect game play for the users? Will they still enjoy the same experience as users on a keypad phone? Instead of catering for both input methods in a single user interface, should a different user interface be developed? For example, instead of listening for the left and right keys, the MIDlet could detect the part of the screen on which the stylus has been pressed; if it is to the left or right of the hero, the character could be moved in that direction. Pressing the stylus on the character itself could invoke the fire mechanism. The jog dial could be used in tandem with the pointer. In other words, instead of emulating the keypad, try to look for other ways of interpreting user input.

Maybe the developers need to ask themselves whether pointer-based devices appeal to a different set of users altogether. Should the game designer be thinking about applications that utilize the features of the device, rather than trying to port an unsuitable game? The best business decision may be not to port at all, but to create a specially-developed concept for that device.

6.3.3 High-Level User Interface Components

Using high-level UI components such as `TextField`, `List` and `Form`, rather than drawing directly to a `Canvas`, generally provides a portable UI. These components and their layout are abstracted, with the device implementation handling the display of the components on the screen. The application is not concerned with the capture of user input or with individual keys, does not define visual appearance, and is unaware of such actions as navigation and scrolling.

This works well for information-based applications, as the developer can be more concerned with organizing information into coherent screens. The developer has little control over look and feel, so the UI retains the look and feel of native applications.

One exception within the high-level API is `CustomItem`, a component that allows developers to define their own `Form` object. Although it is a high-level component derived from `Item`, it behaves more like a `Canvas`. Whereas the other high-level `Form` objects let the implementation manage user interaction and object traversal, the class extending the abstract `CustomItem` class is responsible for implementing this behavior.

The Sony Ericsson P900 and the Nokia 6600 implement `CustomItem` differently, reflecting the different user interaction paradigms of the two phones. It is possible to extend `CustomItem` by redefining the `keyPressed()`, `keyReleased()`, and `keyRepeated()` methods for the Nokia 6600 and the `pointerPressed()`, `pointerDragged()`, and `pointerReleased()` methods for the Sony Ericsson P900. In this way the extended `CustomItem` should behave correctly on both platforms.

6.3.4 Adapting to Proprietary and Optional APIs

MIDP 2.0 has evolved to its current state with the co-operation of many interest groups such as device manufacturers, network operators, and operating system developers including Symbian. In some cases, in order to facilitate the next generation and sometimes in anticipation of forthcoming technology, devices are released with proprietary APIs which provide developers with the ability to create more complex applications using APIs which have not yet (or may never) be standardized. For example, Nokia created a proprietary API for broadcasting SMS messages and a proprietary UI API gave game developers for Nokia MIDP 1.0 devices control of a full-screen canvas. In both cases this functionality has since been incorporated into the standards. JSR 120 supports SMS and MIDP 2.0 provides `Canvas.setFullScreenMode()`. In these circumstances, the Nokia UI API is deprecated, although implementations still ensure backward compatibility.

Developers should be aware of the capabilities of the target device before assuming that all the classes they have used are standard. Code should be written defensively so that when an API is not available the MIDlet will still run, while taking an appropriate action, and not just close the application unexpectedly. It would be even better for the developer to be aware of the device's libraries and perhaps make positive decisions about the functionality of an application prior to release on a new device.

This, however, leaves developers with a quandary. Do they only target particular devices and operators that suit their needs, or do they try to code around the limitations of devices to achieve the same result? Would it be possible, for example, to change the screen layout or menu order to reflect a smaller screen size?

Another area where devices differ in capability is their multimedia support. For example, the MIDP 2.0 Media API (discussed in Chapter 3) provides limited capabilities as a lowest common denominator. Where devices have good native multimedia functionality, such as onboard cameras and microphones, developers would reasonably expect to be able to manipulate the media data. However, at present only some of the more powerful phones, such as the Nokia 3650 and Nokia 6600, implement the fully-featured Mobile Media API (JSR 135), which enables rendering and recording of media data, such as audio and video playback and photo capture. This API enables an application such as the Picture Puzzle MIDlet discussed in Chapter 5 to capture an image from its onboard camera, manipulate it and store it for future use. However, the reach of the application is obviously limited to those devices that support the MMAPI and implement the photo capture functionality (optional under JSR 135).

Fragmentation in the CLDC/MIDP API space is widely acknowledged as a serious issue. The Java Technology for the Wireless Industry (JTWI) expert group was created to address this problem (***http://jcp.org***).

Chapter 3 introduced the JTWI and concentrated on the component JSRs that make up Release 1 of the JTWI roadmap. One of the goals of the JTWI is to provide a lowest common denominator set of APIs and functionality that compliant devices must implement. By targeting their applications at the JTWI platform, developers can be confident that these applications will run on the widest possible range of devices. JTWI also specifies certain minimum requirements both in terms of performance and the implementation of optional functionality within a specific component JSR. This is discussed in more detail in Chapter 3, but here are a few pertinent examples:

- devices should allow JAR files up to 64 KB, with a JAD file of 5 KB and 30 KB of persistent storage

- for graphics, it adds JPEG format files to the PNG support, providing greater flexibility

- a minimum screen size of 125×125 pixels with 12 bits of color depth should be adopted

- devices on GSM/UMTS networks must support SMS push, which works with the push registry to awaken MIDlets upon receipt of an SMS message.

Symbian was a member of the JSR 185 expert group and Symbian's Java implementation is JTWI-compliant from Symbian OS Version 8.0. The ratification of Release 1 of the JTWI postdates MIDP 2.0, but the vast majority of MIDP 2.0 devices are expected to conform to the JTWI initiative in the future.

6.3.5 Download Limitations

Symbian OS devices such as the Nokia 6600 and the Sony Ericsson P900 do not specify limitations on the maximum MIDlet JAR file size; rather, the JAR size is limited by the available persistent storage they have on the device. Typically, Symbian OS devices start with 16 MB, but after the operating system and applications have been added they have around 8 MB. Some devices have memory sticks and MMC cards, so this does, of course, vary. Other considerations include limitations imposed by operators on WAP gateway downloads. An application that is too large will not sell, as no one can download it! Obfuscation (discussed in Chapter 7) provides one way to reduce JAR file size.

Looking further across the market, developers should be aware that some devices impose a maximum download limit. Nokia Series 40 devices have a maximum 64 KB limit, while the Sony Ericsson T610 allows a JAR file size of 60 KB. This gives an idea of where final JAR file sizes should be pitched for the best portability.

The size is, of course, governed by what is inside the file, so it's worth considering exactly what we include. Do sound files really need to be added? For example, the new target device may not be capable of playing certain sounds, or it may not be capable of rendering certain images. To port to a different device we may be able to leave out these extras. Playing a sound on a device with a lower specification may have unwanted side effects on the speed of the MIDlet and the device memory.

It may be that a smaller JAR file size means a smaller game world. Maybe we should consider cutting back on the number of levels for the user to play?

Obfuscation, as well as scrambling the code from prying eyes, has the side effect of reducing the final JAR file size and can improve efficiency, particularly with older VMs. Some obfuscators are more efficient and can reduce the JAR file more dramatically than others, so shop around and try out different ones (Chapter 7 looks briefly at two that are supplied with Sun ONE Studio, Mobile Edition).

6.3.6   Heap Memory

The developer needs to be aware of heap memory, especially when porting to a different device. The heap memory holds all the runtime code, graphics and other objects associated with the MIDlet. Failure to keep within the limits will cause an `OutOfMemory` error and the MIDlet will cease to execute. Too many graphics in a MIDlet may mean not enough heap is left to execute the code. For example, a tiled background needs to be optimized in terms of off-screen buffer for the device in question.

Symbian OS devices typically do not specify a limit on heap memory, leaving the developer with a lot of room to play with. Both the Nokia 6600 and the Sony Ericsson P900/P908 allow for expandable memory up to an 8 MB heap. Of course, the phone's other applications also share that memory space and the application management software may take a different view of what can and cannot be run at any one time. Developers can adopt certain strategies to minimize memory usage. Flyweight design patterns, object factories and object recycling minimize the number of objects in memory at any one time and ensure memory is freed by the application when objects are no longer used, rather than relying on the garbage collector to manage memory.

Porting MIDlets to smaller or different devices may present a different set of challenges. These devices may set a much lower limit on heap memory and developers should be aware of this. An important point to remember here is that the size of the graphics files used to create the application images has a direct impact on the amount of heap used at runtime. A compromise in graphical content may be needed to reduce the overall memory consumption, for instance, by reducing the quality and detail within sprite graphics.

In addition, lower heap memory may cause the garbage collector to kick in more frequently, adversely affecting the overall performance of the MIDlet.

6.4   Summary

In this chapter we have reviewed the techniques and models you should employ to maximize revenue generation by creating flexible and portable applications for mobile devices. We have looked at some of the design patterns you may choose to use and the porting issues you face when writing MIDP 2.0 code. You need to consider the user interface and, in particular, graphical content. We have also looked at some issues arising from using the low-level APIs in game development.

In Chapter 7 we will investigate another important issue in developing applications for constrained devices: optimizing code for the J2ME platform.

7

Writing Optimized Code

7.1   Introduction

This chapter looks at how wireless Java MIDlet developers can get the most from their applications. Optimization is always important, but especially so on mobile phones and other constrained devices such as PDAs. We shall address both improving performance and minimizing memory requirements.

In this chapter we try to help you develop high quality Java applications for Symbian OS. The approach taken is to encourage you to think about the issues involved and to make rational decisions, rather than attempting to provide hard and fast rules for optimization.

We start with a number of general issues including current technology, benchmarking and principles of optimization.

The next few sections discuss several specific areas for optimization: object creation, method and variable modifiers, the use of Strings and using containers sensibly. These ideas are brought together in an example in Section 7.10.

We then look at some more advanced techniques, such as blocking techniques to avoid polling and issues with graphics.

Section 7.14 provides a case study which explores optimization issues in depth. The use of profiling tools is examined in the context of the case study.

Subsequent sections discuss design patterns relevant to optimization, memory issues on constrained devices and the need to cope with out-of-memory situations, and JIT and adaptive compilation technologies.

Useful general references on Java optimization are:

- *Practical Java Programming Language Guide* by Haggar
- *Java 2 Performance and Idiom Guide* by Larman and Guthrie
- *Java Performance Tuning* by Shirazi.

Programming Java 2 Micro Edition on Symbian OS: A developer's guide to MIDP 2.0.   Martin de Jode
© 2004 Symbian Ltd   ISBN: 0-470-09223-8

7.2 What Are We Starting With?

Mobile phones are, by their nature, memory-constrained. In comparison to a desktop computer we have a small screen, a keypad or pointer for input rather than a keyboard or mouse, restricted memory, restricted network and IO performance, and restricted processing power. Of particular concern in this chapter are memory, IO and processor performance.

Mobile phones running Symbian OS typically have between 8 and 16 MB of RAM. The desktop computer on which I am writing this has 512 MB of RAM!

Serial IO on a Symbian OS device is reasonable: both the IR and serial ports operate at 115.2 Kbps. Bluetooth rates are slightly faster, typically several hundred Kbps, but this is still far short of my office network, which runs at 100 Mbps, and my wireless LAN, which operates at 10 Mbps.

Currently, mobile networking is more constrained. GSM provides 9.6 Kbps and GPRS 2.5G technology increases this to over 100 Kbps. 3G UMTS will provide a maximum of 2 Mbps, though typical data rates will be much lower than this. 3.5G UMTS High Speed Downlink Packet Access (HSDPA) could increase the maximum rate to 10 Mbps.

7.3 Benchmarking

Benchmarking wireless devices remains problematic. The Embedded Microprocessor Benchmark Consortium (EEMBC, see **www.eembc. hotdesk.com**) has created a suite of embedded Java benchmarks called GrinderBench, and is working on UI and graphics benchmarks. Grinder-Bench benefits from using engines from real-world applications, such as cryptography, chess and XML parsing.

The table below gives overall results for AMark and CLDCMark tests. AMark is a basic graphics benchmark which can be downloaded from **http://amark.nondove.it**. AMark Version 1.3 is run at a standard size frame, which overcomes the effect of screen size variability. CLDCMark is a benchmark used internally within Symbian; it is purely embedded, with no graphics tests. For both tests, the bigger the number, the faster the device is running. As well as Symbian OS devices, we have included the Motorola A760 (a Linux-based phone with a 200 MHz XScale processor) and Sun's Wireless Toolkit running on a 600 MHz laptop.

	Sun Wireless Toolkit 2.1	Motorola A760	Nokia 9210i	Nokia 7650	Nokia 6600	Sony Ericsson P800	Sony Ericsson P900
AMark 1.3	35.79		8.03	17.13	20.48	19.79	42.63
CLDCMark	248	4726	396	674	3320	4238	5013

The table shows how rapidly Java performance has improved, through faster clock rates and improved VM technology. Since the Nokia 9210, the embedded tests have improved by well over a factor of 10, and the graphics tests by a factor of five. The Nokia 6600 onwards use Sun's CLDC HI VM. The Wireless Toolkit results are intriguing: a very good graphics performance but a very poor embedded performance.

Benchmarks should always be viewed with caution: the only real test is running representative applications on representative hardware.

7.4 General Guidelines for Optimization

This section outlines some general principles for optimizing code. These do not attempt to say anything new; however, restating the obvious is not always a bad thing.

- get the design right
  The biggest gains generally come from getting the overall architecture and design right: how operations should be split between server and client, what technologies to use (e.g. messaging, RMI, object database or relational database), what hardware to use, even what languages are used.

  It is important to design to interfaces, not implementations. This makes it easier to slot in a different or improved algorithm: for example, depending on your data size and how it might already be sorted, there are times when a pigeon sorting algorithm will be the best choice, and times when a bubble sort will be appropriate.

- optimize late: optimizing too early in the process means that you will produce intricate code that gets in the way of good design

- optimize only where necessary: find out where the bottlenecks are and concentrate on sorting them out; this requires access to suitable profiling and heap analysis tools

- do not over-optimize.
  The more you optimize your code, the more highly tuned it becomes to the particular environment. If the environment changes or you want to use the code in a different application, it may run more slowly. Compiler technology in particular can have a profound effect on the benefits or otherwise of a particular optimization.

Optimization can often conflict with other goals for the code:

- clarity and maintainability: improving performance at the code level generally (though not always) means writing more, and often quite obscure, code (we shall see an example of this in the case study in Section 7.14)

- reliability: the corollary of the previous point is that you run the risk of introducing bugs when you optimize

- fast startup time and fast execution
  We can frequently improve startup time by deferring a task until it is required during execution. This is worthwhile if the task may not always be required, and even then may still be worthwhile, especially if the task can be carried out by a background thread.

- reducing memory usage: many of the optimizations require extra code; caching is a vital tool in improving performance, but requires extra memory.

Finally, the behavior of an optimization will vary with the platform. As a Java developer for Symbian OS phones you are likely to be working with three platforms: Java under Windows, the Emulator and a target device. The first two platforms may give a rough idea of the benefits or otherwise of an optimization; however, they cannot be used for a reliable analysis. The performance of the Emulator in particular is very different to that of target hardware, for reasons we shall discuss.

7.5   Feedback and Responsiveness

Performance is in the eye of the beholder, so as well as being fast as measured by a stopwatch, our application also needs to be responsive to the user and to provide feedback. The user should never be confronted with an unresponsive screen that shows no indication that something is happening. Large applications, in particular, can take a long time to initialize. Rather than leave the user with a blank screen, pop up a splash screen.

Unlike on desktop computers, there is generally no wait icon on mobile phones. Therefore it is necessary to have a status area, animated icon or some other way of conveying progress to the user.

Threads are an expensive resource and should therefore be used judiciously; this is why native Symbian OS applications tend to be single-threaded and to rely on cooperative multitasking. You might, however, want to consider loading or saving data in a separate thread, which allows the user to carry on with other work. Windows applications often lock the user out while a file is being saved; this is frustrating and unnecessary. While saving a file, the user should still be able to read it or edit another file of the same type.

7.6   Object Creation

Object creation is an expensive process, so it is worth examining your design to ensure you are not creating large numbers of objects,

Figure 7.1 DiceBox on P900.

particularly short-lived objects, and to consider reusing objects. The AWT, for instance, is notorious for creating lots of short-lived objects; on the other hand, the MIDP designers took great care to minimize object creation, so very few event objects, for instance, are created.

Reusing objects means we do not waste time recreating objects and there is less work for the garbage collector when they are no longer needed.

Figure 7.1 shows the DiceBox MIDlet, which rolls a number of dice in a similar way to a fruit machine rolling fruit.

The following is an extract from the `DiceCanvas` constructor used to display the dice. We create a `List` to change the number of dice in the constructor rather than recreate it every time it is displayed. We also create a pool of dice, six in this case, rather than create new dice every time we change their number.

```
class DiceCanvas extends Canvas implements CommandListener, Runnable{
    ...
    List diceNumberList = new List("Select number of dice",
            List.IMPLICIT, new String[] {"1","2","3","4","5","6"}, null);
    int numberOfDice = 2;
    Dice[] die = new Dice[6];
    public DiceCanvas(DiceBox midlet){
        for(int i = die.length; --i >=0; )
            die[i] = new Dice();
        ...
```

A valid alternative would be to create just the first four dice for our dice pool and then create additional dice only when we increase the number of dice.

It should be emphasized that we have used the DiceBox MIDlet only to illustrate a point. In a program as small as this, such decisions make little practical difference and worrying about them too much should definitely be regarded as over-optimization. Object creation is also less expensive on Sun's CLDC HI VM than on the original KVM.

Consider using object pools for such things as database connections and server connections. For instance, a file server program waits for a request from a client and on receipt of a request returns the appropriate file. The program might use a class called `FileRequestHandler` to listen for, and respond to, file requests from the client. It creates a `FileRequestHandler` for each client it is serving, presumably on the port returned by `ServerSocketConnection.acceptAndOpen()`. Alternatively it can create a pool of `FileRequestHandler` instances at startup and reinitialize an instance with the appropriate port number as needed.

The benefits of using a pool of `FileRequestHandler` instances will be a faster connection time and an implicit limit on the number of clients. This means a client is either guaranteed adequate bandwidth or has to wait for a free `FileRequestHandler`. The downside could be a slower startup time.

Object creation and pooling is discussed in detail in *Smart object-management saves the day* by Sosnoski (***www.javaworld.com/javaworld/jw-11-1999/jw-11-performance.html***).

7.7   Method Modifiers and Inlining

Java provides a number of modifiers to control the scope of methods and variables: `private`, `protected`, `public`, `final`, `static` and `volatile`.

Methods or variables with no modifier have package scope, are non-static (that is, belong to the instance of a class rather than the class itself) and are non-final (that is, can be overridden in a derived class). We tend to use the default without thinking too much about it; it is a reasonably safe compromise. However, we should not be lazy. As good designers we should keep things as private as possible and expose only what we absolutely have to. Invariant data (constants) should, in any case, be marked as `static` and `final`. Such an approach reduces the risk of being stuck with an unsatisfactory public interface; we can always open up our design later, but it is very hard to go back once we make something public.

Performance will also be affected by the scope of our objects and variables. Local variables remain on the stack and so can be accessed directly by the VM (a stack-based interpreter). Static and instance variables are kept on the heap, and can therefore take much longer to access.

```
static int sValue = 1;
int iValue = 2;
void lotsOfVariables(int arg1, int arg2) {
    int value1;
    int value2;

    value1 = arg1;
    value2 = arg2;
    iValue = sValue;
}
```

In the above code snippet, sValue is a static and iValue is an instance variable; both are stored in the heap. value1 and value2 are local variables, arg1 and arg2 are method arguments, and all four are stored on the stack.

The following table shows the performance difference in accessing static, instance, and local variables (see the Microbench MIDlet in the source code for the book, at *www.symbian.com/books*). In each case the executed code was of the form:

```
value1 = value2;
value2 = value3;
value3 = value4;
value4 = value1;
```

where value<n> is either a static, an instance or a local variable. This code was repeated 16 times in each loop, giving 64 read/write operations, with the test looping one million times.

	Sun Wireless Toolkit 2.1	Nokia 9210i	Nokia 7650	Nokia 6600	Sony Ericsson P900
Static variable	20.93 s	547.34 s	312.35 s	4.56 s	2.61 s
Instance variable	36.75 s	48.12 s	24.22 s	2.72 s	1.70 s
Local variable	18.93 s	19.85 s	10.32 s	0.29 s	0.20 s

As can be seen, accessing local variables can be an order of magnitude faster than accessing variables declared on the heap, and static variables are generally slower to access than instance variables.

However, note that for Sun's Wireless Toolkit, access to static variables is faster than to instance variables. This illustrates something we said earlier: optimization behavior is platform-dependent.

Good design encourages the use of getter and setter methods to access variables. As a simple example I might start with an implementation that stores a person's age, but later on change this to store their date of birth, calculating their age from the current date. I can make this change if I have used a getAge() method, but not if I have relied on a public age field. But will getter and setter methods not be slower?

The following code is used to test the speed of getter and setter methods:

```
private int instanceValue = 6;
final int getInstanceVariable(){
    return instanceValue;
}
final void setInstanceVariable(int value){
    instanceValue = value;
}
long instanceMethodTest(int loop){
    long timeStart = System.currentTimeMillis();
    for(int i = loop; --i >= 0; ){
        ...
        setInstanceVariable(getInstanceVariable());
        ...
    }
    return System.currentTimeMillis() - timeStart;
}
```

The line setInstanceVariable(getInstanceVariable()); was repeated 64 times inside the loop. Similar code was used to test getter and setter methods for accessing a static, rather than an instance variable. In this case, the getter and setter methods and the variable being accessed were declared as static. Here are the results for a loop count of one million (in the case of WTK, extrapolated from a loop count of 100 000):

	Sun Wireless Toolkit 2.1	Nokia 9210i	Nokia 7650	Nokia 6600	Sony Ericsson P900
Static accessors	1362.55 s	743.44 s	457.81 s	41.69 s	26.07 s
Instance accessors	1409.42 s	1045.16 s	628.28 s	2.72 s	1.78 s

Again we see platform-dependent differences in behavior. Sun's WTK, Nokia 9210i and Nokia 7650 are all KVM-based, and on all three the static getter and setter accessors are slower than the instance accessors.

Of more interest, though, is comparing the time it takes to access an instance variable directly against accessing it via getter and setter methods. For KVM-based devices, getter and setter methods are very much slower (by about a factor of 20!) However, for CLDC HI-based devices (Nokia 6600 and Sony Ericsson P900), there is no difference. So for the newer devices, there is no excuse for not using getter and setter methods.

What is happening? All method calls are faster after their first execution; the VM replaces lookup by name with a more efficient lookup: virtual methods are dispatched using an index value into the method table for the class, while non-virtual methods are dispatched using a direct link to the method-block for the method. Both approaches offer a similar improvement; however, non-virtual methods can also be inlined.

Public instance methods are virtual. Final methods may be virtual, but can never be overridden. So, depending on the type of object reference to make the call, inlining may still be allowed. Private methods are non-virtual. Static methods are also non-virtual: they cannot be overridden by a derived class, only hidden. In addition, static methods do not have a "this" parameter, which saves a stack push.

The VM attempts the actual inlining at runtime after the first execution. It replaces the method call with an inline version of the method if the method body can be expressed in bytecodes that fit into the method invocation bytespace. In practice this means that simpler getter and setter methods can be inlined by the VM.

This optimization was not implemented in the KVM, which explains the poor performance of static methods on the earlier phones, but is present on the later CLDC HI-based phones.

7.8   Strings

Java is very careful in how it handles Strings in order to minimize storage requirements and increase performance. In particular, Strings are immutable (that is, once a String is created it cannot be modified) and the VM attempts to ensure that there is only one copy of any string in the String literal pool. This section outlines a number of issues that arise from this approach.

7.8.1   Comparing Strings

In general we use equals() to compare two Strings, for example:

```
if(stringA.equals(stringB)) {/* do something */}
```

However, the expression (stringA == stringB) will generally
return true, for example, given:

```
String stringA = "Now is the time";
String stringB = "Now is the time";
```

We have to say 'generally' because Java JDK 1.1 does not guarantee
to maintain a single copy of identical strings. We can, however, force the
issue by using String.intern(). This method returns a string which
is guaranteed to be unique within the pool.

We can therefore do string comparisons using the much faster equality operator:

```
string1 = string1.intern();
...
string2 = string2.intern();
...
if(string1 == string2)) {/* do something */}
```

If your application spends a lot of time comparing Strings (particularly common in database applications), this approach can be of
significant benefit.

Note that String.intern() is not in CLDC 1.0, but has reappeared
in CLDC 1.1.

7.8.2 Concatenating Strings

As we know, Strings are not mutable; in other words, a String cannot
be modified once it has been created. So although concatenating strings
is easy, it is also slow. It may be better to use StringBuffer instead.

The following code reads in characters one at a time from an InputStream and appends each character to a String:

```
String text = "";
while(true){
    int value = inStream.read();
    if(value == -1) break;
    text = text + (char)value;
}
```

The highlighted line is doing a lot more work than is apparent. text
and value are both converted to StringBuffer, concatenated, then
converted back to a String. This can be quite a performance hit in a
tight loop.

The following is a better approach:

```
StringBuffer textBuffer = new StringBuffer(256);
while(true){
    int value = inStream.read();
    if(value == -1) break;
    textBuffer.append((char)value);
}
String text = textBuffer.toString();
```

By default a `StringBuffer` is created with an initial length of 16 characters; however, we know we shall be reading at least 256 characters, so we set this as the initial capacity. The `StringBuffer` will automatically grow if more characters than this are appended.

An alternative to using the + operator to concatenate strings is the `String.concat()` method. Given strings `s1`, `s2` and `s3`,

```
s3 = s1.concat(s2)
```

is more than twice as fast as:

```
s3 = s1 + s2
```

7.8.3   Using Strings as Keys in Hash Tables

Strings are often used as keys in hash tables. Every class, including `String`, implements `hashCode()`, which returns the object's hash code and hash table lookups make use of the key's hash code. However, `String.hashCode()` recalculates the hash code each time it is called. To get around this problem, Larman and Guthrie suggest creating a wrapper class around `String`, called `KeyString`, which looks like this:

```
public final class KeyString{
    private String key;
    private int hashCode;

    public KeyString(String key){
        setKey(key);
    }

    public void setKey(String key){
        this.key = key;
        hashCode = key.hashCode();
    }

    public int hashCode(){
```

```
        return hashCode;
    }

    public boolean equals(Object obj){
        // See later
    }
}
```

The class caches the hash code rather than recalculating it each time. The use of `setKey()` allows a `KeyString` instance to be reused, potentially avoiding unnecessary object creation.

If we re-implement `hashCode()` we are also required to re-implement `equals()`, and this suggests a further refinement that takes advantage of the `String.intern()` method.

First we modify `setKey()`:

```
public void setKey(String key) {
    this.key = key.intern();
    hashCode = key.hashCode();
}
```

Then we need to implement `equals()`:

```
public boolean equals(Object obj) {
    if((obj instanceof KeyString)
        && (key == ((KeyString)(obj)).key)) return true;
    else return false;
}
```

The `if` statement first checks that we are comparing two `KeyString` instances. Because the strings are interned, the `if` statement's second clause can very quickly check if the two `KeyString` instances are equivalent by comparing the identities of the `Strings` used as keys.

7.8.4   The `StringBuffer` Memory Trap

Working with `String` and `StringBuffer` can result in large amounts of memory being used unexpectedly. The problem is this: when `String-Buffer.toString()` creates a `String`, the newly created `String` uses the `StringBuffer` character array. This means that if a `String-Buffer` with a 1 KB capacity only holds a 10-character string, the new `String` will also use a 1 KB character array to store 10 characters. If the `StringBuffer` is modified, the `StringBuffer` array is copied in its entirety and then modified. Now both the `String` and

`StringBuffer` have separate 1 KB character arrays. We have just lost the best part of 1 KB of memory! Repeating the process will continue to use excessive memory as we generate 10-character strings that use 1 KB character buffers.

Here is some code from the Microbench MIDlet that can be run to illustrate the problem:

```
static long bufferTest(int repeat){
    StringBuffer buffer = new StringBuffer(1024);
    String[] strings = new String[repeat];
    Runtime runtime = Runtime.getRuntime();
    long freeMemory;
    long timeStart = System.currentTimeMillis();
    long initialMemory = runtime.freeMemory();
    for(int loop = repeat; --loop >= 0; ){
        buffer.insert(0, "" + loop);
        strings[loop] = buffer.toString();
        freeMemory = runtime.freeMemory();
        Test.test.println("Used: " + (initialMemory -
                freeMemory) + ", total: " +
                runtime.totalMemory() + " " + strings[loop]);
        initialMemory = freeMemory;
    }
    return System.currentTimeMillis() - timeStart;
}
```

A sensible value for the `repeat` argument is 10. This sets up an array of 10 strings. Each pass through the loop inserts a character at the beginning of the `StringBuffer`, creates a `String`, and inserts it into the `String` array. It then prints out the amount of memory used and the contents of the buffer, plus the total memory. (`Test.test.println()` prints a `String` to a `TextBox`.)

What we find is that each pass through the loop uses 2088 bytes. There are 2048 bytes for the 1 KB buffer (Java uses 16-bit Unicode characters), 24 bytes for the `String` (composed of a reference to the character array, a count and an offset into the array) and 16 bytes left over!

There is a slight twist to this, though. If we replace the line:

```
        buffer.insert(0, "" + loop);
```

with:

```
        buffer.append("" + loop);
```

then each time we go through the loop we only use 24 bytes, instead of 2088 bytes! What is happening in this case is that we are adding a character at the end of the `StringBuffer` array on each pass through the loop. This means that each new `String` can reuse the character array from the previous `String`, but with its `count` value set one greater. (It is instructive to watch what is happening in a debugger.)

7.9   Using Containers

CLDC provides four general-purpose containers: `Vector`, `Stack` (which subclasses `Vector`), `Hashtable` and `Array`. The J2SE `BitSet` class, which provides a container for storing arbitrary-length bit patterns, is not supported. There are a few issues to be aware of.

You should avoid using the default constructors for `Hashtable` and `Vector`. Java does not specify the default initial capacity and it could be bigger than we need. If we only want to store a few items, we do not want a 1 KB container; this would be of little concern on a desktop computer, but is a serious issue on a mobile phone. Both `Vector` and `Hashtable` provide constructors that can be used to specify their initial size, respectively `Vector(int initialCapacity)` and `Hashtable(int initialCapacity)`.

The initial capacity for a `Hashtable` should be carefully considered. First, the CLDC 1.0 documentation states that "if many entries are to be made into a Hashtable, creating it with a sufficiently large capacity may allow the entries to be inserted more efficiently than letting it perform automatic rehashing as needed to grow the table". Secondly, as Larman and Guthrie point out, to minimize clustering, the size of a `Hashtable` should be a prime number and powers of two (e.g. 32, 64, 128) should definitely be avoided. Given that a `Hashtable` grows by doubling and adding 1, if we believe our `Hashtable` needs to grow we should choose an initial capacity that can grow and still be prime. A good candidate is 89 (keep doubling and adding 1 and see how long it takes before you get a non-prime number), though 89 may be too large for smaller applications.

Both `Vector` and `Hashtable` can grow indefinitely. We might therefore be using far more memory than we expect and, perhaps worse, using it unpredictably. We have another problem with the KVM, as used for instance on the Nokia 9210 or 7650: although the container shrinks as we remove elements from it or if the container is garbage collected, the recovered memory is only available to our application. The KVM garbage collector does not make this freed memory available to other applications, Java or native. This has changed with the CLDC HI Java VM used on more recent Symbian OS phones: freed memory is returned to the system on a regular basis.

Adding or removing items from `Vector` and `Hashtable` can be slow. These containers grow by copying their internal data into a larger array.

Removing an item from the middle of a `Vector` using `removeElemen-tAt(n)` is achieved by copying all elements from `n` to the end of the array to the preceding slot.

Most of the comments we have made for `Vector` apply to `Stack`. There is, however, no `Stack` constructor that sets its initial size, so you need to use the `setSize()` method inherited from `Vector`.

A `String` is frequently used as a key to a `Hashtable`; however, as we saw in Section 7.8.3, they are not without problems and we suggested that a wrapper class that stores the hash value of the `String` could provide faster lookup. `Integers` also make useful keys because `Integer.hashCode()` simply returns the `Integer` value.

Finally, think about whether an `Array` might provide a faster and more memory-efficient container than a `Vector` or a `Hashtable`. `Vector` can be extremely slow if it is used incorrectly. In *Wireless Java for Symbian Devices*, an example based on a first-in first-out queue is given: a vector-based implementation was around 100 times slower than a reasonably optimized array-based implementation.

7.10 How Not To Do It

We have discussed a number of ideas for improving the performance of our code. This section brings several of these together in an example.

The following code is a slightly extreme example of how not to do it. The code goes through a company database extracting information about each employee:

```
1    float IMP_TO_MET = 1/2.2;
2    String nameList = "";
3    Vector employees = new Vector();
4    for(int id = 0; id < company.getNumberEmployees(); id = id+1){
5        nameList += company.getCompanyName() + "\t";
6        nameList += company.getEmployee(id).getName() + "\t";
7        nameList += company.getEmployee(id).getWeight() * IMP_TO_MET +
                "\n";
8        // do something with nameList
9        nameList = "";
10       employees.addElement(company.getEmployee(id));
11   }
```

Here are the problems:

- Line 1: `IMP_TO_MET` should be declared `static` and `final` (ignoring for the moment that floats are not available in CLDC 1.0, though they are available in CLDC 1.1)

- Line 3: It is unnecessary to use a `Vector`, particularly as we can find out the number of employees; an `Array` would be more appropriate; if we do need to use a `Vector`, we should at least specify its initial size

- Line 4: We should dereference `company.getNumberEmployees` outside the loop and use a local variable

- Line 4: `id++` may optimize better

- Line 5: `getCompanyName()` should be de-referenced outside the loop

- Lines 6, 7, 10: `company.getEmployee(id)` should be obtained only once inside the loop

- Line 6, 7: Should use a `StringBuffer`.

The following code shows how we might resolve these problems. We have defined `tab` and `nl` as `char` rather than as `StringBuffer`: appending one `StringBuffer` to another is no better than appending a `String` to a `StringBuffer`, and significantly slower than appending a `char`.

```
public final static float IMP_TO_MET = 1/2.2;
final char tab = '\t';
final char nl = '\n';
int numberEmployees = company.getNumberEmployees();
Employee[] employees = new Employee[numberEmployees];
StringBuffer nameList = new StringBuffer(128);
StringBuffer companyName
        = new StringBuffer(company.getCompanyName()).append(tab);
for(int id = 0; id < numberEmployees; id++){
    nameList.append(companyName);
    Employee employee = company.getEmployee(id);
    nameList.append(employee.getName()).append(tab);
    nameList.append(employee.getWeight()*IMP_TO_MET).append(nl);
    // Do something with nameList
```

Finally, we reuse the `StringBuffer`, though note that this does not physically resize its internal store:

```
    nameList.setLength(0);
    employees[id] = employee;
}
```

7.11 Copying an `Array`

`System.arraycopy()` is a standard Java method which copies the contents of one `array` into a second `array`, and is generally implemented as a native method. However, rather than JNI, it uses the native interface of the VM, which provides direct access to the `array` contents and type data.

The following is part of a test used to compare `arraycopy()` with our `javaCopy()` method for copying an `array`, taken from the Microbench MIDlet:

```
...
private static Object[] sourceArray = new Object[1000];
private static Object[] destinationArray = new Object[1000];
private static int size;

private static void vmCopy(){
    System.arraycopy(sourceArray, 0, destinationArray, 0, size);
}

private static void javaCopy(){
    for(int i = size; --i >= 0; ){
        destinationArray[i] = sourceArray[i];
    }
}
...
```

The number of elements copied is determined by `size`, which is set by the user interface. `javaCopy()` and `vmCopy()` were called 3 200 000 times and the total durations compared:

size (number of elements copied)	0	1	2	3	10
Nokia 7650:					
arraycopy()	19.53 s	20.47 s	20.94 s	21.41 s	22.66 s
javaCopy()	6.25 s	11.09 s	15.78 s	20.47 s	52.81 s
Nokia 6600:					
arraycopy()	3.30 s	3.83 s	4.28 s	4.78 s	8.13 s
javaCopy()	1.38 s	2.97 s	4.56 s	6.09 s	17.17 s

For small arrays of two or three elements, copying using Java code is faster. For arrays larger than this, using `arraycopy()` is much faster. So, in general, use `arraycopy()` unless you have a very large number of small arrays to copy.

The results under the Emulator were qualitatively different. Native copying was faster except for a zero-length array, emphasizing once again that an optimization must be evaluated on target hardware.

It is not clear how meaningful the results are for zero-length arrays, though dividing the total time of 3.3 s for native copying by the number of calls (3 200 000) suggests a native overhead of about 1 μs per call for the CLDC HI VM on the Nokia 6600.

7.12   Thoughts on Looping

In Section 7.10 we saw that we should not dereference variables inside a loop. In this section we shall look at further issues to do with looping.

7.12.1   Loop Control Statements

In the previous section we used the following Java code to copy the contents of an `array`:

```
private static void javaCopy(){
    for(int i = size; --i >= 0; ){
        destinationArray[i] = sourceArray[i];
    }
}
```

The loop control statement was originally written like this:

```
    for(int i = 0; i < size; i++)
```

However, the loop termination comparison (`>= 0`) used in the final code is built into the Assembler branch opcode and so is quicker. The difference is significant: the final `javaCopy()` ran about 16 % faster than the original.

7.12.2   Recursion

Recursion can be used to create compact code and, if used carefully, code that is also clear. For instance, searching through the contents of a directory structure lends itself to recursive code. In general, however, recursive code is slow and memory-intensive. Each pass has the overhead of a method call and the resulting stack space.

Here is a recursive example that prints out the values of a binary tree (each `Node` in the tree stores a value and references to the two `Nodes` that branch from it):

```
class Node{
    Object value;
    Node smaller;
    Node bigger;
}
class BinaryTree{
    static void print(Node node){
        if(node == null) return;
        System.out.println(node.value);
        print(node.smaller);
        print(node.bigger);
    }
    ...
}
```

The body of the `print()` method calls itself twice unless the `Node` is null, in which case the call returns.

The Microbench MIDlet includes tests to compare recursive and non-recursive implementations. The non-recursive test simply decrements a number (`value`) until it reaches zero, and this is repeated `repeat` times:

```
static long doNonRecursive(int repeat, int value){
    long timeStart = System.currentTimeMillis();
    for(int loop = repeat; --loop >= 0; ) {
        int count = value;
        while (true){
            if(--count == 0) break;
        }
    }
    return System.currentTimeMillis() - timeStart;
}
```

In the recursive version, `decrementCount()` calls itself until `count` is zero. `doRecursive()` does the timing and sets up the first call to `decrementCount()`:

```
private static void decrementCount(int n){
    if (--count == 0) return;
    else decrementCount(n);
}
static long doRecursive(int repeat, int value){
    long timeStart = System.currentTimeMillis();
    for(int loop = repeat; --loop >= 0; ){
        int count = value;
```

```
        decrementCount(count);
    }
    return System.currentTimeMillis() - timeStart;
}
```

We can see from the results below that the recursive option with a depth of 500, repeated 10 000 times, took 7.2 s on the Nokia 6600. The non-recursive solution took just 0.6 s. The message is clear: avoid recursion!

	9210i Personal Java	9210i MIDP 1.0 KVM	Nokia 7650 MIDP 1.0 KVM	Nokia 6600 MIDP 2.0 CLDC HI 1.0	SEMC P900 CLDC HI 1.0
Recursive	34.0 s	19.6 s	15.2 s	7.2 s	6.7 s
Non-recursive	4.6 s	3.4 s	3.1 s	0.6 s	0.4 s

7.12.3 Stack Size and Limits on Recursion Depth

The stack size available with PersonalJava on the Nokia 9210 and KVM on the Nokia 9210 or 7650 is sufficient to allow a recursion depth in excess of 5000 (at least 9000 with PersonalJava on the 9210).

For PersonalJava, the Java stack used to push Java method call frames is set by default to about 400 KB. If you need a greater Java stack depth, the -ossx parameter in the command line can be used. The following command runs the Performance Tests application allowing a huge recursion depth:

```
\epoc32\release\wins\udeb\pjava_g -oss32m -cd j:\examples\PerformanceTests
        -cp PerformanceTests.jar
        com.symbian.devnet.crystal.performance.PerformanceTests
```

The maximum depth that can be achieved with CLDC HI 1.0 is around 500. This reflects the VM's inability to support dynamic stack extension: instead a fixed, albeit generous, stack size was chosen for use by all threads. The unfortunate side effect is an increase in the dynamic footprint per thread (this has been addressed in CLDC HI 1.1).

Sun's KVM allowed thread stacks to be stretched in linked chunks up to the capacity of the dynamic heap. CLDC HI 1.1 can also stretch stacks, but requires a stack to be contiguous. It therefore has to perform a copying realloc on each extension, which is a slower process.

7.12.4 More Examples

Calculating Factorials

We can calculate n! either recursively or non-recursively. The recursive code looks like this:

```
private static long factorialR(int value){
    if(value < 2) return 1L;
    else return value*factorialR(value - 1);
}
```

Here is the non-recursive version:

```
private static long factorial(int value){
    long valueFactorial = value;
    while (--value > 1){
        valueFactorial *= value;
    }
    return valueFactorial;
}
```

These methods are called from `doFactorialRecursive()` and `doFactorialNonrecursive()` respectively. `doFactorialRecursive()` looks like this:

```
static long doFactorialRecursive(int repeat, int value){
    long valueFactorial = 0;
    long timeStart = System.currentTimeMillis();
    for(int loop = repeat; --loop >= 0; ){
        valueFactorial = factorialR(value);
    }
    return System.currentTimeMillis() - timeStart;
}
```

`doFactorialNonrecursive()` is identical to `doFactorialRecursive()` except that it calls `factorial()`, not `factorialR()`.

Calculating 20! recursively one million times on a Nokia 6600 took 6.1 s. Calculating 20! non-recursively took 5.7 s.

However, there is a better way of calculating factorial numbers. The maximum 64-bit `long` value is 9 223 372 036 854 775 807. The largest factorial that can be calculated in a 64-bit `long` is only 20!, which is 2 432 902 008 180 000 000; 21! overflows and returns a negative value. The obvious solution is to use a lookup table of 20 values.

First we need an `array` to store the factorials:

```
private static long[] factorials = new long[20];
```

Then a lookup method:

```
private static long factorialLookup(int value){
    return factorials[value-1];
}
```

These are called by the doFactorialLookup() wrapper. This first populates the array by calling the earlier factorial() method (this could be done much more efficiently, but the startup time is insignificant), then repeatedly calls factorialLookup():

```
static long doFactorialLookup(int repeat, int value){
    for (int index = 0; index < 20; index ++){
        factorials[index] = factorial(index + 1);
    }
    long valueFactorial = 0;
    long timeStart = System.currentTimeMillis();
    for(int loop = repeat; --loop >= 0; ){
        valueFactorial = factorialLookup(value);
    }
    return = System.currentTimeMillis() - timeStart;
}
```

Calculating 20! one million times using this lookup table took just 0.7 s on a Nokia 6600. Here is a complete set of results:

	9210i MIDP 1.0 KVM	Nokia 7650 MIDP 1.0 KVM	Nokia 6600 MIDP 2.0 CLDC HI 1.0	SEMC P900 CLDC HI 1.0
Recursive	39.4 s	26.6 s	6.1 s	4.5 s
Non-recursive	38.0 s	25.5 s	5.7 s	4.4 s
Lookup	3.8 s	2.5 s	0.7 s	0.5 s

Searching a Binary Tree

If a recursive method calls itself just once, then replacing the recursive calls with a loop is trivial: the examples above do this. The problem is a little harder when a method calls itself more than once; for instance, to find a node with a particular value in a binary tree or searching through a directory structure. You do not need recursion for searching if the binary tree is sorted:

```
Node root;

boolean contains(Node nodeToFind){
    Node node = root;
```

```
while (true) {
    if (node == null) return false;
    if (node.compare (nodeToFind) == -1)
        node = node.smaller;
    else if (node.compare (nodeToFind) == 1)
        node = node.bigger;
    else return true;
}
}
```

Avoiding recursion in the `print()` example is harder. In this case we need to maintain a stack containing the branches: we push nodes onto the stack as we go down the tree, then pop them off the stack as we go back up. Details of how to do this can be found in Section 2.3.1 of *The Art of Computer Programming, Volume 1* by Knuth.

These approaches to searching and enumerating are used in the ordered binary tree container discussed in Section 7.14.

7.12.5 Polling

Avoid using loops that poll. The following is a snippet of code that polls the `keepRunning` flag. (`printText(String)` just displays `String` in a UI component.)

```
boolean keepRunning = false;
...
public void run(){
    printText("Started");
    while(keepRunning){
        printText("In loop");
    }
    printText("Stopped");
}
```

Running the loop increased battery consumption from 66 mA to an unacceptable 163mA on my Psion Series 5MX (unfortunately there is no easy way of monitoring battery consumption on more recent mobile phones). The battery consumption returned to 66 mA when keepRunning was set to false. Further, loops like this will hog the CPU and deprive other applications of CPU cycles.

In order to read from an `InputStream` we can sit in a loop polling for the number of available bytes using `InputSteam.available()`. When data becomes available, we read it using `InputStream.read()`. However, it is far better to create a separate reader thread that calls `InputStream.read()` directly. Because this method blocks, the thread will wait until data is present and not consume any unnecessary CPU bandwidth. Although both an event model and a wait–notify model require an extra Thread, this is generally worthwhile.

7.13   Graphics

Graphics coders face two problems: speed and flicker. There are three main causes of flicker:

- before drawing a new frame we need to clear the old frame by painting in the background; we see flicker because the background shows through between frames

- there is insufficient time to paint frames between paint requests, so that we start drawing the new frame before the old frame has been completely drawn

- the underlying OS buffers paint requests, so not every frame is drawn.

There are two main approaches we can take to reducing flicker. We can use a clipping region, so that we only repaint the area that needs to be updated, or we can create the new image in an off-screen buffer and copy this into our graphics context as required.

Using a clipping region is generally faster and will reduce, but not eliminate flicker. An off-screen buffer should eliminate flicker and improve performance, but requires extra memory for the buffer.

However, the graphics on Symbian's Java implementation are already double-buffered so that flickering should not occur, and you should not use double-buffering in your application. In general, you can use `Canvas.isDoubleBuffered()` to check if the implementation is double-buffered and code appropriately. Interestingly, the AMark 1.3 benchmark does not check but does the double-buffering itself. This unfairly penalizes platforms like Symbian OS which provide double-buffering.

7.13.1   The Popcorn Drawing Demonstrator

Popcorn is a test program used to investigate the different approaches to painting. It moves a puck back and forth across the screen without dropping frames (Figure 7.2). The code can be downloaded from **www.symbian.com/books**.

The MIDlet is implemented with three strategies for painting (the user can choose which one to use):

- on each repaint request, paint the whole background, then the puck

- on each repaint request, just paint the background that has changed, then paint in the puck

- create separate images for the background and the puck; on each paint request, paint in only the bits that have changed in the background image and then the puck image.

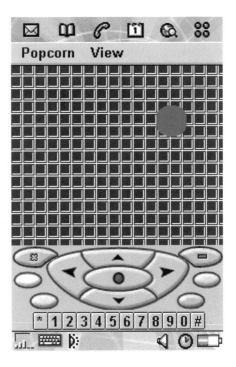

Figure 7.2 Popcorn test program.

The squared background in the playing field gives paint() something to do, as well as adding a bit of interest.

It is instructive to run Popcorn in the Wireless Toolkit emulator with double-buffering enabled and then disabled. In the latter case the basic playing field flickers so badly as to be unusable. The playing field with a clipping region just flickers in the clipped region, which is interesting because it makes the clipping region visible. None of the implementations flicker when run on Symbian OS.

Popcorn is written for MIDP 1.0. The GameCanvas class of MIDP 2.0 can be used to simplify the program logic, and we shall see later how we can modify the MIDlet to use this class.

7.13.1.1 *Painting the Whole Background*

The PlayingField class displays the puck (a filled circle) in a rectangular playing field. It is responsible for painting in the playing field and the puck. Every time PlayingField.move() is called, the puck is redrawn xDelta pixels to the left or to the right. The horizontal size of the playing field is xMax pixels plus the size of the puck (PUCK_SIZE).

PlayingField is a Canvas. It implements Runnable so that we can have a separate thread for the animation, and CommandListener so that we can add Go and Back Command objects (menu entries) to the display. We also define a few constants, including some basic colors. xDelta is the amount we move the puck on each frame (+1 or −1 pixel). xMax is the playing width, the distance the puck moves. paintCount is the number of times paint() is called in order to redisplay the puck in a new position (ignoring paint() requests when part of the screen has been obscured). paintCount should be the same as the number of moves we request; if not, we know we have dropped a frame.

```
class PlayingField extends Canvas implements Runnable, CommandListener{
    private Command goCommand = new Command("Go", Command.SCREEN, 1);
    private Command backCommand = new Command("Back", Command.BACK, 1);
    protected static final int PUCK_SIZE = 30;
    protected static final int Y_POS = 40;
    protected static final int LOOP_COUNT = 500;
    protected static final int BLACK = 0x00000000;
    protected static final int RED = 0x00C12100;
    protected static final int BLUE = 0x000000FF;
    protected static final int GREEN = 0x00008800;
    protected static final int WHITE = 0x00FFFFFF;
    protected static final int GREY = 0x00808080;
    int colourBackground = BLUE;
    protected int xPos = 0;
    protected int xPosOld = 0;
    protected int xDelta = 1;
    protected int xMax;
    int paintCount = 0;
```

The constructor adds the commands and calculates xMax, the distance the puck moves:

```
PlayingField(){
    addCommand(goCommand);
    addCommand(backCommand);
    setCommandListener(this);
    xMax = getWidth() - PUCK_SIZE;
}
```

commandAction() either takes us back to the start screen (which is a simple menu for choosing a repaint method), or starts the animation:

```
public void commandAction(Command c, Displayable s) {
    long timeElapsed = 0;

    if (c == backCommand) {
        Popcorn.popcorn.startApp();
    }
```

```
      else if (c == goCommand){
          new Thread(this).start();
      }
  }
```

run() sits in a loop that repeats 500 times (the number of animations) and records how long it takes. move() is called on each pass to do most of the work. At the end, run() uses a class called OutputTextBox to display the results:

```
public void run(){
    paintCount = 0;
    long timeStart = System.currentTimeMillis();
    for(int i = LOOP_COUNT; --i >=0; ){
        move();
    }
    long timeElapsed = System.currentTimeMillis() - timeStart;
    OutputTextBox.backScreen = this;
    OutputTextBox.println("Time: " + timeElapsed);
    OutputTextBox.println("Count: " + paintCount);
}
```

move() calculates the new position, modifies the direction if necessary and then calls repaint() to request that the screen is repainted with the puck in the new position:

```
public void move(){
    xPosOld = xPos;
    xPos += xDelta;
    if((xPos <= 0) || (xPos > xMax)) xDelta = -xDelta;
    repaint();
    serviceRepaints();
}
```

paint() draws in first the background and then the puck. If the puck has moved, paintCount is incremented:

```
public void paint(Graphics g){
    drawBackground(g);
    g.setColor(RED);
    g.fillRoundRect(xPos, Y_POS, PUCK_SIZE, PUCK_SIZE, PUCK_SIZE,
        PUCK_SIZE);
    if(xPosOld != xPos) paintCount++;
}
```

drawBackground() is called by paint(). It fills in a background color and then paints a pattern of filled and unfilled squares. Interestingly, you get a marginal (1–2 %) increase in performance on Symbian's implementation if you do line and filled drawing separately, rather than interlaced in the same loop as we have done:

```
void drawBackground(Graphics g){
    int width = this.getWidth();
    int height = this.getHeight();
    int pitch = 12;
    int size = 10;
    g.setColor(WHITE);
    g.fillRect(0, 0, width, height);
    g.setColor(colourBackground);

    for (int xPos = 0; xPos < width; xPos += pitch){
        for (int yPos = 0; yPos < height; yPos += pitch){
            g.fillRect(xPos, yPos, size-1, size-1);
            g.drawRect(xPos, yPos, size, size);
        }
    }
}
```

As a general rule it is better to paint a few large areas rather than lots of small areas, even if it means you have to paint in a significantly bigger total area.

7.13.1.2   Using a Clipping Region

We use a clipping region so that we paint only what is needed. To define a clipping region we simply need to modify move() so that we call repaint() with a clipping rectangle (in fact, if you look at the Popcorn source you will see a new class, PlayingFieldWithClipping, that subclasses PlayingField):

```
public void move(){
    int absXDelta = Math.abs(xDelta);
    xPosOld = xPos;
    xPos += xDelta;
    if((xPos <= 0) || (xPos > xMax)) xDelta = -xDelta;
    repaint(xPos - absXDelta, Y_POS, PUCK_SIZE + 2*absXDelta,
            PUCK_SIZE);
    serviceRepaints();
}
```

We need to ensure the clipping region encompasses the old position and the new position of the puck irrespective of the puck's direction, which means we are repainting a bit more than we strictly need to.

Note that paint requests may be buffered so that the actual clipping rectangle will be the union of the clipping rectangles requested by each repaint().

7.13.1.3 Using an Image Buffer

There are various ways in which we could use an image buffer. In this case we have created an image for the background and an image for the puck. On each animation we draw in the background image, then the puck image. To improve performance further, we again call repaint() with a clipping region.

It is worth going through the whole PlayingFieldBuffered class – there is not much to it, as it only has to add a bit to PlayingField.

puckImage and backgroundImage hold the two images:

```
class PlayingFieldBuffered extends PlayingField{
    Image puckImage;
    Image backgroundImage;
```

The constructor calls the PlayingField constructor so that the commands are added to the canvas, sets a background color for later use and calls makeImages():

```
PlayingFieldBuffered(){
    super();
    colourBackground = RED;
    makeImages();
}
```

makeImages() makes the background and puck images. The first three lines create our background image, making use of the superclass drawBackground() method. For the puck it was easier to create a PNG image and load it from the JAR file. This is because we needed a solid circular disc, with the rest of the image transparent. Constructing images with transparency or alpha blending is difficult with MIDP 2.0; the closest method is probably Image.createRGBImage().

```
private void makeImages(){
    backgroundImage = Image.createImage(this.getWidth(),
            this.getHeight());
    Graphics bG = backgroundImage.getGraphics();
    drawBackground(bG);
    try{
        puckImage = Image.createImage("/res/puckSm.png");
    }
    catch (java.io.IOException ioe){
        OutputTextBox.println("Couldn't find puck image");
    }
}
```

`paint()` simply has to paint in the background image, then the puck image in the correct position:

```
public void paint(Graphics g) {
    g.drawImage(backgroundImage, 0, 0, Graphics.TOP|Graphics.LEFT);
    g.drawImage(puckImage, xPos, Y_POS, Graphics.TOP|Graphics.LEFT);
    if(xPosOld != xPos) paintCount++;
}
```

`move()` is identical to the `move()` method in `PlayingFieldWith-Clipping`. We could have subclassed this class and saved ourselves some code, though this approach is less flexible as it becomes harder to change the two classes independently:

```
public void move(){
    int absXDelta = Math.abs(xDelta);
    xPosOld = xPos;
    xPos += xDelta;
    if((xPos <= 0) || (xPos > xMax)) xDelta = -xDelta;
    repaint(xPos - absXDelta, Y_POS, PUCK_SIZE + 2*absXDelta,
            PUCK_SIZE);
    serviceRepaints();
}
}
```

7.13.1.4 *Comparison of the Painting Strategies*

Having gone through the details of the Popcorn MIDlet, it is time to look at the results:

	WTK no buffer	WTK buffered	7650	6600	P900 (full screen)	P900 (with keypad)
Full repaint	36.51 s	25.70 s	38.97 s	23.81 s	30.74 s	21.67 s
Clip region	35.24 s	22.74 s	16.58 s	8.06 s	12.52 s	9.95 s
Buffered	0.90 s	0.80 s	2.88 s	4.56 s	4.53 s	4.56 s

We have deliberately chosen a complex background that takes a long time to draw. On Symbian OS, we can see the benefit of clipping: the less background we have to draw, the faster we can redraw successive screens. Using off-screen images together with a clipping region further improves performance. Indeed, with complex background scenes, this is the only option. The downside is the memory required to store the background image.

The very fast buffered performance of the Nokia 7650 compared to the Nokia 6600 or Sony Ericsson P900 is at least in part because the 7650 has only 4096 colors, whilst the other devices have 65 536 colors. Without buffering on the WTK, our first two options flickered badly.

7.13.1.5 Using GameCanvas in MIDP 2.0

The Popcorn MIDlet was written for MIDP 1.0. However, it is a simple matter to rewrite it for MIDP2.0 to take advantage of the GameCanvas class. Only a few changes are needed to PlayingField, which we have renamed PlayingFieldGameCanvas. We extend GameCanvas, not Canvas, and we need an instance variable for the Graphics object:

```
public class PlayingFieldGameCanvas extends GameCanvas
        implements Runnable, CommandListener {
  Graphics graphics;
  ...
```

Then we change move() so that it calls the paint() method directly, rather than via repaint() (we should really rename the paint() method to save confusion). paint() updates the Graphics object, then we call flushGraphics() to render it to the screen:

```
public void move(){
    xPosOld = xPos;
    xPos += xDelta;
    if((xPos <= 0) || (xPos > xMax)) xDelta = -xDelta;
    paint(graphics);
    flushGraphics();
}
```

Even though in this case we have not saved any code, the logic is now simpler. For instance, I could easily check when the puck hits the edge of the screen, perhaps to change its color or shape, or to add another item to the Graphics object.

However, whether using Canvas or GameCanvas, the implementation has to do broadly the same amount of work, so using GameCanvas made no significant difference to the execution time.

7.13.2 Collision Detection

Figure 7.3 shows a rocket about to collide with an asteroid. How can we tell if they do indeed collide? The MIDP 2.0 Sprite class provides

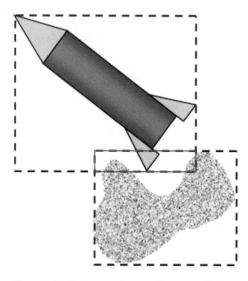

Figure 7.3 Sprites overlapping, but not colliding.

methods for converting an `Image` to a `Sprite` and for detecting whether two sprites are in collision.

In this case the bounding boxes for the sprites overlap. However, the images have not actually collided.

`boolean Sprite.collidesWith(Sprite s, boolean pixelLevel)` returns `true` if the sprites overlap. If `pixelLevel` is false, only the bounding boxes are checked. This is fast, but not accurate. If `pixelLevel` is `true`, first the bounding boxes are checked, then if these overlap, the method checks to see if any non-transparent pixels overlap.

There is no need for you to do a quick check with `pixelLevel` set to `false` followed, if necessary, by an accurate check with `pixelLevel` `true`; just use `collidesWith()` with `pixelLevel` set to `true`. If you need to check collisions between lots of simple sprites, `pixelLevel` should probably be `false`; if you need to check collisions between a few complex objects, `pixelLevel` should probably be `true`. On the other hand, if you have lots of complex objects things can get very complicated.

The number of potential collisions increases with the square of the number of sprites (n sprites means n(n-1)/2 possible collisions). A way to cut this down is to divide the screen into tiles. For each tile you only need to go through all the sprites that are completely enclosed by the tile, or that cross the boundary of the tile.

7.14   LifeTime Case Study

The LifeTime MIDlet is an implementation of Conway's Game of Life. The action takes place on an unlimited field of squares, or cells.

From generation to generation, cells live or die according to three simple rules:

- a cell is created (from nowhere!) if it has 3 neighbors

- a cell stays alive if it has 2 or 3 neighbors

- otherwise a cell dies (of overcrowding or loneliness!) or remains empty.

Near the bottom of Figure 7.4, you can see a block of four cells, a column of three cells and a block of two cells. You might like to convince yourself that in the next generation, using the rules above, the block of four cells remains unchanged because each cell has three neighbors, the column of three changes to a row of three, and the block of two disappears. If you want to know more, *The Recursive Universe* by Poundstone gives an excellent insight into the Game of Life as well as being a thoroughly good read.

Probably the most famous pattern is the r Pentomino. This starts as in Figure 7.5 but explodes into the most amazing patterns. Figure 7.4 is a detail from this pattern after some 70 generations. After 1103 generations, it stabilizes into a predictable, dynamic pattern. Figure 7.6 shows the pattern after 1103 generations at the four zoom levels offered by the program. In the first we see the entire pattern, except for four "gliders" which have traveled beyond the screen and will continue to move out indefinitely. Each cell is represented by a single pixel. At the next zoom level, each cell is represented by a 2 × 2 block of

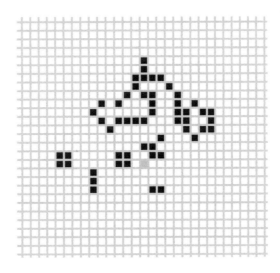

Figure 7.4 Detail of LifeTime.

Figure 7.5 Start of r Pentomino.

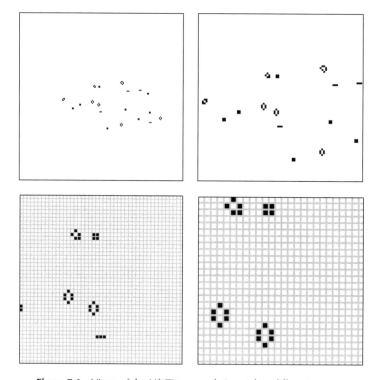

Figure 7.6 Views of the LifeTime population at four different zooms.

pixels, then by a 3 × 3 block, then by a 5 × 5 block at the greatest zoom level.

Figure 7.7 shows the UML class diagram for the LifeTime MIDlet. The classes of particular interest to us are:

- **LifeCanvas**: renders the state of the game to the screen and is responsible for housekeeping functions such as loading and saving games, pan and zoom, and editing functions

- **LifeEngine**: holds the algorithm that interprets Conway's rules to construct a new generation from the old generation

- **GenerationMap**: defines an interface for storing and accessing the data for each generation.

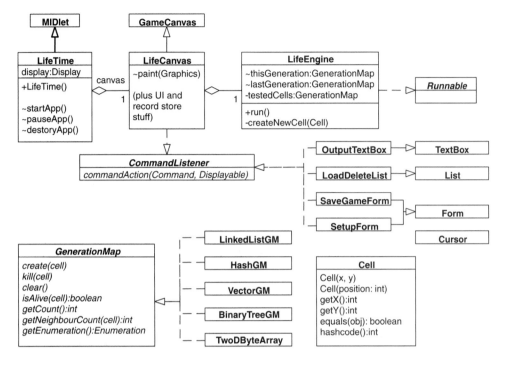

Figure 7.7 UML class diagram for the LifeTime MIDlet.

Four different implementations were tested (the `TwoDByteArray` was not a strict implementation of the interface). In general the location of a cell was stored as one 32-bit integer value, with the top 16 bits holding the y-coordinate and the bottom 16 bits holding the x-coordinate. This meant that the field was limited to 64 K by 64 K, but still much bigger than any screen!

Design choices are driven by the requirements of the game itself, in particular:

- an unlimited playing field; this means that a fixed-size two-dimensional array is not a real option

- maximizing performance

- minimizing memory requirements.

All three classes have to be optimized. `LifeCanvas` needs to paint as fast as possible, not just during a run but also at different zooms, while panning and during editing. The `LifeEngine` algorithm needs to be as quick as possible, at the same time ensuring that the code is straightforward and understandable (a search on the Internet will reveal some very complex, and very fast, Game of Life algorithms). The

GenerationMap implementation needs to provide fast access to the game within a reasonable footprint.

Various auxiliary classes manage loading, saving and deleting games, displaying status information and setting up parameters. They are all implemented as Singletons.

- OutputTextBox: displays status text

- LoadDeleteList: loads a game from the RMS and deletes games from the RMS

- SaveGameForm: saves the current game to the RMS

- SetupForm: sets parameters, such as reporting intervals

- Cursor: simply stores the location of the cursor for editing cells; the MIDlet goes into edit mode when a game is stopped or paused.

When testing different ideas, our standard benchmark is the time taken to generate the first 150 generations starting with the r Pentomino.

7.14.1   Optimizing the LifeCanvas Class

We start our case study by repeating a lesson: optimization is platform-dependent. The main responsibility of the LifeCanvas class is to render the game to the screen when a new generation has been constructed.

The design goal is to ensure fast rendering at all zooms, with rendering independent of screen size (though accepting that rendering could slow down with the number of live cells to be displayed), fast pan and zoom, and fast redraw after editing.

An unsuitable approach is to go through each cell on the screen, check if it is empty or alive, and paint it in accordingly. However, out of interest I recently tried this approach to see how bad it would be. On the Wireless Toolkit using the default color phone emulator it took 109 s to calculate the first 150 generations of the r Pentonimo evolution. This compares to about 48 s using our default rendering.

Version 1

LifeTime was originally developed on the Nokia 9210 using an early implementation of the Wireless Toolkit. Rendering was clearly a bottleneck. As a consequence a great deal of effort went into ensuring that paintCanvas() only updated what had changed; so, for instance, if a cell was alive in both the old generation and the new generation, that location was not updated.

Each call to the painting method carries out the following steps:

1. Fill the whole screen with the background color if we need to repaint the whole screen (e.g. after displaying a dialog or when just started), or if there is no grid (that is, if the zoom is 0 or 1).

2. Paint in the grid lines if we need to repaint the whole screen and the zoom is 2 or 3.

3. Work out the offset of the screen in relation to our origin (the visible area can be panned around the virtual game field).

4. If we did not fill the whole screen with the background color in step 1, then enumerate through the old GenerationMap: for each cell, if it is in the visible area and it does not exist in the new GenerationMap, paint it out with the background color (in fact, because painting was such a bottleneck, it was slightly faster to paint in a prepared image of the empty cell using `Graphics.drawImage()`).

5. Enumerate through the new GenerationMap; for each cell, if it is in the visible area and it did not exist in the old GenerationMap, paint in the live cell image.

6. The cursor may have moved between generations, so paint out the cursor at the old position and paint it in at the new position. The cursor cell is green if there is a live cell at that location and red if the cell is empty.

Version 2

However, on the newer Wireless Toolkit emulator (WTK 2.1) and on Symbian OS phones running the CLDC HI VM, a more straightforward implementation of `paint()` ran just as fast on small screens, and only slightly slower on larger screens.

On each call to our painting method, it carries out the following steps:

1. Fill the whole screen with the background color.

2. Paint in the grid lines if the zoom is 2 or 3.

3. Work out the offset of the screen in relation to the origin (the visible area can be panned around the virtual game field).

4. Enumerate through the new GenerationMap; for each cell, if it is in the visible area, call `Graphics.fillRect()` to paint in the live cell.

5. The cursor may have moved between generations, so paint out the cursor at the old position and paint it in at the new position. The cursor cell is green if there is a live cell at that location and red if the cell is empty.

7.14.2 Optimizing the `LifeEngine` Class

`LifeEngine` contains the algorithm that creates the new generation from the old generation. Rather than go through the code line by line, it is probably less painful to give a description.

The initial implementation used two GenerationMaps: one to hold the new generation (`thisGeneration`), and one to hold the old generation (`lastGeneration`).

- looking at the Game of Life rules, we have to examine each live cell; if it has two or three neighbors it lives, so we create a new cell in `thisGeneration` at the old cell location

- we also have to examine empty cells that have three neighbors. The way the program does this is to examine every cell adjacent to every live cell; if it is empty and has three live neighbors, we create a new cell in `thisGeneration` at the empty location

- having calculated and displayed the new generation, the new generation becomes the old generation and the new generation map is cleared

- `run()` loops once per generation; it goes through all the cells in `lastGeneration` and calls `createNewCell()` to check whether the cell should live or die and to check if the eight neighboring cells should live or die; this translates to a lot of calls to `isAlive()`!

One significant optimization was applied. `testedCells` is a GenerationMap used to hold the tested cells. So, whenever a cell is checked, whether it is empty or not, a cell with the same position is created in `testedCells`. So before testing if a cell should live or die, `createNewCell()` first checks in `testedCells` to see if it has already been tested; if so, it does not test it again. This optimization improved the speed of LifeTime by over 30 % (57 s down to 34 s). However, the extra memory required is significant: if there are 200 live cells in a generation, there will be some 800 tested cells. At 23 bytes per cell, that is about 18 KB.

7.14.3 Tools for Optimization: a Diversion

Taking a guess and test approach to improving performance or reducing memory requirements can work, but is likely to be slow and tedious. We need tools and techniques to help us quickly and accurately identify the bottlenecks.

We shall discuss two tools in this section: profiling and heap analysis. Arguably, the ability to carry out on-target profiling or heap analysis is more important to most wireless application developers than on-target debugging.

The Sun Wireless Toolkit emulator includes a basic profiler and a heap analysis tool. Why these are built into the emulator and not part of the IDE is a mystery. It means we can only profile MIDlets running under the WTK emulator, not under a Symbian OS or any other general emulator, and certainly not on a real device. Perhaps in the not too distant future we can look forward to an extension of the Universal Emulator Interface (UEI). This is currently used to control debug sessions from an IDE in a standardized way, but could be enhanced to cover profiling and heap analysis.

7.14.3.1 *Profiling*

Profiling tools allow us to see how much time is spent in a method and in a line of code in a method, to understand the calling tree, and to see how much time a called method spent servicing calling methods.

The Wireless Toolkit gathers profiling information during a run with no great impact on performance. The results are displayed when the emulator exits. The display is split into two halves:

- on the right is a list of all methods and the statistics for each method: the number of times the method was called, the total number of cycles and the percentage of time spent in the method, and the number of cycles and the percentage excluding time spent in child methods

- on the left is the calling tree, which we can use to drill down and see how much time each method spent executing on behalf of the method that called it.

Figures 7.8, 7.9 and 7.10 show the results from profiling LifeTime on a single run. All three show the same data, rearranged to bring out different aspects. In Figure 7.8, the display has been arranged to show the methods in order of the total execution time. We can immediately see that most of our time was spent in `LifeEngine.run()`. The bulk of this, 73 % overall, was spent in `LifeEngine.createNewCell()`. This method represents the bulk of the Game of Life algorithm. The fact that this method was also called more than 136 000 times suggests that there is room for improvement.

The rendering is handled by `LifeCanvas.paintCanvas1()`. This accounts for only 13 % of the total execution time, so the benefits of optimization here are limited (as we discovered earlier).

We get a different picture if we order methods by the time spent in the method, excluding calls to child methods. Figure 7.9 shows that the most

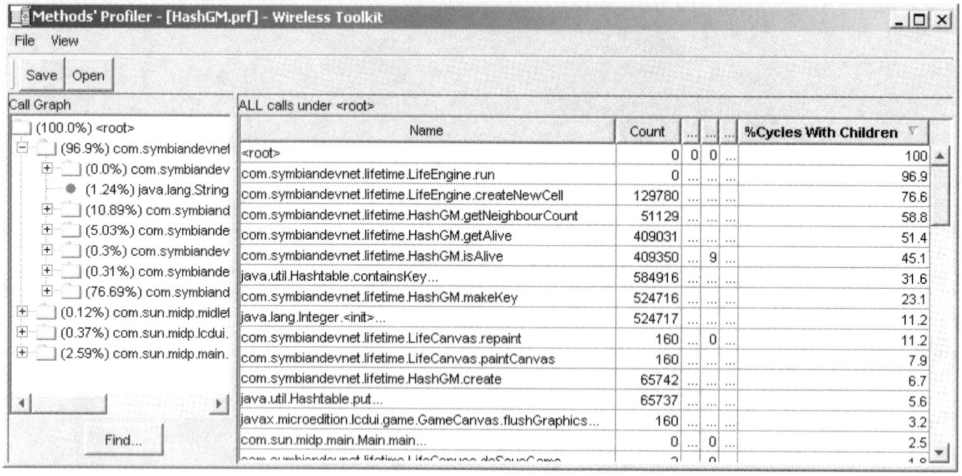

Figure 7.8 Profiling LifeTime by total execution time of the methods.

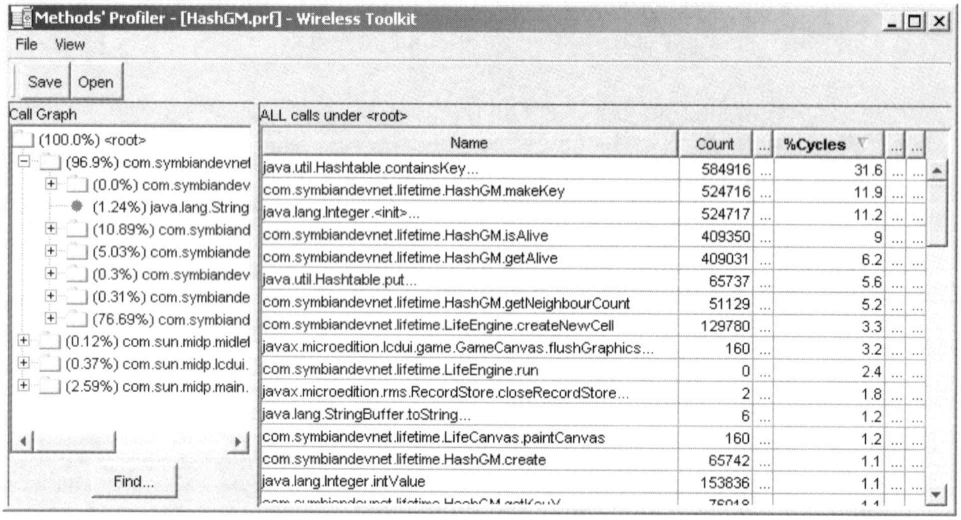

Figure 7.9 Profiling LifeTime by time spent in the methods.

expensive method is `java.util.Hashtable.containsKey()`. The method itself is fairly quick (unfortunately the profiler does not show the average time spent in each method invocation); however, we called it nearly 600 000 times because we are constantly checking to see if a cell is alive or empty.

As we saw in Figure 7.8, some 13 % of the time was spent in `LifeCanvas.paintCanvas()`. However, from the calling graph in Figure 7.10,

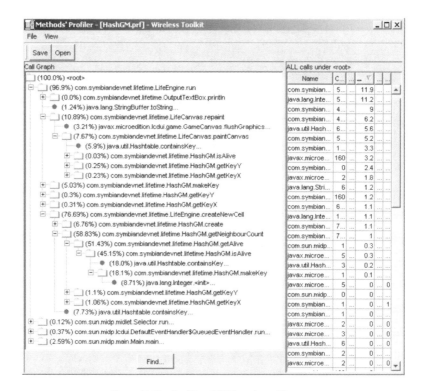

Figure 7.10 Profiling LifeTime by calling tree.

we can see that most of that time was spent in `nextElement()` from the `Hashtable Enumerator`.

53 % of the time was spent in `HashGM.getNeighbourCount()`. The main culprits are `Hashtable.containsKey()` and the `Cell` constructor.

7.14.3.2 Heap Analysis

Heap analysis is the other side of profiling. Profiling is used to identify performance issues; heap analysis to identify memory issues. Sun's Wireless Toolkit heap analyzer displays running data, though with a serious impact on performance, by a factor of about 50.

The tool provides two displays. The first is a graph of overall memory usage (see Figure 7.11). This shows memory gradually increasing, then dropping as the garbage collector kicks in. Remember that this is the KVM garbage collector. It would be quite fascinating to see a similar graph for CLDC HI behavior.

The graph view reports that at the point the emulator was shut down, which was soon after the garbage collector ran, there were 1790 objects, occupying around 52 KB of heap.

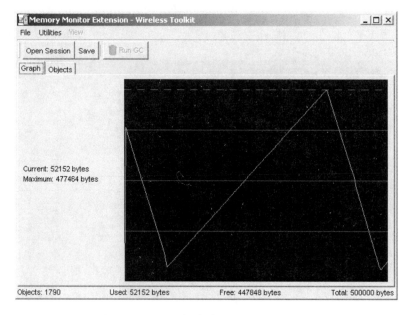

Figure 7.11   Graph of LifeTime memory usage.

The objects view (see Figure 7.12) provides a more detailed break down of the heap utilization. Top of the list are the Cell objects: just over 1500, at 23 bytes each. Again this points to the inefficiency of the algorithm, given that there are typically a few hundred live cells in each generation. Character arrays and Strings are next on the list: these are good targets for obfuscators. The hash tables do not take up as much memory as might be expected.

7.14.3.3   Debugging Flags

What will the compiler do with this code?

```
boolean debug = false;
if(debug){
    debugStream.println("Debug information");
    // other statements
    debugStream.println("Status: " + myClass);
}
```

The compiler will not compile this obviously dead code. You should not be afraid of putting in debug statements in this manner as, provided the debug flag is `false`, the code will not add to the size of your class files. You do have to be careful of one thing: if the debug flag is in a separate file, ensure that you recompile both files when you change the state of the debug flag.

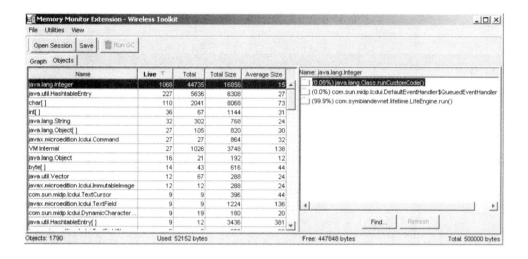

Figure 7.12   Heap Analysis of LifeTime.

7.14.3.4   *What We Should Look Forward To*

The tools for wireless development are still fairly immature. Despite the prospect of more mobile phones running Java than the total number of desktop computers, Wireless IDEs (such as those from IBM, Sun, Borland, Metrowerks and others) are heavyweight J2SE environments modified for wireless development.

We also need real-time tools that work with any emulator and on target devices. To assist this, it is likely that Java VMs on Symbian OS will be at least debug-enabled in the near future, with support for on-target profiling and heap analysis to follow.

Better profiling is needed, for instance to see how much time a method spends servicing each of the methods that call it and how much time is spent on each line of code.

Heap analysis that gives a more detailed snapshot of the heap is required. For instance, the J2SE profiling tools provide a complete dump of the heap so that it is possible to trace and examine the contents of each heap variable.

7.14.4   Implementing the `GenerationMap` Class

The most successful container in LifeTime used a sorted binary tree. Under the Wireless Toolkit emulator (running on a 500 MHz Windows 2000 laptop), LifeTime took about 33 s to calculate and render the first

150 generations of the r Pentomino. As we saw, most of this time was spent in the algorithm.

On a Sony Ericsson P800 and a Nokia 6600 the MIDlet ran dramatically faster, taking around 6 s. Again, most of this was spent in the Game of Life algorithm. We know this because we can disable the rendering (using the LifeTime setup screen); doing so took the execution time down from about 6 s to 4 s, so only about 2 s of the 6 s is spent in rendering.

Here is a summary of some results, all running under the Wireless Toolkit.

GenerationMap implementation	Time	Comparative memory requirements	Comment
2D array	200 s	big!	Need to inspect every cell; limited playing area; not scalable
Linked list	>500 s	3	Fast creation and enumeration, but searching is slow
Vector	>500 s	2	Fast creation and enumeration, but searching is slow
Binary tree	34 s	4	Quite fast creation and searching; enumeration is slow but there is room for improvement Easy access to the source code gave more opportunity for optimization. In particular, we dramatically cut the number of cells created by the `GenerationMap.getNeighbourCount()` method.
Hash table	42 s	7	Searching, enumeration and creation is quite fast but memory-hungry: • a HashTable is sparsely populated • we store a value and a key, when we only need the key. `Hashtable.containsKey(obj)` first checks the `obj` hash code and then checks for equality. In our case, we only need to do one or the other, not both (it would be interesting to download the `Hashtable` source code and reimplement it to meet our requirements).

The linked list and vector implementations performed similarly, and very badly. This is because the searches are linear, with the result that over 90 % of the execution time is spent in the GenerationMap. isAlive() implementation. On the other hand, the binary tree is sorted and the hash table uses hashing for faster lookup. Running on actual phones, the hash table version took 7.5 s on a Nokia 6600 and the binary tree version took 7 s on a Nokia 6600 and 6.5 s on a Sony Ericsson P900.

It is worth looking at the BinaryTreeGM class, but we need to start with the Cell class, which is very straightforward. position combines the x and y coordinates into a single 32-bit integer. next and previous point to the two branches at each node of the tree (LinkedListGM just uses the next pointer and HashtableGM uses neither):

```
package com.symbiandevnet.lifetime;
public class Cell {
    int position;
    Cell next;
    Cell previous;
```

There are two constructors: one takes the packed integer position, the other combines separate x and y coordinates.

```
Cell(int position) {
    this.position = position;
}

Cell(int x, int y) {
    position = (x & 0x0000FFFF) + (y << 16);
}
```

Getter methods for the x and y coordinates:

```
public final int getX() {
    return (short) position;
}

public final int getY() {
    return position >> 16;
}
```

equals() and hashCode() are needed to allow correct searching within a hashtable. In general, equals() should check that obj is not null, returning false if it is. However, we can skip this check because we know this will never be the case.

```
public final boolean equals(Object obj) {
    if ((((Cell)obj).position) == position) return true;
    else return false;
}

public final int hashCode() {
    return position;
}
}
```

The `BinaryTreeGM` class implements the `GenerationMap` interface. `root` is the `Cell` at the start of our binary tree and `size` tracks the number of cells held in the tree. `clear()` clears the tree by simply setting `size` to zero and the root to null. `getCount()` just has to return `size`:

```
package com.symbiandevnet.lifetime;
import java.util.*;
import java.io.*;

class BinaryTreeGM implements GenerationMap {
    private Cell root;
    private int size;

    public final void clear() {
        root = null;
        size = 0;
    }

    public final int getCount(){
        return size;
    }
```

`create(Cell)` inserts a Cell in the correct location in the tree. It returns silently if the tree already contains a Cell in the same position. The algorithm can be found in Section 6.2.2 of *The Art of Computer Programming, Volume 3* by Knuth:

```
public final void create(Cell aCell) {
    Cell cell = new Cell(aCell.position); // Clone cell
    int position = cell.position;

    if (root == null) {
        root = cell;
        size++;
        return;
    }
    Cell node = root;

    while (true) {
        if (node.position < position) {
            if (node.previous == null) {
                node.previous = cell;
                size++;
```

```
                    return;
                }
                else {
                    node = node.previous;
                    continue;
                }
            }
            else if (node.position > position) {
                if (node.next == null) {
                    node.next = cell;
                    size++;
                    return;
                }
                else {
                    node = node.next;
                    continue;
                }
            }
            else return;
        }
    }
```

`isAlive(Cell)` returns true if the tree contains a cell with the same position. Because the tree is sorted it is a fast and simple method:

```
public final boolean isAlive(Cell cell) {
    int position = cell.position;
    Cell node = root;
    while (node != null) {
        if(node.position < position)
            node = node.previous;
        else if(node.position > position)
            node = node.next;
        else return true;
    }
    return false;
}
```

`getNeighbourCount(cell)` returns the number of live cells adjacent to `cell`. It checks whether each of the eight neighboring positions contains a live cell or is empty:

```
public final int getNeighbourCount(Cell cell) {
    int x = cell.getX();
    int y = cell.getY();
    return getAlive(x-1, y-1)
            + getAlive(x, y-1)
            + getAlive(x+1, y-1)
            + getAlive(x-1, y)
            + getAlive(x+1, y)
            + getAlive(x-1, y+1)
            + getAlive(x, y+1)
            + getAlive(x+1, y+1);
}
```

getAlive(int x, int y) is called from getNeighbourCount().
It is similar to isAlive(), but is a private method that returns 0 or 1. It
is used to count the number of neighboring cells:

```
private int getAlive(int x, int y) {
    int position = (x & 0x0000FFFF) + (y << 16);
    Cell node = root;
    while (node != null) {
        if(node.position < position)
            node = node.previous;
        else if(node.position > position)
            node = node.next;
        else return 1;
    }
    return 0;
}
```

The remaining methods implement an Enumeration. copyTreeTo-
Vector() copies the contents of the binary tree to the Vector listV;
getEnumeration() then returns the Enumeration for listV:

```
private Vector listV;
public final Enumeration getEnumeration() {
    copyTreeToVector();
    return listV.elements();
}
private void copyTreeToVector() {
    listV = new Vector(size);
    addToListV(root); // recursive call
}
```

copyTreeToVector() initializes listV to the correct size (to
save resizing during copying, which is expensive) and then calls
addToListV(Cell). This is a recursive method which wanders down
the tree, adding the Cell at each node to the Vector ListV.

```
private void addToListV(Cell node) {
    if(node == null) return;
    listV.addElement(node);
    addToListV(node.previous);
    addToListV(node.next);
}
}
```

7.14.5   Recursion: A Second Look

In Section 7.12.2, we looked at the cost of recursion, both in terms of
memory and performance. We showed how we could avoid recursion
when a method called itself once, but said that even if a method

called itself twice (for instance to enumerate a binary tree) we could avoid recursion.

In the LifeTime `BinaryTreeGM` class, `copyTreeToVector()` used a recursive call to traverse the tree. As promised, here is how we can do it non-recursively:

```
private Vector listV;
private Stack stack = new Stack();

private void copyTreeToVector() {
    listV = new Vector(size);
    if(size == 0) return;
    int count = size;

    Cell node = root;
    while(true) {
        stack.push(node);
        node = node.previous;
        while(node == null) {
            node = (Cell)stack.pop();
            listV.addElement(node);
            count--;
            node = node.next;
            if(count == 0) break;
        }
        if (count == 0) break;
    }
}
```

To explain what is going on, it is easier to think in terms of left and right, rather than next and previous, to describe the branches of the binary tree.

We start at the root and go as far down as we can taking left (previous) branches. Each time we go down, we push that node onto a stack. When we can go no further, we:

1. Pop a node from the stack.

2. Add the node to the `listV`.

3. Decrement `count`.

4. Attempt to take a right branch. If we can, we take the right branch but then continue taking left branches as far as possible. if we cannot, we continue steps 1 to 4 until we can take a right branch, or until we have copied the whole tree to the vector.

5. When `count` is zero we know we have gone through the whole tree, so we return.

This approach is a little ugly because we are copying the whole of the binary tree to a vector. An alternative worth exploring is to take advantage of the fact that the tree is sorted. We would write our own implementation of `Enumeration.nextElement()` that would use the previous `Cell` returned by `nextElement()` as the starting point for a new search. The search would return the next biggest `Cell`.

7.14.6   Summary

There is a further optimization we can consider. The use of `Cells` was driven by the desire to work with standard containers (`Hashtable` and `Vector`), which hold objects, not primitive types. However, we are not interested in the cells themselves, but just their positions (a 32-bit integer). This means we could reduce the number of `Cell` objects created by changing the signatures in the `GenerationMap` interface to take integer values, rather than cells. We would also have to implement our own enumerator interface to return integers, not objects. The result would be a sorted binary tree implementation that was great for our application, but not much use for anything else. However, the goal of this case study is not to make the LifeTime MIDlet as fast (and as memory efficient) as possible, but rather to encourage good design practice in general and consideration of the wider issues.

Each container has its strengths and weaknesses. If insertion is the bottleneck, then a `Vector` would be a good choice; for general ease of use, a `Hashtable` is probably the best choice. `GenerationMap.kill()` was only used during editing, so its performance is not critical. If removing objects has to be done quickly, then `Vector` is a bad choice and `Hashtable` or the sorted binary tree the best choice.

If we have to draw a conclusion from this exercise, it is the need for better containers on wireless devices if we are to run more complex algorithms. Rolling our own containers is a tricky and error-prone business. The ease with which we can optimize our own container has to be offset against the risk of bugs.

The study has hopefully demonstrated a few of our optimization guidelines:

- the benefit of working to interfaces: the `GenerationMap` interface allows us to easily try out different implementations

- reasonably clean architecture and straightforward code: in the interests of maintainability, we have avoided the more exotic Game of Life algorithms and not overspecialized the containers

- the use of profiling and heap analysis tools to identify performance and memory hotspots: we have concentrated our efforts on fixing these areas.

7.15 Arithmetic Operations

Currently there is no hardware assistance available for division and modulo arithmetic in the CPUs used by mobile phones. For an arithmetically-intensive application (such as image analysis or speech decoding), see if you can arrange your divisions so that they are a power of two: you can then use the shift right operator for division. Similarly, for modulo arithmetic you can use a masking operation if the modulus is a power of two.

As an example, you might be using an `array` as a re-circulating buffer, with read and write pointers. The read and write methods will need to wrap their respective pointers when they reach the end of the `array`. If `size` is the size of the array, then on a write we would wrap the pointer with this line of code:

```
writePointer = (++writePointer) % size;
```

Similarly, on a read:

```
readPointer = (++readPointer) % size;
```

If size is a power of two, e.g. 512, we can replace these lines with something a bit faster:

```
writePointer = (++writePointer) & 0x1ff;
readPointer = (++readPointer) & 0x1ff;
```

We can also use a shift right operator to multiply by a power of two. In LifeTime we arranged the cell pitch (`increment`) to be a power of two. In fact, it is equal to two to the power of the `zoomFactor`, where `zoomFactor` is 0, 1, 2, or 3. We could thus replace:

```
g.fillRect(xPos * increment, yPos * increment, cellSize, cellSize);
```

with:

```
g.fillRect(xPos << zoomFactor, yPos << zoomFactor, cellSize, cellSize);
```

There was no measurable performance gain in this case because this line of code was not a bottleneck and because all mobile phone CPUs have hardware multipliers.

7.16   Design Patterns

In Section 7.4, we stated that one of the most important rules for optimization was getting the design right. For instance, it should be possible to defer the choice of sorting algorithm until the trade-offs between bubble sort, quick sort, or some other algorithm can be made intelligently on the basis of performance, memory requirements and the size and distribution of the data set to be sorted. However, this requires designing your code such that substituting one sorting algorithm for another is painless.

This section looks at a couple of patterns that can help achieve a better design.

7.16.1   Caching

Caching can produce very significant improvements in performance. The World Wide Web would probably be unusable if your desktop computer did not cache pages. Disk performance relies on read-ahead caching. Virtual memory is a form of caching. Almost all modern processors use data caches because these can be accessed far more quickly than main memory. Sun's Hot Spot compiler technology, e.g. the CLDC HI VM used by Symbian, caches bytecode as optimized native code.

There are a number of issues to consider when designing a cache (see *A System of Patterns* by Buschmann *et al.*):

- what to cache
  Cache objects which are likely to be reused, are not too big, and are slow to create or to access. A cache will be of most benefit if there is some pattern to the way objects are accessed, e.g. having accessed a web page there is a good chance I shall want to access it again, or having read one sector on a disc there is a good chance the next sector will be wanted.

- how much to cache
  The 80:20 rule applies. Look for the 20 % that is used 80 % of the time. In practice even a small cache can significantly improve performance. On the other hand, a cache that is a similar size to the data set is wasting memory.

- which objects to delete from the cache
  When the cache becomes full, you will have to throw away old items. Strategies include first in–first out, least recently used, least frequently used and random. A random policy works surprisingly well because it is immune to pathological patterns.

- how to maintain integrity between cached data and the data source.
  This takes some thought, as you will be writing data into the cache as well as reading data from the cache. You can maintain cache integrity

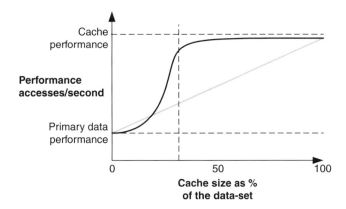

Figure 7.13 Achieving optimum cache size.

using an observer–observable model: read integrity is maintained by making the cache an observer of changes made to the primary data (the cache can also be an observable that is observed by the application), while write integrity is maintained either by using a write-through policy such that data written by the application to the cache is simultaneously written to the primary data source, or by making the primary data an observer of the cache.

Figure 7.13 shows how the optimum cache size depends on the speed of the cache versus the speed of the primary data source, and the size of the primary data set.

The reason for having a cache is that it is faster to access objects in the cache. In this case, the cache is about five times faster to access than the primary data set. Our actual performance (in accesses per second) will not quite reach the cache performance because we shall have to spend some time looking for the object in the cache. Also, of course, the larger the cache the longer it takes to search, so overall performance might even deteriorate with increasing cache size.

The object access pattern implied by this curve suggests a cache size that is 30 % of our primary data set. The lighter-colored straight line gives the performance if objects were accessed randomly.

www.javaworld.com/javaworld/jw-07-2001/jw-0720-cache_p.html provides useful ideas on caching.

7.16.2   Caching Results From a Database

We often want to scroll through records obtained from a database. This might be a remote or local database, or we might be using the PIM APIs (JSR 75) to access our address book.

It is impractical on a constrained device to hold all the data in memory from even a moderate-sized database. Therefore, consider using a cache to hold data already read from the database and predictively load data. The latter can be carried out in a background thread.

For instance, the PIM APIs from JSR 75 access the address book or calendar databases using an Enumeration. Caching ahead will allow the user to look at an entry then quickly iterate through the next few entries. Keeping a small cache of entries that have already been scrolled through will allow the user to scroll back. If the user scrolls back to the beginning of your cache then you have little choice but to reset the Enumeration and read through the database again (which can also be performed in a background thread).

7.16.3   Early or Lazy Instantiation

The Dice Box created its dice at startup time, which is known as early instantiation. Alternatively, we could have created the dice as needed and added them to a pool, which is known as just in time or lazy instantiation. This would reduce startup time at the cost of increasing the time taken to add more dice the first time round. A third alternative would be to create new dice every time we change their number, but being good programmers, we do not give this option too much consideration.

We talked earlier about creating object pools for things like database connections or server connections; we can either create a pool at startup (early instantiation), or build up the pool to some maximum as needed (lazy instantiation).

7.16.4   Larger-Grained Operations

Setting up and tearing down an operation can take a long time compared to the time the operation spends doing real work. It is therefore worth seeing if we can do more in a given operation.

JAR files are used to transfer multiple objects in one HTTP request. Using buffered streams means that we transfer multiple items of data at one time, rather than item by item or byte by byte. It is rare that unbuffered IO is required; buffered IO should always be the default.

7.17   Memory Management

7.17.1   The Garbage Collector

It is rare that a Java application will run out of memory on a desktop computer; however, this is not the case for mobile phones and other constrained devices. We should regard memory exceptions as the rule and handle them gracefully.

The KVM garbage collector does not return memory to the system. Freed memory will only be available to your application: it will not be available to other Java or native applications. If you know you are running on the KVM, do not grab memory just in case you need it; you will deprive other programs of this scarce resource. Even if you are on the CLDC HI VM, it is more socially acceptable to request memory only when you need it. Of course, once your application quits and the KVM exits, the memory it used will become available to other applications. Also remember that `Vectors` and recursive routines have unconstrained memory requirements.

7.17.2 Memory Leaks

Java has a different notion of a memory leak to C++. In C++, a memory leak occurs when a reference to an allocated object is lost before `delete()` is called on the object. If an object is no longer referenced in Java it will be garbage collected, so C++ style memory leaks cannot occur.

However, a similar effect is created by a Java object that is no longer used but is still referenced by another Java object. Care should therefore be taken to de-reference such objects. It is particularly easy to leave objects hanging around in containers. CLDC 1.1 introduces weak references for just this sort of situation.

7.17.3 Defensive Coding to Handle Out-Of-Memory Errors

How can we protect users of our applications from out-of-memory errors? The previous section has highlighted the problem in picking up heap allocation failures. Fortunately, under Java, out-of-memory errors are unlikely to be caused by short-lived objects: the garbage collector should kick in before this happens. Here are some pointers:

- once your application has started, check how much free memory is available (you can use `freeMemory()` from `java.lang.Runtime`) If there is insufficient memory (and only you can judge what that means), give the user the opportunity to take appropriate action such as closing down an application. However, `freeMemory()` and `totalMemory()` should be treated with caution because as memory runs out, more memory will be provided to the MIDlet, up to the limit set at runtime or available in the phone.

- create large objects or arrays in `try-catch` blocks and catch any `OutOfMemoryError` exception that might be thrown; in the `catch` clause, do your best either to shut down gracefully or to take some action that will allow the user to carry on

- never call `Runtime.gc()`: there is no guaranteed behavior for this method; also, the garbage collector knows more about the memory situation than you do, so leave it to get on with its job!

7.18   JIT and DAC Compilers

Most applications benefit from improved compiler technology. This should not be seen as a panacea, though, because Java applications spend a lot of their time executing native code. Many JSRs, for example the Mobile Media API (JSR 135) and Bluetooth APIs (JSR 82), are comparatively thin veneers over native technology.

7.18.1   Just In Time Compilers

JITs have proved popular in enterprise and desktop applications where a lot of memory is available. A JIT is a code generator that converts Java bytecode into native machine code, which generally executes more quickly than interpreted bytecodes. Typically most of the application code is converted, hence the large memory requirement.

When a method is first called, the JIT compiler compiles the method block into native code which is then stored. If code is only called once you will not see a significant performance gain; most of the gain is achieved the second time the JIT calls a method. The JIT compiler also ignores class constructors, so it makes sense to keep constructor code to a minimum.

7.18.2   Java HotSpot Technology and Dynamic Adaptive Compilation

Java HotSpot virtual machine technology uses adaptive optimization and better garbage collection to improve performance. Sun has created two HotSpot VMs, CDC HI and CLDC HI, which implement the CDC and CLDC specifications respectively. HI stands for HotSpot Implementation.

A HotSpot VM compiles and inlines methods that it has determined are used the most by the application. This means that on the first pass Java bytecodes are interpreted as if there were no enhanced compiler present. If the code is determined to be a hotspot, the compiler will compile the bytecodes into native code. The compiled code is patched in so that it shadows the original bytecode when the method is run and patched out again when the retirement scheme decides it is not worth keeping around in compiled form.

CLDC HI also supports "on-stack replacement", which means that a method currently running in interpreted mode can be hot-swapped for the compiled version without having to wait for the method to return and be re-invoked.

An advantage of selective compilation over a JIT compiler is that the bytecode compiler can spend more time generating highly-optimized code for the areas that would benefit most from optimization. By the same token, it can avoid compiling code when the performance gain, memory requirement, or startup time do not justify doing so.

The HotSpot garbage collector introduces several improvements over KVM-type garbage collectors:

- the garbage collector is a "fully-accurate" collector: it knows exactly what is an object reference and what is just data

- the garbage collector uses direct references to objects on the heap rather than object handles: this reduces memory fragmentation, resulting in a more compact memory footprint

- the garbage collector uses generational copying
  Java creates a large number of objects on the heap, and often these objects are short-lived. By placing newly-created objects in a memory "nursery", waiting for the nursery to fill, and then copying only the remaining live objects to a new area, the VM can free in one go the block of memory that the nursery used. This means that the VM does not have to search for a hole in the heap for each new object, and that smaller sections of memory are being manipulated.

  For older objects, the garbage collector makes a sweep through the heap and compacts holes from dead objects directly, removing the need for a free list as used in earlier garbage collection algorithms.

- the perception of garbage collection pauses is removed by staggering the compacting of large free object spaces into smaller groups and compacting them incrementally.

The Java HotSpot VM improves existing synchronized code. Synchronized methods and code blocks have always had a performance overhead when run in a Java VM. HotSpot implements the monitor entry and exit synchronization points itself, rather than depending on the local OS to provide this synchronization. This results in a large improvement in speed, especially for heavily-synchronized GUI applications.

7.19 Obfuscators

Class files carry a lot of information from the original source file, needed for dynamic linking. This makes it fairly straightforward to take a class file and reverse-compile it into a source file that bears an uncanny resemblance to the original, including names of classes, methods and variables.

Obfuscators are intended to make this reverse compilation process less useful. However, they also use a variety of techniques to reduce code size and, to a lesser extent, enhance performance, for example by removing unused data and symbolic names from compiled Java classes and by replacing long identifiers with shorter ones.

Sun ONE Studio Mobile Edition gives access to two obfuscators: RetroGuard and Proguard. RetroGuard is included with the IDE. Proguard has to be downloaded separately (see ***proguard.sourceforge.net***), but the IDE provides clear instructions. As an example, the size of the "straight" LifeTime JAR file is 13 609 bytes; JARing with RetroGuard reduced this to 10 235 bytes and with Proguard to 9618 bytes. The benefits are faster download time and less space needed on the phone.

7.20   Summary

We have looked at a various ideas for improving the performance of our code, and in Section 7.4 we listed a number of guiding principles. Perhaps the most important are these:

- always optimize, but especially on constrained devices

- identify the performance and memory hotspots and fix them

- get the design right.

It is possible on a desktop machine to get away with a poorly-designed Java application. However, this is not true on mobile phones. The corollary is also true: a well-designed Java application on a mobile phone can outperform a badly-designed application on a desktop machine. By thinking carefully about design and optimization we can create surprisingly complex Java applications that will perform just as effectively as an equivalent C++ application.

Finally, an anonymous quote I came across: "I've not seen a well-architected application that was both fast and compact. But then I've never seen a fast and compact application that was also maintainable."

This is perhaps an extreme view, but it is certain that if you have any intention of maintaining your application into the future, or reusing ideas and components for other applications, you should ensure that you have architected it well!

Section 3

The Evolution of the Wireless Java Market

8

The Market, the Opportunities
and Symbian's Plans

8.1 Introduction

Much of this book has dealt with deeply technical aspects of Java development on Symbian OS phones, with the broad goal of helping you to write better and more useful MIDlets for Symbian OS. This chapter looks at the market for Java technology on mobile phones in general and Symbian OS in particular; in other words, at the opportunities you have as a Symbian OS Java developer. It provides estimates for the value of the market, discusses the needs of the various market segments and looks at market opportunities, especially for advanced consumer services.

We will discuss Symbian's approach to Java and how the company is responding to market requirements. This includes a detailed look at Symbian's plans for implementing Java technology over the next couple of years.

We end the chapter with some thoughts on what might be the significant technology trends and related market trends.

8.2 The Wireless Java Market

8.2.1 Market Size

This section looks at what is happening, and what is likely to happen, in the wireless Java market. The rapid growth in the market for mobile phones is legendary. In 2003, there were over a billion mobile phones in use and, for the first time, the number of mobile phones exceeded the number of fixed phones. As shown in Figure 8.1, annual sales are around 400 million (sales dipped in 2002, but picked up again in 2003).

Programming Java 2 Micro Edition on Symbian OS: A developer's guide to MIDP 2.0.   Martin de Jode
© 2004 Symbian Ltd   ISBN: 0-470-09223-8

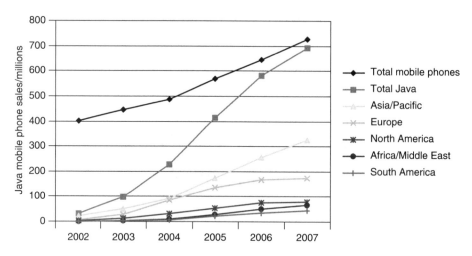

Figure 8.1   Annual sales of mobile phones: total, by region and Java-compatible (source: ARC group).

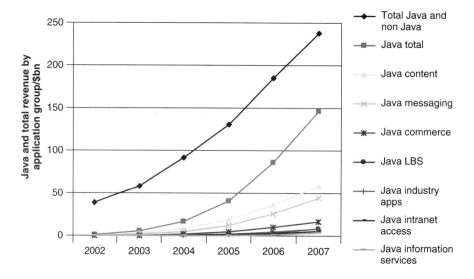

Figure 8.2   Revenue by application group (source: ARC group).

Of particular interest to us, however, is that by 2006 we can expect the vast majority of mobile phones to support Java execution environments.

These figures compare with PC sales of around 130 million per year and an installed base of around 400 million, according to eWeek.com.

Mobile phone manufacturers are including Java functionality in order to generate revenue, which in turn requires that Java content is attractive to end-users. Figure 8.2 shows predictions for worldwide wireless data revenues in excess of $100 billion by 2006 and that most of these revenues will be generated by Java services and applications.

It is worth making a few comments on the above revenue estimates:

- content covers areas such as standalone and multiplayer games, download, storage and playback of music, and video streaming and messaging

- the market for location-based services (LBS) is significantly underestimated: a conservative estimate is that it will be worth more than $30 billion in 2007 (*Location Based Services 2002*, ARC Group)

- games will be worth $4 billion in 2005 (the worldwide games market for PCs and consoles is $25 billion) according to *The Times*, 18 April 2003.

The above statistics suggest that Java consumer services will be worth around $25–30 billion in 2005 (we'll talk about such services in more detail later).

Generating the predicted revenues requires cooperation amongst the players in the value chain: content providers, operators, mobile phone manufacturers and key technology providers must work together.

8.2.2 Java's Significance

The following pie charts indicate the importance of Java as a development language on wireless devices in general and Symbian OS in particular.

Figure 8.3 shows that the industry expects Java to be the most widely used language on wireless devices in 2004. Figures 8.4, 8.5 and 8.6 show

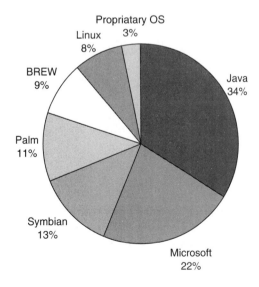

Figure 8.3 Wireless applications to be developed in 2004, by language.

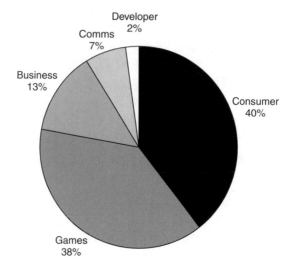

Figure 8.4   Types of application on Symbian OS (all languages), at end of 2003.

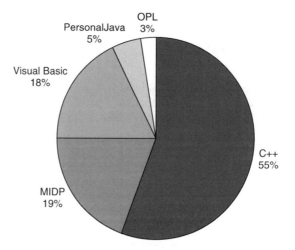

Figure 8.5   Languages used to develop Symbian OS applications, at end of 2003.

the applications and languages on Symbian OS, from internal Symbian data. Note that numbers for MIDP only cover MIDlets specifically sold or marketed for a Symbian OS phone: MIDlets that are not specifically designed for Symbian devices are not included.

Figures 8.5 and 8.6 show that most Symbian applications today are written in C++, with MIDP 1.0 the second most common language. However, MIDP 2.0 is the preferred developer environment and its popularity can only increase as Symbian makes more functionality available to Java developers.

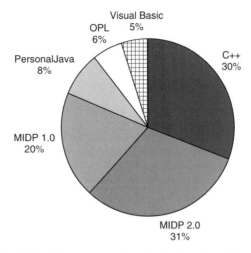

Figure 8.6 Preferred languages used to develop Symbian OS applications.

8.2.3   The Enterprise Market and the Correct Java Configuration

When Symbian was first formed its main focus was on the consumer market, simply because vastly more phones are sold to consumers than to enterprises. However, in the last few years Symbian has been investing heavily in enterprise opportunities.

Here are a few (non rigorous!) features of the enterprise market:

- enterprise projects are high value for middleware vendors (such as IBM Websphere, BEA Weblogic, Oracle Application Server, Sun J2EE)

- for the operators, mobile phone business users are low volume but high average revenue per user (ARPU); consumers are higher volume but lower ARPU

- although the enterprise market is large, manufacturers do not sell many mobile phones into it

- in the US, the growth in wireless devices is being driven by enterprise opportunities; growth in Europe and Asia was driven by the consumer market

- the popularity of WiFi in the US is fueled by business needs for mobile connectivity, email in particular; Europe is promoting Bluetooth as a lower cost, lower power, consumer-oriented alternative; adoption of WiFi in Europe is less than in the US because of the focus on higher bandwidth wide area solutions such as UMTS rather than LAN.

Symbian's Java development is concentrated on MIDP and CLDC, together with the CLDC-compatible wireless Java profiles. This approach is well-suited to the consumer market, even though Symbian OS phones have the power and memory to run CDC-based Java technologies. The emphasis on CLDC rather than CDC is for a number of reasons:

- simpler, fewer and more consistent APIs reduces complexity for the developer and increases developer productivity
- the smaller number of APIs reduces the footprint, which helps to reduce manufacturing and maintenance costs.

Nonetheless, the CDC stack (CDC, Foundation Profile and Personal Profile or Personal Basis Profile) has a couple of significant roles:

- porting existing enterprise applications from desktop to wireless devices, thus extending middleware, such as SAP or Oracle, out to mobile employees, which is made easier by the close relationship between CDC and J2SE
- creating vertical applications where CLDC does not provide the necessary functionality.

Both of these are relatively short-term opportunities; it is hard to see any technical limitations in CLDC that prevent its long-term use for consumer or enterprise segments.

CLDC-based functionality is increasing as wireless JSRs are implemented, to the extent that there is very little functionality in CDC that does not have a CLDC equivalent. This, of course, implies that there are some gaps and we will look at them later in Section 8.7.1.

8.3 Meeting Market Needs

This section identifies some of the key market requirements and Symbian's approach to meeting those requirements. We'll look at these requirements in terms of the value chain comprising consumers, enterprise users, mobile phone manufacturers, developers, operators and service providers.

Consumer Requirements

- games, utilities and simple services
- more advanced added value services.

Enterprise User Requirements

- extension of the organization's information systems to mobile workers.

Service and Content Provider Requirements

- cross-platform standards to maximize the market
- rapid and reliable deployment of new services

- security, PKI and Digital Rights Management solutions
- a provisioning infrastructure.

Developer Requirements

- first class tools and SDKs
- access to necessary functionality
- performance.

Operators

- return on investment
- personalization and branding.

Mobile Phone Manufacturer Requirements

- mass-market compatibility
- time-to-market
- a low bill of materials (this means keeping royalties down, minimizing memory requirements and maximizing performance to allow a slower, and hence lower cost, processor).

So how do we meet the needs of our customers? (If you are a developer, this means your customers as well as Symbian's customers!) Here are few ideas to think about:

- any application or service must add real value, either to the user's leisure time by enhancing their lifestyle, or to their work
- a service that expects the user to spend new money is a harder proposition to sell than one which displaces existing expenditure, even though disposable income is increasing
  For example, young people spend less on confectionery and tobacco to fund mobile phones and messaging in particular. News services may reduce the amount we spend on newspapers. Wireless shopping will reduce the amount we spend on fuel and car parking.
- exploit untapped markets with higher disposable incomes
  Mobile phone services have, at least in Europe and Japan, been driven by the youth market downloading ringtones, wallpapers and games. However, the disposable income of young people is relatively limited. Middle-aged, middle-income groups have a higher disposable income, though are generally more discerning in their expenditure and (usually!) look for clear benefits before purchasing a service.

Also, do not forget older age groups: they have specific needs which are not met by current mobile phones nor the associated services. On the other hand they frequently have access to funds, fewer financial commitments and significant leisure time. Key requirements are simplicity in getting going, ease of use and, most importantly, the service must have a clear, easily understood, benefit and purpose.

- look for subsidies for the service, perhaps through advertising by financial institutions or travel companies

- deliver the service on all available channels: mobile phone, TV, set-top box, Web, etc. This provides the user with task continuity, allowing them to choose when and how to engage with the service.

8.4   Providing Advanced Services

We've seen that simple games and utilities are expected to generate only limited revenue. However, by looking at the market needs and opportunities we've discussed, we can tap into more significant revenue opportunities.

The exciting applications and services, which include multi-user games, location-based services for route planning or localized advertising, entertainment services and wireless commerce, will be those that bring together a wide range of resources and which bring people together. They will be networked, but not reliant on the network, in order that the user can be productive whether online or offline. So a sales application might use a product catalog, route planning services, a timetable and location services.

Figure 8.7 attempts to capture these ideas. Web and WAP browsers present essentially static data, whilst smartphones enable far richer provisioning models. Services are delivered by application providers through channels that include UMTS and Bluetooth, as well as SMS, WAP and Web browsers. Services will have access to data and information that may come from the application provider, but could also come from a variety of other sources.

Providers will use information about the client's capabilities to configure applications for the client device and data will need formatting for both the client and the provisioning channel. Operators will have their own data stores and may also control the services provided to the client. Applications and data will be both pulled by the client and pushed by the operator or service provider.

Client devices will cache data locally, only connecting to the data source to update and synchronize their information. Thus, users will be able to make use of services both offline and online.

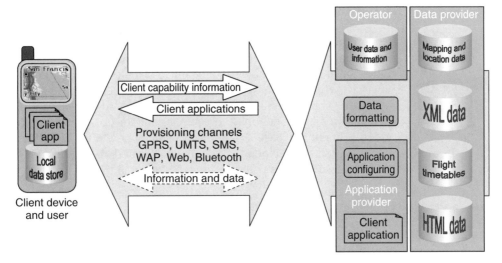

Figure 8.7 The advanced client will be able to work offline and online.

Advanced Consumer Services

- multi-user games: even a simple game like "Snake" can be made more valuable if it allows me to play against my children when I am overseas with a few minutes between meetings

- route planning: routes are stored in a local database and generally accessed offline; if a route is not available, the missing information is downloaded from a server

- localized advertising: receiving information where and when it is relevant

- travel and holiday services

- entertainment services: searching for venues, downloading music; the phone's camera can be used to read a bar code, which takes the user to a relevant web site where the user can download music or video, purchase tickets, or just find more information

- wireless commerce: buying and selling, banking, insurance

- supermarket shopping: the supermarket's stock information would be stored on the mobile phone, allowing me to create a shopping list offline or I could register with a number of supermarkets so that my shopping MIDlet can compare prices and create individual shopping lists; when I am ready to place my order, I synchronize with the supermarkets and my mobile phone is updated with the latest stock details.

Advanced Enterprise Services

- support for mobile employees
  Day-to-day decisions within an organization are typically made by middle management, who also spend much of their time away from the office. They therefore need mobile, and secure, access to a company's systems in general, and communication services in particular. This includes email, calendaring, conference call set up, whiteboarding and document services. So a meeting planner would coordinate meetings by using calendar APIs, contact APIs and messaging APIs to negotiate a suitable time and venue with the attendees.

- sales force automation
  Product catalogs, route planning and timetable information can be stored on the mobile phone.

- field service support.
  Field service applications can use the camera for taking photographs and for reading equipment bar codes, patient bar codes, etc. Email and communications services can be used for transferring and synchronizing records. A touch screen is great for signature capture.

Location-Based Services
Location-based services are rightly regarded as an important source of revenue by operators, service providers and mobile phone manufacturers. Take up will not be as rapid as some have predicted: both mobile phones and infrastructure have to be in place. However, as discussed in Section 8.2.1, the market is expected to be worth over $30 billion in 2007.

At the simplest level, location-based services will allow the user to establish their own location; however, this is merely an enabler for more interesting possibilities:

- how do I get from Paris to Amsterdam? Should I drive, fly, or go by train?

- how do I get from my favorite restaurant back to Joe's place?

- how far is Cambridge?

- where am I? I need an address in the form of town, street, building, company, office and floor (not map coordinates!)

- where is the nearest cinema playing a specific film? Or where are the nearest cinemas in my area?

- what's the weather forecast in my area?

- where is the nearest color printer? The answer might be "4th floor, East end"; the user's coordinates are thus needed in 3D space and probably in the form of an address, rather than numerically; Bluetooth already supports the idea of location "beacons"

- where are my colleagues/family/friends?

- asset tracking: as well as family and friends, non-human assets can be tracked, such as pets or vehicles; this is either for protection against theft or for management

- location-based "to-dos": remind me when I am near home/passing the dry-cleaners/next in Cambridge or when I am near a colleague (this is more challenging because both target and user are mobile)

- location stamping (like time stamping) of user data. Knowing where a data item was created will help with searching and sorting photos, video recordings, voice recordings, etc.; for instance, I could quickly search for all photos of Niagara Falls. Logging calls and messages with a location as well as a time makes them easier to identify and check: "oh yes, I did make that one hour call to Beijing from the Eiffel Tower".

However, there is a danger that the LBS market could fail to achieve its potential if mobile phone manufacturers or operators try to control access to such services. Symbian is taking an agnostic approach to implementing support for location-based services (see Figure 8.8).

Symbian's design means that any location-based service, whether supplied by an operator, a mobile phone manufacturer or a third party, can use any available acquisition technology (A-GPS, translated Cell ID,

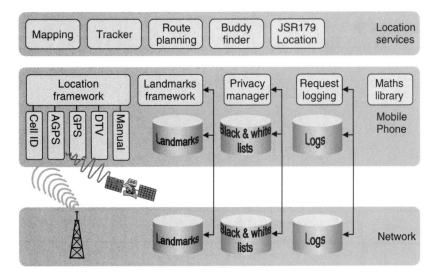

Figure 8.8   Symbian's approach to location-based services.

etc.). Further the service is unaware of whether data such as named landmarks or privacy lists are stored on the network, the mobile phone, or both. Crucially Symbian's implementation of the Location Services API for J2ME (JSR 179) also makes use of this underlying flexibility.

8.5   Why Java?

Sections 8.3 and 8.4 looked at the market segments and opportunities for consumer and enterprise services and identified important market requirements. Let us look at the principal benefits of the Java language for services development and how these meet market needs:

- security: services and applications cannot be subverted

- standardization: more developers and tools mean that more services can be developed

- robustness: fewer faults, fewer recalls

- fast development: faster time-to-market

- ease of porting: service providers can deploy on as many mobile phones as possible.

8.5.1   Security

Wireless services depend on the secure delivery of trusted applications and the secure exchange of information. Security was, and is, one of Java's critical design goals and it is built into Java from the ground up. Features such as the bytecode verifier, preventing random memory accesses and disallowing inappropriate casting, ensure that Java can be used to develop secure systems. Achieving the same watertight security with other languages is much harder.

The absence of pointers and the use of Array objects means that Java code cannot point to either a non-existent object or to the wrong sort of object. It is too easy in C++ code to write or read from an incorrect area of memory (e.g. off the end of an array). The real problem is that the mistake will not be identified immediately, but can generate apparently unrelated misbehavior, frequently a crash, hours or even months later. If a Java application attempts to access an inappropriate object or a non-existent element in an array, an exception will be thrown immediately that identifies both the cause of the problem and where in the source code the problem occurred.

Java's automatic garbage collection results in fewer, or no, memory leaks. In C++, we must be careful to match object construction with object destruction: failing to destroy an object results in a memory leak and attempting to destroy an object twice will cause the program to crash. (As in C++ we must ensure that our Java code does not keep hold of references to unwanted objects; such objects cannot be garbage collected and will effectively cause a memory leak.)

8.5.2 Standardization

At around 3 million, Java developers have overtaken C++ programmers. As a consequence a wide range of development tools, documentation, books, technical support and training is available. Java is the preferred teaching language, and certainly the preferred object-oriented language, in an increasing number of computer science courses.

8.5.3 Robustness and Fast Development

Java code can be developed more quickly and is easier to maintain than C++ code and at the same time is likely to be more robust and contain fewer faults than the equivalent C++ code.

Fewer Faults

Here's an example. This snippet of C++ code is intended to reverse the contents of an array, `ar`:

```
#include <stdlib.h>
void reverseArray(int ar[]) {
    if(ar = NULL) return;
    unsigned int len = sizeof(ar);
    for(unsigned int index = len-1; index >= 0; index--) {
        int temp = ar[index];
        ar[index] = ar[len-index-1];
        ar[len-index-1] = temp;
    }
}
```

The example is based on a genuine piece of code. It actually contains four mistakes: three are coding errors and the fourth is an algorithmic error. These are mistakes which will not generate compiler errors but will cause runtime errors. Let us go through them:

- `if(ar = NULL) return;` is intended to check that `ar` is a valid array; however because the assignment (=) operator has been used rather than the equality (==) operator, `ar` will be set to `null`; the condition evaluates to `false`, so the program will carry on with `ar` equal to `null`

- `sizeof(ar)` is intended to return the number of elements in the array; in fact, it returns the size of an object in bytes so, at best, it will return the size of the array in bytes, not the number of elements; however, even though `ar[]` looks like an array, it is actually a pointer and `sizeof(ar)` will return the size of the pointer, which is typically 4 for a 32-bit machine

- an unsigned integer, `index`, was used for the loop counter; this means `index` will never go negative and therefore the loop will not terminate

- the number of times the code was intended to go through the loop is equal to the number of elements in the array; think about an array of five elements: I want to swap the first with the last, the second with the second to last and the third, or middle element, can stay where it is; in other words, I want to make two swaps, not five!

This is the equivalent Java code:

```
void reverseArray(int[] ar) {
    if(ar == null) return;
    int len = ar.length;
    for(int index = len-1; index >= 0; index--) {
        int temp = ar[index];
        ar[index] = ar[len-index-1];
        ar[len-index-1] = temp;
    }
}
```

The Java compiler expects the argument of an `if` statement to be a `boolean`, therefore we have to use the equality operator. Java arrays are first-class objects and so `ar.length` will return the number of elements in the array. Primitive types in Java (bytes, ints, longs) are always signed so my loop counter will go negative.

We've removed three out of four faults by using Java, allowing us to concentrate on the algorithmic error. Arguably a four-fold improvement in productivity!

Less Code to Write (and Less Code to Deliver)

Java applications also require fewer lines of source code. The following EPOC C++ code sends the message "Hello Imperial" to the server 193.63.255.1 (which belongs to Imperial College in London) on port 7, which is the echo port. The code then reads the echoed reply:

```
RSocketServ ss;
err=ss.Connect();
RSocket sock;
err=sock.Open(ss, KAfInet, KSockStream, KUndefinedProtocol);
const TInt KEchoPort = 7;
TInetAddr imperial(INET_ADDR(193,63,255,1), KEchoPort);
TRequestStatus stat;
sock.Connect(imperial, stat);
User::WaitForRequest(stat);
```

```
TBuf8<14> text = _L("Hello Imperial");
sock.Write(text, stat);
User::WaitForRequest(stat);
sock.Read(text, stat);
User::WaitForRequest(stat);
sock.Close();
```

Although this is Symbian OS C++ code, WIN32 code is very similar. Here's the equivalent Java code:

```
SocketConnection socket
        = (SocketConnection)Connector.open("socket://193.63.255.1:7");
DataOutputStream out = socket.openDataOutputStream();
DataInputStream in = socket.openDataInputStream();
out.writeUTF("Hello Imperial");
out.flush();
String echoedText = in.readUTF();
socket.close();
```

Not only is the code shorter (seven lines rather than 14), but it's a lot clearer as well.

This is not quite the end of the story. Java bytecode itself is compact so that, in general, a line of Java source will generate less code than a line of C++. This is because add, new, etc. are expressed as single bytecodes whereas the C equivalent will expand into word instructions or multiple assembler instructions. On the other hand, we need to be aware of the higher overhead associated with each Java class and that JAR files, if not obfuscated, can be very wordy.

However, in general the consequence of compact bytecode and fewer lines of source is that Java downloads are smaller than C++ equivalents. This is important for over-the-air (OTA) delivery.

8.5.4 Ease of Porting

Java is not a guarantee of success when it comes to device-independence and coping with the huge range of mobile phones; however, it is the least painful solution. APIs are compact and standard user interface classes reduce the worst of the variability. Expert groups such as the Java Technology for the Wireless Industry (JSR 185) initiative are helping to improve portability and reduce fragmentation across mobile phones.

8.6 Symbian and Java

Symbian uses Java to expose the advantages and strengths of Symbian OS through APIs, that, by and large, are standard. Many of the newer wireless Java APIs, such as multimedia, Bluetooth and PIM, are interfaces onto native functionality, which means that a Java implementation is only as good as the underlying platform. Rather than just delivering a vanilla MIDP implementation, Symbian is providing a Java environment that will enable operators and services providers to create revenue through rich, exciting, value-added services.

8.6.1   Current Implementation

Symbian's approach is not only to provide a best of breed environment for standard games and MIDlets (and even here the extra color depth, large screens and good performance will add value as shown in Figures 8.9 and 8.10), but also to enable the large and complex applications and services we discussed earlier.

Symbian's Java implementation ensures that MIDlets are treated in the same manner as native applications (they are "first class citizens") of the platform and, as far as possible, have the appearance of and are managed in the same way as native applications. Here are a few features of Symbian's implementation:

- MIDlets are installed, run and removed like native applications

- MIDlets use native UI components, which are faster and smaller and help to maintain a native look and feel

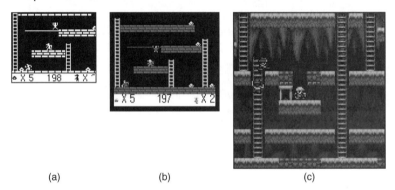

(a)	(b)	(c)

Figure 8.9   Goldminer by Macrospace on a. Siemens SL45i, b. Trium Eclipse and c. Nokia 7650.

Figure 8.10   FunnyBalls by Cybiko, designed for the 9200; good use is made of the screen and the array of control buttons make game play much easier.

- there are no limits on heap size
- there are no limits on characters in a text field or text box, etc.
- there are no limits on the RMS
- the heap can grow and shrink
- there is support for the native color depth
- there is one VM instantiation per MIDlet suite.

Although Symbian's main focus is on CLDC, the Java VM must nonetheless provide uncompromising performance and advanced memory management to deliver the richer services and games we're interested in. Here's a summary of Symbian's VM progress:

- Symbian's first CLDC 1.0 implementation was based on Sun's original KVM, but with the addition of ARM's VTK software acceleration and a heap that can grow; a stack that can grow allows very deep recursion

- Sun's CLDC HI 1.0 uses a dynamic adaptive compiler (DAC) for improved performance
  No debug version is available, so the emulator uses the original KVM configured for debugging. The heap can both grow and shrink, with the heap shrunk on the basis of the percentage used after major garbage collection. This means, on the one hand, that applications should not run out of memory (within the limits of the available system memory) but, on the other, that memory no longer needed by a MIDlet can be recovered by the system for use by other applications.

- CLDC HI 1.1: improves the static and ROMization footprint, which reduces the size of all preinstalled JSRs
  Changing from native to lightweight threads also reduces the footprint. There are small performance gains, around 10% measured against EEMBC benchmarks. The heap and stacks have associated grow and shrink heuristics, with shrink heuristics applied during garbage collection. In addition, ARM is developing the Jazelle technology for use with CLDC HI 1.1, which is a promising combination.

It is worth noting that there is a close correlation between Symbian OS functionality and the wireless JSRs, to the extent that is there is little significant Symbian technology that cannot be exposed via the appropriate JSR.

8.6.2 Future Plans

Having looked in depth at the market and opportunities, it's now time to consider Symbian's plans and how they meet market needs. The

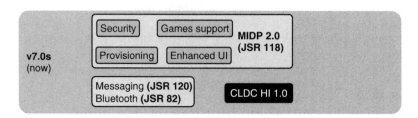

Figure 8.11 Java technology in Symbian OS Version 7.0s.

markets of interest are, broadly, games, location services, web and advanced consumer services, enterprise mobility and mobile commerce. This discussion should be seen as a rough guide only!

Symbian OS Version 7.0s (see Figure 8.11) is used, for instance, on the Nokia 6600 and provides the basic requirements for connected games and utilities. There are many thousands of simple games and utilities running on MIDP 1.0; however, the number of Java APIs in Symbian OS Version 7.0s is an order of magnitude greater than in MIDP 1.0. It will be interesting to see how the number of MIDlets will increase as a consequence.

8.6.2.1 Bluetooth

Java APIs for Bluetooth (JSR 82) enables MIDlets to communicate over Bluetooth. However mobile phones can also use these APIs to host and share services, such as games, printer controllers and rendering services. A Java MIDlet registers itself as a Bluetooth service using the Service Discovery Protocol (SDP). Applications on other mobile phones (either MIDlets using the Java Bluetooth APIs or native applications) can then "discover" the registered MIDlet. The Java APIs return an array of URIs of discovered devices and then an array of URIs for services registered on a particular device. If the registered MIDlet is not already running, the Bluetooth push implementation will launch it. It will even be possible to enable mobile code: the Bluetooth OBEX APIs can be used to transfer a MIDlet from one device to the inbox of a Symbian OS phone, from where the user can install it on their phone. Here is Symbian's roadmap for Bluetooth:

- basic Bluetooth APIs: now
- Bluetooth push: next release (Version 8.0)
- Bluetooth OBEX: end 2004 or early 2005.

8.6.2.2 Symbian OS Version 8.0

Symbian OS Version 8.0 (see Figure 8.12) was released to Symbian licensees early in 2004. Multimedia and 3D graphics were added to the platform, enabling more exciting games and entertainment services.

Figure 8.12 Java technology in Symbian OS Version 8.0.

Symbian's implementation of Mobile Media API (JSR 135) gives developers access to all natively supported media types, which in general will also include dynamically installed codecs. The Mobile 3D Graphics API for J2ME (JSR 184) sits on top of the native OpenGL ES API (***www.khronos.org/opengles***), so that it will benefit from any native hardware graphics acceleration.

The File Generic Connection Framework (GCF) provides access to media files (audio, video, etc.), shared areas and private scratch areas. It is important for both generic consumer applications and services as well as enterprise applications.

Symbian OS Version 8.0 is compatible with Java Technology for the Wireless Industry (JSR 185). It also implements the UEI (Universal Emulator Interface), enabling any Symbian OS phone emulator to be debugged with any UEI-compliant IDE.

8.6.2.3 *Symbian OS Version 8.x*

Symbian will release the next version of Symbian OS in 2004 (see Figure 8.13). PIM provides access to contacts and calendaring information. This can be used to enhance games, provide additional services and deliver mobile support for enterprises. 2D graphics provide vector drawing facilities appropriate for mapping, engineering drawings and kitchen designs.

In the same time frame, Symbian is working on improved Java tools, e.g. for debugging, profiling and heap analysis.

Towards the end of 2004 and into 2005 Symbian will add Java APIs needed to meet the essential needs of the market sectors we identified earlier (see Figure 8.14), making it easier to create advanced consumer and enterprise services. In particular, the example services we've looked at had a number of common themes:

- interaction with back-end services

- the need for local persistence and data storage

- the need to synchronize data with remote services.

Figure 8.13 Java technology in Symbian OS Version 8.x.

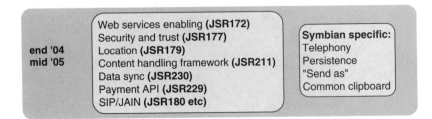

Figure 8.14   Forthcoming Symbian Java technology.

JSR 172

The J2ME Web Services Specification (JSR 172) will be used to interact with net-based consumer and enterprise services. In general, clients for web services tend to be fairly thin, providing little more than a browser interface. The possibilities are wider on Symbian OS, where different web services, for instance weather forecasting and traffic flow information, may be aggregated in the same application. JSR 172 relies on Simple Object Access Protocol (SOAP). This is a wire protocol similar to the IIOP for CORBA, ORPC for DCOM, or Java Remote Method Protocol (JRMP) for Java Remote Method Invocation (RMI). However, while IIOP, ORPC and JRMP are binary protocols, SOAP is a text-based protocol that uses XML. It therefore remains to be seen in practice whether SOAP's wordiness will cause bandwidth problems on wireless networks.

The RMS provides a very basic persistent store in a flat structure. However, there is no CLDC-compatible JSR for persistent object storage or database access. JDBC Optional Package for CDC/Foundation Profile (JSR 169) provides a JDBC subset for CDC; however, a CLDC-compatible API is yet to be defined. We should also carefully look for the right model: JDBC supports industry standard SQL, however an object database may be more natural for the Java language.

JSR 230

Data Sync API (JSR 230) is currently being defined. It should allow applications to synchronize data with back-end stores and take part in platform data sync operations. It should be independent of the communication protocol, though SyncML is likely to be the most common implementation.

JSR 177

Security and Trust Services (JSR 177) is important for wireless commerce, micropayments, billing, etc. It provides access to a smart card (usually a SIM) using either Application Protocol Data Unit (APDU) commands or RMI access. It also provides a certificate store and cryptography library.

JSR 179

We've touched on Location API for J2ME (JSR 179). The Location APIs will allow many location-based services to be developed in Java. It gives Java developers access to whatever location acquisition methods are provided on the mobile phone, such as A-GPS, GPS, or basic translated Cell ID. The `Criteria` class is used to select an acquisition method based on criteria such as accuracy, speed of fix, cost and power. It also provides a Landmarks store that stores coordinate–name pairs: location positions are stored and handled internally as WGS 84 latitude–longitude coordinates, so the ability to convert between a named location and coordinates is essential as users generally work with named locations, for instance, "How far is the Bowling Alley from the supermarket?"

JSR 180

Session Initiation Protocol (SIP) is an application-layer control protocol that can establish, modify and terminate multimedia sessions, as well as inviting participants to join existing sessions. SIP transparently supports name mapping and redirection services, enabling personal mobility whereby users can maintain a single externally visible identifier regardless of their network location.

Five facets of establishing and terminating multimedia communications are supported:

- user location: determining the end system to be used for communication

- user availability: determining the willingness of the called party to engage in communication

- user capabilities: determining the media and media parameters to be used

- session setup: establishing session parameters for both called and calling party

- session management: including session transfer and termination, modifying session parameters and invoking services.

A useful summary of Java, SIP, and JAIN can be found at **www.cs.columbia.edu/sip/Java-SIP-Specifications.pdf**. SIP is probably best known for Instant Messaging and Presence (IM&P) session control. SIP has been adopted as the baseline signaling protocol for the 3GPP IP Multimedia Subsystem (IMS), which will be available in 3GPP Release 5. SIP could be used for mobile phone management, a new application area.

There are other use cases, though these assume that the operators have built the corresponding infrastructure:

- IP telephony applications and IP-based telephone networks

- game billing
  In a multiplayer game, the game could send a SIP signal to the back-end server saying who lost the game, supporting a "loser pays" payment model. In many cases, only the MIDlet running on the mobile phone knows about the status of the game, so that SIP signaling is the only way to use this knowledge for charging.

- game management
  SIP can be used to maintain a game play session until the game is over, even if the mobile phone was turned on and off several times between. The charge applied can still be a fixed fee for the game, independent of time.

- charging and billing for SIP-unaware applications.
  Games and services may not use SIP interfaces directly, but instead could be using open connection, or send message APIs. Underneath, the mobile phone would use SIP signaling appropriate to the application and the API, so enabling SIP-based charging and billing integration even for legacy applications.

The SIP for J2ME (JSR 180) specification extends the GCF pattern, which means new SIP connections are obtained through the `Connector` factory. The specification follows the same simple and lightweight structure as all other MIDP protocol frameworks, e.g. `HttpConnection` and `SocketConnection`. SIP for J2ME is defined at the transaction level in the same way as `HttpConnection`. This makes the API specification multipurpose, without any assumptions about its intended usage. As a consequence, a MIDlet that is implemented at the transaction level must handle message flow. This HTTP-like functionality has been extended to support receiving `Requests` that exist in SIP and HTTP, so blocking calls are extended with an event mechanism that allows application developers to choose their optimal programming style.

Java APIs for Integrated Networks

Java APIs for Integrated Networks (JAIN) provides wireless devices with a uniform interface to a variety of networks such as wireless, proprietary Internet, the public switched telephone system, and Asynchronous Transfer Mode (ATM) networks. JAIN is used to reshape proprietary interfaces into uniform Java interfaces, enhancing application portability.

There are four CLDC-compatible APIs for IM&P that use the JAIN APIs. Whereas the SIP APIs are very low level, these are high-level service-oriented APIs:

- JAIN Presence (JSR 164) provides a standard, portable and secure interface to manipulate presence information between a SIMPLE client (known as a watcher) and a presence server (known as a presence agent); SIMPLE extends SIP with support for presence and instant messaging

- JAIN SIMPLE Instant Messaging (JSR 165) provides an interface to exchange messages between SIMPLE clients; it is a peer-to-peer protocol

- JAIN Presence (JSR 186) is a generic API for presence that is independent of the communication protocol (whereas JSR 164 is based on SIMPLE)

- JAIN Instant Messaging (JSR 187) is an API for instant messaging that is independent of the communication protocol, whereas JSR 165 is based on SIMPLE, and it uses a presence server for message handling.

JSR 186 and 187 require underlying protocol support for specific IM&P services. Some popular choices are OMA Wireless Village, IETF SIP and IETF XMPP, which are all standard protocols. There are also proprietary protocols such as AOL, Yahoo and MSN. The selection of protocol stacks (which all run over TCP/IP) is implementation-specific: a mobile phone which is to be used with specific ISP services should provide the appropriate protocol stacks.

JSR 229

Payment API (JSR 229) enables application developers to initiate mobile payment transactions in MIDlets. It defines a generic API to initiate payment transactions and the syntax to describe the associated provisioning information. This enables different payment instruments to be supported, such as operator charging, stored value accounts, or third-party payment services. Transactions can take place over a variety of transports, such as SMS or the Internet, though the JSR assumes a secure channel is available.

JSR 211

Content Handler API (JSR 211) will allow MIDlets to handle actions on a URI based on the MIME type or scheme. So, for instance, clicking on a specialist audio file in a browser starts up the appropriately registered MIDlet decoder. Further, an application can use the URI and/or MIME type to invoke another application. This will allow the applications to run sequentially, passing parameters and returning results.

8.6.3   Symbian-Specific Extensions

Figure 8.14 listed a number of potential Symbian specific extensions: telephony, persistence, "Send as" and common clipboard. Synchronization used to be on this list, but fortunately Siemens initiated JSR 230, the Data sync APIs! Ideally all these APIs should be defined by standard JSRs.

We have already discussed the need for persistence or database access. This could either be straight SQL, i.e. a subset of JDBC, or an object store.

Telephony APIs are needed to provide access to telephony-related features (we are not discussing APIs needed to create a telephony client: that was the purpose of JTAPI). The functionality would include:

- access to IMEI and IMSI numbers, which uniquely identify a mobile phone; this is especially useful for games and DRM – currently the best a game can do is use the Wireless Messaging APIs to obtain the phone number

- reacting to telephony events, e.g. to detect ringing events, call pickup, call termination and, importantly, caller id; this enables a MIDlet to identify a caller and display a relevant contact card or other related information

- providing information such as signal strength, battery level and power status, IR and Bluetooth status

- launching the mobile phone's telephony application: this should not require a separate API as it should be achievable either from the user interface using a `TextBox` or `TextField` with a PHONENUMBER constraint, or programmatically using `platformRequest()`.

A "Send as" menu option is provided in many Symbian OS applications, e.g. Word, and is used to send the document via IR, Bluetooth, email, SMS, etc. The "Send as" API would provide a MIDlet with the same functionality and is part of making MIDlets first class citizens.

The common clipboard API continues the theme of making MIDlets first class citizens. As the name suggests, it allows MIDlets to copy data to and from the system clipboard, in the same manner as native applications.

8.7   Java and Digital Rights Management

Increasingly, suppliers of content such as games, videos, audio, other multimedia material and applications in general, are keen to prevent illegal use of the content or to control its use. Digital Rights Management (DRM) is about how rights of use can be associated with content. Such rights could prevent a MIDlet suite being passed on to another mobile phone, allow the game to be played only until a certain date, or allow a piece of music to be played only a set number of times. See ***www.openmobilealliance.org/tech/release.html*** for the specification, or ***www.openmobilealliance.org/docs/DRM%20Short%20Paper%20DEC %202003%20.pdf*** for a top level description.

The first phase, OMA DRM Version 1.0, is moderately easy to break and is intended for low value content (simpler games and applications, or ringtones). It consists of three options:

- forward lock, which prevents content from being forwarded to other phones
  The content is downloaded within a wrapper and the wrapper has a MIME type which indicates that this content should not be forwarded (the wrapper header includes the MIME type of the content, for instance, a video clip). It is then up to the platform to decide how to handle this content to prevent forwarding, for instance by ensuring that it is not installed in a user-accessible location or by encrypting it with a hidden key.

- combined delivery, which is similar to forward lock, except that the wrapper includes a rights object
  The rights object defines in detail how the content can be used, for example the number of hours for which a game can be played, or how many times a music track can be listened to. Again how this is implemented is down to the platform.

- separate delivery, in which content and the rights object are sent separately.
  The content is encrypted into a DRM Content Format (DCF) file using a Content Encryption Key (CEK) – a symmetric key using the Advanced Encryption Standard (AES) – and can then be downloaded over an insecure channel such as the Internet. However the rights object must be downloaded over a secure channel, for instance SMS, because it contains the CEK (a bit like whispering a password in someone's ear). The CEK is then used to decrypt the DCF file.

MIDlet suites already come with JAD and JAR files, so that separate delivery, for instance, would work like this:

1. The user clicks on a URL in a browser, which, as for an unprotected MIDlet suite, initiates the JAD download.

2. The user decides whether to download the application based on the information from the JAD (cost, size, required support, etc.) as they would for an unprotected suite.

3. The JAD, rather than pointing to a JAR file, points to the DCF file containing the JAR, which is then downloaded by the platform's DCF recognizer.

4. Meanwhile, WAP push is used to send the rights object to the phone, where it is used by the installer to decrypt the DCF file, extract the JAR file and install the MIDlet suite.

The second phase of OMA DRM should be finalized by the middle of 2004. It will offer more security, making it suitable for higher value content. It will encrypt both the rights object and the content encryption key with the phone's public key, binding them to the phone. Both the content and the rights object will protected against tampering through the use of hash keys.

Symbian provides APIs for the OMA DRM Version 1 specification. Content publishing tools for use with the Nokia 6600 and Sony Ericsson P800 and P900 are available from the respective manufacturer's website.

8.8   The Java Verified Program

The Java Verified program (**www.javaverified.com**) is intended to test the basic functionality of a MIDlet: does it start, does it stop and exit gracefully, does it hog bandwidth or other resources? It does not check conformance with corporate branding, nor does a pass or fail depend on whether or not the MIDlet is socially acceptable, though unacceptable content will not be allowed to use the Java logo.

The members of the program are Sun, Motorola, Nokia, Siemens and Sony Ericsson. Sun host a portal where developers can register information about the MIDlet they want verified. The program will not generate revenue, indeed the only transactions are between the developer and the test house (the website provides details of test houses and pricing). Most of the verification can be carried out by the test house and this is where most of the work has to be done. However, the last 10% is carrier-specific, e.g. the type of download server, billing wrapper, or any DRM implementation.

The scope of the program is currently limited: it is for untrusted MIDlets only and is aimed at the service provider, operator, or aggregator who wants to provision the MIDlet. The provider receives the MIDlet encrypted and uses a public key supplied by the program to decrypt it before publishing it. The provider is thus assured that the MIDlet has been through the Java Verified program, that the author is who he claims to be and that the MIDlet has not been tampered with since testing.

The end-user downloads the unencrypted MIDlet to a mobile phone and may have no knowledge that the MIDlet has been through the program. This is in contrast to the Symbian signing program for native applications, which delivers signed MIDlets to the mobile phone.

It is to be hoped that in the near future the program will create a Public Key Infrastructure (PKI) that will be agreed by all parties: operators, mobile phone manufacturers and developers. This will provide a signing mechanism so that developers can create trusted, signed, MIDlets that can offer more interesting services.

8.9 Beyond Advanced Consumer Services

We've talked about services mainly in the context of a client running on a mobile phone talking to back-end services (JSR 172 will be important in delivering such services). However there is potentially a bigger opportunity for what might be called "ubiquitous services", where services are provided by many small embedded devices such as home appliances, drinks machines, teller services, even light switches. The service might be executed on the device, or loaded onto the mobile phone and run as a MIDlet. There is also no reason why mobile phones themselves cannot host and share services.

To achieve these ubiquitous services we need an infrastructure that covers:

- service registration: the ability to register a service for discovery by other devices, mobile or otherwise
- service discovery: this could be by the user searching through a browser type interface, or by an application searching for a particular type of service
- remote service access: this can be achieved by JSR 172 and SOAP (though SOAP may require too much bandwidth for wireless networks)
- service lifecycle: existing technologies are probably adequate for service start up (e.g. push technology from Bluetooth, WAP or MIDP), however, many services will be transient and should be deleted after use; this would have to handled by the system AMS, perhaps in response to a message
- transfer of executable content: once a service has been discovered, it can be transferred as a MIDlet using OTA-type protocols and executed on the mobile phone.

OSGi provides a partial answer (see, for instance, Mobile Operational Management (JSR 232)). However, this is a very heavyweight option and is only applicable to CDC. The Bluetooth discussion in Section 8.6.2.1 gives an idea of how we can enable ubiquitous services today or in the near future.

8.10 Trends in Technology

To end this chapter (and the book), let us gaze into a crystal ball, starting with the technology:

- CPU power will continue to increase in accordance with Moore's law
- combinations of software and hardware acceleration will remove the gap between Java and native performance

- network bandwidth will improve, though not so dramatically

- network connections will always be available, reducing latency

- costs for persistent storage will continue to tumble and access speeds will increase dramatically as new memory technologies, such as Ferroelectric RAM, Magnetic RAM and Ovonic memory, replace NOR and NAND flash

- the resolution of screen displays will continue to improve, through a decrease in dot pitch as screen sizes will be limited by overall mobile phone ergonomics.

There will also be market changes:

- "smart houses" will become a reality: climate control, entertainment and security systems will be controlled by a variety of devices, including mobile phones

- digital consumer goods will converge.

Today, video cameras can take still images and digital cameras can record video, and quite often both include MP3 players. These capabilities are moving into mobile phones: the current phones only support VGA, however the next generation of mobile phones will have megapixel resolution cameras (indeed a number of Japanese cameras already do). Many of today's mobile phones come with FM radios and in the future we are likely to see the inclusion of Digital Audio Broadcast radios. In Korea, people can now use their mobile phones for credit card purchases. The consequence will be an explosion in the amount of data users store on their mobile phone: audio, video, images, email and messaging. This will amount to gigabytes of storage.

So, we leave you with a simple challenge: to use your development skills, and the knowledge and insight that we hope you have gained from this book, to create the next killer Java service or application on Symbian OS.

Appendix 1

CLDC Core Libraries

System Classes

`java.lang.Class`	Instances of `Class` represent classes and interfaces in a running application.
`java.lang.Object`	The `Object` class is the root of classes.
`java.lang.Runtime`	Every Java application has a single instance of the `Runtime` class, which allows the application to interface with the environment in which it is running. Note that the `Exit()` method always throws a `java.lang.SecurityException`.
`java.lang.System`	The `System` class contains several useful fields and methods and it cannot be instantiated. Note that the `Exit()` method always throws a `java.lang.SecurityException`.
`java.lang.Thread`	A Thread is a unit of execution in a program. Multiple threads may be executed concurrently.
`java.lang.Runnable` (interface)	This interface should be implemented by any class which is intended to be executed as threads. A `run()` method must be defined by such a class.
`java.lang.Throwable`	The `Throwable` class is the superclass of all errors and exceptions.

Data Type Classes

`java.lang.Boolean`	The `Boolean` class wraps a value of the boolean primitive type in an object.
`java.lang.Byte`	The `Byte` class wraps a value of the byte primitive type in an object.
`java.lang.Character`	The `Character` wraps a value of the char primitive type in an object.
`java.lang.Integer`	The `Integer` class wraps a value of the int primitive type in an object.
`java.lang.Long`	The `Long` class wraps a value of the long primitive type in an object.
`java.lang.Short`	The `Short` class wraps a value of the short primitive type in an object.
`java.lang.String`	The `String` class represents character strings.
`java.lang.Stringbuffer`	A `StringBuffer` implements a mutable sequence of characters.

Collection Classes

`java.util.Vector`	The `Vector` class implements an array of objects that can grow.
`java.util.Stack`	The `Stack` class represents a last in first out stack of objects.
`java.util.Hashtable`	This class implements a hashtable, which maps keys to values.
`java.util.Enumeration` (interface)	An object that implements the `Enumeration` interface generates a series of elements, one at a time.

Input/Output Classes

`java.io.InputStream`	This abstract class is the superclass of all classes representing an input stream of bytes.
`java.io.OutputStream`	This abstract class is the superclass of all classes representing an output stream of bytes.
`java.io.ByteArrayInputStream`	A `ByteArrayInputStream` has an internal buffer that contains bytes that may be read from the stream.

`java.io.ByteArrayOutputStream`	This class implements an output stream in which the data is written into a byte array.
`java.io.DataInput` (interface)	The `DataInput` interface provides for reading bytes from a binary stream and reconstructing from them data in any of the primitive types.
`java.io.DataOutput` (interface)	The `DataOutput` interface provides for converting data from any of the primitive types to a series of bytes and writing to a binary stream.
`java.io.DataInputStream`	A `DataInputStream` lets an application read primitive data types from an underlying input stream in a machine-independent way.
`java.io.DataOutputStream`	A `DataOutputStream` lets an application write primitive data types to an output stream in a portable way.
`java.io.Reader`	An abstract class for reading character streams.
`java.io.Writer`	An abstract class for writing character streams.
`java.io.InputStreamReader`	An `InputStreamReader` is a bridge from byte streams to character streams. It reads bytes and translates them into characters according to a specified character encoding.
`java.io.OutputStreamReader`	An `OutputStreamReader` is a bridge from character streams to byte streams. Characters written to it are translated into bytes according to a specified character encoding.
`java.io.PrintStream`	A `PrintStream` adds functionality to another output stream, namely the ability to print representations of various data values conveniently.

Calendar and Time Classes

`java.util.Calendar`	The `Calendar` is an abstract class for getting and setting dates using a set of integer fields such as YEAR, MONTH, DAY, etc.

`java.util.Date`	The `Date` class represents a specific instant in time with a millisecond precision.
`java.util.TimeZone`	The `TimeZone` class represents a time zone offset and also works out daylight savings.

Additional Utility Classes

`java.util.Random`	An instance of this class is used to generate series of pseudo-random numbers.
`java.lang.Math`	The `Math` class contains methods for performing basic numeric operations.

Exception Classes

`java.lang.Exception`	The `Exception` class and its subclasses are a form of `Throwable` that indicates conditions that a reasonable application might want to catch.
`java.lang.ClassNotFoundException`	Thrown when an application tries to load in a class through its string name using the `forName()` method in `Class` class.
`java.lang.IllegalAccessException`	Thrown when an application tries to load in a class but the executing method does not have access to the class definition, because the class is in another package and is not public.
`java.lang.InstantiationException`	Thrown when an application tries to create an instance of a class using the `newInstance()` method in `Class` class, but cannot instantiate it because it is an interface or an abstract class or it doesn't have a default constructor.
`java.lang.InterruptedException`	Thrown when a thread is waiting, sleeping or otherwise paused and another thread interrupts it.
`java.lang.RuntimeException`	This is the superclass of exceptions that can be thrown during the normal operation of the Java Virtual Machine.

`java.lang.ArithmeticException`	Thrown when an exceptional arithmetic condition occurs.
`java.lang.ArrayStoreException`	Thrown to indicate that an attempt has been made to store the wrong type of object in an array of objects.
`java.lang.ArrayIndexOutOfBoundsException`	Thrown to indicate that an array has been accessed with an illegal index.
`java.lang.ClassCastException`	Thrown to indicate that the code has attempted to cast an object to a subclass of which it is not an instance.
`java.lang.IllegalArgumentException`	Thrown to indicate that a method has been passed an illegal or inappropriate argument.
`java.lang.IllegalThreadStateException`	Thrown when starting a Thread for the second time.
`java.lang.NumberFormatException`	Thrown when trying to read an Integer from a malformed String.
`java.lang.IllegalMonitorStateException`	Thrown to indicate that a thread has attempted to wait on an object's monitor or to notify other threads waiting on an object's monitor without owning the specified monitor.
`java.lang.IndexOutofBoundsException`	Thrown to indicate that an index of some sort (such as an index to an array, to a string, or to a vector) is out of range.
`java.lang.StringIndexOutOfBoundsException`	Thrown by the charAt() method in class String and by other String methods, to indicate that an index is either negative or greater than or equal to the size of the string.
`java.lang.NegativeArraySizeException`	Thrown if an application tries to create an array with negative size.
`java.lang.NullPointerException`	Thrown when an application attempts to use null in a case where an object is required.
`java.lang.SecurityException`	Thrown by the security manager to indicate a security violation.
`java.util.EmptyStackException`	Thrown by methods in the Stack class to indicate that the stack is empty.
`java.util.NoSuchElementException`	Thrown by the methods of an Enumeration to indicate that there are no more elements in the enumeration.

`java.io.EOFException`	Signals that an end of file or end of stream has been reached unexpectedly during input.
`java.io.IOException`	Signals that an I/O exception of some sort has occurred.
`java.io.InterruptedIOException`	Signals that an I/O operation has been interrupted.
`java.io.` `UnsupportedEncodingException`	Signals that the character encoding is not supported.
`java.io.UTFDataFormatException`	Signals that a malformed UTF8 string has been read in a data input stream or by any class that implements the data input interface.

Error Classes

In contrast to the exception classes, the error-handling capabilities of CLDC are limited to just three:

`java.lang.Error`	`Error` is a subclass of `Throwable` that indicates serious problems that a reasonable application may not try to catch.
`java.lang.VirtualMachineError`	Thrown to indicate that the Java Virtual Machine is broken or has run out of the resources necessary for it to continue operating.
`java.lang.OutOfMemoryError`	Thrown when the Java Virtual Machine cannot allocate an object because it is out of memory and no more memory can be made available by the garbage collector.

Catching an `OutOfMemoryError` is very good practice when developing for a resource-constrained device. It allows the developer to try to free all the memory he can and maybe give the application another chance to perform the requested action. In the worst case scenario, the application should be able to display a previously allocated dialog box to inform the user that the application cannot continue.

Appendix 2

MIDP Libraries

Networking Package

`javax.microedition.io.Connection`	This interface is the most basic type of generic connection.
`javax.microedition.io.Connector`	This class is a placeholder for the static methods used to create all the connection objects.
`javax.microedition.io.CommConnection`	This interface defines a logical serial port connection.
`javax.microedition.io.ContentConnection`	This interface defines the stream connection over which content is passed.
`javax.microedition.io.Datagram`	This is the generic datagram interface.
`javax.microedition.io.DatagramConnection`	This interface defines the capabilities that a datagram connection must have.
`javax.microedition.io.HttpConnection`	This interface defines the necessary methods and constants for an HTTP connection.
`javax.microedition.io.HttpsConnection`	This interface defines the necessary methods and constants to establish a secure network connection.
`javax.microedition.io.InputConnection`	This interface defines the capabilities that an input stream connection must have.

`javax.microedition.io.OutputConnection`	This interface defines the capabilities that an output stream connection must have.
`javax.microedition.io.PushRegistry`	This class maintains a list of inbound connections.
`javax.microedition.io.SecureConnection`	This interface defines the secure socket stream connection.
`javax.microedition.io.SecurityInfo`	This interface defines the methods for accessing information about a secure connection.
`javax.microedition.io.` `ServerSocketConnection`	This interface defines the server socket stream connection.
`javax.microedition.io.SocketConnection`	This interface defines the socket stream connection.
`javax.microedition.io.StreamConnection`	This interface defines the capabilities that a stream connection must have.
`javax.microedition.io.` `StreamConnectionNotifier`	This interface defines the capabilities that a connection notifier must have.
`javax.microedition.io.` `UDPDatagramConnection`	This interface defines a datagram connection which knows the local end point address.

Exception

`javax.microedition.io.` `ConnectionNotFoundException`	Signals that the protocol for the connection is not supported by the device.

User Interface Classes

`javax.microedition.lcdui.Alert`	A screen that shows data to the user and waits for a certain period of time before proceeding to the next screen.
`javax.microedition.lcdui.AlertType`	Provides an indication of the nature of alerts.

`javax.microedition.lcdui.Canvas`	The base class for writing applications that need to handle low-level events and to issue graphics calls for drawing to the display.
`javax.microedition.lcdui.Choice`	This interface defines an API for user interface components that enable the user to select from a predefined number of choices.
`javax.microedition.lcdui.ChoiceGroup`	A group of selectable elements intended to be placed within a `Form`.
`javax.microedition.lcdui.Command`	A construct that encapsulates the semantic information of an action.
`javax.microedition.lcdui.CommandListener`	This interface is used by applications which need to receive high-level events from the implementation.
`javax.microedition.lcdui.CustomItem`	A customizable element which can be subclassed to introduce new visual and interactive elements to a `Form`.
`javax.microedition.lcdui.DateField`	An editable component for presenting date and time (calendar) information that may be placed in a `Form`.
`javax.microedition.lcdui.Display`	Represents the manager of the display and GUI capabilities of the system.
`javax.microedition.lcdui.Displayable`	An object that can be placed on the display.
`javax.microedition.lcdui.Font`	Represents fonts and font metrics.
`javax.microedition.lcdui.Form`	A `Screen` that contains an arbitrary mixture of items: read-only text fields, editable text fields, editable date fields, gauges, choice groups and custom items.

`javax.microedition.lcdui.Gauge`	Implements a graphical display, such as a bar graph, of an integer value.
`javax.microedition.lcdui.Graphics`	Provides simple 2D geometric rendering capability.
`javax.microedition.lcdui.Image`	Used to hold graphical image data.
`javax.microedition.lcdui.ImageItem`	An `Item` that contains an image.
`javax.microedition.lcdui.Item`	A superclass for components that can be added to a `Form`.
`javax.microedition.lcdui.ItemCommandListener`	This interface is a listener type for receiving notification of commands that have been invoked on `Item` objects.
`javax.microedition.lcdui.ItemStateListener`	This interface is used by applications which need to receive events that indicate changes in the internal state of the interactive items within a `Form` screen.
`javax.microedition.lcdui.List`	A screen containing a list of choices.
`javax.microedition.lcdui.Screen`	The common superclass of all high-level user interface classes.
`javax.microedition.lcdui.Spacer`	A blank, non-interactive `Item` that has a settable minimum size.
`javax.microedition.lcdui.StringItem`	A non-interactive `Item` that can contain a string.
`javax.microedition.lcdui.TextBox`	A screen that allows the user to enter and edit text.
`javax.microedition.lcdui.TextField`	An editable text component that may be placed in a `Form`.
`javax.microedition.lcdui.Ticker`	Implements a "ticker tape", a piece of text that runs continuously across the display.

Game API

`java.microedition.lcdui.game.GameCanvas`	This class provides the basis for a game user interface.

`java.microedition.lcdui.game.Layer`	An abstract class representing a visual element of a game.
`java.microedition.lcdui.game.LayerManager`	The `LayerManager` manages a series of Layers.
`java.microedition.lcdui.game.Sprite`	A basic visual element that can be rendered with one of several frames stored in an image; different frames can be shown to animate the `Sprite`.
`java.microedition.lcdui.game.TiledLayer`	A visual element composed of a grid of cells that can be filled with a set of tile images.

Media API

`java.microedition.media.Control`	A superclass for objects used to control some media processing functions.
`java.microedition.media.Controllable`	An interface for obtaining the `Controls` from an object.
`java.microedition.media.Manager`	The access point for obtaining system-dependent resources such as `Players` for multimedia processing.
`java.microedition.media.MediaException`	Indicates an unexpected error condition in a method.
`java.microedition.media.Player`	Controls the rendering of time-based media data.
`java.microedition.media.PlayerListener`	An interface for receiving asynchronous events generated by `Players`.
`java.microedition.media.control.ToneControl`	An interface that enables the playback of user-defined monotonic tone sequences.
`java.microedition.media.control.VolumeControl`	An interface for manipulating the audio volume of a `Player`.

Midlet Classes

`javax.microedition.midlet.Midlet`	Superclass for all MIDP applications.
`javax.microedition.midlet.Midlet.StateChangeException`	Signals that a requested MIDlet state change failed.

Persistent Storage

`javax.microedition.rms.InvalidRecordIDException`	Thrown to indicate an operation could not be completed because the record ID was invalid.
`javax.microedition.rms.RecordComparator`	An interface used to compare two records. An implementation checks whether they match or what their relative sort order is.
`javax.microedition.rms.RecordEnumeration`	An interface representing a bi-directional record store record enumerator.
`javax.microedition.rms.RecordFilter`	An interface used to filter records matching a criterion
`javax.microedition.rms.RecordListener`	A listener interface for receiving record changed, added or deleted events from a `RecordStore`.
`javax.microedition.rms.RecordStore`	A class representing a record store.
`javax.microedition.rms.RecordStoreException`	Thrown to indicate a general exception was encountered in a `RecordStore` operation.
`javax.microedition.rms.RecordStoreFullException`	Thrown to indicate that the operation could not be completed because the `RecordStore` is full.
`javax.microedition.rms.RecordStoreNotFoundException`	Thrown to indicate that the `RecordStore` could not be found.
`javax.microedition.rms.RecordStoreNotOpenException`	Thrown to indicate that the operation was attempted on a closed `RecordStore`.

End-to-End Security

`java.microedition.pki.Certificate`	Interface common to certificates.
`java.microedition.pki.CertificateException`	Encapsulates an error that occurred while a certificate is being used.

Core Packages

`java.io`	Provides the system input and output through data streams and serialization.
`java.lang`	Provides the classes that are fundamental to the design of the Java language. For example, `Object`, which is the root of the class hierarchy.
`java.lang.ref`	Provides the reference object classes, which support a limited degree of interaction with the garbage collector.
`java.lang.reflect`	Provides the classes and interfaces for obtaining reflective information about classes and objects.
`java.math`	Provides classes for performing arbitrary-precision integer (BigInteger) and decimal arithmetic (BigDecimal).
`java.net`	Provides classes for implementing networking applications.
`java.security`	Provides classes and interfaces for the security framework.
`java.security.cert`	Provides classes and interfaces for parsing and managing certificates.

`java.text`	Provides classes and interfaces for handling text, dates, numbers and messages in a manner independent of natural languages.
`java.util`	Provides classes which contain the collections framework, legacy collection classes, event model, date and time facilities, internationalization and miscellaneous utility classes such as string tokenizer and random number generator.
`java.util.jar`	Provides classes for reading and writing the JAR file format, which is based upon standard ZIP file format with an optional manifest file.
`java.util.zip`	Provides classes for reading and writing the standard ZIP and GZIP file formats.
`javax.microedition.io`	Provides classes for the generic connection framework.

Appendix 3

Using the Wireless Toolkit Tools at the Command Line

This appendix provides developers with an insight into how the compile, pre-verify and packaging process works when using the Wireless Toolkit at the command line.

In the first instance we should make sure we have all the relevant binaries within the view of our command line. Some paths, therefore, need to be set. Assuming the J2ME Wireless Toolkit 2.1 has been installed to `C:\WTK21` we should set the development platform's PATH environment variable to that directory. On a Windows desktop computer, the path to the binaries should be set as follows:

```
C:> SET PATH=%PATH%;<install dir>\WTK21\bin
```

We will also need a Java compiler. We should already have the latest J2SE SDK installed on the machine, so we can use that compiler. Set PATH as follows:

```
C:> SET PATH=%PATH%;<install dir>\JavaSoft\j2sdk1.4.2\bin
```

Now we should be able to use both the compiler and pre-verifier quite easily. However, before we proceed we should also add a couple of environment variables to make MIDlet creation a little easier. We need to direct the commands towards the MIDP API and the other J2ME classes. Therefore we should set the following variables:

```
C:> SET J2MEHOME=<install dir>\WTK21
C:> SET MIDPAPI=%J2MEHOME%\lib\midpapi20.jar
C:> SET J2MECLASSPATH=%J2MEHOME%\wtklib\kenv.zip;
        %J2MEHOME%\wtklib\kvem.jar;%J2MEHOME%\wtklib\lime.jar;
        %J2MEHOME%\lib\cldcapi10.jar
```

Programming Java 2 Micro Edition on Symbian OS: A developer's guide to MIDP 2.0.   Martin de Jode
© 2004 Symbian Ltd   ISBN: 0-470-09223-8

Now that some handy variables have been set, we can try to create a MIDlet suite. Once the classes have been written, they need to be compiled. The following command should be used to compile all the classes in the current directory and then put them in a previously created directory, `tmpclasses`. Note that we have specified the classpath of the MIDP API to make sure the compiler knows to compile against the CLDC and MIDP classes, otherwise the classes may be compiled against the J2SE SDK.

```
C:\WTK20\apps\Example\src>javac -d tmpclasses -bootclasspath %MIDPAPI%
        -classpath %J2MECLASSPATH% *.java
```

Once this has been completed, all the compiled class files can be seen in the `tmpclasses` directory. We should now pre-verify them. By typing the word `preverify` at the command line the following help information appears showing the options available.

```
Usage: preverify [options] classnames|dirnames ...
where options include:
    -classpath      <directories separated by ';'> Directories in which to look
for classes
    -d <directory> Directory in which output is written (default is
./output/)
    -cldc           Checks for existence of language features prohibited by
CLDC (native methods, floating point and finalizers)
    -nofinalize     No finalizers allowed
    -nonative       No native methods allowed
    -nofp           No floating point operations allowed
    @<filename>     Read command line arguments from a text file Command line
arguments must all be on a single line; directory names must be enclosed in
double quotes(")
```

There are two options of interest to us here. The -classpath option, which will specify which target API should be verified against, and the -d option, which specifies the output directory for these verified files. The following command should be issued in the current directory:

```
C:\WTK20\apps\Example\src > preverify -classpath %MIDPAPI%;tmpclasses
        -d classes tmpclasses
```

The pre-verified files will now be in the `classes` directory. These files are ready for packaging into a MIDlet suite. For this we use the `jar` command:

```
C:\WTK20\apps\Example\src> jar -cvf MyMidlet.jar classes/*
```

In this case we have asked the `jar` command to create a JAR file called `MyMidlet.jar` from all the files stored in the directory structure under `classes/`.

Appendix 4

Developer Resources and Bibliography

Download code for this book from
www.symbian.com/books/pjso/pjso-source.html

Symbian

Corporate	***www.symbian.com***
Developer	***www.symbiandevnet.com***

Symbian Licensees

Arima	***www.arima.com.tw***
BenQ	***www.benq.com***
Fujitsu	***www.fujitsu.com***
Lenovo	***www.legendgrp.com***
LG Electronics	***www.lge.com***
Motorola	***www.motorola.com***
Nokia	***www.nokia.com***
Panasonic	***www.panasonic.com***
Psion	***www.psion.com***
Samsung	***www.samsung.com***
Sanyo	***www.sanyo.com***
Sendo	***www.sendo.com***
Siemens	***www.siemens.com***
Sony Ericsson	***www.sonyericsson.com***

Online Developer Resources

Motorola
http://idenphones.motorola.com/iden/developer/developer_home.jsp
Nokia
www.forum.nokia.com

Programming Java 2 Micro Edition on Symbian OS: A developer's guide to MIDP 2.0.   Martin de Jode
© 2004 Symbian Ltd   ISBN: 0-470-09223-8

NTT DoCoMo
   www.nttdocomo.com/corebiz/imode/why/tech.html
Sendo
   www.sendo.com/dev
Siemens
   www.siemens-mobile.com/developer
Sony Ericsson
   http//developer.sonyericsson.com and
   www.sonyericsson.com/developer
Sun Microsystems
   http://java.sun.com/j2me
UIQ
   www.uiq.com/developer

Tools manufacturers

AppForge
   www.appforge.com
Borland
   http://bdn.borland.com
Metrowerks
   www.metrowerks.com/MW/Develop/Wireless/Default.htm

Resources Mentioned in This Book and Additional Material

Chapter 1

Java Community Process, JSR 30: CLDC
   http://jcp.org/en/jsr/detail?id=30

Chapter 2

Antenna
   http://antenna.sourceforge.net
Apache, Jakarta project
   http://jakarta.apache.org
Apache, Ant download
   http://ant.apache.org/srcdownload.cgi
Apache, Ant project
   http://ant.apache.org/index.html
Borland, Jbuilder
   www.borland.com/products/downloads/
download_jbuilder.html
Eclipse
   www.eclipse.org

Forum Nokia
   www.forum.nokia.com
jEdit
   www.jedit.org
Proguard
   http://proguard.sourceforge.net
Retrologic Systems
   www.retrologic.com
Sony Ericsson Developer Network, P900 Emulator for the
Wireless Toolkit
   http//developer.sonyericsson.com
Sun, J2ME Wireless Toolkit 2.1 Download
   http://java.sun.com/products/j2mewtoolkit/download-2_1.html
Sun, J2SE downloads
   http://java.sun.com/j2se/downloads.html
Sun ONE Studio 4
   www.sun.com/software/sundev/jde/studio_me/index.html
Symbian Developer Network, UIQ2.1 SDK
   www.symbian.com/developer/sdks_uiq21.asp
Xinox Software, Jcreator
   www.jcreator.com

Chapter 3

Forum Nokia, *Camera MIDlet: A Mobile Media API Example*
   http://ncsp.forum.nokia.com/csp
Forum Nokia, *Known Issues in the Nokia 6600 MIDP 2.0
   Implementation* Version 1.2,
   www.forum.nokia.com
Java Community Process, JSR 30: CLDC 1.0 specification
   http://jcp.org/en/jsr/detail?id=30
Java Community Process, JSR 118: MIDP 2.0 specification
   http://jcp.org/en/jsr/detail?id=118
Java Community Process, JSR 120: Wireless Messaging API specification
   http://jcp.org/en/jsr/detail?id=120
Java Community Process, JSR 135: Mobile Media API specification
   http://jcp.org/en/jsr/detail?id=135
Java Community Process, JSR 139: CLDC 1.1 specification
   http://jcp.org/en/jsr/detail?id=139
Java Community Process, JSR 185: JTWI specification
   http://jcp.org/en/jsr/detail?id=185
Java Verified Program for J2ME
   www.javaverified.com
Sony Ericsson, *Developer Guidelines: Java MIDP 2.0 for P900/908*
   Version R3A
   http://developer.sonyericsson.com

Sun (2003) *The CLDC HotSpot Implementation Virtual Machine*,
White Paper
  http://java.sun.com
Symbian, *Symbian on Java*
  www.symbian.com/technology/standard-java.html
Symbian Phones
  www.symbian.com/phones

Chapter 4

Bluetooth SIG, *Assigned numbers: Bluetooth baseband*
  https://www.bluetooth.org/foundry/assignnumb/document/
  baseband
Bluetooth SIG, *Specification of the Bluetooth System, Volume 1.*
  www.bluetooth.com
Casira Development System for Bluetooth
  www.csr.com
Forum Nokia, Nokia Developer's Suite for J2ME 2.0
  http://forum.nokia.com
Forum Nokia, Series 60 MIDP SDK 1.2.1 for Symbian OS, Nokia Edition
  http://forum.nokia.com
Forum Nokia (2003) *Setting Up and Using the Bluetooth Testing*
Environment for Series 60 Platform
  http://forum.nokia.com
Hopkins, B. and Anthony, R. (2003) *Bluetooth for Java*, Apress.
Java Community Process, JSR 82: Java APIs for Bluetooth Wireless
  Technology
  http://jcp.org/en/jsr/detail?id=82
Rococo Impronto Simulator
  www.rococosoft.com
Symbian, UIQ 2.1 SDK
  www.symbian.com

Chapter 5

kXML library
  http://xmlpull.org
Nokia, Wireless Toolkit
  http://forum.nokia.com
Proguard Obfuscation Library
http://proguard.sourceforge.net
Sony Ericsson Developer Network, P900 Emulator for the Wireless
Toolkit
  http//developer.sonyericsson.com

Sun, J2ME Wireless Toolkit 2.1 Download
   http://java.sun.com/products/j2mewtoolkit/download-2_1.html
Sun, Java Web Services Toolkit
   http://java.sun.com/webservices/webservicespack.html

Chapter 6

Java Community Process, JSR185: JTWI specification
   http://jcp.org/en/jsr/detail?id=185
W3, CC/PP information
   www.w3.org/Mobile/CCPP

Chapter 7

Allin, J. (2001) *Wireless Java for Symbian Devices*, Wiley.
Buschmann, F., Meunier, R., Rohnert, H., Sommerland, P. and Stal, M. (1996) *Pattern-Oriented Software Architecture: A system of patterns*, Wiley.
Embedded Microprocessor Benchmark Consortium, GrinderBench
   www.eembc.hotdesk.com
Grand, M. and Knudsen, J. (1997) *Java Fundamental Classes Reference*, O'Reilly
Haggar, P. (2000) *Practical Java Programming Language Guide*, Addison-Wesley.
Knuth, D. E. (1997) *The Art of Computer Programming* Addison Wesley.
Larman, C. and Guthrie, R. (1999) *Java 2 Performance and Idiom Guide*. Prentice Hall.
Lurie, J. (2001) *Develop a Generic Caching Service to Improve Performance*, Java World
   www.javaworld.com/javaworld/jw-07-2001/jw-0720-cache_p.html
Nondove, Amark 1.3
   http://amark.nondove.it
Poundstone, W. (1985) *The Recursive Universe: Cosmic complexity and the limits of scientific knowledge*, William Morrow.
Proguard
   http://proguard.sourceforge.net
Shirazi, J. (2003) *Java Performance Tuning*, O'Reilly.
Sosnoski, D. M. (1999) *Smart Object-management Saves the Day*
   www.javaworld.com/javaworld/jw-11-1999/jw-11-performance.html

Chapter 8

ARC Group
   www.arcgroup.com

eWeek, Enterprise news and reviews
www.eweek.com/article2/0,4149,893492,00.asp
Java Community Process, JSR 75: PDA Optional Packages for the J2ME
Platform
http://jcp.org/en/jsr/detail?id=75
Java Community Process, JSR 135: Mobile Media API
http://jcp.org/en/jsr/detail?id=135
Java Community Process, JSR 172: J2METM Web Services Specification
http://jcp.org/en/jsr/detail?id=172
Java Community Process, JSR 177: Security and Trust Services API for
J2ME
http://jcp.org/en/jsr/detail?id=177
Java Community Process, JSR 179: Location API for J2ME
http://jcp.org/en/jsr/detail?id=179
Java Community Process, JSR 180: SIP API for J2ME
http://jcp.org/en/jsr/detail?id=180
Java Community Process, JSR 184: Mobile 3D Graphics API for J2ME
http://jcp.org/en/jsr/detail?id=184
Java Community Process, JSR 205: Wireless Messaging API 2.0
http://jcp.org/en/jsr/detail?id=205
Java Community Process, JSR 211: Content Handler API
http://jcp.org/en/jsr/detail?id=211
Java Community Process, JSR 226: Scalable 2D Vector Graphics API for
J2ME
http://jcp.org/en/jsr/detail?id=226
Java Community Process, JSR 229: Payment API
http://jcp.org/en/jsr/detail?id=229
Java Community Process, JSR 230: Data Sync API
http://jcp.org/en/jsr/detail?id=230
Java Community Process, JSR 232: Mobile Operational Management
http://jcp.org/en/jsr/detail?id=232
Java Verified Program
www.javaverified.com
Khronos Group, OpenGL ES
www.khronos.org/opengles
Macrospace
www.macrospace.com
O'Doherty, P. (2003) *SIP Specifications and the Java Platforms*, Sun
www.cs.columbia.edu/sip/Java-SIP-Specifications.pdf
OMA DRM Version 1.0, Specification
www.openmobilealliance.org/tech/release.html
OMA DRM Version 1.0, Top-level description
www.openmobilealliance.org/docs/DRM%20Short%
20Paper%20DEC%202003 %20.pdf

Appendix 5

Specifications of Symbian OS Phones

Additional technical information on a range of phones can be found at *www.symbian.com/phones*.

Please note that this is a quick guide to Symbian OS phones. For full specifications, C++ developers retrieve extended information using HAL APIs or check the manufacturer's website.

Programming Java 2 Micro Edition on Symbian OS: A developer's guide to MIDP 2.0.   Martin de Jode
© 2004 Symbian Ltd   ISBN: 0-470-09223-8

Nokia 9210i

Java APIs	CLDC 1.0 MIDP 1.0 PersonalJava 1.1.1 JavaPhone
OS Version	Symbian OS v6.0
UI/Category	Series 80
Memory available to user	40 MB
Storage media	Yes
Screen	640 × 200; 4096 colors
Pointing device	No
Camera	No
GSM/HSCSD/GPRS/3G	
GSM 900	Yes
GSM 1800	Yes
GSM 1900	No (GSM 900/1900 on 9290)
HSCSD	Yes
GPRS	No
3G	No
Connectivity	
Infrared	Yes
Bluetooth	No
USB	No
Serial	Yes
Browsing	
WAP	WAP 1.1
XHTML (MP)	Yes
Browser available	Yes (built-in and third-party)

Nokia 7650

Java APIs	**MIDP 1.0** **CLDC 1.0** **Nokia UI**
OS Version	Symbian OS v6.1
UI/Category	Series 60
Memory available to user	4 MB NOR flash user data storage
Storage media	No
Screen	176 × 208; 4096 colors
Pointing device	No
Camera	Yes; 640 × 480 resolution
GSM/HSCSD/GPRS/3G	
GSM 900	Yes
GSM 1800	Yes
GSM 1900	No
HSCSD	Yes
GPRS	Yes (2 + 2, 3 + 1, class B and C)
3G	No
Connectivity	
Infrared	Yes
Bluetooth	Yes
USB	No
Serial	No
Browsing	
WAP	WAP 1.2.1
XHTML (MP)	No
Browser available	Yes (third-party)

Nokia 3600/3650

Java APIs	**MIDP 1.0** **CLDC 1.0** **Nokia UI** **WMA** **MMAPI**
OS Version	Symbian OS v6.1
UI/Category	Series 60 (v1)
Memory available to user	3.4 MB
Storage media	Yes; MMC
Screen	176×208; 4096/65 536 colors
Pointing device	No
Camera	Yes; 640×480 resolution
GSM/HSCSD/GPRS/3G	
GSM 900	Yes
GSM 1800	Yes
GSM 1900	Yes
HSCSD	Yes
GPRS	Yes (2 + 2, 3 + 1, class B and C)
3G	No
Connectivity	
Infrared	Yes
Bluetooth	Yes
USB	No
Serial	No
Browsing	
WAP	WAP 1.2.1
XHTML (MP)	Yes
Browser available	Yes (third-party)

Nokia 3620/3660

Java APIs	**MIDP 1.0** **CLDC 1.0** **Nokia UI** **MMAPI** **WMA**
OS Version	Symbian OS v6.1
UI/Category	Series 60 (v1)
Memory available to user	4 MB
Storage media	Yes; MMC
Screen	176 × 208; 4096/65 536 colors
Pointing device	No
Camera	Yes; 640×480 resolution
GSM/HSCSD/GPRS/3G	
GSM 850	Yes
GSM 1800	No
GSM 1900	Yes
HSCSD	Yes
GPRS	Yes
3G	No
Connectivity	
Infra-red	Yes
Bluetooth	Yes
USB	No
Serial	No
Browsing	
WAP	WAP 1.2.1
XHTML (MP)	Yes
Browser available	Yes

Siemens SX1

Java APIs	MIDP 1.0 WMA MMAPI
OS Version	Symbian OS v6.1
UI/Category	Series 60
Storage media	Yes; MMC
Screen	176 × 208; 65 536 TFT
Pointing device	No
Camera	Yes; 640 × 480 and 160 × 120 resolution
GSM/HSCSD/GPRS/3G	
GSM 900	Yes
GSM 1800	Yes
GSM 1900	Yes
HSCSD	Yes
GPRS	Yes (class 10, B (2Tx, 4Rx))
3G	No
Connectivity	
Infra-red	Yes
Bluetooth	Yes
USB	Yes
Serial	No
Browsing	
WAP	WAP 2.0
XHTML (MP)	Yes
Browser available	Yes (third-party)

Nokia N-Gage

Java APIs	**MIDP 1.0** **CLDC 1.0** **Nokia UI** **WMA** **MMAPI**
OS Version UI/Category Memory available to user Storage media	Symbian OS v6.1 Series 60 4 MB NOR flash user data storage Yes; MMC
Screen Pointing device Camera	176 × 208; 4096 colors No No
GSM/HSCSD/GPRS/3G GSM 900 GSM 1800 GSM 1900 HSCSD GPRS 3G	 Yes Yes Yes Yes Yes (2 + 2, 3 + 1, class B and C) No
Connectivity Infra-red Bluetooth USB Serial	 No Yes Yes No
Browsing WAP XHTML (MP) Browser available	 WAP 1.2.1 Yes Yes (third-party)

Sendo X

Java APIs	**MIDP1.0**
	WMA
	Bluetooth
	Nokia UI
	MMAPI
OS Version	Symbian OS v6.1
UI/Category	Series 60
Memory available to user	12 MB
Storage media	Yes; MMC and SD
Screen	176×220; 65 536 colors
Pointing device	No
Camera	Yes; 640×480 resolution
GSM/HSCSD/GPRS/3G	
GSM 900	Yes
GSM 1800	Yes
GSM 1900	Yes
HSCSD	No
GPRS	Yes, Class 8 (4 + 1)
3G	No
Connectivity	
Infrared	Yes
Bluetooth	Yes
USB	Yes
Serial	Yes
Browsing	
WAP	WAP 2.0
XHTML (MP)	Yes
Browser available	Yes (third-party)

BenQ P30

Java APIs	**MIDP 2.0**
	PersonalJava 1.1.1
	BTAPI
	WMA
OS Version	Symbian OS v7.0
UI/Category	UIQ 2.1
Storage media	Yes; MMC and SD
Screen	208×320; 65 536 colors TFT
Pointing device	Yes
Camera	Yes; 604×480 resolution
GSM/HSCSD/GPRS/3G	
GSM 900	Yes
GSM 1800	Yes
GSM 1900	Yes
HSCSD	Yes
GPRS	Yes (4 + 2, class 10)
3G	No
Connectivity	
Infrared	Yes
Bluetooth	Yes
USB	Yes
Serial	No
Browsing	
WAP	Yes 2.0
XHTML (MP)	Yes
Browser available	Yes

Sony Ericsson P800

Java API	CLDC 1.0
	MIDP 1.0
	PersonalJava 1.1.1

OS Version	Symbian OS v7.0
UI/Category	UIQ
Memory available to user	12 MB
Storage media	Yes; Sony MS Duo
Screen	208×320 (Flip Open); 208×144 (Flip Closed); 4096 colors
Pointing device	Yes
Camera	Yes; 640×480 resolution
GSM/HSCSD/GPRS/3G	
GSM 900	Yes
GSM 1800	Yes
GSM 1900	Yes
HSCSD	Yes
GPRS	Yes (4 + 1)
3G	No
Connectivity	
Infra-red	Yes
Bluetooth	Yes
USB	Yes (high speed serial connector with a USB->Serial adapter built into the desk stand)
Serial	Yes
Browsing	
WAP	WAP 2.0
XHTML (MP)	Yes
Browser available	Yes (inbuilt and third-party)

Motorola A920/A925

Java APIs	MIDP 1.03 PersonalJava 1.1.1a
OS Version	Symbian OS v7.0
UI/Category	UIQ
Memory available to user	8 MB
Storage media	Yes; MMC and SD
Screen	208×320; 65 536 colors TFT
Pointing device	Yes
Camera	Yes
GSM/HSCD/GPRS/3G	
GSM 900	Yes
GSM 1800	Yes
GSM 1900	Yes
HSCD	Yes
GPRS	Yes
3G	Yes
Connectivity	
Infrared	Yes
Bluetooth	A920 No/A925 Yes
USB	Yes
Serial	Yes
Browsing	
WAP	No
XHTML (MP)	Yes
Browser available	Yes (third-party)

Sony Ericsson P900

Java APIs	**MIDP 2.0** **PersonalJava 1.1.1** **BTAPI** **WMA**
OS Version	Symbian OS v7.0 (+ security updates and MIDP2.0)
UI/Category	UIQ 2.1
Memory available to user	16 MB
Storage media	Yes; Sony MS Duo
Screen	208 × 320 (Flip Open); 208 × 208 (Flip Closed); 65 536 colors TFT
Pointing device	Yes
Camera	Yes; 640 × 480 resolution
GSM/HSCSD/GPRS/3G	
GSM 900	Yes
GSM 1800	Yes
GSM 1900	Yes
HSCSD	Yes
GPRS	Yes
3G	No
Connectivity	
Infrared	Yes
Bluetooth	Yes
USB	Yes (high speed serial connector with a USB->Serial adapter built into the desk stand)
Serial	No
Browsing	
WAP	WAP 2.0
XHTML (MP)	Yes
Browser available	Yes

Nokia 6600

Java APIs	MIDP 2.0 CLDC 1.0 Nokia UI MMAPI WMA BTAPI
OS Version	Symbian OS v7.0s
UI/Category	Series 60 (v2)
Memory available to user	6 MB NOR flash user data storage
Storage media	Yes; MMC
Screen	176×208; 65 536 colors TFT
Pointing device	No
Camera	Yes; 640×480 resolution
GSM/HSCSD/GPRS/3G	
GSM 900	Yes
GSM 1800	Yes
GSM 1900	Yes
HSCSD	Yes
GPRS	Yes (2 + 2, 3 + 1, class B and C)
3G	No
Connectivity	
Infra-red	Yes
Bluetooth	Yes
USB	No
Serial	No
Browsing	
WAP	WAP 2.0
XHTML (MP)	Yes
Browser available	Yes

Nokia 6620

Java APIs	**MIDP 2.0**
	CLDC 1.0
	Nokia UI
	MMAPI
	WMA
	BTAPI
OS Version	Symbian OS v7.0s
UI/Category	Series 60 (v2)
Memory available to user	6 MB NOR flash user data storage
Storage media	Yes; MMC
Screen	176 × 220; 65 536 colors TFT
Pointing device	No
Camera	Yes; 640 × 480 resolution
GSM/HSCSD/GPRS/3G	
GSM 850	Yes
GSM 1800	Yes
GSM 1900	Yes
HSCSD	No
GPRS	No
3G	No
EDGE	Yes
Connectivity	
Infra-red	Yes
Bluetooth	Yes
USB	Yes
Serial	No
Browsing	
WAP	WAP 2.0
XHTML (MP)	Yes
Browser available	Yes

Nokia 7700

Java APIs	**MIDP 2.0**
	CLDC 1.0
	Nokia UI
	WMA
	MMAPI
	BTAPI
OS Version	Symbian OS v7.0s
UI/Category	Series 90
Memory available to user	64 MB
Storage media	Additional memory slot
Screen	640 × 320; 65 536 colors
Pointing device	Yes
Camera	Yes; 640×480 resolution
GSM/HSCSD/GPRS/3G	
GSM 900	Yes
GSM 1800	Yes
GSM 1900	Yes
HSCSD	Yes
GPRS	Yes
3G	No
EDGE	Yes
Connectivity	
Infra-red	Yes
Bluetooth	Yes
USB	Yes
Serial	No
Browsing	
XHTML (MP)	Yes (+ HTML)
Browser available	Yes

Index

Abstract Window Toolkit (AWT)
7, 29
access codes   215
access control   405
additional utility classes   426
advanced services   402–6, 421
alarms, Push Registry   122
Alert objects   34–5
<AllowedSender> field   120
alpha blending   146–9
AMark test   336–7
AMS see application management
software
animation
Game API   136–9
Helloworld – Turbo Edition
46–54
synchronization forms   269–70
threading   42–3
annual sales of mobile phones
395–6
Ant see Apache Ant
Antenna   59–63
Apache Ant   59–63
APIs
protected   96, 187–8
see also individual APIs
application controller   299
application management software
(AMS)   23–7, 86–9

application types, Symbian OS
398
arithmetic operations   385
Array
copying   351–2
optimizing code   348, 349,
350, 351–2
arraycopy() method   351–2
Array Objects   406
asset tracking   405
audio media   155–72
Audio Player MIDlet   164–72
authentication   227–8
authorization   100–1, 228–9
automatic garbage collection
406–7
AWT see Abstract Window
Toolkit

backgrounds
code portability   327
painting   358–65
battery consumption   357
benchmarking   336–7
BenQ P30   453
bibliography   439–4
billing   416
bill of materials   401
binary trees   356–7

Bitmap (BMP) formats   183
blanket interaction mode   101
blended images   146–9
Bluetooth Wireless Technology
205–45
access codes   215
authentication   227–8
authorization   228–9
BT demo sample code   230–40
CoD records   217
development tools   241–4
device discovery   214–18
encryption   229
future plans   412
JSR 82   206, 207–8, 244, 412
L2CAP service connections
226
master–slave roles   222
MIDlet installation   84–5
MIDP 2.0 security model
229–30
profiles   207
protocol stack   206–7
"quick and dirty" service
connection   222–3
RFCOMM service connections
222–3
security   227–30
Sendo X   452
server creation   212–14

Programming Java 2 Micro Edition on Symbian OS: A developer's guide to MIDP 2.0.   Martin de Jode
© 2004 Symbian Ltd   ISBN: 0-470-09223-8

Bluetooth Wireless... (*continued*)
   service discovery   218–21
   service records   209–11
   service registration   208–14
   UUIDs   211–12
Borland   66–8
BREW   397
BTAPI
   BenQ P30   453
   Nokia 6600   460
   Nokia 6620   461
   Nokia 7700   462
   Sony Ericsson P900   459
BT Demo MIDlets   230–40
business logic/presentation code
   separation   263
bytecode   409

C++
   memory leaks   389
   preferred languages on Symbian
      OS   399
   Symbian OS applications
      proportion   398
CA *see* certificate authorities
caching and cached devices
   223–4, 386–8
calculating factorials   355–6
calendar classes   425–6
callback methods   172
called methods   373–5
calling trees   373–5
camera phones   178–9, 182–3,
   188, 294
Canvas   31, 41, 291–2
Canvas.isDoubleBuffered()
   method   358
capture   159, 160
captured images   294, 302–5,
   311–15
case studies
   Demo Racer game   247,
      282–93
   expense application   247,
      248–81
   Life Time   366–84
   Picture Puzzle   248, 294–315

CC/PP *see* Composite
   Capability/Preference Profiles
CDC (Connected Device
   Configuration)   16–20
   core packages   17–18
   device specifications   17
   HotSpot Implementation   390
   JSR 36   16
   optional packages   18–19
   Personal Profile   19–20
   stack   400
   uses   5
certificate authorities (CA)
   97–100, 103–4
certificate management   56
charging and billing   416
ChatMIDlet   193–9
checkPermission() method
   146
ChoiceForm class   300–2
ChoiceGroup objects   37
Choice interface   40, 126
Class of Device/Service (CoD)
   records   217
classes
   additional utility   426
   calendar   425–6
   collection   424
   data type   424
   error   428
   exception   426–8
   input/output   424–5
   Midlet   434
   system   423
   time   425–6
   user interface   430–2
CLDC (Connected Limited Device
   Configuration)   7–12
   classes   9–11
   core libraries   423–8
   device capabilities   7–8
   differences from CDC   8–9
   functionality based on   400
   general-purpose containers
      348–9
   HotSpot Implementation   94–5,
      354, 390
   JSR 30   7
   JTWI   92

MIDlet creation   27
networking   11–12
Nokia 3600/3650   448
Nokia 3620/3660   449
Nokia 6600   460
Nokia 6620   461
Nokia 7650   447
Nokia 7700   462
Nokia 9210i   446
Nokia N-Gage   451
portability   8
Sony Ericsson P800   454
Symbian OS   94–5
uses   5
virtual machines   8–9
CLDCMark test   336–7
ClientConnection class
   117–18
client devices   402–3
client mode connection formats
   190
clipping region   358, 362
close() method   162
CoD *see* Class of Device/Service
code
   different device platforms
      263–4
   Java benefits   408–9
   optimized   335–92
   see also portable code
CodeWarrior Wireless Studio 7
   68–71
collection classes   424
collision detection   139, 286, 288,
   328, 365–6
combined delivery   419
commandAction() method
   170, 310, 360
Command class   33–4
command line   437–8
CommandListener   40, 42, 360
comparing strings   343–4
compilation   390–1, 437–8
Composite Capability/Preference
   Profiles (CC/PP) UAProf
   standard   326
concatenation   344–5

configurations
  uses 5
  see also CDC; CLDC
Connected Device Configuration
  see CDC
Connected Limited Device
  Configuration *see* CLDC
connecting to services 222–3,
  226
connection framework 108–19
<ConnectionURL> field 120
constrained devices 3, 5
consumers 399–400, 403
containers, optimizing code
  348–9
Content Handler API (JSR 211)
  417
content provider requirements
  400–1
Control 158, 162–3
Controller *see*
  Model–View–Controller
  design pattern
Conway's Game of Life 366, 367
copying an Array 351–2
core functionality 14–16
core game classes 324–5
core libraries 9–11, 17–18
core packages 435–6
correct Java configuration
  399–400
createRGBImage() method
  146–7
cryptography 96, 229
CustomItem
  class 37–8, 125
  event handling 258–62
  expense application case study
    253–64
  item painting 257–8
  item size 257
  KeyPad MIDlet 130–131
  series 60/UIQ interfaces
    253–6, 262–4

DAC *see* Dynamic Adaptive
  Compilation
data access objects (DAOs)
  264–9

databases 16, 387–8
datagram support 113–14
data providers 402–3
data storage 44–5
Data Sync API (JSR 230) 414
data type classes 424
DateField 38
deallocate() method 162
debugging 376, 377
decrementCount() 353–4
defensive code 330, 389
defineCollisionRect-
  angle() 328
delay 111
delivery, OMA DRM Version 1.0
  419
Demo Racer game
  background 282–4
  case study 247, 282–93
  layer manager 288–92
  MIDlet lifecycle 292–3
  sprites 284–8
design, optimizing code 337
design patterns
  Model–View 322–3
  Model–View–Controller
    320–2
  optimizing code 386–8
  portable code 320–5
  practical application 323–5
desktop applications 29
destroyApp() method 170
Developer's Suite *see* Nokia
  Developer's Suite
development
  expense application case study
    249
  resources 439–4
  time 407–9
  tools 54–66, 241–4, 249
device 159–60
deviceDiscovered() method
  214
device discovery 214–18
device emulators 76–82
device identification 326
device look and feel 262–3
DiceBox MIDlet 339–40

Digital Rights Management (DRM)
  418–20
digital signatures 96–8, 102–5
DiscoveryAgent class 215,
  223–4
DiscoveryListener interface
  214–15, 218–21
discType values 214
Displayable objects 31
Display class 123–4
Display object 252
disposable incomes 401–2
DoJa 6, 456, 457, 458
doRecursive() method 353
double buffering 358
download limitations 331–2
drawBackground() method
  361–2, 363
drawImage() method 41
drawRGB() method 147, 148–9
DRM *see* Digital Rights
  Management
Dynamic Adaptive Compilation
  (DAC) 390–1

early instantiation 388
EEMBC *see* Embedded
  Microprocessor Benchmark
  Consortium
embedded devices 421
Embedded Microprocessor
  Benchmark Consortium
  (EEMBC) 336
embedded tests 336–7
employees, advanced enterprise
  services 404
emulators
  device emulators 76–82
  Sony Ericsson P900 J2ME SDK
    81–2
  UIQ SDK 76–82
  Unified Emulator Interface
    74–6
encoding records 265–7
encryption 96, 229
end-to-end security 16, 435
Engine *see* Model
enterprise market 399–400

enterprise services, advanced 404
enterprise user requirements 400
entertainment services 403
Enumeration 388
Enumeration.nextElement()
    method 384
enumeration of records 267–9
error classes 428
event handling 258–62
event model 32–3
exception classes 426–8
expense application
    case study 247, 248–81
    custom items 253–64
    development environment 249
    MIDlet 251–3, 279–81
    record stores 264–9
    requirements 249–51
    synchronization 269–77
    Web Server implementation
        277–8
extensions, Symbian-specific
    417–18
extensive connectivity 15

factorials 355–6
fast development 407–9
faults, Java benefits 407–8
feedback, optimizing code 338
field service support 404
FileRequestHandler class
    340
final methods 343
FIRE key events 310
flicker 358
flushGraphics() 365
form-based applications 253–64
Form class 124–5
Form object 36
forward lock 419
Foundation Profile 6–7, 19–20
fragmentation 330
frames 136–9
freeMemory() method 389
Fujitsu F900i 458
Fujitsu F2051 456
Fujitsu F2102V 457
FullCanvas class 182

function groups 106, 114–15
future plans 411–17

GameActions 328
Game API 14–15, 43–4, 46–54,
    131–44, 282, 432–3
GameCanvas class 43, 49–51,
    132, 358, 365
Game of Life 366, 367
GameMIDlet class 295–300
games
    actions 42
    advanced consumer services
        403
    billing 416
    Demo Racer 282–93
    design patterns 324–5
    functionality 14–15
    logic 306–11, 324–5
    low-level API 30–1
    management 416
    worldwide revenue predictions
        397
garbage collection 388–9, 391,
    406–7
GCF see Generic Connection
    Framework
General/Unlimited Inquiry Access
    Codes (GIAC) 215
GenerationMap class 368, 369,
    370, 377–82
Generic Connection Framework
    (File GCF) 11, 413
getConnectionURL() method
    222, 226
getControls() method 163–4
getMajorDevice() method
    217
getMinContentHeight()
    method 130
getMinContentWidth()
    method 130
getMinimumHeight() method
    124
getMinimumWidth() method
    124
getPrefContentHeight()
    method 130

getPrefContentWidth()
    method 130
getPreferredHeight()
    method 124
getPreferredWidth() method
    124
getter methods 342–3
GIAC see General/Unlimited
    Inquiry Access Codes
graphics
    benchmarks 336–7
    collision detection 365–6
    LCDUI low-level API 40–2
    low-level graphical content
        portability 326–8
    optimizing code 358–66
    Popcorn Drawing demonstrator
        358–65
Graphics.drawImage()
    method 371
Graphics.fillRect() method
    371
GrinderBench 336

hashCode() method 345–6
Hashtable containers 348–9
hash tables 345–6
HCI see Host Controller Interface
heap analysis 375–6, 377
heap memory 332–3
'Helloworld' –, Turbo Edition
    46–54
high-level API 30, 33–40
high-level user interface
    components 329
Host Controller Interface (HCI)
    206–7
HotSpot garbage collector 391
HotSpot technology 94–5, 354,
    390–1
HTTP 45, 108–9, 272, 326
HTTPS 109

IDEs see integrated development
    environments
image buffer 363–4

image capture 178–9, 182–3, 188, 294, 302–5
Image.createRGBImage() method 363
ImageItem 38–9
image manipulation 294, 306–11
IMP *see* Information Module Profile
Impronto Simulator *see* Rococo Impronto Simulator
Information Module Profile (IMP) 6
infrared, MIDlet installation 83–4
initDisplayMode() method 176
inlining 340–3
input classes 424–5
input devices 29
input methods 328–9
InputStream 357
instance accessors 342–3
instance variables 341–3
instantiation time 388
integrated development environments (IDEs)
  CodeWarrior Wireless Studio 7 68–71
  JBuilder 9 66–8
  NDS integration 65–6, 72
  Sun ONE Studio 4 72–4
  Unified Emulator Interface 74–6
I/O implementation 11–12
isAuthenticated() method 228
isAuthorized() method 229
isDoubleBuffered() method 358
isEncrypted() method 229
Item class 36–7, 124–5
ItemCommandListener 40, 126, 130–1
Item painting 257–8
Item size 257
ItemStateChanged() method 171–2
ItemStateListener interface 40

J2EE (Enterprise Edition) 3–4
J2ME Connected Device Configuration *see* CDC
J2ME Connected Limited Device Configuration *see* CLDC
J2ME Web Server access 56
J2ME Web Services Specification (JSR 172) 414
J2ME Wireless Toolkit 2.1 *see* Wireless Toolkit
J2SE relationship 3–4
JAD files
  expense application case study 280
  MIDlet creation 27–8
  over-the-air MIDlet installation 84–5
JAIN, future plans 416–17
JAIN Instant Messaging (JSR 187) 417
JAIN Presence (JSR 164) 416–17
JAIN Presence (JSR 186) 417
JAIN SIMPLE Instant Messaging (JSR 165) 417
Jakarta 59–63
JAR files 99, 100, 331–2
Java
  benefits for services development 406–9
  wireless applications significance 397–9
  wireless devices proportion 397
Java APIs for Bluetooth (JSR 82) 412
Java APIs for Integrated Networks *see* JAIN
Java API for XML Binding *see* JAXB
Java application descriptor *see* JAD files
javaCopy() method 351, 352
Java Developer Kit 1.4 249
Java HotSpot technology 94–5, 354, 390–1
java.lang.runnable interface 270–3
JavaPhone 446
Java Technology for the Wireless Industry *see* JTWI

Java Verified Program 420
JAXB 273, 277–8
JBuilder 9 66–8, 69
JIT *see* Just In Time
JSR 30 (J2ME Connected Limited Device Configuration) 7, 92
JSR 36 (J2ME Connected Device Configuration) 16
JSR 37 (Mobile Information Device Profile for the J2ME Platform) 29
JSR 82 (Java APIs for Bluetooth) 206, 207–8, 244, 412
JSR 118 (Mobile Information Device Profile 2.0) 12, 92
JSR 120 (Wireless Messaging API) 92
JSR 135 (Mobile Media API) 92
JSR 164 (JAIN Presence) 416–17
JSR 165 (JAIN SIMPLE Instant Messaging) 417
JSR 172 (J2ME Web Services Specification) 414
JSR 177 (Security and Trust Services) 414
JSR 179 (Location API for J2ME) 415
JSR 180 (SIP API for J2ME) 415–16
JSR 185 (JTWI deliverables) 93
JSR 186 (JAIN Presence) 417
JSR 187 (JAIN Instant Messaging) 417
JSR 211 (Content Handler API) 417
JSR 229 (Payment API) 417
JSR 230 (Data Sync API) 414
JTWI
  code portability 331
  component JSRs 92
  deliverables 93
  introduction 91–4
  optional APIs 155–201
  specification requirements 92–3
  Symbian 93–4
Just In Time (JIT) compilers 390
just in time instantiation 388

Kauai/Kilo Virtual Machine (KVM) 8
keepalive 111
keypad entry 328, 329
KeyPad MIDlet 126–31
keyPressed() method 41, 42, 310
keys
  in hash tables 345–6
  MIDP 2.0 security model 96–8, 102–5
KeyString wrapper class 345–6
KToolbar 27, 29
KVM see Kauai/Kilo Virtual Machine
KVM garbage collector 388–9
kXML parsing 274–5

L2CAP protocol 206–7, 224–6
Landmarks store 415
larger-grained operations 388
Layer 44
LayerManager class 44, 140–4, 282
layout 124–5
lazy instantiation 388
LBS see location-based services
LCDUI 13–14
  architecture 33
  Displayable objects 31–2
  event model 32–3
  expense application 251
  high-level API 30, 33–40
  interfaces 40, 42
  low-level API 30, 40–4
  MIDP 2.0 123–31
  model 31–2
  origins 29–30
  structure 30–1
  threading animation 42–3
LIAC see Limited Dedicated Inquiry Access Codes
libraries
  CLDC core 423–8
  MIDP 429–36
licensees, websites 439
LifeTime case study 366–84

Limited Dedicated Inquiry Access Codes (LIAC) 215
linger 111
Linux 397
List object 35
localized advertising 403
local variables 341
Location API for J2ME (JSR 179) 415
location-based services (LBS)
  advance services provision 404–6
  Symbian's approach 405–6
  worldwide revenue predictions 397
location-based "to dos" 405
location stamping of user data 405
lookup method 356
looping 352–7
low-level API 30, 40–4
low-level graphical content 326–8

major device bit values 217
makeImages () method 363
Manager 158
manufacturers
  requirements 401–2
  tools (websites) 440
mapping 42
market issues 395–402
master–slave roles 222
maximum transmission unit (MTU) 224–5
Media API 15, 45, 145, 433
media players 158
memory
  constraints 336
  heap analysis 375–6, 377
  leaks 389, 406–7
  management 388–9
  mobile phones versus computers 336
  traps 346–8
messages
  exchange 275–7
  receiving of SMS 191–2

sending using WMA 190–1
method modifiers 340–3
Metrowerks 68–71
Microsoft, wireless devices proportion 397
middleware vendors 399
MIDlet class, MIDP 2.0 145–6
MIDlet-Jar-RSA-SHA1 attribute 100
MIDlet-Permissions attribute 100–1, 122, 187–8, 200, 229
MIDlet-Permissions-Opt attribute 100–1
MIDlets
  AMS interaction 25
  application management software installation 86–9
  building 279–81
  classes 434
  creating 27–9
  current implementation 410
  DESTROYED state 311
  Helloworld.java 47–9
  Java Verified Program 420
  lifecycle 25, 26, 292–3
  model 23–9
  running on devices 82–9
  running on emulators 74–83
  signing 55
  states 24–6
  structure 27
  transfer to devices 83–5
  untrusted 105–6, 188, 200
  see also individual MIDlets
MIDlet suites
  authentication of signed 100
  separate delivery 419
  signing 98–100, 102–5
  trusted 96
MIDP (Mobile Information Device Profile) 12–16, 23
  libraries 429–36
  Symbian OS applications proportion 398
  toolkits 54–66
  user interfaces 29–43
  uses 6
MIDP 1.0 (Mobile Information Device Profile) 12–16

BenQ P30   453
classes   13–15
core functionality   14–16
Game API   43–4
GameCanvas class   365
JSR 37   29
JSR 118   13
limitations   95, 155–6
Networking   45
Nokia 3600/3650   448
Nokia 3620/3660   449
Nokia 6600   460
Nokia 6620   461
Nokia 7650   447
Nokia 7700   462
Nokia 9210i   446
Nokia N-Gage   451
OTA provisioning   15–16
packages   13–14
preferred languages on Symbian
     OS   399
Sendo X   452
Siemens SX1   450
Sony Ericsson P800   454
Sony Ericsson P900   459
Sprite class   365–6
Symbian OS phones   89
user interfaces   29
WMA   192–3
MIDP 1.03 (Mobile Information
     Device Profile)   455
MIDP 2.0 (Mobile Information
     Device Profile)   95–155
audio subset   181–2
Bluetooth security model
     229–30
case studies   247–315
connection framework   108–19
JTWI   92
LCDUI additions   123–31
Media API   45
Networking   45–6
new features   95, 145–55
Push Registry   119–23
Recommended Security Policy
     for GSM/UMTS Compliant
     Devices addendum   230
security model   96–107,
     187–9, 200–1

Symbian OS phones   89, 201–2
minor device bit values   218
MMAPI (Mobile Media API)
     14–15, 155–80
architecture   158–9
J2ME Wireless Toolkit   56
MIDP 1.0 security model
     187–9
Nokia 3600/3650   448
Nokia 3620/3660   449
Nokia 6600   460
Nokia 6620   461
Nokia 7700   462
Nokia N-Gage   451
Picture Puzzle application   294
Sendo X   452
Siemens SX1   450
Symbian OS phones   180–7
mobile employees   404
Mobile Information Device Profile
     see MIDP
Mobile Media API see MMAPI
Mobile User Interface (LCDUI)   14
Model–View–Controller (MVC)
     design pattern   320–2
Model–View (MV) design pattern
     322–3
modifiers, optimizing code
     340–3
Monty (CLDC HI)   94–5, 354, 390
Motorola A920/A925   455
MTU see maximum transmission
     unit
multimedia functionality   14–15
multimedia support   330
multi-user games   403
mustBeMaster argument   222
MV see Model–View
MVC see Model–View–Controller

NDS see Nokia Developer's Suite
Net Access function group
     114–15
Network Address Translation (NAT)
     gateways   115–16
networking   11–12, 45–6,
     429–30
Nokia 3600/3650   448

Nokia 3620/3660   449
Nokia 6600
     MIDP 2.0 Symbian OS   89,
          93–4, 107, 201, 202
     Push Registry   123
     security policy   115
     specifications   460
Nokia 6620   461
Nokia 7650   447
Nokia 7700   462
Nokia 9210   370
Nokia 9210i   446
Nokia
     MMAPI implementation on
          Symbian OS phones
          180–1, 182–5
     Series 60 MIDP Concept SDK
          63
Nokia Developers' Suite for J2ME
     2.0 (NDS)   63–6, 241–2
Nokia N-Gage   451
Nokia UI
     Nokia 3600/3650   448
     Nokia 3620/3660   449
     Nokia 6600   460
     Nokia 6620   461
     Nokia 7650   447
     Nokia 7700   462
     Nokia N-Gage   451
     Sendo X   452
notifyIncomingMessage
     interface   195–6

OBEX see Object Exchange
     Protocol
obfuscation
     CodeWarrior   69
     expense application case study
          279–80
     J2ME Wireless Toolkit   56
     JAR file size   331, 332
     JBuilder   67
     optimizing code   391–2
object creation, optimizing code
     338–40
Object Exchange Protocol (OBEX)
     208, 244
object interaction   321, 322

object pools   340
Observer pattern   322
OMA DRM Version 1.0   419–20
oneshot interaction mode   102
online developer resources
   439–40
on-stack replacement   390
opening recordstores   149–50,
   264–5
openRecordStore() method
   149–50
operating systems   54–5
operators   401, 402–3
OPL   398, 399
Optimization test MIDlet   351
optimizing code   335–92
   arithmetic operations   385
   Array copying   351–2
   benchmarking   336–7
   design patterns   386–8
   Dynamic Adaptive Compilation
      390–1
   feedback   338
   general guidelines   337–8
   graphics   358–66
   Just In Time compliers   390
   LifeTime case study   366–84
   looping   352–7
   memory management   388–9
   method modifiers and inlining
      340–3
   obfuscators   391–2
   object creation   338–40
   responsiveness   338
   strings   343–8
   tools   372–7
   using containers   348–9
optional APIs   330–1
-ossx parameter   354
OTA see over-the-air
out-of-memory errors   332, 389,
   428
output classes   424–5
OutputTextBox class   361
over-optimization   337
over-the-air (OTA)
   emulation   55
   MIDlet installation   84–5
   provisioning   15–16, 107

packages
   core   435–6
   networking   429–30
packaging process   437–8
packet based protocols   224
paintCanvas() method   370–1
paintCount   360, 361
painting
   clipping region   362
   image buffer   363–4
   Popcorn drawing demonstrator
      358–65
   strategies comparison   364–5
   whole background   359–62
paint() method   41
   alpha blending   148–9
   code optimization   364, 365
   KeyPad class   130
   LifeTime   372
   Popcorn test program   359
   SpriteCanvas   138
paired remote devices   228–9
Palm OS   6, 397
parsing XML, synchronization
   274–5, 277
patterns, game of life   366–70
pauseApp() method   48,
   169–70, 293, 298
paused states   47–8, 53–4, 293,
   298
Payment API (JSR 229)   417
PC operating systems   54–5
performance issues, profiling
   373–5, 377
persistent storage   16, 44–5, 422,
   434
   see also Record Management
      system
Personal Basis Profile   7, 20
PersonalJava   398, 399
   BenQ P30   453
   Nokia 9210i   446
   Sony Ericsson P800   454
   Sony Ericsson P900   459
   Motorola A920/A925   455
   PersonalJava technology   7,
      398, 399
Personal Profile   7, 19–20
Picture Puzzle MIDlet

case study   248, 294–315
choice form   300–2
game logic   306–11
image capture   178–9, 302–5
image names/IDs   306, 314–15
image record stores   311–15
MIDlet lifecycle   295–300
PIN codes   227–8
pixelLevel   366
PKI see Public Key Infrastructure
platformRequest() method
   145–6
Player   159, 160–1
PlayerListener interface   158,
   164
playerUpdate() method   171
playing media content   161–4
PNG see Portable Network
   Graphics
pointer-based devices   328, 329
pointerDragged() method
   130
pointerPressed() method
   41, 42, 130
pointerReleased() method
   130
polling   328, 357
Popcorn drawing demonstrator
   358–65
portable code   319–33
   CLDC   8
   design patterns   320–5
   download limitations   331–2
   heap memory   332–3
   high-level user interface
      components   329
   input methods variation   328–9
   key codes   42
   low-level graphical content
      326–8
   Model–View–Controller design
      pattern   320–2
   Model–View design pattern
      322–3
   portability issues   326–33
   problems   319
   proprietary and optional APIs
      330–1
   user interfaces   29, 30–1

Portable Network Graphics (PNG)
183
porting
design patterns 323–4
heap memory 332
Java benefits 409
predicted worldwide revenue
396–7
prefetch() method 161, 162
PREKNOWN devices 223–4
presentation code/business logic
separation 263
pre-verification 280, 437–8
privacy 340, 343
profiles 5–6, 207
profiling tools 372–5, 377
ProGuard obfuscation 56,
279–80
proprietary APIs 330–1
proprietary operating systems 397
protected APIs 96, 187–8
protection domains 101–2, 106,
107, 113
protocol monitoring 56
protocol stack 206–7
provisioning channels 402–3
public instance methods 343
Public Key Infrastructure (PKI)
96–8, 420
Publisher–Subscriber pattern 322
pucks 358–65
Push Registry
Bluetooth 244
J2ME Wireless Toolkit 56
MIDP 2.0 119–23
Networking 46
WMA 192–3, 195, 199

"quick and dirty" Bluetooth service
connection 222–3

racing game see Demo Racer game
RAM see memory
rcvbuf socket option 111
realize() method 161, 162
realloc 354
Real Time Protocol (RTP) 160

Receiver class 196–8
receiving messages 191–2
Recommended Security Policy
(RSP) for GSM/UMTS
Compliant Devices 106–7,
230
RecordControl 184–5, 186
record IDs 314–15
Record Management System (RMS)
44–5
captured images 294, 311–15
expense application case study
264–9
MIDP 2.0 149–55
Picture Puzzle application
311–15
RecordStore 45
recursion 352–7, 382–4
registerAlarm() method 122
registerConnection()
method 121
registration 208–14
rendering 370–1
repaint() method
alpha blending 149
clipping region painting 362
image buffer painting 363
sprite animation 138
whole background painting
361
repaint strategies 358
requirements overview 249–51
resources 439–44
responsiveness 338
retrieveDevices() method
223–4
revenue predictions, worldwide
396–7
RFCOMM protocol 206–7, 213,
224
RMS see Record Management
System
RMSReader MIDlet 153–5
RMSWriter MIDlet 150–2
robustness 407–9
Rococo Impronto Simulator 241
root certificates 98
root keys 98
route planning 403

r Pentomino pattern 367, 368
RSP see recommended security
policy
RTP see Real Time Protocol
run() method
AudioPlayer class 166–7
MIDlet animation 143–4
Receiver class 197–8
synchronization worker threads
270–3
VideoPlayer class 175
run scripts 281
Runtime.gc() method 389
runtime support 326

sales, annual 395–6
sales force automation 404
sample applications 46–54,
247–315
screen display resolution 422
Screen objects 34
screen size 327–8
SDDB see Service Discovery
Database
SDKs 63, 76–82, 242–4
SDP see Service Discovery Protocol
searchServices() method
219
secure socket support 112–13
security
Bluetooth 227–30
CLDC devices 12
end-to-end 435
Java benefits 406–7
MIDP 2.0 96–107, 187–9,
200–1, 230
MIDP 16
network connections 114–15
Push Registry 122–3
Recommended Security Policy
for GSM/UMTS Compliant
Devices 230
Security and Trust Services (JSR
177) 414
selector item 253–6
selectService() method 223
sending SMS messages 190–1
Sendo X 452

separate delivery   419
Series 60 Developer Platform
    1.0/2.0 182–5, 188
Series 60 MIDP SDK   63, 242–3
series 60 phones   253–6
server creation   212–14, 225
ServerSocketConnection
    interface   111
server socket support   110–12
service connection   222–3, 226
service discovery   218–21
Service Discovery Database
    (SDDB)   209, 219
Service Discovery Protocol (SDP)
    412
service provider requirements
    400
ServiceRecords   209–11, 219,
    226
service registration   208–14
servicesDiscovered()
    method   218
Session Initiation Protocol (SIP)
    415–16
session interaction mode   102
setCell() method   136
setLayout() method   124
setPosition() method   138
setter methods   342–3
short-lived objects   339
Siemens SX1 specifications   450
signatures, digital   96–8, 102–5
SIMPLE clients   416–17
SIP see Session Initiation Protocol
SIP API for J2ME (JSR 180)
    415–16
SIP-unaware applications   416
slave-master roles   222
"smart houses"   422
SMS messages   189–201
sndbuf socket option   111
SocketConnection interface
    111
Socket Demo MIDlet   116–19
socket support   109–10
Sony Ericsson P800   454
Sony Ericsson P900
    J2ME SDK   81–2

MIDP 2.0   89, 93–4, 107, 182,
    201, 202
Push Registry   123
security policy   115
specifications   459
UIQ SDK   76
Sony Ericsson P908
    MIDP 2.0   89, 93–4, 107, 182,
        201, 202
    Push Registry   123
    security policy   115
sound download limitations   332
Spacer class   39, 126
specifications, Symbian OS phones
    445–62
speed, graphics problem   358
Sprite class   44
    code portability   327–8
    collision detection   365–6
    Demo Racer game   284–8, 290
    Game API   136–9
    Helloworld   51–3
Stack containers   348–9
stack size   354
standardization, Java benefits   407
startApp() method
    paused states   47–8, 169, 293,
        298
    Push Registry   121
    SMS ChatMIDlet   195
    use   299
start() method   161, 162
startPlayer() method   167
startup time, optimizing code
    338
static variables, optimizing code
    341–3
stop() method   162
storage
    persistent   16, 44–5, 422, 434
    see also Record Management
        system
stream based protocols   224
StringBuffer   344–5, 346–8,
    350
StringItem class   39, 125
strings
    comparing   343–4
    concatenating   344–5

keys in hash tables   345–6
optimizing code   343–8
StringBuffer memory trap
    346–8
Sun
    Java history   21
    Java Verified Program   420
    virtual machines   8
Sun J2ME Wireless Toolkit, see also
    Wireless Toolkit
Sun ONE Studio   72–6, 392
supermarket shopping   403
support capability determination
    186–7
Symbian
    specific extensions   417–18
    websites   439
    wireless devices proportion
        397
Symbian OS
    CLDC   94–5
    Java history   21
    JTWI   93–4
    push architecture   123
    Version 8.0   185–6, 412–13
    Version 8.x   413–14
Symbian OS phones
    MIDP support   89
    Mobile Media API   180–7
    security model   107
    specifications   445–62
    WMA   201
synchronization   269–77
System.arraycopy() method
    351–2
system classes   423

task continuity   402
technology trends   421–2
telephony APIs   418
TextBox object   36
TextField   39–40
thisGeneration   372
threading   42–3, 338
Ticker   40
TiledLayer class   44, 132–6,
    284, 310, 327
time classes   425–6
time issues   407–9

Timer Task 269–70
tone generation 157, 179–80
tools
    MIDP 54–66
    optimization 372–7
    websites 440
    see also Wireless Toolkit
totalMemory() method 389
touch screen devices 324
transparency 146–9
trends in technology 421–2
trust anchors 98, 99
trusted MIDlet suites 96
trusted protection domain 230

ubiquitous services 421
UEI *see* Unified Emulator Interface
UIQ SDK 76–82, 242–4
UIQ user interface 253–6, 262–4
UML class diagrams 321, 323, 324, 369
UML sequence diagrams 322
Unified Emulator Interface (UEI) 74–6
Universally Unique Identifiers (UUIDs) 211–12, 219, 223
untapped markets 401–2
untrusted MIDlets 105–6, 188, 200
untrusted protection domain 230
user interfaces
    business logic separation 263
    classes 430–2

design patterns 324–5
MIDP 29–44
UIQ 253–6, 262–4
see also LCDUI
UUIDs *see* Universally Unique Identifiers

value-added services 410
variables, optimizing code 340–3
Vector 348–9, 350
verification 420
video media 157, 172–8
    image capture 302–5
    paused states 298
Video Player MIDlet 172–8
View *see* Model–View–Controller design pattern; Model–View design pattern
virtual machines 8–9
Visual Basic 398, 399
vmCopy() method 351
VM progress 411

Web Server components 277–8
website resources 439–44
whole background painting 359–62
WiFi 399
wireless Java market 395–400
Wireless Messaging API (WMA) 189–201

BenQ P30 453
emulation 55
JTWI 92
Nokia 3600/3650 448
Nokia 3620/3660 449
Nokia 6600 460
Nokia 6620 461
Nokia 7700 462
Nokia N-Gage 451
Sendo X 452
Siemens SX1 450
Sony Ericsson P900 459
wireless networking 115–16
Wireless Toolkit (WTK) 54–9, 104–5, 371–2
    benchmarking 336–7
    command line 437–8
    expense application case study 249
    heap analysis 375–6, 377
    LifeTime 370–1
    limitations 29
    profiling 372–5
WMA *see* Wireless Messaging API
worker threads 270–3
wrappers, OMA DRM 419
WTK *see* Wireless Toolkit

X.509 PKI 96–8
XML parsing 274–5, 277

zoomFactor 385